Advance praise for *Clearing the Thickets: A History of Antebellum Alabama*

"Jim Lewis' *Clearing the Thickets* is narrative history in the grand old style—a spirited effort to make sense of the ideas, human beings, and events that came together to shape Alabama's first tumultuous decades. In addition to historical knowledge gained by years of research and reading, Lewis possesses a professional's understanding of law. Thus he is able to account for the considerable influence that legal doctrines, not to mention lawyers, had upon the state's formative period. Students of Alabama history will be reminded of Thomas P. Abernethy's analytical skills. Anyone interested in antebellum Alabama will be grateful for what Lewis has accomplished."

— Paul Pruitt, Jr.
Special Collection Librarian, Bounds Law Library, University of Alabama
Author of *Taming Alabama: Lawyers and Reformers, 1804–1929* (2010)

"Lewis has carefully crafted a thoughtful, deliberate, and well-balanced history of antebellum Alabama. Perhaps not coincidentally, we are now in the decade of Alabama's bicentennial. In days such as these, Lewis' book should be on the shelf of anyone interested in Alabama's early history."

— James L. Noles, Jr.
Chairman, Alabama Humanities Foundation

"In the grand tradition of A.J. Pickett and A.B. Moore, Jim Lewis has produced a richly detailed, encyclopedic in scope, history of antebellum Alabama. Gracefully written, with unique insights provided by a career in government and law, his book weaves the rich diversity of the state's early history into a compelling tale replete with assorted heroes and heroines, scoundrels and statesmen, and fools and filibusterers. From wandering Spaniards to the "fire-eating" politicians of the 1850s, he does not miss a stitch in the crazy quilt that became Alabama. Lewis obviously loves Alabama history. After reading *Clearing the Thickets*, you will too."

— Martin Everse
Retired Director, Tannehill Ironworks Historical State Park and
Brierfield Ironworks Historical State Park

CLEARING

THE

THICKETS

CLEARING
THE
THICKETS

A History of Antebellum Alabama

Herbert James Lewis

History & Heroes Series

QUID PRO BOOKS

New Orleans, Louisiana

Published in 2013 by Quid Pro Books.

ISBN 978-1-61027-165-3 (pbk.)
ISBN 978-1-61027-169-1 (hbk.)
ISBN 978-1-61027-166-0 (eBook)

QUID PRO BOOKS
Quid Pro, LLC
5860 Citrus Blvd., Suite D-101
New Orleans, Louisiana 70123
www.quidprobooks.com

qp

Publisher's Cataloging-in-Publication

Lewis, Herbert James.

Clearing the thickets: a history of antebellum Alabama / Herbert James Lewis.

p. cm. — (History & heroes)

Includes bibliographical references and index.

ISBN 978-1-61027-165-3 (pbk.)

1. Alabama—History. 2. Alabama—Politics and government. 3. Slavery—Alabama—History—19th century. I. Title. II. Series.

F326 .L443 2013   321'.02'15—dc22

                                                                               2013533672

The cover images are used with the generous permission of the Alabama Department of Archives and History, as are many images in this book (as marked). The author and publisher thank them for their important contribution. Map images are used by permission of Barry Lawrence Ruderman Antique Maps, www.RareMaps.com. Other images are used with permission as credited, or derive from material in the public domain.

This book is dedicated

to the memory of my parents

Myra Koenig Lewis and Herbert James Lewis, Jr.

CONTENTS

CLEARING

THE

THICKETS

INTRODUCTION

In his book *Rivers of History: Life on the Coosa, Tallapoosa, Cahaba, and Alabama*, Harvey H. Jackson III introduces the chapter entitled "Settling the Alabama" with this quote from Harper Lee's *To Kill a Mockingbird*:

> I said if he wanted to take a broad view of the thing, it really began with Andrew Jackson. If General Jackson hadn't run the Creeks up the creek, Simon Finch would never have paddled up the Alabama, and where would we be if he hadn't?

This succinct and cogent observation poses important questions that all native Alabamians should address concerning where we would be had our ancestors not traveled the Federal Road, sailed into the Port of Mobile, or paddled up the Alabama River to start anew their lives. More important, however, are the questions of why they came to Alabama, what conditions they faced upon their arrival in an untamed frontier, and what they contributed to the establishment of an ordered society. Although a lawyer by profession, I majored in history in undergraduate school and have a passion for the history of early Alabama. My father, who was also a lawyer, instilled this passion in me at an early age. During the 1950s when Davy Crockett—as packaged by Walt Disney—was the rage, I remember a Sunday afternoon excursion to Lowndes County with my father, where we searched for the point where William Weatherford, later dubbed "Red Eagle" by poet A. B. Meek, purportedly jumped into the Alabama River to escape American soldiers at the Battle of the Holy Ground. Other weekend family trips included visits to Horseshoe Bend National Park, Moundville, the ruins of old Cahaba, and antebellum homes in the Black Belt, such as Kirkwood in Eutaw, Gaineswood in Demopolis, and Rosemount located between Demopolis and Eutaw in Greene County.

Ever since those weekend excursions, I have had a keen interest in Alabama's early history and the people who brought order to its frontier society. This interest was further fueled when I researched and wrote an entry for the *Alabama Review* concerning my third great grandfather, Henry Wilbourne Stevens, who sailed from Connecticut to Mobile in 1814. He arrived just in time to serve in the Mississippi territorial militia at the end of the War of 1812. Having graduated from one of America's first law schools, in Litchfield, Connecticut (a proprietary law school that also educated Aaron Burr, who features colorfully in the history that unfolds here), Stevens then practiced law for a short while near Natchez before succumbing to Alabama fever and becoming Montgomery County's first justice of the peace and the register of its orphans' court.

A few months before the publication of my article concerning Henry

Stevens, I retired after thirty-one years of service as an attorney with the federal government, twenty-six years of which were served as an Assistant United States Attorney in Birmingham. Soon after, I became involved with the *Encyclopedia of Alabama* as a freelance writer and editor. In that capacity, I have contributed forty-seven entries, nearly half of which pertain to early Alabama history. The research inspired the idea of writing a book that tells the story of Alabama from frontier times—a fascinating period of colonization, settlement, and unparalleled expansion not examined in depth over the past two decades. My weekend excursions became a full-time mission.

The name *Alabama* comes from the Choctaw word meaning "clearers of the thickets," hence the title of this volume. The book's purpose is to examine modern Alabama's early history beginning with the era of European colonization and culminating with Alabama's secession from the Union after just forty-one years as a state (recognizing, of course, that the actual history began long before this emigration, with civilizations that include such native nations as the Choctaw, Muskogee Creek, and Chickasaw tribes). In so doing, the book traces how Alabama emerged from a raw frontier of European settlement into a fully functioning state that provided much-needed order to its new citizens. Specifically, a government was formed to provide protection for many who had suffered from the violence associated with an untamed frontier. This violence emanated from both a rough and rowdy element that flourished in the absence of lawful authority and from Native Americans, whose lands they had invaded upon their arrival in the territory that was to become Alabama.

Organization and Subject Matter

This book presents a narrative (chronologically, for the most part) of Alabama's antebellum period, emphasizing the political, constitutional, and military developments that led to bringing order to its frontier society. The book begins in Chapter 1 with an examination of the colonial period during which three European powers—Spain, France, and Great Britain—continually vied for control of what was to become part of Alabama. These powers imposed their own legal codes, each of which brought some measure of order to the emerging frontier of the lower Gulf region and readied the region to become a territory of the United States. Next, Chapter 2 takes an in-depth look at the formation of the Mississippi Territory, whose eastern section was comprised of the future state of Alabama. The controversial implementation of Sargent's Code within the Mississippi Territory kept a growing, raucous population from achieving total chaos. As more settlers reached the Tombigbee region of Alabama, Washington County was created to bring organized American government to Alabama soil for the first time. Chapter 3 thus examines the many roles played by Judge Harry Toulmin, a federal official presiding in the Alabama section of the territory, in transforming the remote "Bigbee District" into a civilized community ready for statehood.

Before delving into the politics of statehood, Chapter 4 chronicles the legendary and compelling story of the Creek War of 1813–1814, which started out as a civil war between rival Creek factions before American involvement after the massacre at Fort Mims. After defeating the Red Sticks at Horseshoe Bend, Andrew Jackson forced a treaty upon the Creeks that resulted in the cession of approximately 22 million acres of land located in the future state of Alabama—a majority of the state, in fact. This cession contributed to an "Alabama fever" that resulted in the emigration of droves of new settlers to the area. As the population massively swelled, statehood was attained within a little over five years.

Chapter 5 outlines land booms in the Tennessee Valley that led to the development of Huntsville as well as in the central part of the state that led to the founding of Montgomery. The chapter also looks in depth at the formation of a separate Alabama Territory and the organization of its government. Chapter 6 chronicles the Constitutional Convention of 1819 in Huntsville and the writing of the state of Alabama's first constitution. Elections were soon held under that regime, but statehood also catalyzed national compromise which at best postponed, and in some ways made inevitable, the Civil War. Thus the very creation of the Alabama state both birthed a new political home and laid the seeds for the eventual downfall of its original construction.

With the advent of statehood, Chapters 7 through 9 examine in some detail the various governors' administrations and legislative sessions as the state capital moved from Cahaba to Tuscaloosa and then from Tuscaloosa to Montgomery, its current home and eventual capital of the Confederate South as well. These chapters examine the development of Alabama's state government in its formative stages, the politics involved in the efforts to decide upon a permanent seat of government, the downfall of the Georgia political faction that had been influential in achieving statehood for Alabama, banking issues that dominated early state politics, and Alabama's confrontation with the federal government with regard to Indian removal policy. Chapter 10 breaks from the chronological narrative to treat separately the issue of the dominant power of King Cotton and the slave labor upon which it was based. The chapter substantively examines Alabama's "peculiar institution" of slavery that would only end by force of arms as a result of the Civil War.

Chapter 11 returns to a chronological review of events in the 1850s leading up to Alabama's secession from the Union. It particularly looks at the rise of the fiery states' rights advocate William Lowndes Yancey who would push Alabamians toward secession—and a war which would set the state back socially, politically, economically, and psychologically for generations to come. Alabama's frontier stage ended with a war rather than a period during which its cotton-based economy could be diversified by the development of the state's plentiful natural resources.

Although most of the book focuses on the political, constitutional, and military developments of the antebellum period, the twelfth and final chapter takes a closer look at the social and economic transformations that were occurring during this time frame and how they were interrupted and stunted by the tragedy of secession and war.

Perspective

As Alabama's bicentennial approaches in 2019, I hope that Alabamians, both native and transplanted, and other interested readers, will devote closer attention to the state's early history and become more familiar with the events and circumstances that led to the settlement and development of the state. Some have scoffed at an alleged over-romanticization of our early history that includes the glorification of Indian fighters and land seizures, the portrayal of wealthy planters as chivalrous and moralistic leaders of an aristocratic ruling class, and the soft-peddling of the condition of hundreds of thousands of African Americans held in human bondage. It is hoped, however, that those who read this account will find a balanced examination of Alabama's formative period, which includes a report of atrocities committed by both Native Americans and white settlers; a realistic look at the planter class versus the yeoman farmers with regard to political power; and a frank portrayal of slavery within the state.

Alabama's early history cannot be sugar-coated—in today's vernacular, "it is what it is." While our early history includes acutely troubling aspects with regard to the treatment of Alabama's native inhabitants and African slaves brought into the state to serve white masters, Alabamians were hardly pioneers in these matters. English settlers in Virginia and New England had warred with local Indian tribes almost two hundred years before the Creek War of 1813–1814. By the time Alabama became a state, Native American tribes in New England had been essentially eradicated by this warfare, in combination with diseases introduced by the English settlers. As the frontier expanded southward and westward, the initial federal policy of assimilation of Native Americans gave way to a policy of removal and relocation of tribes. Reflecting this change, Andrew Jackson, who defeated the Creeks at Horseshoe Bend in 1814, forced the cession of over 34,000 square miles of tribal lands within Alabama. Jackson continued a harsh policy of removal when he became president in 1829. In any case, Alabama's confrontation with its native peoples was not singular but, instead, was part and parcel of a national Indian policy.

As for slavery, it had been introduced on the American continent in 1619 while Alabama remained uncolonized and peopled only by its native inhabitants. Slavery quickly spread, particularly within the South, and was implicitly sanctioned by the United States Constitution at the nation's beginning. Slavery became particularly profitable and flourished in Alabama as a result of the introduction of the cotton gin and the opening up for cultivation of the fertile soils of the Black Belt. It existed without interference until the Civil War in all of the eleven southern states that would comprise the Confederate States of America, as well as the border states of Missouri, Kentucky, Maryland, and Delaware. Although Alabamians were obviously not uniquely responsible for the introduction of slavery into their midst, they—shamefully, like their neighbors throughout the South—refused to give up the economic benefits of slavery and thus allowed the abomination to continue until the South was made by force of arms to accept emancipation.

Historical Overview

Many fascinating people and events dot the landscape of Alabama's antebellum history. One of the most intriguing events in Alabama history occurred with the arrival of the first major European expedition led by Hernando de Soto of Spain in 1540. De Soto's expedition is wrapped in mystery to this day because none of the accounts of the expedition reveal with any degree of certainty his precise route through Alabama or the locations of the Mississippian Indian villages he passed through—including the village of Mabila (Mauvila, Maubila, or Mavilla), where an epic battle ensued during which de Soto's Spaniards killed anywhere from 2,500 to 5,000 Native Americans. A symposium of scholars recently focused on three possible sites including Bogue Chitto in Dallas County, and Gee's Bend and Miller's Ferry in Wilcox County, all of which are near the Alabama River in central Alabama. Other possibilities remain, including a site where Cahaba—Alabama's future capital—was later located at the confluence of the Alabama and Cahaba rivers.

Spain's failure to colonize the lower Gulf region left Alabama virtually free of European influence and settlers for nearly another century and a half when, in 1699, the French arrived. The French ruled the region for the next sixty-four years. Many of those years were under the leadership of Jean-Baptiste Le Moyne, Sieur de Bienville, who founded La Mobile and the associated Fort Louis de la Louisiane in 1702 on the Mobile River at a site now known as Twenty-seven Mile Bluff near present-day Mount Vernon, Alabama. La Mobile served as the first permanent capital of the Louisiana colony of France. In 1711 the settlement was relocated to a site at the head of Mobile Bay where the current city of Mobile is located.

Under French rule, there were two important firsts in what was to become Alabama—the employment in 1712 of *La Coutume de Paris*, which was the region's first western legal code, and the arrival in 1721 of the first slaves in Mobile on the ship *Africane*. The arrival of slaves into the colony prompted the implementation of the *Code Noir*, which regulated slavery and constituted a religious edict forbidding the public practice of any religion within the colony other than Roman Catholicism.

French control of Alabama ended with the signing of the Treaty of Paris in 1763 at the conclusion of the French and Indian War. Mobile then became subject to British rule for the first time as it was now a part of British West Florida. Under British rule, the common law of England was instituted and would lay the foundation for Alabama's system of jurisprudence when it became a territory of the United States. British governor George Johnstone allowed the first form of representative government on Alabama soil when he called for the election of representatives of the freeholders to serve in a lower chamber (Common House) to the governor's appointed Council.

During the American Revolution, Spain wrestled control of Mobile and British West Florida from Great Britain to become the last of the revolving door European powers to rule Mobile. Eventually Spain tailored the colonial laws and customs of her *Recopilación de Leyes de los Reinos de las Indias* to fit the frontier conditions existing along the gulf coast of Alabama and Mississippi. One of the more interesting aspects of life in Spanish Mobile was the role played by "free persons of color." Free blacks amounted to 20 percent of Mobile's total free population in 1788, increasing to 30 percent by 1805. Their status as free persons enabled them to enter into contracts, buy and sell property, manage businesses, and sue and be sued. In 1812 the U.S. Congress annexed the Mobile District of West Florida to the Mississippi Territory. On April 13, 1813, Spanish Captain Cayetano Pérez surrendered his garrison, and Mobile was at last a part of the United States.

Fifteen years earlier, on April 8, 1798, the U.S. Congress had enacted a law creating the Mississippi Territory, which included present day Alabama north of the 31st parallel. President John Adams appointed a seemingly unlikely Harvard-educated, New England Puritan by the name of Winthrop Sargent as the territory's first governor. To Sargent fell the task of bringing order to a region composed of escaped prisoners, fugitives from justice, border rowdies, debtors, and slaves on the run to freedom. To this end, he implemented what was derisively referred to as Sargent's Code. These laws were considered repressive and unconstitutional by the frontier populace to whom they were applied. There was particular concern with the harshness of criminal punishments, the exorbitance of fees and licenses, and the implementation of "blue laws," which prohibited working, hunting, fiddling, bear-baiting, and slaves playing "chuck-penny" on Sunday. As a Federalist opposed by constituents who were mostly Jeffersonian Republicans, Sargent failed to get reappointed governor; President Jefferson instead appointed William C. C. Claiborne as the second governor of the Mississippi Territory.

Before leaving office, on June 4, 1800, Governor Sargent issued a proclamation creating Washington County, finally bringing organized government to the banks of the Tombigbee and Tensaw rivers and the Alabama section of the territory. The superior court of Washington County held its first session at McIntosh Bluff in September 1802 with Seth Lewis, chief justice of the Mississippi Territory, presiding. In 1803, President Thomas Jefferson appointed Ephraim Kirby, a land-speculating Connecticut lawyer and former Revolutionary War soldier, and Robert Carter Nicholas of Kentucky, as land commissioners in the eastern part of the territory—the first federal officials to serve in the area. On July 6, 1804, Kirby took on substantial extra duties when he received a personal appeal from President Jefferson to accept an appointment as the first federal judge for the Alabama portion of the Mississippi Territory.

Late in the year of 1804, Harry Toulmin left Kentucky to replace Ephraim Kirby, who had died that year on October 20. Toulmin was a Dissenting minister in Lancashire, England, before leaving for America in 1793 in search of religious freedom. Before becoming Alabama's second federal judge, Toulmin had served as president of Transylvania College in Kentucky and as Kentucky's Secretary of State. Far from simply presiding over the territorial district court, Toulmin assumed many additional responsibilities as the chief federal civil official in a remote wilderness frontier, an extension of duties that in effect made him czar of the Tombigbee settlements. During his fourteen-year rule from his log courthouse in Wakefield, Toulmin strove to keep in check local filibusterers who had their eyes on taking Mobile from the Spanish, and he played a role in the arrest of former Vice President Aaron Burr who was accused of treason. Harry Toulmin's rule of the Tombigbee district earned him the name "the Frontier Justinian."

Toulmin courageously transformed his remote frontier outpost into a civilized community ready for statehood. Prior to achieving statehood, however, the Alabama region would be embroiled in a war between the encroaching white settlers and native Creek Indians. American encroachment into the lower part of the Mississippi Territory bordering Spanish Florida brought settlers increasingly into contact with the Creek Nation. Under Alexander McGillivray's leadership, the Creeks were able to avoid major hostilities with the Americans in the Mississippi Territory. But after McGillivray died, relations among different factions of the Creek Nation, as well as between the Creeks and Americans, deteriorated to the point of war in the summer of 1813. The Creek War of 1813–1814 began as a civil war between two principal factions of the Creek Nation. The traditionalist faction, known as the Red Sticks, resented what they viewed as the accommodationist actions of the Creek National Council, which favored cooperating with encroaching settlers. In retaliation for an ambush of warriors returning from Spanish-held Pensacola where they had purchased gun powder and supplies, on August 30, 1813, the Red Stick faction of the Creek Nation attacked Fort Mims near present-day Bay Minette in Baldwin County. The attack resulted in the massacre of between 250 and 300 men, women, and children, including both white Americans and settler-friendly Creeks who had opposed the Red Stick faction.

News of the massacre at Fort Mims spread quickly throughout the old Southwest, prompting outraged cries for revenge and calls to arms. In response, the governors of Tennessee, Georgia, and the Mississippi Territory called up militias commanded by Andrew Jackson, John Floyd, and Ferdinand L. Claiborne to lead a multi-pronged retaliatory invasion into Red Stick territory within Alabama. These men led attacks at Red Stick villages such as Tallushatchee, Talladega, Emuckfau, Enitachopco, Autossee, Callabee, Ikanachaki (the Holy Ground), and Tohopeka (Horseshoe Bend).

The fighting during the Creek War was brutal, as demonstrated by the massacre at Fort Mims as well as the aggressiveness with which American soldiers attacked Red Stick towns. For example, legendary frontier hero Davy Crockett reported that forty-six warriors were shot "like dogs" and then consumed by fire when the house in which they had sought refuge was set ablaze by the troops that had attacked Tallushatchee. The war also produced heroic feats of its participants, including the "Canoe Fight," which pitted a small band of Americans led by Samuel Dale in hand-to-hand combat with a larger group of Red Sticks on the Alabama River, as well as William Weatherford's celebrated leap on his horse into the Alabama River to escape capture during the Battle of the Holy Ground.

The Creek War ended when Andrew Jackson defeated the Red Sticks at Horseshoe Bend on March 27, 1814. More than 800 Red Stick warriors lost their lives during that conclusive battle, while only forty-nine Americans were killed and 153 wounded. Approximately 350 Indian women and children were taken as prisoners. As with most other battles of the war, the Red Sticks were defeated by superior firepower and manpower. In a peace treaty signed after the battle, the Creeks ceded approximately 22 million acres of land to the United States. Alabama was now ready to be opened up for settlement and statehood.

With the cession of Creek lands, the influx of settlers into the future state of Alabama was so great that it was called "Alabama Fever." These first settlers were mostly yeoman farmers who lived a demanding and grueling life just scratching out an existence in the wilderness abounding in dangerous animals and rowdy neighbors. As a result of the unprecedented influx of new settlers, a movement began to make Alabama a separate territory. Alabama did not become a territory, however, until Mississippi was admitted into the Union as a state in 1817. William Wyatt Bibb was appointed territorial governor and St. Stephens was designated as the territory's capital. Alabama would become a state itself within two years largely due to the efforts of a group of Georgia politicians, sometimes referred to as the "Broad River Group," of which Governor Bibb was a member.

The Broad River Group was a closely knit social and political community that had initially settled on the Broad River in northeastern Georgia. Before members of this group moved to Alabama, they had become politically powerful in Georgia, producing a governor, three senators, and a number of congressmen and state legislators. Of these, several would play a major role in Alabama's road to statehood, including senators William Wyatt Bibb and Charles Tait, as well as U.S. Secretary of the Treasury William H. Crawford. Members of this Georgia faction were instrumental in settling Huntsville and Montgomery.

During this territorial period, land booms occurred in north Alabama and in the area surrounding Montgomery. In one of the more colorful adventures of the times, the U.S. Congress also granted a tract of land near present-day Demopolis to a group of French expatriates to cultivate the donated lands with grape vines and olive trees, presumably with the hopes of making America competitive in the wine industry. While the venture ultimately failed, many of the French colonists remained in the area and took advantage of the area's rich soil to contribute to the cotton production of the emerging Black Belt of Alabama. One of the major political issues addressed by the Alabama territorial government was the selection of a permanent seat of government. Two major factions vied to have a site in their part of the state chosen as the capital—the Alabama/Cahaba River basin group and the Warrior/Tombigbee system group. However, Governor Bibb, who owned land in central Alabama near Coosada on the Alabama River, used his influence in Washington to outmaneuver the Warrior/Tombigbee group to have the capital moved from St. Stephens to Cahaba rather than Tuscaloosa.

When Alabama's Enabling Act became law on March 2, 1819, the stage was finally set for Alabama to become a state once a constitution was adopted by a duly elected convention and submitted to Congress for approval. On July 5, 1819, the convention assembled in Huntsville. The forty-four delegates assembled selected John W. Walker, a member of the Broad River Group, as president of the convention. They then appointed a Committee of Fifteen, chaired by Clement Comer Clay, to write an original draft. The convention adopted one of the most liberal state constitutions of the time, concluding their work on August 2, 1819. On December 14, 1819, President Monroe signed Congress' resolution of admission and Alabama became the nation's twenty-second state.

William Wyatt Bibb defeated Marmaduke Williams to become the state of Alabama's first governor. Political maneuvering involved in the naming of Alabama's first two senators centered on the north-versus-south sectional jealousies, as well as a growing opposition to the Broad River Group from Georgia. In the end, the combined houses of the General Assembly elected John W. Walker and William Rufus King as Alabama's first U.S. Senators.

During Governor Bibb's administration, the General Assembly went about the business of forging a state government in accordance with the recently adopted constitution. In order to provide for the peace and security of its citizens, the Assembly provided for the organization of a state militia and created a comprehensive court system. The Assembly also passed several acts with respect to public roadways and navigable waterways, and an engineer was tasked with locating "the nearest and most eligible approaches" between the Mobile and Tennessee River systems "for facilitating the commercial intercourse of this State." Shortly after the capital relocated to Cahaba, Alabama's first governor died as a result of complications from injuries sustained when he fell off of his horse. He was succeeded by his brother Thomas Bibb who was the president of the state senate. Thomas Bibb was basically a caretaker governor and did not seek reelection.

Thomas Bibb's decision not to run for office opened the way for the election of Israel Pickens, who had rejected his prior allegiance to the Georgia faction. Pickens became Alabama's third governor by taking advantage of public resentment that had been intensifying against the Merchants and Planters Bank of Huntsville, whose capital was primarily under the control of wealthy former Georgians then dominating state government and federal patronage within the state. He easily defeated the Georgia faction's candidate and was inaugurated on November 9, 1821. The establishment of a state bank and the Assembly's vote to move the capital to Tuscaloosa were the major achievements of his administration. During his term in office, Governor Pickens also presided over the celebrated visit to the state of Revolutionary War hero French General Marquis de Lafayette in 1825. Of political significance, the Georgia faction was rendered virtually powerless with the election of William Rufus King and William Kelly to the U.S. Senate, both of whom were opposed by the once influential Georgians.

The focus in Cahaba had been on organizing a state government and providing for the basic needs of its citizens. About the time that the state's government and its officers settled in Tuscaloosa, however, citizens began to focus upon national issues such as tariffs, internal improvements, slavery, Indian policy, and states' rights. Two of these issues, slavery and states' rights, would remain dominant as the state government left Tuscaloosa for Montgomery twenty years later. In the interim, the government in Tuscaloosa grappled with thorny issues of both national and local consequence.

The seat of government remained in Tuscaloosa for twenty years. The banking issue continued to dominate politics during this time. Reform proposals in the legislature eventually gave way to the termination of the State Bank of Alabama amidst allegations of fraud and corruption and because of gross mismanagement. Also during this time, Governor John Gayle became embroiled in Alabama's first confrontation with the federal government concerning the management of lands that had been ceded to the United States by the Creeks in the Treaty of Cusseta of 1832. The confrontation created a crisis that nearly led to a military clash with the national government. Cooler heads prevailed when President Jackson sent Francis Scott Key—a United States Attorney in Maryland who had, more famously, authored the "Star-Spangled Banner"—to Alabama in 1833, to negotiate a truce and to avert a military confrontation between the two governments. Other challenges facing the state while the capital was in Tuscaloosa were the Creek War of 1836 and the Panic of 1837.

The 1844 census revealed a shift of population eastward as result of nine new counties carved out of the Creek land session. This in turn propelled a movement to relocate the capital from Tuscaloosa. Moreover, political power was shifting from north Alabama to the Black Belt as cotton was beginning to dominate the state's economy. As a result, Montgomery became the state's fifth capital, with "King Cotton" ensconced as the predominant economic and political force within the state. By 1846, when the capital moved to its present home, there were approximately 300,000 slaves within the state. Alabama's politics were consumed with the defense of slavery and the advocacy of the right to take slaves into the new western territories that began to emerge after the 1846–1848 Mexican-American War.

Reuben Chapman, who was the first governor to be inaugurated in Montgomery, was a strong supporter of states' rights, and spent the overwhelming majority of his inaugural address ranting against the "General Government"—Washington, D.C. This sentiment would increase exponentially until Alabama eventually seceded from the Union. William Lowndes Yancey emerged as the leader of Alabama's states' rights advocates in the late 1840s after the death of Senator Dixon Hall Lewis. Under Yancey's leadership, these groups—known as *fire-eaters*—would become more extreme in their views and eventually began to push wholeheartedly for an independent Southern nation.

Ironically, Andrew B. Moore, the last governor to serve Alabama prior to leaving the Union, came into office as a moderate with regard to the issue of secession. Moore soon changed his mind and became more open to immediate secession after the raid led by abolitionist John Brown at Harpers Ferry, Virginia, in October 1859. Indeed, Governor Moore secured the passage of several acts to ready the state to defend itself from attacks such as that carried out at Harpers Ferry. The election of Abraham Lincoln as president in November 1860 ended all doubt that Alabama would secede from the Union, of which it had only been a member for forty-one years. As a result, Alabama's formative stage ended with a war rather than a period during which its cotton-based economy could be diversified by the development of the state's plentiful natural resources.

All of the state's attainments and developments during its formative antebellum period lay in utter ruins after the Civil War. One redeeming and inspirational effect of the war was the freedom accorded to hundreds of thousands of African American Alabamians who had been held in bondage all of their lives.

1

❧

EUROPEAN INVASION OF NATIVE LANDS

Hernando de Soto

Prior to the creation of the Mississippi Territory in 1798, three foreign nations and the state of Georgia had at various times exercised different measures of sovereignty over the area which now includes the state of Alabama. None of these, however, provided a permanent, organized government to dispense justice and maintain order on a sustained basis. Nor did they exercise jurisdiction over the several indigenous tribal nations that were occupying the area when white settlers began to intrude upon the natives' lands.

The revolving-door reigns of France, Great Britain, and Spain, and the concomitant lack of a continuous established government, attracted fugitive murderers, escaped prisoners, frontier rowdies, and outcast Tories to the area. Nevertheless, each foreign power during the colonial period made some progress toward transforming this rough frontier into a more ordered society by providing its own system of laws and jurisprudence. From a feminine revolution over food to a court-martial concerning stolen handkerchiefs, from religious intolerance to an implementation of representative government, from harsh treatment of slaves to a remarkable protection of the rights of free blacks, the colonial period's dichotomies readied future Alabamians for their hand at self-government and the ordering of their society.[1]

The indigenous peoples of Alabama preceded European explorers by thousands of years. Hunters and gatherers were among the first definite groups to roam Alabama during the Paleo-Indian period ranging between

---

[1] Most of the discussion of the colonial period centers on Mobile and the surrounding Tensaw and Tombigbee districts, since there were very few European settlers in the rest of present-day Alabama until Native Americans were forced to cede large quantities of land in the early 1800s.

approximately 9000 and 8000 BC. Further stages in the development of Alabama's indigenous population occurred during the Archaic period (approximately 8000 to 4000 BC), the Gulf Formational period (approximately 2500 to 100 BC), and the Woodland period (approximately 300 BC to AD 1000), prior to the emergence of the mound-building culture of the Mississippian period ranging from approximately AD 1000 to AD 1550. Agriculture was important in the Mississippian culture, which produced corn as the staple of its society. Settlements were located in fertile river valleys and featured large earthen mounds that were believed to have served as monuments to the dead, homes of the elite, or sites of religious temples. As the Mississippian period came to a close, these mounds were gradually abandoned. The Mississippian people were nevertheless still vibrant and were led by powerful chieftains, making them a force to be reckoned with by invading foreign forces from Europe.[2]

Christopher Columbus' discovery of North America in 1492 was soon followed by a wave of further expeditions that eventually resulted in Spanish exploration of the Gulf of Mexico, including Ponce de León's journey to Florida in 1513. As early as 1519, Spaniards accompanying the expedition of Alonso Álvarez de Pineda likely ventured into Mobile Bay as they explored the rivers and bays of the northern coast of the Gulf of Mexico. In 1528, conquistadors under the command of Pánfilo de Narváez stopped in Mobile Bay on their way to Mexico after an ill-fated attempt to settle Florida. It was not until July 1540, however, that the first Europeans explored the interior of what is today Alabama. These pioneering explorers were led by Spain's Hernando de Soto, governor of Cuba and *adelantado*, or military ruler, of Florida. De Soto explored the Southeast in search of riches with an *asiento* from the Spanish government to conquer, subjugate, and colonize.[3]

According to Albert James Pickett, author of Alabama's first history, the chief of Coosa was one of the first Native American chiefs encountered by

---

[2] The dates of these formational periods are approximated based on a composite of the following references: John A. Walthall, *Prehistoric Indians of the Southeast: Archeology of Alabama and the Middle South* (Tuscaloosa: University of Alabama Press, 1990), 20–184; Ned J. Jenkins and Richard A. Krause, *The Tombigbee Watershed in Southeastern Prehistory* (Tuscaloosa: University of Alabama Press, 1986), 30–49; William Warren Rogers et al., *Alabama: The History of a Deep South State* (Tuscaloosa: University of Alabama Press, 1994), 3–7 (all references herein to this work are contained in Part One, "From the Early Times to the End of the Civil War," by Leah Rawls Atkins).

[3] Albert Burton Moore, *History of Alabama* (1934; repr., Tuscaloosa: Alabama Book Store, 1951), 36–38; Rogers et al., *Alabama*, 19–24; Albert James Pickett, *History of Alabama, and Incidentally of Georgia and Mississippi, from the Earliest Period* (1851; repr., Birmingham, Ala.: Birmingham Book and Magazine Co., 1962), 17–57; Jay Higginbotham, "The Battle of Mauvila, Causes and Consequences," *Gulf South Historical Review* 6 (Spring 1991): 19–27. A highly controversial and unsubstantiated legend maintains that Prince Madoc of Wales was the first European to land on Alabama's gulf coast in 1170 near Fort Morgan, some three hundred years prior to Columbus' voyage to the Americas. According to this legend, Madoc went on to explore the interior of Alabama, Georgia, and Tennessee, leaving Indian tribes in the Southeast with their language and their propensity for blue eyes and light skin. While references to Madoc appeared in a few grade school Alabama history textbooks in the early 1980s, Madoc's alleged exploration remains merely a legend with no basis in proven facts. John C. Hall, "Prince Madoc and the Stubborn Persistence of a Legend," *Alabama Heritage*, Spring 2010, 30–37.

de Soto's men in the future state of Alabama. The chief invited de Soto to establish a large Spanish colony within his realm near the Coosa River between the mouths of two creeks now known as Talladega and Tallushatchee in present-day Talladega County. De Soto declined this offer, and instead temporarily took the chief hostage to guarantee the expedition's continued safe journey in its quest to find riches.[4]

After nearly half of a millennium, much is still unknown about de Soto's journey through Alabama, despite the fact that four different chronicles were kept of the journey. The chroniclers were de Soto's private secretary, Rodrigo Ranjel; the factor of the expedition, Hernandez de Biedma; the so-called "Gentleman of Elvas"; and Inca Garcilaso de la Vega, known as the Inca. Their diaries were in agreement with regard to some important aspects of the journey, while differing with regard to others. None of these accounts, however, reveal with any degree of certainty de Soto's precise route through Alabama or the locations of the villages he passed through. In any event it is widely accepted that as de Soto traveled through Alabama, he cruelly enslaved natives to serve as porters for his troops' provisions, frequently putting them into leg and neck irons; shamelessly captured women to service his men sexually; and shrewdly captured province leaders, as was the case with the chief of Coosa, to ensure cooperation from a town's or province's inhabitants as they traveled through different tribal provinces.[5]

After passing through several Indian villages along the Coosa, Tallapoosa, and Alabama rivers, de Soto and his men arrived at the town of Atahachi, believed by some to be located near present-day Montgomery and by others further west within Durant Bend on the Alabama River between Montgomery and Selma. At this village they came across an imposing Indian chief named Tascaluza, royal ruler of the province of Mabila (Mauvila, Maubila, or Mavilla). Reportedly towering over most of the Spaniards by more than a foot and adorned with a stately turban as well as a feathered cloak reaching to his feet, chief Tascaluza undoubtedly astounded de Soto and his soldiers as he sat royally upon comfortable cushions while one of his Indians protected him from the sun with a shield made of painted deerskin. This encounter would not only prove to have a profound effect on the remainder of de Soto's explorative journey through the Southeast, but it also would have a profound effect on Alabama's future development.[6]

Keeping within his modus operandi, de Soto asked Tascaluza to provide men to carry his supplies and women for the pleasure for his soldiers. When he refused this request, Tascaluza was put under arrest. Unhappy with his predicament, Tascaluza decided to provide the requested porters

[4] Pickett, *History of Alabama*, 30–33.

[5] Jay Higginbotham, "Discovery, Exploration, and Colonization of Mobile Bay to 1711," in *Mobile: The New History of Alabama's First City*, ed. Michael V. R. Thomason (Tuscaloosa: University of Alabama Press, 2001), 11–12; Rogers et al., *Alabama*, 19–24.

[6] Theda Perdue and Michael D. Green, *The Columbia Guide to American Indians of the Southeast* (New York: Columbia University Press, 2005), 37.

and promised that women and food would be made available in Mabila. With this assurance, de Soto's expedition pulled up stakes to continue on to Mabila, described by de Biedma as "a very small and very strongly palisaded town." Shortly after de Soto's conquistadors arrived at this small fortress on October 18, 1540, they were attacked by Mabila's villagers. All chroniclers essentially agree that an angered Tascaluza had deceptively led de Soto into a planned ambush.[7]

One contemporary historian questions whether the attack was planned, or instead resulted from a spontaneous emotional reaction to a shoving match between the invading Spaniards and the indigenous Indian tribes. However it commenced, de Soto's forces nevertheless quickly rebounded from the attack and their cavalry was deployed to surround the town and prevent natives escaping. Troops were then sent in to set the village afire. De Biedma, in describing the ensuing brutality, stated "we fought that day until it was night, without one Indian surrendering to us, rather they fought like fierce lions. Of those who came out, we killed them all, some with fire, others with swords, others with lances." One surviving Indian made the massacre complete by hanging himself from a tree with the cord of his bow.[8]

Some historians consider the battle at Mabila to be one of the most decisive ever fought on North American soil considering the number of Indians slain, estimated from anywhere between 2,500 and 5,000. The enormity of the battle and the resulting change in de Soto's plans played a significant role in delaying permanent European colonization of the lower South for another 150 years. Although victorious in this battle, the Spanish suffered greatly nonetheless due to the loss of key soldiers, horses, equipment, and overall morale. Surprisingly, 472 years after the fact, Alabama scholars have not unraveled the mystery as to where the important village of Mabila was located. A recent book combining the research of noted historians, archeologists, geographers, and geologists, among others, have focused on three possible sites including Bogue Chitto in Dallas County, and Gee's Bend and Miller's Ferry in Wilcox County, all of which are near the Alabama River in central Alabama. Nevertheless, there is still no consensus as to one site and there are still other possibilities, including a site where Cahaba, Alabama's future capital, was later located at the confluence of the Alabama and Cahaba rivers.[9]

Wherever located, the Battle of Mabila dramatically altered de Soto's strategy. After recovering from the battle, de Soto and his men fled north into Mississippi and Arkansas rather than rendezvousing with supply ships

---

[7] Higginbotham, "Discovery, Exploration, and Colonization," 11–12; Rogers et al., *Alabama*, 20–24; Perdue and Green, *Columbia Guide to American Indians*, 37–38; Lawrence A. Clayton, Vernon J. Knight, and Edward C. Moore, *The De Soto Chronicles: The Expedition of Hernando de Soto to North America in 1539–1543* (Tuscaloosa: University of Alabama Press, 1993), 1:233–35.

[8] Higginbotham, "The Battle of Mauvila," 19–27; Vernon J. Knight, ed., *The Search for Mabila: The Decisive Battle between Hernando de Soto and Chief Tascalusa* (Tuscaloosa: University of Alabama Press, 2009), 15, 173, 182–90.

[9] Higginbotham, "Battle of Mauvila," 29; Knight, *Search for Mabila*, 224.

on the gulf coast. Doubling back from Arkansas, de Soto died upon reaching the Mississippi River in May 1541. Pursued by members of the Quigualtam chiefdom—believed to be ancestors of the Natchez Indians—de Soto's surviving soldiers constructed brigantines and escaped down the Mississippi River. They then sailed westward in the Gulf of Mexico to Pánuco in Mexico.[10]

In 1559, determined to protect its shipping lanes to the riches of Mexico and the West Indies, Spain made another futile attempt led by Don Tristán de Luna y Arellano to settle the coastal region of the northern Gulf coast. De Luna's expedition commenced soon after Guido de las Bazáres had scouted the area looking for a possible site for a new colony. Bazáres, concerned that the Mississippi Delta was too mushy and swampy, advocated the advantages of Mobile Bay, which he named the Bay of Filipina. After receiving Bazáres' report, de Luna struck out from Vera Cruz with 500 soldiers—some of who were veterans of de Soto's earlier expedition—and approximately 1,000 settlers, including women and children. De Luna passed up Bazáres' recommended Filipina Bay for the deeper harbor at Ochuse (Pensacola). Five days after anchoring in Pensacola Bay, a hurricane struck, destroying most of de Luna's ships and supplies, and killing many of his people. After sending scouting parties inland, de Luna established an outpost at the large village of Nanipacana on the Alabama River where de Luna's men had discovered an abandoned supply of corn and beans that would barely get them through the winter. Perhaps remembering de Soto's legacy of destruction and disease, the village's inhabitants had run off as the conquistadores approached. Relying upon the glowing accounts given by de Soto's veterans of their previous visit to the area, de Luna sent a detachment of men further north to the Coca village on the Coosa River when Nanipacana's meager food supply ran out. For the most part, however, the lands they traversed were barren and the Indian villages were not as thriving as they had been when de Soto visited the area. As a result, de Luna's famished men beseeched him to return to Mexico "in order that we may not see ourselves perish and our wives and children die." De Luna relented and returned his men to the gulf coast, where they were eventually rescued by a Spanish fleet heading for the east coast of Florida.[11]

Spain's failure to colonize the lower Gulf region left Alabama free of European influence and settlers for nearly another century and a half. Then in 1699, French Canadian brothers Pierre Le Moyne, Sieur d'Iberville, and Jean-Baptiste Le Moyne, Sieur de Bienville—sons of a 1641 French émigré to Canada who profited handsomely from the fur trade—began exploring

[10] Higginbotham, "Discovery, Exploration, and Colonization," 11–12; Rogers et al., *Alabama*, 23–24; Higginbotham, "Battle of Mauvila," 29; Peter J. Hamilton, *Colonial Mobile* (1910; repr., Tuscaloosa: University of Alabama Press, 1976), 27.

[11] Rogers et al., *Alabama*, 23–24; Hamilton, *Colonial Mobile*, 32; Woodbury Lowery, *The Spanish Settlements Within the Present Limits of the United States, 1513–1561* (New York: G.P. Putnam's Sons, 1901), 351–77; Herbert I. Priestley, *Tristán de Luna: Conquistador of the Old South, A Study of Spanish Imperial Strategy* (Glendale, Cal.: Arthur H. Clark Co., 1936), 138.

the Alabama coastal region on behalf of France. Their explorations took them to Mobile Point, Dauphin Island (named by Iberville "Massacre Island" because of a large pile of human bones found there), and Mon Louis Island. Further explorations of the area led to the founding of La Mobile and the associated Fort Louis de la Louisiane in 1702 on the Mobile River at a site now known as Twenty-seven Mile Bluff near present-day Mount Vernon, Alabama. Named for the neighboring Mobilian Indians—perhaps descendants of the Mauvilla tribe subdued by de Soto—the colonial village of La Mobile served as the first permanent capital of the Louisiana colony of France. The French colonists were able to survive in this location for almost a decade primarily because of their amity with the local Native American tribes, or *petites nations*, which allowed them to settle on their tribal lands, enter into military alliances with them, trade with them, and provide them most of their food. The locale of their village, however, would prove to be tremendously inconvenient. Since Mobile Bay was then too shallow to support ocean-going vessels, imported goods and supplies for the settlement had to be rowed twenty-three miles up the bay from a port on Dauphin Island and then twenty-seven more miles up the Mobile River.[12]

Due to this inconvenience, as well as swampy living conditions, in 1711 the settlement was relocated to a site at the head of Mobile Bay where the current city of Mobile is located. Historian A. B. Moore compared the early French settlement at Mobile—now referred to as *Vieux Mobile*, or Old Mobile—to that of the earlier English settlement at Jamestown. They both endured Indian troubles, times of starvation, periods of unrest, and settlers who were not very industrious. Rowdy Canadian rangers were the settlement's only line of defense against the native tribes. In an effort to domesticate these Canadian defenders, Iberville arranged for twenty-three young French women to be sent over on a ship, named the *Pelican*, in 1704.[13]

Within a month nearly all the women had married, bringing some stability to the settlement. Ill prepared for the primitive life style awaiting them in the wilderness of Alabama, these "Pelican girls" proved to be quite feisty themselves, instigating the first known rebellion on Alabama soil in protest of having to eat cornbread rather than the French bread to which they were accustomed. This episode, known as the "petticoat insurrection," was significant enough that an exasperated Bienville noted in one of his dispatches to the crown that "the males in the colony [are] reconciled to corn, as an article of nourishment; but the females, who are mostly Parisians, have for this kind of food a dogged aversion," causing them to "inveigh bitterly against his grace, the Bishop of Quebec, who, they say, has enticed

---

[12] Grace Elizabeth King, *Jean Baptiste Le Moyne Sieur de Bienville* (New York: Dodd, Mead, and Company, 1892), 1–10; Moore, *History of Alabama*, 39–41; Rogers et al., *Alabama*, 26–28; Higginbotham, "Discovery, Exploration, and Colonization," 17; Gregory Waselkov, *Old Mobile Archeology* (Tuscaloosa: University of Alabama Press, 2005), 2–3, 36.

[13] Moore, *History of Alabama*, 39–41; Rogers et al., *Alabama*, 26–28. Unfortunately, the *Pelican* also brought with it yellow fever that had been contracted by crew members while in port at Havana and resulted in the death of over forty of the colonists and hundreds of neighboring Indians, including the Mobilians as well as the Tomé who were located further north along the Tombigbee River. Waselkov, *Old Mobile*, 2–3, 23–25, 37–38.

them away from home under the pretext of sending them to enjoy the milk and honey of the land of promise."[14]

The French exercised dominion over Mobile and much of Alabama for almost sixty years. During this period, for the first time ever, a western legal code was officially employed within the confines of present-day Alabama. Initially the colony of Louisiana was just a military outpost with no civil government. Its commandant was fully in charge, ruling under the prevailing French maritime law, the *Ordonnance de la Marine* of 1681.[15]

In 1712, however, King Louis XIV issued an edict requiring French colonists in Louisiana to utilize the laws of their native France, or *La Coutume de Paris*. First published in 1510 under the direction of Charles VII, *La Coutume de Paris* was a compilation of local customs dating back to the Teutonic invasion that had achieved the force of law in the vicinity of Paris and had been largely modified by Roman civil law. It was revised in 1580 to include 362 articles pertaining principally to civil law. It dealt specifically with issues of feudal law, property, possession, mortgages, family law, guardianship, gifts, wills, and successions. One of the most important attributes of French law was the community ownership of property between husband and wife. Feudal law principles of the Old World were certainly more relaxed in their application in Louisiana, however, as the French king recognized the need to provide his colonists a less restrictive form of ownership of property akin to the fee simple ownership available under English law to British colonists along the Atlantic seaboard of America.[16]

Iberville and Bienville laid the foundations of a proposed colony for France in the New World. Shortly after their discoveries along the gulf coast, Iberville sailed for France in May 1700 to lobby for a permanent French colony. He left M. de Sauvolle in charge at Fort Maurepas near present-day Biloxi, Mississippi, with his nineteen-year-old brother, Bienville, second in command. Bienville became commandant when Sauvolle died in 1701. At that time the main settlement of the proposed colony had not yet located in Mobile. During Iberville's absence, Bienville began developing a keen knowledge of local Indian cultures and languages and actively sought Indian allies amongst the Choctaw and Chickasaw. Iberville returned from France in December 1701 and shortly thereafter tasked Bienville with moving the expedition's military outpost from Biloxi to a spot twenty-seven miles up the Mobile River from present-day Mobile, which

---

[14] Charles Gayarré, *Louisiana; Its Colonial History and Romance* (New York: Harper & Brothers, 1851), 1: 93.

[15] General maritime law evolved from various maritime codes including Rhodian law (circa 800 BC), Roman law, the Rôles of Oléron (circa 1190), and the *Ordonnance de la Marine* (1681). All of these were relied on in the English Admiralty Court and in the maritime courts of Europe of the day. William Tetley, "Maritime Law as a Mixed Legal System, With Particular Reference to the Distinctive Nature of American Maritime Law . . .," *Tulane Maritime Law Journal* 23 (Spring 1999): 317.

[16] Jerah Johnson, "La Coutume de Paris: Louisiana's First Law," Louisiana History 30 (Spring 1989): 150–54; Peter Hamilton, *The Founding of Mobile: 1702–1718: Studies in the History of the First Capital of the Province of Louisiana, with Map Showing Its Relation to the Present City* (Mobile, Ala.: Commercial Print Co., 1911), 78–82; Moore, *History of Alabama*, 44.

would serve as a permanent capital for the proposed colony. Illnesses had become too frequent in Biloxi; Iberville wanted a location closer to the Indians and one from which he could keep a better eye upon British traders from the Carolinas. On July 20, 1703, Jean-Baptiste de La Croix de Chevrières de Saint-Vallier, the bishop of Quebec, added Mobile as a new parish to his North American diocese and soon thereafter assigned Henri Roulleaux de La Vente as its priest. It was Bishop Saint-Vallier who had spearheaded the effort in 1704 to bring over brides for the Canadian rangers defending Mobile in response to Iberville's request.[17]

Iberville died in Havana, Cuba, in July 1706, just after capturing the English possession of Nevis in the Caribbean and while waiting to attack the English province of Carolina. Upon Iberville's death, Nicolas Daneau de Muy was appointed governor of Louisiana, but never took office because he died as his ship was approaching Havana's harbor. Bienville had been passed over for the formal appointment because of a number of enemies he had acquired in the colony as a result of his suspected complicity in the questionable business practices of his brothers, Iberville and Joseph Le Moyne de Sérigny, both of whom had accumulated a sizeable wealth as a result of alleged profiteering. While these allegations impaired Bienville's reputation in Paris, he nevertheless was able to avoid recall by the French government and continued as the de facto ruler of the colony that he and his brother had founded. Continuing his quest for Indian allies, Bienville succeeded in aligning the Louisiana colony with the Choctaw Nation against the Chickasaw, who were suspected of being aligned with the British. Over the next several years, while France concentrated its resources on the War of Spanish Succession in Europe, Bienville kept the colony going by the support provided by his Choctaw allies and by trading with the reviled Spanish in Mexico.[18]

On September 14, 1712, the French crown chartered Louisiana to Antoine Crozat, a successful merchant, for a period of fifteen years. Strapped by the costs of the War of Spanish Succession, the crown expected Crozat to use his own resources to develop the colony. Crozat's charter, in addition to decreeing *La Coutume de Paris* in effect, called for the establishment of a *conseil supérieur* (Superior Council) to administer it. Although Antoine de la Mothe Cadillac was chosen to replace Bienville as governor of the colony, Cadillac reluctantly retained Bienville as his lieutenant governor, recognizing his superior diplomatic and administrative skills. Arriving in Mobile in 1713 to assume his duties, Cadillac observed "here is nothing more than piled up dregs of Canada, jailbirds who escaped the rope, without any subordination to Religion or Government, steeped in vice, principally in their concubinage with savage women, whom they prefer to French girls."

---

[17] Russell W. Strong, "Governor Bienville and the Fate of French Louisiana," *Gulf Coast Historical Review* 8 (Spring 1993): 7; Rogers et al., *Alabama*, 25–27; Higginbotham, "Discovery, Exploration, and Colonization," 19–20. As we have seen above, due to its inconvenient location and swampy conditions, in 1711 Mobile was moved down to the mouth of the Mobile River at Mobile Bay where the current city of Mobile is located.

[18] Strong, "Governor Bienville," 7–8; Higginbotham, "Discovery, Exploration, and Colonization," 22–23.

Health permitting, Cadillac pledged to "put the colony on a firm founda-tion," noting that at the moment, however, "it is not worth a straw." His pledge proved to be a tall order considering that the Superior Council was the only instrument within the colony available to administer justice to, and command the respect of, these disreputable citizens.[19]

The Superior Council was given a three-year license "to judge in last re-sort . . . all law suits and disputes criminal as well as civil commenced and intended among our subjects . . . without costs." The council was to be comprised of the governor; the Intendant of Justice, Police, and Finance; the first Councilor; an attorney general; and a clerk. Judgments in civil matters required the concurrence of three of the council members; criminal matters required the concurrence of five. Despite his enthusiasm to put the colony on a firm foundation, Cadillac had about as much confidence in this council as the citizens it was to regulate, describing it as composed "of ignorant and scandalous men . . . entirely devoted to their passions."[20]

The records of the Superior Council demonstrate that it had a wide-ranging jurisdiction over the legal affairs of the colony. It handled such civil matters as recordation of wills, sales of real property, renunciation of estates, acknowledgements of indebtedness, petitions for the recovery of debts, execution of marriage contracts, recordation of acts of partnership, sales of slaves, confirmations of the manumission of slaves, and reports of judgments entered in civil suits. A great percentage of the civil suits were petitions to recover debts. An example of the council's ability to enforce its judgments in these cases is an attachment proceeding recorded on Novem-ber 15, 1731, reflecting that the sheriff of the colony seized four horses and other unspecified property in satisfaction of a debt of 56 Spanish dollars. The creditor was the master gunner of the French ship *Dromadaire*.[21]

A typical early criminal prosecution heard by the Superior Council in-volved a defendant charged with theft from the King's Store on December 30, 1721. Justice was swiftly imposed less than three weeks later when the defendant was convicted in the council's chamber at Biloxi on January 16, 1722, and was sentenced to keelhauling. A common punishment of Europe-an navies, keelhauling consisted of dragging the offender underneath the ship across the keel from side to side. It was a dreaded sentence because of the possibility of serious lacerations from barnacles or even drowning in some cases. On September 13, 1722, the council imposed an arguably harsher sentence of flogging and six years of incarceration on a free black person also charged with theft from the company's store. Of course this sentence was only harsher than keelhauling if one makes the important assumption that the person punished survived the keelhauling! The incon-

---

[19] Johnson, "Coutume de Paris," 154; Richard F. Brown, "Colonial Mobile, 1712–1813," in Thomason, *Mobile*, 31.

[20] Henry Plauchè Dart, "The Legal Institutions of Louisiana," *Louisiana Historical Quarterly* 2 (January 1919): 76–79.

[21] Héloise H. Cruzat, trans., "Records of the Superior Council of Louisiana," *Louisiana Historical Quarterly* 7 (October 1924): 678–705; Héloise H. Cruzat, trans., "Records of the Superior Council of Louisiana," *Louisiana Historical Quarterly* 5 (April 1922): 246.

sistency in the disbursement of justice by the Superior Council is further demonstrated by a sentence of "whipping at the crossings" with no incarceration imposed on May 29, 1728, for a defendant convicted of a violent crime involving the stabbing of his victim.[22]

While the Superior Council provided some amount of domestic tranquility for the colony, Bienville concentrated his efforts on providing for its common defense. In 1708, following two failed expeditions led against them by Bienville, the Alabamas, the southernmost tribe of the Upper Creeks known to the French as the "Alibamons," formed an alliance with other tribes in opposition to the French. As a rejoinder to this alliance Bienville reacted vehemently by offering a gun and five pounds of ammunition for each Alibamons scalp taken. The skirmishes between the French and the Alibamons continued for a number of years. By the time Cadillac became governor in 1713, the Creeks were cozying up to British traders from South Carolina. Bienville thought it best to negotiate with the Indians and obtain the right for the French to construct a trading post in Creek country up the Alabama River. Although colonial authorities in Paris agreed, Governor Cadillac, always at odds with Bienville with respect to Indian policy, instead, thought it more important to establish a fort at Natchez on the Mississippi River.[23]

Just as the British were about to beat out the French to gain a foothold in Upper Creek territory in Alabama, fortune intervened on the side of the French with the advent of the Yamasee War in April 1715, in which numerous Indian tribes—including the Yamasee, Creek, Cherokee, and Chickasaw—rebelled against overreaching English traders and encroaching settlers. As a result of this war, in the fall of 1715, the Upper Creeks sent a delegation to Fort Louis in Mobile seeking an alliance with the French and delivering an invitation to the French to send traders to their country to supplant the British. As luck would have it, Bienville was in command while Cadillac was away on a prolonged mission up the Mississippi River. Taking advantage of the situation, Bienville eagerly agreed to send French traders to Creek country. As for the construction of a fort, however, Cadillac once again resisted the idea upon his return and, instead, sent Bienville to Natchez to oversee the construction of Fort Rosalie. In the interim, the Creeks sought to renew friendly relations with the British. This time, though, the French government in Paris had become more adamant that a post be established among the Alibamons Indians. Cadillac was notified in 1716 that "this post is absolutely necessary" to "place the savages in our interest." Later that year Cadillac was recalled and the way was cleared for the construction of the second inland fort within the Louisiana colony.[24]

---

[22] Cruzat, "Records of the Superior Council of Louisiana (1924)," 676–78, 686; Leland P. Lovette, *Navy Customs, Traditions and Usage* (Annapolis, Md.: United States Naval Institute, 1939), 69, 143; Louis Sicking, *Neptune and the Netherlands: State, Economy, and War at Sea in the Renaissance* (Leiden, Netherlands: Brill, 2004), 474.

[23] Daniel H. Thomas, *Fort Toulouse: The French Outpost at the Alabamas on the Coosa* (1960; repr., Tuscaloosa: University of Alabama Press, 1989), 5.

[24] Ibid., 6–10.

Jean Baptiste Le Moyne, Sieur de Bienville
Courtesy of Alabama Department of Archives and History

Under the direction of Bienville, once more serving as governor after Cadillac was removed from office, construction was begun in 1717 on a French post at the confluence of the Coosa and Tallapoosa rivers near present-day Wetumpka, Alabama. To be garrisoned by twenty to fifty French marines, its purpose was to encourage the fur trade and to serve as a buffer against the British. It was never intended to serve as point from which to attack the Alibamons, with whom Bienville had worked so hard to obtain as trading partners. The new post was officially named Fort Toulouse in honor of Admiral Louis Alexandre de Bourbon, the Count of Toulouse and a member of the Council of Marine, the French department that functioned as the ministry of the navy and of colonies from 1715 to 1718. However, the French usually referred to its posts in reference to their geographical location rather than by their official names. Thus, the fort was usually referred to as the "Post aux Alibamons" or "Fort des Alibamons." The fort was well underway as the British raced to reestablish themselves among the Creeks. Arriving as Fort Toulouse was nearing completion, a group of British bearing gifts were almost successful in winning the Alibamons back over to their side. But the French managed to prevail and maintained the post until the surrounding territory was ceded to the British by the Treaty of Paris in 1763. In the winter of 1763–1764, the last French commandant spiked the fort's cannons and dumped excess gun powder into the Coosa River prior to evacuating the post.[25]

The Superior Council, which had been empowered to act for only three years, had its authority extended "perpetually and irrevocably" on September 18, 1716. It thus survived the charter of its origin, which was surrendered in 1719 by a disillusioned Crozat who was losing money on his Louisiana venture. The crown next turned the Louisiana colony over to the Western Company, also known as the Company of the Indies and the Mississippi Company. This company was under the leadership of John Law, a colorful Scottish promoter with a passion for gambling and women. Law had fled to the continent after having been convicted of murder for killing a man in a duel and sentenced to death. Although pardoned by the crown, the victim's brother had taken an appeal, the outcome of which Law chose not to await. Law's exaggeration of the wealth of Louisiana resulted in an economic boom that soon spiraled out of control. Its speculative fever, known as the "Mississippi Bubble," eventually burst, bringing Louisiana back under the direct control of the royal crown and a return of Bienville as governor.[26]

During Law's monopoly, the colony's capital was moved from Mobile to New Biloxi in 1720 because Law's energies were focused upon the Mississippi River region and because of the closing of Fort Dauphin due to a hurricane-created sandbar. Mobile nevertheless became the seat of one of nine judicial districts created by the new company in order to bring justice

---

[25] Ibid., 10–12, 66; Moore, *History of Alabama*, 45 n.2; Daniel H. Thomas, "Fort Toulouse—In Tradition and Fact," *Alabama Review* 13 (October 1960): 243–48; Rogers et al., *Alabama*, 29. This site would have further significance in the legal and political development of Alabama when the Creeks surrendered to General Jackson there in 1814 and when the first courts of Montgomery County convened there in 1817 and 1818 while Alabama was still a territory. Clanton W. Williams, *The Early History of Montgomery and Incidentally of the State of Alabama* (University, Ala.: Confederate Publishing Company, 1979), 20; James W. Parker, "Fort Jackson after the War of 1812," *Alabama Review* 38 (April 1985): 128–29.

[26] Dart, "Legal Institutions of Louisiana," 82; Lucille Griffith, *Alabama: A Documentary History to 1900*, rev. ed. (Tuscaloosa: University of Alabama Press, 1972), 23; Moore, *History of Alabama*, 42–43; Brown, "Colonial Mobile," 31; Gayarré, *Louisiana*, 201; Rogers et al., *Alabama*, 30–32.

within closer grasp of the colonists, who were by then dispersed over an increasingly expanding area. The districts included the capital city of Biloxi, as well as Mobile, Alibamons (site of Fort Toulouse), Natchez, Yazoo, Natchitoches, Arkansas, and Illinois. Under this new system, each of the colony's districts had a local judge of its own assisted by two appointed citizens for hearing civil cases and four appointed citizens for hearing criminal cases. The judgments of these courts could be appealed to the Superior Council, which served as the colony's supreme court in addition to a court of first resort for the capital district in which it sat, first in Biloxi, and then in New Orleans after 1723.[27]

Even after Mobile lost its status as the capital of the colony, it nevertheless remained as the colony's largest town for a while. The labor required for improving the town, running the surrounding plantations, and working the wharves resulted in the importation of African slaves for the first time and the implementation of a legal code in addition to *La Coutume de Paris*. In March 1724, King Louis XV ordered Bienville to promulgate the *Code Noir* in Louisiana, patterned after a slave code first implemented within the French West Indies. The *Code Noir* was as much a religious edict as it was a system of laws for the purpose of controlling the increasing number of slaves in the colony. Indeed, it prohibited the public practice of any religion within the colony other than Roman Catholicism. In furtherance of its stranglehold on religious freedom, the *Code Noir* ordered the expulsion of Jews from the colony in the face of confiscation of property and imprisonment, invalidated the marriage of non-Catholics, declared children born of unions between non-Catholics as illegitimate, and forbade work on Sundays or religious holidays by anyone, including slaves. Additionally, only persons of the Catholic faith could be assigned authority over slaves, and slaves were required to be baptized and receive religious instruction in the Catholic faith.[28]

Although the *Code Noir* provided more protection to slaves than similar English codes, it nevertheless placed severe restrictions upon them to prevent insurrections, such as prohibiting the gathering of slaves of different masters at any time of day or night, with recidivists of this offense subjected to a possible death penalty; forbidding them from carrying weapons, unless hunting with the permission of their master; and forbidding slaves from selling any commodities without the express permission of their masters. Any slave who struck his master or his family members in the face or drew blood was punished by death. More humane provisions were included to protect the wellbeing of the slave population, such as prohibitions against torture, separation of husbands and wives by sale, and separation of young children from their mothers. Social relationships between the races were of concern to the Crown, however, as reflected in the *Code Noir*'s prohibition

---

[27] Johnson, "Coutume de Paris," 154.

[28] Moore, *History of Alabama*, 43; Donald E. Everett, "Free Persons of Color in Colonial Louisiana," *Louisiana History* 1 (Winter 1966): 21–22; Rogers et al., *Alabama*, 30; Dart, "Legal Institutions of Louisiana," 94; *Édit du Roi, Touchant la Police des Isles de l'Amérique Francaise* (Paris, 1687), 28–58.

of marriage between whites and blacks, whether slave or free. Whites were also forbidden to have extramarital trysts with slaves, and concubinage was outlawed between free blacks and slaves. A black person's status as a slave or as a free person was determined by the status of his or her mother, i.e., the children of a free father and a slave mother were slaves and, conversely, the children of a slave father and a free mother were free persons. Finally, the *Code Noir* provided for emancipation of slaves under certain conditions. Any owner twenty-five years or older could manumit his slaves if he so chose, but only with the approval of the Superior Council. Indeed, transcribed records of the Superior Council dated October 1, 1733, indicate that Bienville freed a male slave and his wife "in recognition of their good and faithful service . . . during 26 years." The *Code Noir* made it clear that manumitted slaves were granted "the same rights, privileges, and immunities which are enjoyed by free persons."[29]

The French Crown did not give the colonization of Louisiana precedence and thus many commercial interests shied away from investing in its development. Likewise the leaders of the Catholic Church were reluctant to send missionaries. Since it was difficult to lure French citizens to immigrate to Louisiana, a systematic deportation of criminals was employed between 1717 and 1720, resulting in the colony being populated during this period by petty criminals, deserters, vagrants, and the destitute. Most of the female immigrants had been convicted of minor offenses such as blasphemy and prostitution. Occasionally more hardened criminals were deported. The French king stopped the deporting of prisoners in May 1720 in response to a prison riot protesting the policy.[30]

Bienville, Louisiana's off-and-on governor, was removed from power in 1724 and recalled to France to respond to vague charges of maladministration. Replacing Bienville as interim governor was his cousin, Pierre Sidrac Dugue de Boisbriand. In 1727, Étienne de Périer, a veteran employee of the Company of the Indies, was appointed permanently to replace Bienville. Périer pursued an aggressive agricultural policy that encouraged the cultivation of tobacco in the area surrounding Fort Rosalie near Natchez. Unfortunately, this policy resulted in French encroachment on tribal lands of the Natchez Indians. As a consequence, on November 28, 1729, the Natchez attacked Fort Rosalie and brutally massacred 145 men, thirty-six women, and fifty-six children. The French replied in kind by nearly wiping out the Natchez tribe. Those that were not killed were either sold into West Indian slavery or escaped and allied with the Chickasaw to attack white settlements near New Orleans and Mobile. The Company of the Indies soon

---

[29] *Édit du Roi*, 28–58; Everett, "Free Persons of Color," 22–23; Rogers et al., *Alabama*, 30; Cruzat, "Records of the Superior Council of Louisiana" (1922), 250. The status of a person as either in bondage or free being determined by the status of the mother had previously been codified into law in 1662 by English colonists in Virginia. William Waller Hening, *The Statutes at Large, Being a Collection of All the Laws of Virginia from the First Session of the Legislature in the Year 1619* (New York: R & W & G. Bartow, 1823), 2:170.

[30] Rogers et al., *Alabama*, 31; Brown, "Colonial Mobile," 29, 37.

had enough and surrendered control of Louisiana back to the French government in July 1731.[31]

French colonial authorities once again turned to Bienville with the mandate for him to end the war with the Chickasaw. In his last term as Louisiana's governor from 1733 to 1742, Bienville restored order to a colony that was short of food and patched up strained relations with the Choctaw and Alabamons. He immediately began to recruit Choctaw warriors for an assault upon the Chickasaw. After only a few scattered Choctaw successes, around 1735 Bienville sought to strengthen the colony within the interior by establishing Fort Tombecbé, located along the Tombigbee River in present-day Sumter County, Alabama. The lack of a major offensive by the Choctaw, combined with growing concerns of British influence not only among the Chickasaw but the Choctaw as well, convinced Bienville that he must commit French troops to take on the Chickasaw. Thus in 1736 Bienville directed two campaigns against the Chickasaw, who were aided by the British and surviving Natchez Indians. One campaign was led by Bienville himself and consisted of an army of six hundred French soldiers and an additional six hundred Choctaw allies. The other campaign led by Lieut. Pierre d'Artaguette was much smaller, consisting of just 100 French colonial troops and 325 Indians. Both ended in failure. After a few more unsuccessful campaigns from 1736 to 1742, an ailing and aging Bienville returned to France for the remainder of his days.[32]

That the French were able to hold onto the Louisiana colony for the better part of six decades despite a lack of enthusiasm for colonization can be credited in some small degree to the implementation of *La Coutume de Paris* and the *Code Noir* that, in combination, gave a sense of direction and security to the settlers of the colony. Bienville deserves a much larger degree of credit due to his service to the colony for over forty years in one capacity or another. Historian Peter Hamilton believed Bienville to be "the controlling spirit in Louisiana as long as he was in it, no matter who was governor." Faced not only with France's neglect, but also with starvation, the hostility of surrounding Native Americans, and the rivalry of neighboring colonies belonging to Spain and Great Britain, the colony persisted under Bienville's recurrent leadership. An early biographer of Bienville summarized his feats as "bulwarking himself against the Spaniards in the east, spying out their land in the west, fending off the British at the north, keeping his channel of the Mississippi well open, scouring the Gulf with his little vessels, arming the Indians against one another and against everybody, but himself, . . . borrowing food, quartering his men in times of dearth upon the Indians, . . . punishing savages, repressing his own bandits,

---

[31] Brown, "Colonial Mobile," 32–33; Strong, "Governor Bienville," 11–15; Rogers et al., *Alabama*, 30–31; King, *Jean Baptise Le Moyne*, 306–21.

[32] Brown, "Colonial Mobile," 32–33; Strong, "Governor Bienville," 11–15; Rogers et al., *Alabama*, 30–31; King, *Jean Baptise Le Moyne*, 306–21.

building, sowing, [and] carrying out with a handful of soldiers and a pittance of money the great Mississippi and Gulf policy of Iberville."[33]

French control of Alabama ended with the signing of the Treaty of Paris in 1763 at the conclusion of the French and Indian War. By the terms of the treaty France ceded Louisiana west of the Mississippi River to Spain, and Canada and the rest of its territory east of the Mississippi River to Great Britain. Great Britain then ceded New Orleans to Spain in exchange for Florida. The British crown decided to establish two provinces out of the lands surrendered by France and Spain. Under this division of territory, the peninsula of Florida became East Florida, with St. Augustine as its capital, and the remainder from Apalachicola over to the Pearl River became West Florida, with Pensacola its capital. Mobile was within the area between the Perdido and Pearl Rivers, and thus became subject to British rule for the first time.[34]

On October 20, 1763, the French commander at Fort Condé officially surrendered Mobile to Major Robert Farmar, an American-born British Army officer. Fort Condé was then renamed Fort Charlotte in honor of the British queen. Although Major Farmar allowed the French to continue to practice the Roman Catholic faith and keep their property, he recognized English as the official language and the Anglican Church as the official church of the colony. He also instituted the common law of England, which would endure well beyond Great Britain's rule and would lay the foundation for Alabama's system of jurisprudence when it became a territory of the United States.[35] Major Farmar ruled Mobile as a military commander for a year until George Johnstone was named governor of British West Florida and established a civil government in Pensacola. Governor Johnstone had a belligerent and domineering demeanor that kept him at odds with civil and military authorities. His confrontations with Major Farmer eventually resulted in Farmar being court-martialed amidst allegations of embezzlement.[36]

---

[33] Hamilton, *Founding of Mobile*, 71; King, *Jean Baptiste Le Moyne*, 147–48. That Bienville possessed the callousness necessary to survive the challenges of this wild frontier is demonstrated by his ordering the decapitation of seventeen of eighteen deserters accused of treason in an action against the Spanish at Pensacola. The other deserter was hanged on Dauphin Island. Pickett, *History of Alabama*, 218.

[34] Rogers et al., *Alabama*, 31; Moore, *History of Alabama*, 47. The northern boundary of the British colony of West Florida was that of 38° 28' and thus included much of present-day south Alabama. However, the area above this line situated just south of present-day Birmingham was then included within the British province of Illinois. Pickett, *History of Alabama*, 320.

[35] The common law of England had been decreed applicable to England's current and future colonies by the Board of Trade in 1720. Edward Channing, *A History of the United States*, vol. 1, *The Planting of a Nation in the New World, 1000–1600* (New York: Macmillan, 1905), 174. English common law, the origin of which encompasses too broad a topic to discuss herein, was a body of law based upon centuries of customs which evolved into precedents as determined and declared by the English courts as opposed to legislative enactments. See generally James Kent, *Commentaries on American Law* (New York: O. Halsted, 1826), 471–72.

[36] Rogers et al., *Alabama*, 33. After returning from an expedition to Illinois where he helped establish British rule, Farmar was eventually acquitted, and he retired as a planter on the Tensaw River near present-day Stockton, Alabama, in Baldwin County. Farmar continued to

Not only did the British introduce their common law to the future state of Alabama, they also gave it its first form of representative government.[37] While earlier French settlers had been content to be governed from Paris, the English settlers coming into West Florida, like their kindred in the Crown's other colonies in America, believed in the right of self-governance. Johnstone described the colony's incoming immigrants as "the refuse of the Jails of great Citys [*sic*] and the overflowing Scum of the Empire." Thus, seeing the need for a strong government to deal with these rowdies, he appointed a council that enjoyed considerable power and regulatory authority. But in order to pass new laws of a local nature he eventually called for the election of representatives of the freeholders, which included those he had previously denigrated as scum, to serve in a lower chamber to the Council. The resulting General Assembly met in a rented house in Pensacola and was divided into the appointed Council and the elected Common House of Assembly. Legislation passed by these bodies required the approval of the governor and, even with his approval, could be vetoed by the Board of Trade, which was an agency of the British government with administrative authority over the Crown's colonies.[38]

The governor of the colony alone had the authority to convene a general assembly and to determine the constituencies and the number of delegates to be elected to the Commons House, or lower house. The governor also had sufficient discretion in defining the electorate so as to allow him to extend the vote to householders as well as freeholders. The constituencies, or electoral districts, consisted of Mobile, Pensacola, and Campbelltown, a few miles east of Pensacola on the Escambia River. By 1778 the population had shifted such as to result in the addition of the districts of Manchac and Natchez and the elimination of Campbelltown. Approximately 54 percent of the West Florida legislators were merchants; planters made up 23 percent of the delegates; military officers comprised 12 percent; and lawyers closed the ranks at 11 percent. Planters and lawyers were somewhat more prevalent in the Mobile district, while military candidates were more favored by the Pensacola electorate.[39]

Four governors convened seven General Assemblies during the eighteen years of British rule in West Florida. The first session called by Governor Johnstone on November 3, 1766, was by far the most productive,

---

yield considerable influence in the area as a substantial landowner with many slaves and as a five-time elected representative in the General Assembly of West Florida. His plantation, known as Farm Hall, became an important meeting place for traders and travelers coming in and out of Mobile. In the summer of 1775 Farmar hosted William Bartram, the renowned American naturalist and botanist. Brown, "Colonial Mobile," 42; Hamilton, *Colonial Mobile*, 196, 202; Robert R. Rea, *Major Robert Farmar of Mobile* (Tuscaloosa: University of Alabama Press, 1990), 81–111.

[37] Robert R. Rea and Milo B. Howard, comps., *The Minutes, Journals, and Acts of the General Assembly of British West Florida* (Tuscaloosa: University of Alabama Press, 1979), ix.

[38] Moore, *History of Alabama*, 44; Robin F. A. Fabel, *Bombast and Broadsides: The Lives of George Johnstone* (Tuscaloosa: University of Alabama Press, 1987), 33–46, quoted in Rogers et al., *Alabama*, 33; Rea and Howard, *Minutes, Journals, and Acts*, x.

[39] Rea and Howard, *Minutes, Journals, and Acts*, xiv–xvii.

passing twenty-three acts between November 24, 1766, and June 6, 1767. Governor Montford Browne convened the second and third General Assemblies, which sat between December 1767 and February 1769. These two assemblies produced a total of only ten statutes. Governor John Eliot called the election for the fourth General Assembly, but due to Eliot's suicide soon thereafter, Montford Browne was named by the Crown to again lead the Assembly. It passed eight acts between March 19 and May 18, 1770. Governor Peter Chester, the colony's longest serving governor, called the fifth General Assembly, which passed five acts between June 21 and July 15, 1771.[40]

The acts passed by these assemblies responded to the needs of a frontier colony and imposed measures to regulate the conduct of its citizens. Most important for an ordered society were a number of statutes that addressed the organization and refinement of the local government, including acts regulating elections, setting the number of assemblymen, regulating the duration of assemblies, instituting a court of requests (a court to review equitable petitions of the citizens), regulating the method of appointing constables, appointing vestries and parish officers for Mobile and Pensacola, and creating a separate judicial system for the newly created Charlotte County that included Mobile and its environs. To further promote the well-being of the colony through commerce and settlement, acts encouraged immigration, the building of wharfs in Mobile and Pensacola, and better regulation of the Indian trade. Concerns for maintaining order were addressed by such laws as "An Act to Restrain Drunkenness and Promote Industry," "An Act Empowering the Magistrates and Freeholders of Charlotte County Occasionally to Prohibit the Selling of Rum or Other Strong Liquors to the Indians," "An Act to Prevent Stealing of Horses and Neat Cattle and for the More Effectual Discovery and Punishment of Such Persons as shall Unlawfully Brand, Mark, or Kill the Same," "An Act Punishing All Persons Who May Infringe Any of the Treaties Made with the Indians," and "An Act for the Punishment of Vagabonds and Other Idle and Disorderly Persons, and to Prevent Persons Hunting on the Indians' Grounds and Trespassing on the Lands of the Crown."[41]

The first General Assembly made extensive provisions for both indentured servants and slaves by the passage of "An Act for the Regulation of Servants" and "An Act for the Regulation and Government of Negroes and Slaves." Like the French before them, the British felt the need for strict control of slaves and made life for them even harsher. Slaves could be put to death or dismembered if found guilty of felonies such as burglary, robbery, burning of houses, or rebellious conspiracies. At least two justices and a panel of freeholders would determine the slave's innocence or guilt. Upon a finding of guilt they could, within their discretion, impose a sentence of death or a lesser sentence consisting of a form of corporal punishment or deportation from the colony. However, if a slave was found guilty of murdering a white person, the death penalty was mandatory. Also, when more

---

[40] Ibid., x–xi.

[41] Ibid., 397–98.

than one slave participated in a capital crime other than murder, only one was put to death to serve as a deterrent example to the others, who were returned to their owners after receiving such corporal punishment as the justices and freeholders saw fit to inflict.[42]

The movement of slaves within the colony was strictly regulated. For example, a slave was not allowed to be more than two miles from his plantation or residence unless with a white person or in possession of a ticket specifying from what place and to where he or she was traveling. Slaves were also prohibited from meeting or feasting together in numbers of more than six after nine o'clock at night. Slaves caught at gaming were "whipped through the streets of the town" where the offense was committed. Likewise, retailers of rum or other spirituous liquors would be fined forty shillings if slaves were allowed to meet and drink or game in their establishment. Other provisions regarding slavery made manumission very expensive and pronounced that no slave could be made free by becoming a Christian. The law further provided that if a slave were executed for a crime, his master was reimbursed the slave's full value.[43]

The most significant legislation pertaining to the political development of the future state of Alabama was "An Act to Erect Mobile into a County and to establish a Court of Common Pleas Therein," passed by the General Assembly on January 2, 1767. Recognizing the great expense to Mobilians in attending the courts at Pensacola, the assembly created Charlotte County, including Mobile and its immediate vacinity, and established a court to service its citizens. The three Justices of the Peace residing in the new county were given full power and authority to sit as a Court of Common Pleas, having jurisdiction over all cases not exceeding thirty pounds sterling. Their judgment in such cases was to be final. This court sat in Mobile on the second Tuesdays in February, May, August, and November each year. The justices were empowered to appoint their own clerk, whose duties included keeping a fair record of the court's proceedings and issuing writs and other legal process returnable to the court. Justices were expected to attend each session of the court upon penalty of forfeiting forty shillings sterling, to be donated to the poor of Mobile, for each day of an unexcused absence. Mobile's experiment in home rule ended after five years when the Privy Council disallowed the act creating Mobile's court.[44]

Between 1771 and 1778, the colonial government operated without the benefit of a General Assembly. Although a sixth assembly was called by Governor Chester in March 1772, it never convened primarily due to the Mobile assembly members' objections to Chester's decision to remove term limitations. The Pensacola delegation's decision not to take their seats if Mobile was not represented resulted in the necessity of the governor ruling without an assembly. This stalemate lasted until a seventh assembly was

---

[42] Ibid., 342–46; Brown, "Colonial Mobile," 45.

[43] Rea and Howard, *Minutes, Journals, and Acts*, 342–46.

[44] Ibid., 324; Peter J. Hamilton, *Colonial Mobile: An Historical Study Largely from Original Sources, of the Alabama-Tombigbee Basin and the Old South West . . .*, rev. ed. (Boston: Houghton Mifflin Co., 1910), 244–45.

finally convened in response to the growing dangers of the American Revolution nearing the colony's borders. This assembly sat between October 1 and November 5, 1778, but was unable to pass any legislation due in part to the continuing dispute with the fractious Mobilians, as well as the interruption of proceedings by a ravaging hurricane that struck Pensacola during mid-October. Chester, irritated with the squabbling of members over prerogatives and property, adjourned the assembly, which was not to be convened again due to the Spanish accession of the colony in 1781.[45]

Chester's unwillingness to work with an assembly to pass a militia bill no doubt hastened the fall of the western portion of the colony. With Spain's entry into the war against England, the Spanish governor of Louisiana saw the opportunity to attack Mobile on behalf of Spain. Governor Bernardo de Gálvez thus sailed from New Orleans on January 11, 1780, with a total force of 754 men. He was joined just off Mobile Bay by five ships from Havana, carrying another 1,412 men. Vastly outnumbered, Mobile's commander, Elias Dunford, eventually surrendered. On March 14, 1780, de Gálvez took possession of Fort Charlotte and raised the Spanish flag over the future Alabama city. Pensacola would subsequently fall in May of 1781, and all of West Florida became a Spanish Colony.[46]

José de Ezpeleta became the first Spanish commandant at Fort Charlotte, and on May 16, 1780, he ordered the inhabitants of the Mobile district to take a loyalty oath to the Spanish government. The majority of inhabitants took the required oath and were rewarded with a mild Spanish rule that allowed for a gradual eradication of the well-established French law and customs. Eventually Spain tailored the colonial laws and customs of her *Recopilacion de Leyes de los Reinos de Indias* to fit the frontier conditions existing along the gulf coast of Alabama and Mississippi. The *Recopilacion* acquired its legal concepts from a vast body of ancient Spanish law, particularly the *Siete Partidas* commissioned by King Alfonso X and completed around 1265. This seven-part code dealt with almost all aspects of life, from political and canon law to civil and criminal law. The *partidas* also addressed political, philosophical, moral, and theological topics in addition to serving as a compilation of laws.[47]

---

[45] Rea and Howard, *Minutes, Journals, and Acts*, xi–xii, 272–78, 314–15. Chester alleged that the merchants of Mobile did not want an assembly for fear that it would regulate their activities in the Indian trade. Brown, "Colonial Mobile," 49–50.

[46] Brown, "Colonial Mobile," 51–52.

[47] Hamilton, *Colonial Mobile* (1910), 321–22; Brown, "Colonial Mobile," 52; Jack D.L. Holmes, "The Role of Blacks in Spanish Alabama: The Mobile District, 1780–1813," *Alabama Historical Quarterly* 37 (Spring 1975): 6; Roger Bigelow Merriman, *The Rise of the Spanish Empire in the Old World and in the New*, vol. 1, *"The Middle Ages"* (New York: Macmillan, 1918), 241–43. The *partidas* also expounded on the ideal qualities and characteristics that rulers and institutions should possess, with such topics as, "How a king should be moderate in eating and in drinking," "How the children of the king should be trained to be well dressed and clean," "How doctors and surgeons who represent themselves as learned and are not so deserved to be punished if any one dies through their fault," and "That no monk should be permitted to study physic or laws"; Ulick Ralph Burke, *A History of Spain from the Earliest Times to the Death of Ferdinand the Catholic*, 2nd ed. (London: Longman's, Green, and Co., 1900), 1: 281–83.

Throughout Spain's reign in Alabama territory, military officials governed Mobile under the orders of the Spanish governor in New Orleans until the Louisiana Purchase in 1803, and then from that date until 1813 under the orders of the governor of Spanish West Florida at Pensacola. Mobile's commandant decided all military, political, and judicial matters. Employing the Spanish paternal system of colonial government, the commandant in each district was supreme in political and military matters that governed the soldiers. Additionally, he appointed inferior judges called *alcaldes*, or *syndics*, but the commandant remained the superior judge with final authority. He also was the district's notary and custodian of all legal records. The record keeper received fees of fifty cents per signature, a fact which historian Peter Hamilton surmised accounted for the ample number of notices, certificates, and other legal documents in the records.[48]

The commandant exercised a broad, and often very summary, jurisdiction over most kinds of civil disputes, including contract, attachment, and damages for personal injury. The tribunals, or courts, held in Mobile were very formal. Instead of lawyers, in the sense of present day private practitioners, clerks and notaries who were public officials aided the parties in their petitions. Criminal cases were tried before the same tribunals as civil, often with an officially recognized defending representative. Appeals could be taken to the supreme tribunal of the colony in New Orleans if a security was given for costs. Further appeals could be taken to St. Jago de Cuba and finally to Spain. The *alcalde*, similar to a justice of the peace, tried civil and criminal cases summarily without a written record of the proceedings. The *alcalde*'s jurisdiction was limited to civil matters in which the amount in dispute did not exceed twenty dollars.[49]

One of the more interesting aspects of life in Spanish Mobile was the role played by "free persons of color." Free blacks amounted to twenty percent of Mobile's total free population in 1788, increasing to thirty percent by 1805. Their status as free persons enabled them to enter into contracts, buy and sell property, manage businesses, and sue and be sued. Mobile also had a black militia unit with a first sergeant and twenty-one militiamen. The unit was kept separate from the white troops and ironically was used at times to track down runaway slaves. Important positions in the community held by free blacks included sailors ferrying supplies between Dauphin Island and Mobile, a nurse at the royal hospital, a maintenance man for the coast guard, a master mason, and a baking contractor for Fort San Esteban. Spanish officers lived openly with their mulatto concubines and officially recognized their offspring by naming them as their natural children in the local parish registers. Some free blacks and mulattoes lived alongside whites in the prominent section of town.[50]

A court-martial over two handkerchiefs allegedly stolen by soldiers of

---

[48] Hamilton, *Colonial Mobile* (1910), 321–22; Brown, "Colonial Mobile," 54.

[49] Hamilton, *Colonial Mobile: An Historical Study Largely from Original Sources, of the Alabama-Tombigbee Basin and the Old South West* . . . (Boston: Houghton Mifflin Company, 1898), 280–81.

[50] Brown, "Colonial Mobile," 56–58; Holmes, "Role of Blacks in Spanish Alabama," 11–17.

the Crown from a free mulatto woman in Mobile further demonstrates the equality afforded to the free blacks of the colony. Although the accused soldiers were acquitted by a court-martial convened in Pensacola, governor-general Francisco Luis Hector, el Baron de Carondelet, in his role as the Inspector General of the armies of the colony, refused to accept the verdict and forwarded the case to the Supreme Council of War in Spain with his objections as to how the case had resulted in a "white wash" of the guilty parties. While there is no record of the results of this appeal, the fact such an appeal was even made demonstrates how diligently the local Spanish authorities sought to protect the rights of "free persons of color." Governor-General Carondelet showed similar sympathy for a free black woman in a case of slander brought by Capt. Don Pedro Favrot in 1795 against Maria Cofignie, who allegedly insulted and berated his wife by addressing her daughter as the "daughter of a whore." Based upon the testimony of two witnesses presented by Favrot, Carondelet placed Cofignie temporarily under house arrest, as there was no women's prison at that time. Cofignie was then allowed to provide her side of the story and played on the sympathies of the court as a single working woman with several children to support. Eventually Carondelet encouraged Favrot to settle for an apology to his wife and daughter, which Cofignie reluctantly gave.[51]

Extensive plantations and ranches along the rivers and coast helped propel agriculture to be the leading industry in the Mobile and Tensaw districts under Spanish rule. Mobile and its environs were thus moving closer to a slave-based economy. By 1795, the Mobile district had a total of forty-nine planters who owned 284 slaves. Although Spain initially continued the relatively mild *Code Noir* that had been instituted by the French to regulate those in human bondage, slave insurrections at Saint-Domingue (Haiti) and at Point Coupée in Louisiana resulted in Carondelet issuing a more stringent slave code and ordering a suspension of the slave trade. Worsening conditions prompted some slaves to flee into the backwoods of the surrounding "Indian country." These slaves were called "cimarrones" or "cimarrons" and they had a price on their heads. Despite these worsening conditions, slaves under Spanish rule had the right to petition the government to be transferred to another owner if physically abused by his or her current master. Also, slaves could be bestowed freedom if the commandant granted emancipation after the owner was paid a price fixed by arbitration.[52]

---

[51] Holmes, "Role of Blacks in Spanish Alabama," 11–17; Kimberly S. Hanger, "'The Most Vile Atrocities': Accusations of Slander against Maria Cofignie, Para Libre (Louisiana 1795)," in *Colonial Lives: Documents in Latin American History, 1550–1850*, ed. Richard Boyer and Geoffrey Spurling (New York: Oxford University Press, 2000), 269–78. Don Pedro Favrot served as Mobile's commandant from 1783 to 1787. See Jack D. L. Holmes, "Law and Order in Spanish Natchez, 1781–1798," *Journal of Mississippi History* 25 (July 1963): 186–201, for examples of how justice was imposed by the Spanish in the nearby Natchez district in litigation that was similar to that carried on throughout Spanish Louisiana.

[52] Moore, *History of Alabama*, 56–57; Brown, "Colonial Mobile," 56–58; Holmes, "Role of Blacks in Spanish Alabama," 7–13; Jack D. L. Holmes, "The Abortive Slave Revolt at Point Coupée, Louisiana, 1795," *Louisiana History* 11 (Fall 1970): 354–57; Hamilton, *Colonial Mobile* (1910), 349.

Don Pedro Favrot, who served as Mobile's commandant from October 14, 1783, until June 28, 1787, was one of the more intriguing leaders during the colonial period of Mobile and of the lower portion of what would become Alabama. Born Pierre Joseph Favrot in Louisiana in July 1749 to French parents, he had a forty-two-year military career, serving under King Louis XV of France and Kings Carlos III and IV of Spain. Following a long line of military officers in his family, Favrot first served in the French army and was assigned to the Arkansas Post. After his mother's death he went on leave to join his father, who had gone back to Paris. When his leave was over, he was ordered to Saint-Domingue for a brief period and then returned to France where he served as a recruiting officer on the Isle de Ré for a year and a half. After briefly taking command of a force embarking for Martinique, Favrot was allowed to retire from the French army upon his father's death in order to return to Louisiana where his sister still lived. Since Louisiana was now a Spanish colony, Favrot had to enter the service of the King of Spain to continue his military career in Louisiana. With the help of a benefactor in the Spanish royal court, he was allowed to transfer to the Spanish army. On November 20, 1778, Favrot was commissioned a captain of a company in the second battalion of the Regiment of Infantry of Louisiana and was thenceforth known as Don Pedro José Favrot.[53]

When Favrot arrived in New Orleans in April 1779 to assume his new position, he was assigned to Spanish Governor Don Bernardo de Gálvez. Favrot quickly gained the confidence of de Gálvez and was given a high place in his councils. Soon thereafter he accompanied de Gálvez on his famous campaign against the British forts of Bute at Manchac and New Richmond at Baton Rouge, which resulted in the British abandoning the Mississippi River valley. De Gálvez's faith in this French Creole officer was confirmed when he left Favrot in command of the newly acquired fort at Baton Rouge while de Gálvez went back to New Orleans. Favrot served as the Commandant of the Post of Baton Rouge for almost two years and was commended by de Gálvez for his efforts in remodeling the fort and for the abilities he displayed in both civil and military affairs. In August 1781 he surrendered his Baton Rouge command and reported to New Orleans, where he served for nearly two years before being reassigned to Mobile to replace the ailing Enrique Grimarest.[54]

Mobile's commandants, including Favrot, generally relied on appointed *alcaldes* to handle routine civil and criminal matters so that they could focus their attention on making land grants, protecting Spanish trade with the Indians, and defending settlers from attack. Favrot was highly successful in maintaining peace and amiable relations with area Indians by conducting his negotiations through Alexander McGillivray, a Creek chieftain of Scottish and French descent who was hailed as the "Alabama Talleyrand" by historian A.J. Pickett. Also of great assistance to Favrot in keeping order in the territory was John Linder, appointed civil administrator (*alcalde*) of

---

[53] Helen H. Parkhurst, "Don Pedro Favrot, a Creole Pepys," *Louisiana Historical Quarterly* 28 (July 1945): 679–94.

[54] Ibid., 694–98.

the Tensaw District in September 1785. Linder, a native of Switzerland, was influenced by McGillivray at the time of the American Revolution to leave Charleston, where he had been an engineer and surveyor, to settle in the Tensaw district near Mobile. Linder and his son quickly became leading landowners in what was to become south Alabama, growing corn, tobacco, rice, and chickpeas. They also already owned eighty-two slaves, twenty-seven horses, and seventy-two head of cattle. Presumably, by this time the younger Linder had reformed from his previous exploits as the leader of a group of "disbanded men from the British and American Armies, together with some Vagrants from the different Provinces" who engaged in "repeated acts of robbery and rebellion."[55]

In addition to his skills in diplomacy, Favrot ably handled a myriad of administrative and legal matters that helped to keep order in and around Mobile. In this regard he assisted the governor of Pensacola in supplying meat to his post until the Indians could bring in venison; fixed prices and regulated the sale of merchandise to Indians; took measures to prevent the spread of rabies in the colony; had runaway slaves captured and returned to their owners; and collected money from a resident of Mobile owed to a free man of color. As part of a very early major law enforcement initiative, he also ordered the capture of William Drue, the leader of a gang of frontier ruffians who were wreaking havoc throughout the Tensaw country of lower Alabama looting homes; stealing livestock, equipment and weapons; capturing and killing slaves; and tearing down fences and ruining crops.[56]

More mundane duties of the commandant included serving as the official before whom marriage contracts were executed and sealing up the personal effects of deceased citizens in anticipation of proper administration of their estates. An example of a prenuptial agreement executed before Commandant Favrot in May 1786 provided for a Catholic marriage as soon as either party requested it, that neither party was responsible for the antenuptial debts of the other, and that all property was to be held in common in accordance with the custom of Spain. Favrot knew something about the formalities involving marriages as he himself, while serving as Mobile's commandant, filed a petition with His Catholic Majesty on December 7, 1783, seeking permission to marry. In an accompanying fifty-four-page document that had taken him two years to prepare, Favrot made the case that his fiancée possessed the requisite qualifications imposed by royal ordinances to serve as the spouse of a Spanish soldier. Apparently viewing this tedious process as a mere formality, Favrot and his lover solemnized their marriage in church soon after dutifully sending their petition to His Majesty, but well before officially receiving royal consent.[57]

As rumors reached Mobile that Favrot was to be removed from command, leading citizens petitioned the governor in opposition to his removal,

---

[55] Parkhurst, "Don Pedro Favrot," 700; Jack D. L. Holmes, "Alabama's Forgotten Settler: Notes on the Spanish Mobile District, 1780–1813," *Alabama Historical Quarterly* 33 (Summer 1971): 89, 90–91, 96; Pickett, *History of Alabama*, 369.

[56] Parkhurst, *Don Pedro Favrot*, 700–01.

[57] Hamilton, *Colonial Mobile* (1910), 346–47; Parkhurst, "Don Pedro Favrot," 699.

praising his fairness in the administration of justice and his success in keeping the Indians at peace, which was essential to the safety and security of their homes. Residents of the surrounding Tensaw and Tombigbee districts also signed similar petitions. Despite these efforts, he was relieved of his command and replaced by Don Vicente Folch on June 28, 1787. Favrot subsequently served at Natchez and at the Post of Plaquemines below New Orleans before retiring to a plantation in West Baton Rouge in 1804, where he became an American citizen. He went on to serve in the Louisiana state legislature before his death in 1824.[58]

The Spanish rule over Mobile and its surrounding areas was inevitably destined to end as a result of several momentous geopolitical events occurring in a relatively short span of time, including the end of the American Revolution in 1783, the Treaty of San Lorenzo in 1795, the Louisiana Purchase in 1803, and the Napoleonic invasion of Spain in 1808. The first of these events culminated with the signing of the Peace of Paris in 1783, which extended the western boundary of the United States to the Mississippi River and established the southern boundary at the thirty-first parallel. Spain did not recognize this boundary, instead claiming territory up to the line of 32° 28'. In the 1795 Treaty of San Lorenzo, however, Spain finally acknowledged the thirty-first parallel as the boundary of West Florida, conceded free navigation rights on the Mississippi River to the United States, and agreed to mutual protection against Indian attacks. Although the treaty also provided that Spain was to withdraw from all of its forts north of the thirty-first parallel, no one could agree where that line fell.[59]

With increasing numbers of settlers coming to the area, the United States wanted once and for all to establish its southern boundary. Thus in 1797, Andrew Ellicott, surveyor general of the United States, was given the responsibility of surveying and establishing the boundary line. Despite initial resistance from Spain and area Indians and after encountering slow going through the Lower Creek Territory, Ellicott was successful in establishing the southern boundary of Mississippi and Alabama in 1799. Nevertheless, the United States' jurisdiction over this area was not completely clear due to the state of Georgia's claim of a sea-to-sea charter. In furtherance of this claim, in 1785 Georgia organized part of the area into Bourbon County, which was located on the Mississippi River and included the future city of Natchez and several counties in the present state of Mississippi. Under pressure from a national government concerned about conflicting Spanish and Native American claims, Georgia dissolved the county in 1788. But in 1789, the state sold fifteen million acres of land in this area to three Yazoo speculative land companies. President Washington asserted federal authority over the area and revoked the sale as illegal, but some speculators refused to comply. Despite purchasing the lands at dirt-cheap prices, the companies defaulted on their payments to the state of Georgia and the

---

[58] Parkhurst, "Don Pedro Favrot," 700–34. Two of Don Pedro's sons went on to serve as state judges in Louisiana. His son Philogene predeceased him, ironically losing his life in a fierce duel of sabers with another judge in 1822.

[59] Rogers et al., *Alabama*, 39–43.

sales were canceled. In 1795, Georgia attempted a second Yazoo land sale, this time selling 21,500,000 acres, much of which was in Alabama, for $500,000, amounting to about 2.5¢ per acre. Speculators in turn sold the land on credit for one dollar per acre, foisting spurious titles on innocent purchasers. Claims of some bona fide purchasers were ultimately paid by Georgia, leaving other claims to be settled by congressional intervention. Conflicting Spanish land grants and bogus Yazoo titles would set the stage for many legal disputes during the territorial period of Alabama.[60]

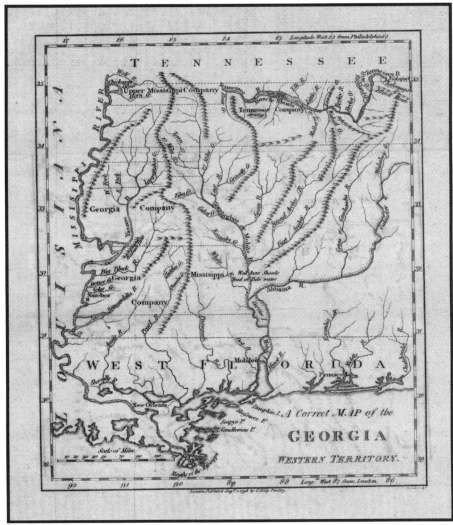

"A Correct Map of the Georgia Western Territory"
1798, published by London mapmakers Jedidiah Morse & Charles Dilly

Courtesy Barry Lawrence Ruderman Antique Maps, www.RareMaps.com, used by permission

---

[60] Ibid., 43–44.

The withdrawal of Spain from the territory north of the thirty-first parallel and the land-grabbing activities of the Yazoo land companies combined to draw settlers into the Tombigbee and Natchez districts. Many of these settlers began pouring into the Fort St. Stephens area of Alabama from Tennessee, Kentucky, the Carolinas, Georgia, and Virginia over the Natchez Trace, down the Tennessee River and then crossing over to the Tombigbee River, or down the Alabama River basin. Responding to an increasing population, Congress organized the Mississippi Territory in 1798, taking in all of the present states of Mississippi and Alabama between the lines of 31° and 32° 28'. However, it was not until 1802 that the state of Georgia formally relinquished its claim to lands within the Mississippi Territory. In 1804 the northern border was extended to the Tennessee line. Subsequent cessions of land made by the Chickasaw in 1805 and the Cherokee in 1806 opened up the Huntsville area for settlement.[61]

The colonial period had not quite ended in all of Alabama, however, as Spain continued to hold on to the territory south of the thirty-first parallel, including Mobile. In 1802 Spanish influence in the area began to unravel when Spain returned Louisiana to France. Then in 1803 Napoleon sold Louisiana to the United States for $15 million, resulting in the United States' negotiators claiming that Mobile was included within the deal. Spain in turn imposed a twelve percent duty on goods transported on the Mobile River in an effort to discourage Anglo-American settlement in the area. Congress responded in 1804 by enacting the Mobile Act declaring the annexation of all navigable waterways within the United States flowing into the Gulf of Mexico and created a special customs district at the newly constructed Fort Stoddert, located just north of Mobile. Distracted by the Napoleonic invasion of 1808, Spain slowly began to lose control of its North American territory as the number of its troops dwindled to only fifteen hundred. Citizens of Baton Rouge took advantage of this situation in the summer of 1810 by driving the Spanish out of their garrison and requesting admission to the United States. Asserting that Baton Rouge was also part of the Louisiana Purchase, President James Madison annexed the area, and the United States took possession on December 6, 1810.[62]

Efforts by U.S. citizens to seize Spanish West Florida were temporarily foiled by the calming intervention of Edmund P. Gaines, the commandant of Fort Stoddert, and Harry Toulmin, a federal district judge in the Tensaw District of the Mississippi Territory.[63] Seeing the handwriting on the wall,

---

[61] Moore, *History of Alabama*, 57; Rogers et al., *Alabama*, 43–44; "An Act for an Amicable Settlement of Limits with the State of Georgia, and Authorizing the Establishment of a Government in the Mississippi Territory, 1798," sec. 3, 1 *Stat.* 549.

[62] Brown, "Colonial Mobile," 59.

[63] Toulmin to His Excellency D. Holmes, Governor of the Mississippi Territory, September 16, 1810, Mississippi (Territory), Judge of the Superior Court, Correspondence, SG3111, Alabama Department of Archives and History, Montgomery, Alabama (ADAH). In this letter, Toulmin indicated to Governor Holmes that he had taken what he considered to be the "best course to suppress the projected expedition" against Mobile "by exposing the folly of it in an address to the grand jury, which I repeated on Sunday last to a body of citizens in another settlement." See also Jacqueline Anderson Matte, *The History of Washington County, First County in Alabama* (Chatom, Ala.: Washington County Historical Society, 1982), 31–32. Toulmin

however, West Florida's Governor Vicente Folch thought it best to begin informal negotiations with the United States to cede West Florida to the United States. Pressing the issue, in 1812 the U.S. Congress annexed the Mobile District of West Florida to the Mississippi Territory, and territorial Governor David Holmes immediately began organizing a militia and municipal government for the area. Spain maintained its claim over the area for a while, peacefully coexisting with the Americans in the territory. However, in the following year, the area was occupied by a military force under the leadership of General James Wilkinson, commander-in-chief of the U.S. Army. The Spanish commandant offered no resistance. Accordingly, on April 13, 1813, Spanish Captain Cayetano Pérez surrendered his garrison, and Mobile was at last a part of the United States.[64]

With the seizure of Mobile, Alabama's colonial period finally ended. With no more European powers to answer to, Americans were left to organize their own government and commence the process of bringing order to a frontier inhabited by "Indian countrymen," fugitives from justice, frontier rowdies, outcast Tories, and escaped slaves.[65] In spite of removal of the final European forces from the territory and resolution of the Georgia land claims, the new territorial government would still be faced with the resistance of the Creek Indians, the most powerful Native American populace in the southeast. The ensuing eruption of the Creek War after the attack upon Fort Mims in the Tensaw District in August 1813 would play a major role in bringing order and peace to the new territory.

The Muskogees or Muscogees, better known to Americans as Creeks, were the largest of the Native American groups in Alabama, occupying two-thirds of modern-day Alabama. Like other tribes in the southeast, the Creeks descended from the Muskogean-speaking immigrants that began drifting into the area from the west during the late Mississippian period circa AD 1200, assimilating native populations into their ranks. These peoples were thus subjected to the diseases and widespread warfare brought to the region by de Soto's expedition in 1540. The resulting depopulation and disbursement was overcome during the seventeenth century as diverse tribes joined together into the Creek Confederacy. The town, or *talwa*, was the center of Creek political and social life. Most of the Alabama towns were located along the lower Tallapoosa and central Coosa rivers, but included displaced members of tribes from the lower Alabama River.[66]

The Creeks give us an example of a government and a limited system of laws indigenous to North America. Their government was decentralized,

---

realized the importance of Mobile to the area, but he thought annexation should come through official military or diplomatic action by the United States and not through the intrigues of local filibusterers.

[64] Brown, "Colonial Mobile," 59–61.

[65] Moore, *History of Alabama*, 64–66; Rogers et al., *Alabama*, 36; Justus Wyman, "A Geographical Sketch of the Alabama Territory," *Transactions of the Alabama Historical Society* 3 (1898–99): 121.

[66] Kathryn E. Braund, *Deerskins & Duffels: The Creek Indian Trade with Anglo-America, 1685–1815* (Lincoln: University of Nebraska Press, 1993), 3–7.

allowing each town to rule its people through civil and religious leaders and a head warrior. The most important of these was the *mico*, or village chief. The *mico* supervised all public and domestic functions of the village and served as its diplomatic representative, welcoming all foreign representatives and traders. The *mico* and his counselors and warriors met every day in the public square, the ceremonial and governmental center of town, where complaints were brought up, addressed, and remedied while all smoked tobacco and drank a dark-colored tea called *cassina*. The *mico* was a hereditary position held for life or during a period of good behavior, and was passed down upon a *mico*'s death to a maternal nephew, if the man was deemed fit; if not, a successor was chosen from the next of kin in the female line of descent.[67]

Kinship amongst Creeks was matrilineal, meaning that family descent came through the mother's line. While a young woman could indicate her preference for a mate, marriages could only be arranged by female relatives of the husband-to-be negotiating with the female relatives of the desired wife. Even after a woman's clan approved a marriage, the husband-to-be had to prove that he was a good provider before he was allowed to consummate the marriage. Polygamy was acceptable in Creek society, but a man had to obtain his first wife's consent before he could take on an additional wife or wives. Upon the death of her husband, unless she was released from mourning by her husband's clan, a woman was required to endure a difficult four-year widowhood. To avoid this period, widows often persuaded the deceased husband's brother or other near relation to marry her, thereby releasing her from the required mourning.[68]

The Creek criminal justice system was based upon an "eye for an eye" philosophy, with established rules for reprisal and retribution of crimes. Offenses were dealt with swiftly, and the family of the victims often participated in the administration of the punishment. For example, if a murder was committed, only the family and the tribe, or clan, of the victim had the right of taking satisfaction. Also, if a person was adjudged guilty and fled, the tribe could administer the punishment to the next of kin instead. Indeed, a clan was legally bound to seek retribution for any offenses committed against one of its members or to recompense for any harm caused by the illegal acts of a fellow clan member. As a matter of fact, until a dead person was avenged, it was believed that the spirit of the deceased contaminated the public square of his town and frustrated normal religious life. Adultery was dealt with in a particularly harsh manner and was also punished by the family or the tribe of the victim. If proof of the adultery was clear they hunted down the offenders, beat them severely with sticks, and cut off their ears. Abraham Mordecai, a Jewish trader from Pennsylvania residing in the "Indian country" in present-day Montgomery County, unfortunately found himself a recipient of the brutal ear cropping punishment in 1802 when a local chief heard of his dalliance with a married woman of

---

[67] Thomas Foster, ed., *The Collected Works of Benjamin Hawkins, 1796–1810* (Tuscaloosa: University of Alabama Press, 2003), 67s–75s; Braund, *Deerskins & Duffels*, 15–16, 20.

[68] Braund, *Deerskins & Duffels*, 12–14.

his clan. The chief led twelve warriors to Mordecai's house where they beat him with poles until he was senseless, cut off his ear, destroyed his boat, and burned down his gin-house. Thus, according to Pickett, the first cotton gin in Alabama was destroyed as the result of a roving eye.[69]

During Alabama's colonial period, dynamic leaders from different cultures implemented several significant western bodies of law, or legal codes. The French instituted *La Coutume de Paris*, with its governing Superior Council, and the *Code Noir*, a slave code first implemented in the French West Indies; the British introduced the common law and gave the area its first form of representative government; and the Spanish instituted a paternal system of government tailored to the needs of its colonies and derived from the ancient *Siete Partidas*. While these bodies of law all played a role in bringing order to the people they governed, none of them had any practical application to, or recognized jurisdiction over, the Native Americans who occupied most of the lands claimed by these European powers. That a significant portion of these Native Americans chose not to be assimilated into the society of the newcomers to their lands set the stage for a showdown between the citizens of the newly created Mississippi Territory and the predominant Native American nation of the region.

---

[69] Foster, *Collected Works of Benjamin Hawkins*, 74s–75s; Braund, *Deerskins & Duffels*, 12; Joel Martin, *Sacred Revolt: The Muscogees' Struggle for a New World* (Boston: Beacon Press, 1991), 34; Pickett, *History of Alabama*, 421, 469–70.

LE
CODE NOIR,
O U
R E C U E I L
DES REGLEMENS RENDUS
jufqu'à prefent,

CONCERNANT le Gouvernement, l'Ad-
miniftration de la Juftice, la Police,
la Difcipline & le Commerce des Ne-
gres dans les Colonies Françoifes.

*Et les Confeils & Compagnies établis
à ce fujet.*

A PARIS,
Chez PRAULT pere, Imprimeur de
Monfeigneur le Chancelier, Quai
de Gêvres, au Paradis.

M. DCC. XLII.
AVEC PRIVILEGE DU ROI.

Le Code Noir
1742 edition, published in Paris by Chez Père (Pierre) Prault

Winthrop Sargent
Governor of Mississippi Territory
1798–1801

Courtesy of Alabama Department of Archives and History

2

♨

IMPLEMENTATION OF SARGENT'S CODE

While the Spanish tenaciously held onto Mobile, Spain ceded the rest of present-day Alabama and Mississippi above the thirty-first parallel to the United States in the Treaty of San Lorenzo of 1795. As settlers began pouring into this region, Congress organized the Mississippi Territory in 1798, taking in all of the area between the lines of 31° and 32° 28'. Many veterans of the war for independence began to respond to the lure of the Old Southwest as economic opportunities in the Upper South began to diminish because of a dwindling supply of good lands and the decline of the markets for their tobacco and rice. Lacking modern farming techniques, farmers and their families were forced to abandon the exhausted soils of Virginia, the Carolinas, and Georgia for the virgin lands of the newly opened Mississippi Territory and its emerging cotton culture. This first wave of immigration began when the territory opened in 1798 and subsided with the beginning of the War of 1812. A stronger wave of immigrants would come after the Treaty of Fort Jackson in 1814, which ended the Creek War, and peaked in 1818 and 1819 immediately preceding Alabama's admission into the Union. In the interim, the Mississippi territorial government was formed and dealt with the intrigues of the Spanish government, treasonous activities, and the increasing hostility of much of the Creek Nation.[1]

In furtherance of securing the southwestern frontier, President John Adams signed a bill creating the Mississippi Territory on April 8, 1798. This act authorized the institution of a territorial government "in all respects similar to that now exercised in the territory north-west of the river Ohio." The Mississippi territorial assembly thus co-opted the major provisions of the Northwest Ordinance of 1787, with the important exception of its provision prohibiting slavery, so as to quickly institute American legal and governmental principles within the new territory. The Northwest Ordinance had been enacted by the Congress of the Confederation on July 13, 1787, and was subsequently adopted by the first U.S. Congress. The ordinance provided for the establishment of governments within the territories and outlined how they were to be admitted into the Union. Significantly, it contained a prototype for the Bill of Rights of the U.S. Constitution, including provisions allowing for the orderly exercise of religion, the benefits of the writ of habeas corpus, the right to trial by jury, the right to bail except for capital offenses, and a prohibition against cruel and unusual punish-

---

[1] An Act for . . . Establishment of a Government in the Mississippi Territory; Charles D. Lowery, "The Great Migration to the Mississippi Territory, 1798–1819," *Journal of Mississippi History* 30 (August 1968): 175–79.

ments. In addition to these rights, it encouraged education and mandated a benevolent relationship with Native American inhabitants.[2]

During the first stage of territorial government, Congress was authorized to appoint a governor to a three-year term. It also was authorized to appoint a court consisting of three judges whose terms remained in force during "good behavior." Any two of these judges could convene court and exercise a common-law jurisdiction. The governor and judges, or a majority of them, were directed to adopt and publish in the territory whatever civil or criminal laws of the original states they deemed necessary for the particular circumstances of their territory. The laws they chose to adopt in this regard were to remain in effect until a General Assembly (legislature) could be organized and convened in the territory, unless sooner disapproved by Congress. Once organized, however, the General Assembly thereafter had the authority to alter these laws as it deemed appropriate.[3]

In 1798 the region constituting the Mississippi Territory, including an area now part of present-day Alabama, was in desperate need of organized government. The territory at that time had two major areas of settlement that were not near any older American settlements and were separated from each other by hundreds of miles of treacherous wilderness. The major settlements of the Mississippi section of the territory were located on the Mississippi River and were referred to as the Natchez district. The only settlements in the Alabama portion of the territory were along the Tombigbee and Tensaw rivers and were referred to as the Tombigbee-Tensaw or "Bigbee" settlements. Both were hemmed in to the south by Spanish territory. The Spanish holdings in this area had always served as a refuge for escaped prisoners, fugitives from justice, border rowdies, debtors, and slaves on the run to freedom. Populating the Bigbee settlements were a considerable number of Tories avoiding the American Revolution and a few respectable French planters, in addition to the more plentiful fugitives and escaped prisoners. When Americans gained control of the territory, frontiersmen began arriving by Indian trails through the territory's immense wilderness to supplement its mostly disreputable population. Typically, but not universally, ignorant, cruel, and violent, these frontiersmen spent most of their time fighting a hostile environment just to survive. Their limited free time was devoted by many to vices such as gambling, heavy drinking, profanity, and fighting. Those so inclined felt secure in their vices and vicious natures because the territory was without any civil control and would be so until the first governor arrived in the territory to

---

[2] An Act for . . . Establishment of a Government in the Mississippi Territory; John Wunder, "American Law and Order Comes to the Mississippi Territory: The Making of Sargent's Code, 1798–1800," *Journal of Mississippi History* 38 (May 1976): 131; William N. Ethridge Jr., "An Introduction to Sargent's Code of the Mississippi Territory (1798–1800)," *American Journal of Legal History* 11 (April 1967): 148–51; An Ordinance for the Government of the Territory of the United States, North-West of the River Ohio, July 13, 1787, Second Continental Congress (the Northwest Ordinance); Mabel Hill, *Liberty Documents, with Contemporary Exposition and Critical Comments, Drawn from Various Writers* (London: Longmans, Green, and Co., 1901), 227.

[3] Northwest Ordinance; Wunder, "American Law and Order," 132–33.

formally organize a government.[4]

The arduous task of bringing order to this raucous society fell first to a seemingly unlikely Harvard-educated, New England Puritan. President John Adams appointed Winthrop Sargent to serve as the first governor of the Mississippi Territory on May 7, 1798. Sargent came from an old Gloucester, Massachusetts family of successful merchants. After graduating from Harvard in 1771, he briefly served aboard one of the family's merchant ships before joining the American forces fighting for independence. He eventually accepted an officer's appointment in the artillery regiment of Gen. Henry Knox. Ultimately achieving the rank of major, Sargent participated with his artillery in many engagements including those at Long Island, White Plains, Trenton, Brandywine, and Monmouth. He also was with General Washington's army during the harsh winter at Valley Forge.[5]

At the end of the war, reduced to only a sword and six months' worth of "Morris notes," Sargent sought a recommendation from General Washington to accompany his application for a commission in the armed services of Holland.[6] Washington readily provided a statement praising Sargent for his early entry into the war and his continual display of "zeal, integrity and intelligence which did honor him as an officer and gentleman." Sargent never made it to Holland, opting instead for the Ohio country, better known as the Northwest Territory, which was made available for settlement by Congress in 1785. In June 1786 Sargent was appointed as a surveyor for the new territory to aid in laying out its townships. When the Northwest Ordinance of 1787 organized the government for the territory, Congress appointed Sargent secretary. Sargent also served as adjutant-general during the war against the Miami Indians and was wounded in action on November 4, 1791. Arthur St. Clair, the territory's governor, was more seriously wounded in battle than Sargent, thus catapulting Sargent into the role of acting governor for a significant period of time. This invaluable experience boded well for his future appointment as governor of the Mississippi

---

[4] Robert V. Haynes Jr., "Law Enforcement in Frontier Mississippi," *Journal of Mississippi History* 22 (January 1960): 27–28; James F. Doster, "Early Settlements on the Tombigbee and Tensaw Rivers," *Alabama Review* 12 (April 1959): 84; Wyman, "Geographical Sketch," 121; Moore, *History of Alabama*, 64.

[5] Mary Joan Elliott, "Winthrop Sargent and the Administration of the Mississippi Territory, 1798–1801" (PhD diss., University of Southern California, 1970), 4; Dunbar Rowland, ed., *The Mississippi Territorial Archives, 1798–18. . .* (Nashville: Brandon Print. Co., 1905), 1: 9–10; *Mississippi Territorial Statutes* (Birmingham, Ala.: Historical Records Survey, 1939), iii. His brother Fitz-William founded the successful India Company, which engaged in business with Calcutta, China, Russia, and other foreign countries. His sister Judith Sargent Murray was a writer and poet who was one America's first advocates of women's equality. Winthrop Sargent also was a poet and was a member of such educational societies as the American Academy of Arts and Sciences in 1788, the American Philosophical Society in 1789, and the Massachusetts Historical Society in 1794. Vena Bernadette Field, *Constantia: A Study of the Life and Works of Judith Sargent Murray, 1751–1820* (Orono, Me.: University Press, 1931), 13–14.

[6] "Morris notes"—backed by the personal fortune of Superintendent of Finance Robert Morris—replaced the virtually worthless Continental paper currency issued by the Bank of North America. James J. Kirschke, *Gouverneur Morris: Author, Statesman and Man of the World* (New York: Thomas Dunne Books, 2005), 140–41.

Territory.[7]

At first glance Winthrop Sargent, with his puritanical New England upbringing, did not seem a likely candidate to lead an emerging rough frontier government in the Old Southwest. However, his military experiences in the American Revolution and the Indian wars in Ohio, together with his service as secretary and acting governor of the Northwest Territory, certainly gave him the bona fides to hold such a position. When it became apparent that Sargent had little prospect of becoming the governor of the Northwest Territory, he looked southward for such an opportunity in the Mississippi Territory. His bona fides notwithstanding, Sargent almost lost out to William Matthews, governor of Georgia, who received the initial appointment from President Adams. Matthews, however, would never make it to Natchez to assume office due to his involvement in the Yazoo land speculation scandal. With opposition mounting in the Senate to Matthews, President Adams withdrew the nomination and appointed Sargent instead. Senator James Ross of Pennsylvania warned Sargent that the position would be "troublesome beyond calculation and difficult of execution, all this to be encountered for very inadequate compensation."[8]

Despite such counsel, Winthrop Sargent arrived in Natchez on August 6, 1798, to accept his appointment to lead the Mississippi Territory. He came with a preconceived notion of a lawless and chaotic society in the territory: he wrote to Secretary of State Timothy Pickering before his arrival in Natchez that he understood that the inhabitants of the territory were of a "refractory and turbulent Spirit," and led by men of "perverseness and Cunning." He further believed that it was imperative to rein in this supposed wild populace by the imposition of the rule of law as soon as possible, noting that "every moments [sic] delay in adoption of rules and regulations amongst them must be productive of growing evils and discontent." These observations reflect what historian Robert V. Haynes described as Sargent's "distaste for western mannerisms" acquired during his ten-year stay in the Northwest Territory. Haynes reported that Sargent's haughtiness and austere attitude toward the masses even caused concern among his friends, one of whom declared that "a man so frigid and sour" could not expect to endear himself with "a free people."[9]

---

[7] Elliott, "Winthrop Sargent," 6-9; Rowland, *Mississippi Territorial Archives*, 9-10; *Sargent's Code: A Collection of the Original Laws of the Mississippi Territory Enacted 1799-1800 by Governor Winthrop Sargent and the Territorial Judges* (Jackson, Miss.: Historical Records Survey, 1939), i. Captain William Henry Harrison, future President of the United States, succeeded Sargent as secretary of the Northwest Territory. John Anthony Caruso, *The Great Lakes Frontier: An Epic of the Old Northwest* (Indianapolis: Bobbs-Merrill, 1961), 209.

[8] Wunder, "American Law and Order," 133; Ross to Sargent, July 15, 1798, Winthrop Sargent Papers (Boston: Massachusetts Historical Society), quoted in Elliott, "Winthrop Sargent," 17–18.

[9] Sargent to Pickering, June 16, 1798, in Rowland, *Mississippi Territorial Archives*, 1:22; Robert V. Haynes, "The Formation of the Territory," in *A History of Mississippi,* ed. Richard Aubrey McLemore (Jackson: University & College Press of Mississippi, 1973), 1: 179; Wunder, "American Law and Order," 135–36. Sargent's "disdain for the common man" was summed up as follows by John Anthony Caruso: "He scoffed at public opinion and wore his Harvard education on his sleeve. Like the Bourbons, he learned nothing and forgot nothing. Trained for

On August 18, 1798, Sargent first addressed the people of the territory, declaring to them that personal merit and a firm attachment to the United States would be the leading prerequisites for appointment to office during his administration. Despite the urgency for law and order, he made it clear that he would put off any such appointments until he familiarized himself with the dwellers of this new territory. His promised familiarization led him to characterize to Secretary of State Pickering the overall condition of the territory as "truly deplorable" and its inhabitants as "Aliens of various Characters," including "the most Abandoned Vilians [*sic*] who have escaped from the Chains and Prisons of Spain and convicted of the Blackest of Crimes." Indeed, a friend of Sargent's stated that the population was as unsuited to legal authority "as a bride is generally for the first night or two of her marriage."[10]

To assist Governor Sargent in bringing organized government to the backwoods of the Mississippi Territory, President Adams appointed John Steele as secretary and Peter Bryan Bruin, Daniel Tilton, and William McGuire as judges. Secretary Steele was from Virginia where he had served in the Revolution as a commissioned Second Lieutenant. Of the judges, only William McGuire, also of Virginia, was actually a lawyer. He had studied law at the College of William and Mary before practicing law in Fredericksburg, Virginia, and winning election to the state legislature in 1796. Although Daniel Tilton of New Hampshire was a Harvard College graduate, he had never practiced law. Peter Bryan Bruin, a native of Ireland and a veteran of the Revolution, was the only judicial appointee to then reside in the Territory, having settled in Natchez in 1788. Unfortunately, Bruin had no formal education, legal or otherwise; his appointment was apparently based upon his status as a loyal Federalist.[11]

Governor Sargent was eager for Judges Tilton and McGuire to arrive so that he could begin the task of joining with them to adopt laws necessary for the governance of the territory and to address such concerns as the establishment of a militia, settlement of complex land claims, and improving relations with the Indian tribes. Although Judge Bruin was already on the scene in Natchez, it took him, the governor, and at least one other judge to commence legislation. In a letter to Secretary of State Pickering dated August 20, 1798, Sargent expressed concern over McGuire's and Tilton's

---

military life, he preached the supremacy of discipline; he saw no merit in the roaming and liberal-minded frontiersman. An unyielding and unimaginative Puritan, he denounced as a vice every pleasure he felt he must not enjoy." Caruso, *Great Lakes Frontier*, 184.

[10] *Sargent's Code*, i–ii; Lewis Evans to Andrew Ellicott, August 7, 1798, Andrew Ellicott Papers, MSS Division, Library of Congress, quoted in Haynes, "Law Enforcement in Frontier Mississippi," 31–32; "Address to Inhabitants of Mississippi Territory" and Sargent to Pickering, December 20, 1798, in Rowland, *Mississippi Territorial Archives*, 1: 27, 89.

[11] Joseph A. Waddell, *Waddell's Annals of Augusta County, Virginia, from 1726 to 1871*, Roane County, TN Family History Project, http://roanetnhistory.org/bookread.php?loc=WaddellsAnnals&pgid=326#section68 (accessed January 11, 2013), 314; Wunder, "American Law and Order," 134–35; *Sargent's Code*, ii; John D. W. Guice, "The Cement of Society: Law in the Mississippi Territory," *Gulf Coast Historical Review* 1 (Spring 1986): 82; Dunbar Rowland, *Courts, Judges, and Lawyers of Mississippi, 1798–1935* (Jackson: State Department of Archives and History and the Mississippi Historical Society, 1935): 11–13.

delay in arriving and an overall concern as to the quality of these appointments: "My great source of uneasiness is the want of Judges___ I pray God
Mr. McGuire will soon arrive, or some law character___ In a court from
which is no appeal, most certainly there should be law knowledge___ Judge
Bruin a worthy and sensible man, is beyond doubt deficient, and Judge
Tilton cannot have had more reading or experience. Under these circumstances might it not be advisable to make compensation to some gentleman
learned in the law, to reside here as an attorney for the United States, and
Territory?"[12]

While he was waiting for the arrival of these two judges, he nevertheless
proceeded to form a temporary ad hoc government. He had to do so even
without the services of the territory's new secretary. Although Steele had
arrived in the fall of 1798, he was too ill to assume his duties for several
months. Notwithstanding the temporary unavailability of Steele and the
requisite judges, on September 9, 1798, Sargent took it upon himself to
appoint the first local Anglo-American judges in the hopes of quickly
bringing a semblance of law and order to the new territory. These local
judges, named "conservators of the peace," were authorized "to keep and
preserve the peace___ To Suppress all riots and affrays, and to take notice of
all Treasonable or Seditious language and to Commit the Authors, unless
they shall give Security for good Conduct and to answer for their crimes at a
first Session of a Court of general Quarter Sessions of the peace." Two of
these so-called "conservators of the peace" were empowered to convene
court and issue warrants to a sheriff appointed by them to apprehend and
hold persons over to answer for alleged crimes before the supreme court of
the territory when it next sat within the district where the alleged crime
occurred.[13]

When reporting the offices he had taken upon himself to define and fill
to Secretary Pickering, Sargent admitted to a usurpation of power forced upon
him by the absence of the officers necessary to legislate for the territory:

> From the Continued Absence of the Civil officers of Government, we real-
> ly suffer extremely. . . . Every day and hour Multiply Complaints, some of
> them amounting to felonies and very high Misdemeanors; I have been
> Constrained to some Civil appointments, and to the define of duties
> thereof, which was the province of the Legislature; and am to be Justified
> only by the imperious necessity existing.[14]

Sargent realized that these appointments were temporary and would
have to be confirmed when at least one more judge arrived in the territory,
but he had decided to actively govern until then. Accordingly, he fulfilled a
perceived urgent need to provide security for the territory by issuing an

---

[12] Elliott, "Winthrop Sargent," 66; Sargent to Pickering, August 20, 1798, in Rowland, *Mississippi Territorial Archives*, 1: 30.

[13] Elliott, "Winthrop Sargent," 81–83; *Sargent's Code*, ii; "Information to the Inhabitants of
the Mississippi Territory," in Rowland, *Mississippi Territorial Archives*, 1: 42–43.

[14] Elliott, "Winthrop Sargent," 83; Sargent to Pickering, September 18, 1798, in Rowland,
Mississippi Territorial Archives, 1: 47–48.

Order for the Regulation of the Militia. The territorial militia he decreed was divided into two legions, one for each of the districts carved out for the implementation of civil government. A lieutenant colonel was appointed to command each legion. Sixty-four men constituted a company of infantry, riflemen, or a troop of cavalry. Service in the militia was required of all free male inhabitants between the ages of sixteen and fifty, with the exception of governmental officers, ministers, and "regular educated practicing physicians." Persons over the age of fifty were required to "arm and accoutre [*sic*] themselves" for service in their choice of the cavalry, infantry, or riflemen. However, they were not liable for military service except during actual invasions of the territory, and then only under the direct command of the governor who was commander-in-chief.[15]

The soldiers of this hastily formed militia were required to provide their own arms and equipment. Infantrymen were to bring a musket and bayonet, cartridge boxes, thirty rounds of cartridges, six flints, priming wires and brushes, and knapsacks. Riflemen were to furnish good rifles, tomahawks, powder horns, bullet pouches, six flints, one pound of powder, four pounds of bullets, priming wires and brushes, and knapsacks. Horse soldiers were to provide "a sword of straight blade (if such could be procured) and one pistol," twelve rounds of cartridges, three flints, a priming wire, and a small portmanteau (leather suitcase). All these items were to be brought to a company level training muster to be held on the first Saturday afternoon of each month at a location deemed most convenient by the company commander. The company was required to drill for at least two hours, receiving training in marching, wheeling, firing their weapons, and, in the case of the infantry, the use of the bayonet. A soldier found deficient in any of the required arms or accoutrements on the day of his muster was to be fined fifty cents for each failure to correct the deficiency after being given a reasonable amount of time to procure the necessary item.[16]

The necessity of a territorial militia notwithstanding, those opposed to Sargent sought to undermine the militia's effectiveness by frequently ignoring call-up orders. This avoidance of service resulted from a deep resentment of not being allowed to elect the officers who would lead them. Instead they were led by men unfamiliar to them, who were appointed by and loyal to Governor Sargent. Furthermore, Sargent enraged the territory's citizens when he suggested that the militia be used to end the debauchery he perceived was being conducted by the masses on Sunday afternoons in Natchez. Most inhabitants simply viewed this "debauched" activity as traditional Sunday afternoon picnics following mass for which no military interference was warranted.[17]

Having usurped power out of necessity to pull together a rag-tag militia and to appoint a rudiment of civil officers, Sargent was delighted when Judge Daniel Tilton finally arrived in Natchez in January 1799, making it

---

[15] "Order for the Regulation of Militia," in Rowland, *Mississippi Territorial Archives*, 1: 36–40.

[16] Ibid.

[17] Wunder, "American Law and Order," 147–48.

possible for him to officially enact legislation with the concurrence of the requisite number of judges. As thrilled as Sargent was with Tilton's belated arrival, he was extremely disappointed to learn that the boat upon which the judge had arrived was not big enough to bring the bulky books containing the laws of the original states from which he and the judges could pick and choose to establish an extensive code for their citizens. To his further dismay, it consequently became necessary to base the territory's first laws upon those of the Old Northwest Territory, considered a poor model by Sargent. Compounding his disappointment, Judge William McGuire, the only lawyer among the territory's appointed judges, arrived only to quickly return to Virginia in September 1799, not finding the pay to his liking.[18]

With a duly constituted government now in place, forty-six laws were enacted between February 28, 1799 and October 30, 1800. Derisively referred to as Sargent's Code, these laws were considered repressive and unconstitutional by the frontier populace to whom they were applied. There was particular concern with the harshness of criminal punishments, such as the death penalty, forfeiture of all property, and corporal punishment. The pioneers also resented what they considered exorbitant fees for marriage licenses, tavern licenses, and passports. Despite these concerns, the first nine laws enacted by Sargent and the judges laid the foundation for bringing orderly government to this unruly society. Of paramount importance were the establishment of the first court system for the territory and the permanent establishment of a militia. Initial laws were also enacted pertaining to marriage, oaths of office, taverns, sheriffs, coroners, recorders, and treasurers.[19]

With the creation of the territory's first court system, Sargent's Code initiated a system in which the English common law was to be applied. William Hamilton, a student of early Mississippi common law, waxed poetic in describing the significance of the transportation of common law to America: "The Thames flowed into the muddy waters of the majestic Mississippi and transformed them, engulfed them, Anglicized them forevermore." This was not the first implementation of the common law on Alabama soil, as the British applied it to the governance of British West Florida from 1763 until 1781, but it was its first application during American control of the region.[20]

Similar to the system which had been established in the Northwest Territory, Sargent's Code created a General Quarter Sessions of the Peace court

---

[18] Ethridge, "Introduction to Sargent's Code," 148–54; Guice, "Cement of Society," 82.

[19] Elliott, "Winthrop Sargent," 103–06; Haynes, "Formation of the Territory," 1: 181-82; Ethridge, "Introduction to Sargent's Code," 154. Frontier citizens argued that instead of "adopting" laws from the other states as required by Congress, Sargent and his judges "made" laws which were in their opinion in contravention of the U.S. Constitution and ran afoul of the common law. It should be noted here that Sargent's Code was applicable in the eastern reaches of the territory that would become part of the state of Alabama, but there was no governmental structure in place in the Bigbee and Tensas settlements to enforce the code. Organized government would not come to these areas until the Mississippi territorial Legislature created Washington County on June 4, 1800.

[20] Guice, "Cement of Society," 76–77.

in each county, which was authorized to hear charges of all crimes and misdemeanors to the extent that the punishment for the offense did not involve a death sentence, a forfeiture, or imprisonment for more than a year. Sargent's Code also created a Court of Common Pleas to hear civil cases in each county. The governor of the territory appointed judges for both of these courts, which met for four three-day sessions per year. To the chagrin of the local citizenry, Sargent's Code also established an intricate probate court system, allowing the governor to appoint judges who could exercise power over very valuable estates within the territory. As under the common law, defendants had the right to a jury trial and could take an appeal from both the General Quarter Sessions court and the Court of Common Pleas to a territorial supreme court which met once a year in each county. In addition to its appellate jurisdiction, the Supreme Court had original jurisdiction over all felonies, suits initiated by the United States, and complaints of misconduct against territorial officials. Decisions of the court could not be appealed until 1805, when Congress authorized writs of error from territorial courts to the U.S. Supreme Court. Despite the power that went with the finality initially bestowed upon their decisions, supreme court justices also performed menial tasks such as certifying notary publics, consecrating marriage ceremonies, and recording deed acknowledgements.[21]

Notwithstanding the relatively broad jurisdiction that had been conferred upon the territory's courts, Sargent's Code made no provision for the granting of divorces within the judicial system. Citizens were thus at the mercy of Governor Sargent and two judges to legislate their divorces. The difficulty of obtaining divorces legislatively is reflected by the fact that only two divorces were included in the forty-six statutes comprising Sargent's Code.[22]

Elizabeth Hutchins earned the distinction of being the first person granted a divorce within the Mississippi Territory when Sargent, McGuire, and Bruin enacted a law to that effect on October 3, 1799. Elizabeth had petitioned for a legislative divorce in response to scurrilous allegations made by her husband, John Hutchins, that she had put poison in his coffee in an effort to rid herself of him in favor of extra-marital suitors. In denying these allegations, Elizabeth averred in her divorce petition that her husband's unfounded jealously had resulted in her running away from their conjugal home after only fifteen months of marriage. "For good causes shown," Sargent, McGuire, and Bruin sided with Elizabeth by granting her a divorce from John and by authorizing her, "by her next friend," to institute appropriate legal actions against her former husband to recover property that was rightfully hers and "which was given of her advancement in marriage." The only other legislative divorce contained within Sargent's Code was granted to John Walton on May 27, 1800. Favoring the husband

[21] Elliott, "Winthrop Sargent," 106–07; Guice, "Cement of Society," 77–78; Ethridge, "Introduction to Sargent's Code," 160–65; Wunder, "American Law and Order," 138–40; "An Act to Extend Jurisdiction in Certain Cases, to the Territorial Courts, 1805," 2 *Stat.* 338.

[22] Wunder, "American Law and Order," 148–49.

in this conflict, Sargent and the judges found Nancy Walton to be guilty of an adulterous affair resulting in a pregnancy.[23]

It was not the court structure itself that caused dismay to those who fell under its jurisdiction. Instead there was great concern among inhabitants of the territory that unelected appointees of the governor were given unreasonably broad powers to preserve the peace, whether on the bench or not, including the power to commit persons to jail for an indefinite period pending trial and to sentence a person on the spot for crimes committed in the judge's presence. Additionally citizens resented the broad investigatory powers given to probate judges in the probate of estates and their authority to issue writs requiring the sheriff to summon jurors to determine whether an alleged "idiot, lunatic, or distracted person" was incapable of caring for him or herself and, if so determined, to appoint a guardian to manage that person's personal and business affairs. Even more troublesome to these democratic frontiersmen was the fact that Sargent's Code provided for the assessment of taxes by appointed commissioners, unlike the more democratic system of electing assessors as implemented in the Northwest Territory. Undoubtedly echoes of the cries of "taxation without representation" during the American Revolution were continuing to reverberate on the southwest frontier.[24]

The harshness of penalties imposed for violations of the territory's criminal code, although resented by the inhabitants, nevertheless graphically reflected the unruliness of the rugged frontier. Frontiersmen particularly loathed the forfeiture of all property for the crimes of treason and arson, a punishment they deemed unconstitutional. They also undoubtedly resented the whip and pillory reserved as punishment for crimes such as burglary, larceny, and robbery. Other sore spots included the imposition of personal servitude for up to seven years in lieu of the ability to give restitution in the case of larceny exceeding the value of three dollars, and the loss of the ability to give testimony, serve as a juror, or hold civil or military office in the case of a perjury conviction. Yet no one seemed to complain of lesser consequences reserved for "unlawfully cut [ting] out or disabl[ing] the tongue, put[ting] out an eye, slit[ting] or bit[ting] the nose, ear, or lip, or cut[ting] off or disabl[ing] any limb or member, with intention in doing so, to maim or disfigure." Such vicious conduct incurred a meagerly incarceration of one to six months and a fine of fifty to one thousand dollars. Overall, however, punishments for most minor crimes were fairly severe and included cropping, whipping, branding, placing in stocks, and fines up to one

---

[23] Ironically, both John and Elizabeth Hutchins were the offspring of leading opponents of Governor Sargent: Anthony Hutchins and Thomas M. Green. Haynes, "Formation of the Territory," 1: 186. See also "Divorce Petition to Governor and Legislature," September 16, 1799, Governor's Records, Administration of Winthrop Sargent, May 1798–April 1801, series A volume 1, Mississippi Department of Archives and History, Jackson, Mississippi (MDAH), quoted in Elliott, "Winthrop Sargent" 121–22; *Mississippi Territorial Statutes*, 134, 151.

[24] Guice, "Cement of Society," 78; Ethridge, "Introduction to Sargent's Code," 174; Elliott, "Winthrop Sargent," 117–19; Wunder, "American Law and Order," 137–39. Governor Sargent appointed William Dunbar to serve as the first probate judge in the Mississippi Territory.

thousand dollars.[25]

Sargent's Puritanism was reflected by a number of "blue laws" which prohibited working, hunting, fiddling, bear-baiting, and slaves playing "chuck-penny" on Sunday. Most of these laws were generally ignored and went unenforced. Although sex offenses were rare, in 1802 adultery was made punishable by a fine of one hundred dollars. It was not until 1812 that fornication became an offense. Gambling and dueling were made offenses, but these violations were not consistently enforced.[26]

Other laws enacted by Sargent and the judges which helped bring order to the frontier society covered such subjects as the building of jails and regulating aliens. To effectively deal with the raucous society, each county was directed to build a courthouse, jail, whipping post, and stocks, as soon as the necessary funding became available. Concern over treasonous activities being stirred up by aliens resulted in a law empowering the governor to require "sufficient Testimonials" as to the reputation and character of aliens entering the territory. Once in the territory, aliens were to register with local conservators of the peace. In so registering, an alien was required to provide "his age, place of nativity, the country whence he came, the nation to which he belongs and owes allegiance, his occupation, and the arms and ammunition that he is possessed of." The failure of an alien to register was punishable by a fine not exceeding three hundred dollars.[27]

Although the laws pertaining to slavery were very strict, they were nevertheless not as controversial as most of the other regulatory enactments. Since the imposition of the *Code Noir* by the French in parts of the territory in 1724, citizens were used to restrictions being placed upon their slaves' rights to assemble, travel, possess weapons, and even sell commodities. Sargent's Code placed additional restrictions on a slave's right to own animals such as dogs and horses or "to keep hogs running at large, and to keep more in enclosures than they can conveniently maintain." While Sargent's Code contained many of the same restrictions first imposed by the *Code Noir*, it did not adopt the French code's more humane provisions such as prohibitions against separation of husbands and wives by sale and separation of young children from their mothers, nor did it provide for emancipation under any circumstances. Sargent's Code nevertheless did purport to adopt a "humane policy" toward slaves within the territory by prohibiting cruel and unusual punishments and by empowering courts to impose fines of up to one hundred dollars on slave owners found guilty of authorizing or permitting such punishments. However, in an address to militia officers on January 12, 1801, Governor Sargent expressed concern that "a Mild and humane Treatment" would only temporarily assuage an increasing number of slaves who had the potential to take revenge upon

[25] Ethridge, "Introduction to Sargent's Code," 166–72; Guice, "Cement of Society, 78.

[26] Haynes Jr., "Law Enforcement in Frontier Mississippi," 38.

[27] Haynes Jr., "Law Enforcement in Frontier Mississippi," 38; Elliott, "Winthrop Sargent," 110–11; Ethridge, "Introduction to Sargent's Code," 191.

their outnumbered masters as a result of being deprived of "the sacred Boon of Liberty."[28]

Overcoming opposition from the local populace and the paucity of legal experience possessed by his judges, Sargent was able to institute a legal code that, while sometimes overbearing and unpopular, provided at least some stability to the expanding southwestern frontier. More stability in leadership would be needed though, as Sargent and two of his appointed judges would not serve long following the passage of Sargent's Code. The harshness of frontier life, the political volatility resulting from the imposition of the code, and poor pay resulted in the quick departure of judges Tilton and McGuire, who both left the territory after less than a year of service in their judicial posts. They were replaced by Seth Lewis and David Ker. Further stability was brought to the court with the appointment to the bench of Thomas Rodney of Delaware, who arrived in Natchez on December 1, 1803. In addition to his commission as a territorial judge, Rodney was also appointed as a land commissioner for the area west of the Pearl River. Judge Bruin, who had no legal experience and who had a serious drinking problem, was able to stay in office until forced to resign in 1808 after steps were taken to have him impeached.[29]

Sargent's eventual removal began with the concerted effort of a group under the leadership of Cato West, Narsworthy Hunter, and Col. Anthony Hutchins. This faction had formed in opposition to Sargent and his administration with the passage of laws they considered arbitrary and unconstitutional. They were fed up with strict regulations, exorbitant fees, harsh criminal penalties, and appointed tax assessors and other unelected officials. To express their dismay, they presented lists of grievances to the grand juries of Adams and Pickering counties and to higher authorities. In a petition to Congress dated October 2, 1799, a "committee of inhabitants" particularly complained that the "executive, legislative, and Judicial authorities so carefully separated in the Elder States, are here mingled together in the hands of three or four individuals." Although a congressional committee found no cause to proceed against Sargent for alleged mismanagement of the territory, on May 10, 1800, Congress did vote to advance the territory to its second stage of government. In this stage, more power was vested in the legislative branch, which included a popularly elected lower house with the power to override the veto of the governor.[30]

Although Sargent avoided any adverse action by Congress, he could not survive the change of administrations in Washington. Having received word of Thomas Jefferson's election to the presidency, Sargent temporarily

---

[28] *Édit du Roi*, 28–58; Everett, "Free Persons of Color," 22–23; *Mississippi Territorial Statutes*, 53–58; Ethridge, "Introduction to Sargent's Code," 192–96; Elliott, "Winthrop Sargent," 113; "Address to Militia Officers," in Rowland, *Mississippi Territorial Archives*, 1:325; Wunder, "American Law and Order," 151.

[29] Guice, "Cement of Society," 82–84; William Baskerville Hamilton, *Anglo-American Law on the Frontier: Thomas Rodney and his Territorial Cases* (Durham, N.C.: Duke University Press, 1953), 74.

[30] Robert V. Haynes, "The Revolution of 1800 in Mississippi," *Journal of Mississippi History* 19 (October 1957): 234–51; *Sargent's Code*, ii–iii.

turned over the reins of the territorial government to Secretary Steele on April 3, 1801, and headed to Washington in a futile attempt to save his job. As a Federalist opposed by constituents who were mostly Jeffersonian Republicans, Sargent had no chance. Inevitably, on May 25, 1801, Sargent was notified by Secretary of State James Madison that President Jefferson deemed it "expedient" that the office of governor be filled by someone else. Jefferson appointed William C. C. Claiborne as the second governor of the Mississippi Territory. Claiborne was only twenty-six years old at the time of this appointment, but he was already a leading congressional proponent of western democratic ideals and Jeffersonian liberalism. Upon his arrival in Natchez, Claiborne quickly gave his constituents hope of change when, in his first address to the Territorial Assembly, he called for a "strict adherence to the Federal Constitution" and "justice in the most cheap, easy, and expeditious manner . . . conformably to the Law." The assembly then proceeded to enact a new code of laws that involved the establishment of a new judicial system. Governor Claiborne quickly notified President Madison of the repeal of the "greatly defective" Sargent's Code.[31]

Historian John Wunder nevertheless believes that Sargent's Code "managed to cover many areas that Governor Sargent felt were necessary to hold the Mississippi Territory for the United States" and provided the basic laws he believed were necessary "to maintain and increase American predominance over an unstable frontier outpost." In this regard, Sargent's Code provided for a civilized means of settling disputes within a structured judicial system, which in turn ensured that principles of English common law were fully integrated into territorial jurisprudence. Further order was brought to the territory with the establishment of a militia, the creation of county governments, and the implementation of a tax system. Sargent kept a tight rein on the territory's governmental structure and direction by reserving the power of appointment to territorial office, controlling the certification of attorneys, and imposing a stringent criminal justice system.[32]

Upon his removal from the office of governor, Sargent retired to his estate near Natchez, where he lived the life of a gentleman planter until his death in 1820.[33] Before retiring, however, he took action with respect to two matters which, at long last, had a direct impact on the eastern portion of the territory in the Tombigbee and Tensaw districts. On June 4, 1800, Governor Sargent issued a proclamation creating Washington County, finally bringing organized government to the banks of the Tombigbee and Tensaw rivers. The boundaries given to this new county included the area

---

[31] *Sargent's Code,* iv; Guice, "Cement of Society," 78; Haynes, "Formation of the Territory," 196.

[32] Wunder, "American Law and Order," 154.

[33] Sargent's removal left him with a bitter taste in his mouth, as reflected by a vindictive pamphlet he published in Boston, *Political Intolerance,* in which he accused President Jefferson of lying and duplicity in the way he was forced from office. Merrill D. Peterson, *Thomas Jefferson and the New Nation: A Biography* (London: Oxford University Press, 1975), 681.

east of the Pearl River and covered an area four times larger than either of the other two counties in the Mississippi Territory. Sargent was also forced to deal with implementing the second stage of territorial government, which had been authorized by Congress. In this regard he had to provide the mechanism for the first popular election to a portion of the legislature. Now that future Alabamians had an officially recognized county government, they were provided representation in the territory's new popularly elected legislature. William McGrew had the distinction of being elected Washington County's first representative to the Territorial Assembly.[34]

The stage had thus been set for the ultimate division of the territory, with the western portion achieving statehood as Mississippi and the eastern portion becoming the Alabama Territory in 1817. In the meantime, much work needed to be done in newly created Washington County to establish a judicial system and to bring more order to that isolated portion of the territory.

---

[34] *Sargent's Code*, 22; Robert V. Haynes, "Early Washington County, Alabama," *Alabama Review* 18 (July 1965): 190–91; Haynes, "Formation of the Territory," 194.

3

❧

REIGN OF JUDGE HARRY TOULMIN

When Governor Winthrop Sargent created Washington County in June 1800, American government was implemented at the local level for the first time in what was to become the state of Alabama. McIntosh Bluff, situated on the west bank of the Tombigbee River approximately forty miles north of Mobile, was named county seat at the recommendation of Secretary of State John Steele due to its central location in the newly created eastern governmental component of the territory. McIntosh Bluff got its name from Captain John McIntosh, a British officer who had served in West Florida and had received a land grant in 1775. Washington County at that time had a total population of 1,227, including 399 white males, 334 white females, and 494 African American slaves. This population was confined to the west bank of the lower Tombigbee or in the Tensaw settlement south of the confluence of the Alabama and Tombigbee rivers. The concentration of population in these two areas was due to the presence of increasingly hostile Creek Indians in the forks east of the Tombigbee River and west of the Alabama River.[1]

Sargent struggled to find appropriate leaders to appoint to the offices of the new county. Just had he done when he appointed the initial territorial officers, Sargent spent a great deal of time gathering information so as to make the right selections. Receiving discouraging information from military officers, federal officials, and Secretary Steele (who had recently toured the region), Sargent considered going there himself to assess the situation. Instead he stayed at home and made his decisions based in part on the grave picture painted by those hoping to secure their own political appointments. Finally, in June 1800, Sargent appointed James Fair, John Johnson, John Chastang, John Caller, Joseph Thompson, and Flood McGrew as justices of the county's first courts. Other county officials appointed at this time included Wilson Carman as sheriff; John Pierce as county coroner; David Mims as treasurer; and Samuel McCarkle as prothonotary to the Court of Common Pleas, clerk of the General Quarter Sessions court, and county recorder.[2]

The superior court of Washington County held its first session at McIntosh Bluff in September 1802 with Seth Lewis, chief justice of the Mississippi Territory, presiding. During this first session of the court, Nicholas Perkins took the oath of office as the attorney general of the court and

---

[1] Haynes, "Early Washington County," 183–200; Matte, *History of Washington County*, 22; Theodore Bowling Pearson, "Early Settlement around Historic McIntosh Bluff: Alabama's First County Seat," *Alabama Review* 23 (October 1970): 243.

[2] Matte, *History of Washington County*, 22–23.

attorneys Lemuel Henry, Robert Knox, and Leonard D. Shaw became the first attorneys admitted to practice in what was to become the state of Alabama. During this term of court David Matthias became one of the first recipients of the area's frontier justice when a jury found him guilty of stealing a barrel of flour worth ten dollars for which he was "ordered to receive 25 lashes on his bear [sic] back, pay the $10 for the barrel of flour and that he stand committed until the cost of suit be paid."[3]

In 1803, President Thomas Jefferson appointed Ephraim Kirby, a land-speculating Connecticut lawyer and former Revolutionary War soldier, and Robert Carter Nicholas of Kentucky as land commissioners in the eastern part of the territory, the first federal officials to serve in the area. Kirby had distinguished himself in Connecticut in 1789 by publishing *Reports of Cases Adjudged in the Superior Court and Court of Errors of the State of Connecticut from the Year 1785 to May 1788,* the first fully developed case law reports ever compiled in America. More importantly for his future, he had also been instrumental in the creation and development of the Jeffersonian Republican party in Connecticut and ran for lieutenant governor on a slate of candidates in the spring of 1801. Unsuccessful in the race and land poor due to over-speculation, Kirby took advantage of his connections with President Jefferson and sought a patronage position. The Congressional Act of March 3, 1803, enacted for the purpose of "regulating the grants of land, and providing for the disposal of the lands of the United States, south of the State of Tennessee," allowed President Jefferson to appoint Kirby and Nicholas as land commissioners in the Mississippi Territory. Like Kirby, Nicholas had political ties to Jefferson, undoubtedly receiving his commission as a reward for his father's service as a Jeffersonian leader in the state of Kentucky in the 1790s.[4]

Kirby and Nicholas were to report to Fort Stoddert, an American outpost of fewer than eighty men on the Mobile River just six miles above the 31° parallel boundary with Spain. Fort Stoddert had been built in 1799 on a site known as Ward's Bluff, a few miles south of the confluence of the Tombigbee and Alabama rivers, to provide settlers protection against Spanish and Indian aggression. A rapidly growing settlement soon sprung up around this military outpost and became the center of all legal business

---

[3] Washington County Superior Court Records (1802–1804), Probate Records, 1799–1964 (Salt Lake City: Genealogical Society of Utah, 1979 and 1991), microfilm, ADAH, quoted in Pearson, "Early Settlement around Historic McIntosh Bluff," 248–49. A county court (inferior court) met at McIntosh Bluff in 1803, presided over by Justices John Caller, John Johnston, and Cornelius Rain.

[4] Alan V. Briceland, "Ephraim Kirby: Mr. Jefferson's Emissary on the Tombigbee-Mobile Frontier in 1804," *Alabama Review* 24 (April, 1971): 83–88. The law was necessary because before 1803, four governments—France, Great Britain, Spain, and the State of Georgia—had exercised successive sovereignty over the region. Each of the three foreign governments had granted title to lands along the Mobile, Tensaw, and Tombigbee rivers upon private individuals. On April 24, 1802, Georgia ceded its claims and titles to the area to the United States. Alan V. Briceland, "Land, Law, and Politics on the Tombigbee Frontier, 1804," *Alabama Review* 33 (April 1980): 92–93; Haig A. Bosmajian, *Metaphor and Reason in Judicial Opinions* (Carbondale: Southern Illinois University Press, 1992), 25; Richard J. Purcell, *Connecticut in Transition: 1775–1818* (Middletown, Conn.: Wesleyan University Press, 1963), 147–53.

within the Alabama section of the Mississippi Territory and a port of entry and customs for goods arriving into the territory from Spanish-held Mobile. Fort Stoddert also had the distinction of housing former Vice President Aaron Burr as prisoner for two weeks in 1807, printing the first newspaper in Alabama in 1811, and serving as the staging point from which Maj. Gen. James Wilkinson's troops marched into Mobile to accept the Spanish commander's surrender of that city in 1813.[5]

Kirby and Nicholas arrived at Fort Stoddert on January 26, 1804, where they met up with the third member of the Board of Land Commissioners, Joseph Chambers, who had also been the agent of the Choctaw trading house located at Fort St. Stephens. The Board of Land Commissioners was convened on February 3, 1804, to adjust land titles east of the Pearl River in the Mississippi Territory. The board met from mid-March until July 16, 1804, receiving evidence from claimants to land in the area. Holding sessions six days a week, the commissioners toiled to adjudicate claims under the laws of the United States so as to provide claimants with clear title to their lands where appropriate.[6]

On July 6, 1804, Kirby took on substantial extra duties when he received a personal appeal from President Jefferson to accept an appointment as the first federal judge for the Alabama portion of the Mississippi Territory. Undoubtedly busy in his dual positions, Kirby nevertheless grew weary of the remoteness of the territory, stating "should I continue here any great length of time, cut off from all intercourse with the intelligent part of my species I shall forget the relation in which I stand to them," thus wishing for "the termination of my official duties in this wild region." However, he was not inclined to leave right away, as President Jefferson had also imposed tasks beyond his official duties involving the providing of intelligence to the government concerning the area's physical features, the characteristics of the American settlers, and the strength of nearby Spanish settlements, including information relating to reinforcements at Mobile and Pensacola.[7]

On April 1, May 1, and July 1 in 1804, Kirby provided three lengthy reports assessing these factors in letters written to President Jefferson and Treasury Secretary Albert Gallatin. Kirby's first observations concerned the economic potential of Mobile Bay and the necessity of America's control of it so as to take full advantage of its abundant interior river system. Kirby was less impressed with the populace of the area, describing them as "generally without integrity, morality, industry or any other good quality."

---

[5] William H. Jenkins, "Alabama Forts, 1700–1838," *Alabama Review* 12 (July 1959): 169–70.

[6] Briceland, "Ephraim Kirby," 89–90. There were four categories of claims: those based upon British patents, Spanish warrants of survey, occupancy, and right of preemption. Claimants under the first three categories did not have to pay anything other than small fees for surveying and registration, as the lands were "donations" by the board on behalf of the United States. A person receiving a right of preemption would, on the other hand, have to pay two dollars an acre to obtain ownership of the claim. Despite grievances lodged by Tombigbee citizens over the paucity of donations validated, eighty-one percent of the claimants obtained a right to some part of their lands. Briceland, "Land, Law, and Politics," 97, 114.

[7] Briceland, "Ephraim Kirby," 90–92.

A few months later in another report to Jefferson, Kirby reiterated his initial thoughts by stating that "the present inhabitants (with few exceptions) are illiterate, wild and savage, of depraved morals, unworthy of public confidence or private esteem; litigious, disunited, and knowing each other, universally distrustful of each other." Kirby even described local officials as being "without dignity, respect, probity, influence or authority," resulting in local justice being in an "imbecile and corrupt" state. The militia was described as being "without discipline or competent officers."[8]

Kirby reasoned that the populace was in the described dire consequences due to its physical, economic, and psychological isolation. Realizing that such isolation prevented the people from solving their own problems, Kirby advocated the need of federal intervention. He stressed that intervention was needed to provide clear land titles to the area's inhabitants, to establish boundaries with Indian nations so as to provide access to more fertile lands on the east bank of the Tombigbee River, to bring stability to the area's system of justice, and to improve commerce by providing access to the Mobile River running through Spanish West Florida. Although usually accurate in his assessments, Kirby faltered in his reports to administration officials concerning the Creek Nation surrounding local settlements. Describing the Creeks as more "disposed to industry" and better understanding "the value and use of property," he erroneously predicted that they would "become perfectly peaceful and harmless."[9]

Gaining access to Mobile Bay was important to the future of the American citizens of Washington County. Accordingly, Kirby reported to Jefferson that he was concerned that anti-Spanish sentiments among the population would lead local leaders to take matters into their own hands in regard to Spain and Mobile. It was not that Kirby did not sympathize with those opposed to the imposition of exorbitant Spanish duties, but he strived to convince them to await the formal intervention of the federal government and, in his capacity as a federal judge, worked to put a stop to American filibustering against Spanish territory or property. In this regard, he led an investigation into the activities of James Caller, a prominent local citizen and a colonel in the militia, believed by Kirby to be involved in illegal movements against the Spanish and thus posing a threat to peaceful relations with Spain. Although death would prevent Kirby from finishing his investigation of Caller, the investigation put Caller's activities in check for a while. He nevertheless resumed his filibustering and presented problems for Kirby's successor a decade later.[10]

Kirby's service in the Alabama section of the Mississippi Territory was limited to nine short months. In August 1804, his judicial and land commission activities were severely curtailed when he suffered an attack of "billous fever" after a trip up the rain-swollen Tombigbee River to St. Stephens. After recovering somewhat in September, he realized that he

[8] Ibid., 92–98; Doster, "Early Settlements," 87.

[9] Briceland, "Ephraim Kirby," 98–99, 102.

[10] Ibid., 104–11.

would have to leave the Mississippi Territory in order to improve his health. To this end he was planning to return to Litchfield, Connecticut, to rejoin his wife and eight children when he was again inflicted by fevers indigenous to the area. Late in the afternoon of October 20, 1804, he died in his quarters at Fort Stoddert and was buried the next day with military honors in the fort's cemetery. Although the business of the Board of Land Commissioners had ended in July, Kirby had not signed the certificates before his death and it took commissioner Joseph Chambers another year to get them completed. As previously indicated, Kirby was successful in at least temporarily checking the filibustering activities in the region. Although there was some relaxation in Spain's control of American trade, Spain continued to hold on to Mobile. Much was left to challenge Ephraim Kirby's successor.[11]

Upon Kirby's death, citizens of Fort Stoddert signed a petition drawn up by anti-Spanish activist John Caller recommending that Rodominick H. Gilmer of Virginia be appointed as Kirby's successor as territorial judge. Gilmer defeated his own chances, however, by expressing reluctance to take the job in a letter to President Jefferson, who instead chose Harry Toulmin, son of Reverend Joshua Toulmin, a prominent English separatist and friend of theologian and scientist Joseph Priestly. Born in 1766 in Taunton, England, Harry Toulmin was a Dissenting minister in Lancashire before leaving for America in 1793 in search of religious freedom. According to historian Albert James Pickett, Toulmin had become "an object of suspicion to the [British] government," and he was "frequently threatened with personal injury, and often surrounded by mobs." Escaping to America, he landed in Norfolk, Virginia, and soon became acquainted with Thomas Jefferson and James Madison, who shared his liberal views. With a letter of recommendation from Jefferson, Toulmin in 1794 moved on to Kentucky, where he secured the position of president of Transylvania Seminary. His two-year tenure at Transylvania was contentious because his liberal Unitarian views conflicted with those of the Presbyterians who had founded the seminary. Toulmin resigned when James Garrad, a former liberal member of the Transylvania board, was elected Governor of Kentucky in 1796 and appointed him Secretary of State. During his term, Toulmin undertook a major compilation of Kentucky's laws in an effort to make them accessible to all of its citizens, publishing *Description of Kentucky* in 1792, *Magistrate's Assistant: Collection of the Acts of Kentucky* in 1802, and *Review of the Criminal Law of Kentucky with James Blair* in 1804. More importantly, Toulmin signed the 1798-1799 Kentucky Resolutions, protesting the Alien and Sedition Acts passed by a conservative Federalist Congress, thus casting himself as an advocate of "states' rights" and positioning himself for a future presidential appointment.[12]

---

[11] Ibid., 110–13.

[12] Paul M. Pruitt Jr., *Taming Alabama: Lawyers and Reformers, 1804–1929* (Tuscaloosa: University of Alabama Press, 2010), 1–13. (Toulmin continued to publish legal authorities upon his arrival in the Mississippi Territory. In 1806 he published a self-help law book tediously entitled, *The Clerk's Magazine and Conveyancer's Assistant: Being a Collection Adapted to the United State of the Most Approved Precedents*. He next compiled the laws of the new territory, entitled *1807 Statutes of the Mississippi Territory*.) See also Doster, "Early

Judge Harry Toulmin
"The Frontier Justinian"
Courtesy of Transylvania University Photographic Archives

Late in the year of 1804, Toulmin left Kentucky to replace Ephraim Kirby. He came to the territory by the way of the Ohio and Mississippi rivers by barge and further by way of New Orleans and Mobile on the same craft. He then ascended the Mobile River and finally embarked at Fort Stoddert, a short distance below the confluence of the Tombigbee and

Settlements," 88–89; Rowland, *Courts, Judges, and Lawyers,* 21; Niels H. Sonne, *Liberal Kentucky, 1780–1828* (New York: Columbia University Press, 1939), 33–34; Pickett, *History of Alabama,* 480–81; Philip Beidler, "Toulmin and Hitchcock: Pioneering Jurists of the Alabama Frontier," *Alabama Heritage,* no. 81 (Summer 2006): 20–21; Guice, "Cement of Society," 84; Thomas McAdory Owen, *History of Alabama and Dictionary of Alabama Biography* (Chicago: S. J. Clarke Publishing Company, 1921), 4: 676–77.

Alabama rivers. Upon his arrival, he decided to move the Washington County seat from McIntosh Bluff to a site about eight miles north, which he named Wakefield in remembrance of Oliver Goldsmith's novel *The Vicar of Wakefield*. Ephraim Kirby had never actually held court during his short tenure as territorial judge, as he was preoccupied with his duties as land commissioner and envoy for President Jefferson, as well as his investigation into the filibustering activities of James Caller. Thus Judge Toulmin held the first permanent federal court in Washington County in the fall of 1804. Far from simply presiding over the territorial district court, Toulmin assumed many additional responsibilities as the chief federal civil official in a remote wilderness frontier that in effect made him czar of the Tombigbee settlements. Like Kirby before him, he was an envoy for and reported to federal officials in Washington and Natchez. He served as the area's post-master, and from 1806 to 1810 he contracted to operate a mail route from Fort Stoddert to Natchez. He also officiated at marriages and funerals, practiced medicine, and later made patriotic speeches supportive of America's role in the War of 1812. He was further strengthened in the community by the fact that one of his daughters married Edmund Pendleton, the commander of Fort Stoddert, another daughter married the son of Gen. James Wilkinson, the controversial senior officer of the United States Army, and his son married the daughter of rival filibusterer James Caller.[13]

Toulmin's immediate goal as the area's first permanent territorial judge had been to bring order and stability to this remote frontier. In this regard, he later reflected that he was against what he called "that baneful ascendancy which the most abandoned men, have obtained among us." He further acknowledged Judge Kirby's curtailed efforts against this group of unrefined frontiersman and those efforts of others who had left the area "shudder[ing] at the idea of sacrificing [themselves] to such men." Toulmin nevertheless commenced what would be a fourteen-year period of dispensing justice from a log courthouse in Wakefield. This crude courthouse and a necessary jail sat across from each other on the road from St. Stephens to Mobile. The few court files that survive indicate an active frontier docket of torts and criminal cases, with the leading lawyers being Nicholas Perkins, Joseph P. Kennedy, Lemuel Henry, Rodominick H. Gilmer, Samuel Acre, and Joseph Carson.[14]

Toulmin did not just hold court in Wakefield. His territorial jurisdiction extended over an area 340 miles long and 330 miles wide, covering seven current counties mostly in present-day Alabama. In each of these counties he had to hold court twice a year, and he complained in a letter to William Lattimore, a territorial delegate to Congress, that two additional judges

---

[13] Appendix, "Mississippi Territorial Register of Appointments, Civil and Military, 1805–1817," cited in Matte, *History of Washington County*, 29; Pruitt, *Taming Alabama*, 5–6; "Portrait of Judge Toulmin Presented," *Alabama Lawyer* (April 1950): 157; Owen, *History of Alabama*, 4: 676; Rowland, *Courts, Judges, and Lawyers*, 21; Guice, "Cement of Society," 84–85.

[14] Toulmin to James Madison, May 1, 1804; Caleb Wallace to Madison, Apr. 30, 1804; and Toulmin to John Graham, Feb. 25, 1812; all in Clarence E. Carter, ed., *Territorial Papers of the United States*, vols. 5 and 6, *Mississippi* (Washington, D.C.: Government Printing Office, 1937), 5: 320–21, 6: 272.

were necessary to provide adequate coverage of the area. Toulmin covered this vast circuit on horseback, usually accompanied by Tony, his young African American slave. These were long, hazardous journeys through a deep wilderness sparsely settled by white Europeans but thriving with Native Americans, many of whom were members of hostile tribes.[15]

As chief law enforcement officer in the area, Toulmin was quite naturally pitted against the robust backwoods citizenry, humorously described by some as "half-horse, half-alligator." While his efforts to civilize the territory and his relationship with the community would improve with the immigration of more and more stable farm families, he initially had to contend with a contentious faction. As discussed previously, a group led by John Caller had unsuccessfully pushed for the nomination of Rodominick H. Gilmer for territorial judge instead of Toulmin. The Caller brothers were not easily dissuaded and continued to promote Gilmer for public office. In a January 3, 1805 letter to Cato West, acting governor of the Mississippi Territory, John Caller recommended the appointment of Gilmer to the position of clerk of the county court to replace Richard Lee, who Caller alleged had been drunk during the whole term of court and had totally neglected its business. It appears, however, that Gilmer was of dubious character himself. Theodore Brightwell, the sheriff of Washington County, responded to what he described as "prejudicial and malicious" allegations made against him by Gilmer by portraying Gilmer as "a restless Practitioner whose professions have no sincerity; guided by no rule of reason, and limited by no law of principle, the only art or pursuit he seems to have in view is, if possible to deprecate the characters of others, so as to gain ascendancy over his superiors by adding to the number of his equals." This is just the sort of local rascal that Toulmin had to overcome in bringing civility to the Tombigbee settlements.[16]

The need to restrain locals led by the Caller brothers and Joseph P. Kennedy from taking on the nearby Spanish in Mobile was one of Toulmin's priorities upon taking office. The "Bigbee" settlers, however, were extremely agitated by Spain's imposition of a 12 percent duty on ships bound to and from Fort Stoddert through Mobile. James and John Caller vented their fellow settlers' resentment over these heavy duties on essential imports by threatening to capture and burn any Spanish vessel straying

---

[15] Malcom Cook McMillan, *Constitutional Development in Alabama, 1798–1901: A Study in Politics, the Negro, and Sectionalism* (Chapel Hill: University of North Carolina Press, 1955), 9; G. H. Toulmin, comp., "Judge Harry Toulmin—A Sketch," The Northern Toulmins, http://www.toulmin.family.btinternet.co.uk/GeorgesWebPage/AppL.htm (accessed April 26, 2008, no longer active; see http://archive.is/PbWd).

[16] Matte, *History of Washington County*, 29–30; Theodore Brightwell to Robert Williams, July 20, 1805, "General Correspondence, 1795–1815," *Mississippi Territorial Transcripts*, 1, 37–38. James Caller himself later spoke of Gilmer in 1809 as one of the "most frivolous, vicious, and abandoned characters in the country," accused him of legal malpractices, and threatened to reveal his alleged reprehensible "exploits in the mountainous forest of North Carolina." Doster, "Early Settlements," 89.

into American territory above the 31st parallel.[17] Toulmin realized the importance of Mobile to the area and expressed disdain in a letter to Secretary of State James Madison for the duty imposed by Spain: "such an extraction as this, you may well conceive, must be ruinous to this country, and is moreover the source of perpetual heartburnings [*sic*] and contention between our citizens and the subjects of his Catholic majesty."[18]

Judge Toulmin nevertheless thought annexation should come through official military or diplomatic action by the United States and not through the intrigues of local filibusterers known as the "Mobile Society," which included the Caller brothers, Kennedy, Reuben Kemper, and Sterling Dupree.[19] Several of these, however, had clout in the community as military officers and justices of the peace. Toulmin's courageous efforts to keep this filibustering faction in check resulted in a threat of assassination against him by Kennedy and in his narrow escape from an angry mob. Despite these acts of intimidation, Toulmin successfully rebuffed attempts by this group to take Mobile by illegal means. To this end, he convened a grand jury to inform them of the government's opposition to such efforts and later distributed to every militia commander in the area a copy of a proclamation from President Madison declaring these filibustering activities as illegal and ordering the arrest of its participants.[20]

The filibustering reached its climax in 1810 when Kemper, after successfully conducting an insurrection in Spanish-held Baton Rouge, led a force of drunken combatants into Mobile. Toulmin put an end to this attack on Spanish sovereignty by having Kemper and his leading abettors arrested. Not surprisingly, Kemper labeled Toulmin as "a base Devil, filled with deception and bloody rascality." That most residents of the area shared Kemper's opinion of the judge contributed to a local jury's acquittal of Kemper and his marauders. In retaliation, Kemper's men bad-mouthed Toulmin and even convinced a grand jury in newly created Baldwin County to indict him on charges of abusing his judicial powers by utilizing military procedures in questioning witnesses. He defended his actions, which had been characterized as overzealous, by asserting that a judge on the frontier "must perpetually take a more active part in the early stages of prosecutions

---

[17] Philip Beidler, in describing the Caller brothers, states, "there seems to have been no end to their energies for participation in corrupt schemes." Philip D. Beidler, *First Books: The Printed Word and Cultural Formation in Early Alabama* (Tuscaloosa: University of Alabama Press, 1999), 17.

[18] Haynes, "Law Enforcement in Frontier Mississippi," 35; Toulmin to Secretary of State James Madison, July 6, 1805, "General Correspondence, 1795–1815," *Mississippi Territorial Transcripts*, 58-A.

[19] In a letter to the Spanish Commandant in Mobile discussing what course to take with a Spanish subject who had murdered a Tensaw settler and then had escaped back into Spanish territory, Toulmin expressed his philosophy concerning the relations between the two governments by concluding "as far as it depends upon me, I shall always be ready to cooperate with good men of both governments in the suppression of villainy and licentiousness." Hamilton, *Colonial Mobile* (1898), 345–46.

[20] Haynes, "Law Enforcement in Frontier Mississippi," 35; Matte, *History of Washington County*, 33; Isaac J. Cox, *The West Florida Controversy, 1798–1813: A Study in American Diplomacy* (Baltimore: John Hopkins Press, 1918), 176–87.

than is customary in societies more established, and composed of better materials." Toulmin weathered the storm as there was insufficient evidence presented in support of the indictment to either the territorial assembly or to Congress.[21]

In addition to his interaction with local filibusterers, Toulmin also played a prominent role in an intriguing matter involving the arrest of former Vice President Aaron Burr. Since the infamous duel in which he killed Alexander Hamilton, Burr had become an anathema politically in the East and had sought refuge in the expanding western frontier. Even while serving as Vice President, Burr had begun to devise a scheme that many believe involved the conquest of Mexico and the separation of the western states and territories from the established states in the East.[22] By denying the part of his scheme that involved hostile designs on the United States, Burr was able to enlist support for a while from future president Andrew Jackson, who favored war with Spain. Jackson soon decided it best to keep an eye on the mysterious Burr, however, vowing that he would "die in the last ditch before I would . . . see the Union disunited."[23]

In furtherance of his grandiose plan, Burr assembled a small group of men on the Ohio River's Blennerhassett Island, home to Herman Blennerhasset, a wealthy Irish immigrant who was completely enamored of the former Vice President. Charges of levying war against the United States would ultimately be brought against Burr as a result of the assemblage of men and material at this location. In the meantime, Burr enlisted the support of Gen. James Wilkinson, who—despite the fact that he was the senior officer in the American Army and the first governor of the Louisiana Territory—was secretly on the Spanish payroll and had taken an oath of loyalty to Spain. The duplicitous general turned on Burr, however, when it became clear to him that the conspiracy had been compromised and that he would be in danger of losing his position as the commanding officer of the U.S. Army if he continued to participate. Accordingly, he quickly moved to expose Burr's scheme by informing President Jefferson in a letter that he had uncovered "a deep, dark, and wicked conspiracy" to capture New Or-

---

[21] Haynes, "Law Enforcement in Frontier Mississippi," 35–36; Doster, "Early Settlements," 92; Pruitt, *Taming Alabama,* 8–9; William C. Davis, *The Rogue Republic: How Would-Be Patriots Waged the Shortest Revolution in American History* (Boston: Houghton Mifflin Harcourt, 2011), 218–35; Jay Higginbotham, *Mobile: City by the Bay* (Mobile, Ala.: Azalea City Printers, 1968), 45–47. As discussed hereafter, the Mobile question finally resolved itself when a military force under Gen. James Wilkinson brought Mobile under American control for good on April 13, 1813, by accepting the surrender of Spanish Capt. Cayetano Pérez. Brown, "Colonial Mobile," 59.

[22] Historians have had a difficult time in nailing down with any precision the object of Burr's designs because, as Thomas Perkins Abernethy put it, "the whole trouble with the Burr Conspiracy is that there were too many liars mixed up in it." Thomas Perkins Abernethy, "Aaron Burr in Mississippi," *Journal of Southern History* 15 (February 1949): 15. For a recent and thorough examination of the Burr conspiracy and the trial that followed, see R. Kent Newmyer, *The Treason Trial of Aaron Burr: Law, Politics and the Character Wars of the New Nation* (Cambridge, UK: Cambridge University Press, 2012).

[23] Aaron Welborn, "A Traitor in the Wilderness: The Arrest of Aaron Burr," *Alabama Heritage,* no. 83 (Winter 2007): 10–19; H. W. Brands, *Andrew Jackson: His Life and Times* (New York: Doubleday, 2005), 113–27.

leans and to establish an independent western nation.[24]

Jefferson responded by issuing a proclamation on November 27, 1806, exposing the conspiracy and calling for Burr's arrest. Burr was not aware of this proclamation until he landed his forces in Bayou Pierre, Louisiana, on January 10, 1807. Nevertheless, the citizens of the Mississippi Territory had been abuzz with the possibility of Burr's arrival as indicated by a letter from Silas Dinsmore to Col. John McKee, both Choctaw Indian agents. Dinsmore wrote McKee, "we are all in a flurry here hourly expecting Colonel Burr & all Kentucky & half of Tennessee at his [back] to punish General Wilkinson, set the negroes free, Rob the banks & take Mexico," adding "come & help me to laugh at the fun." Perhaps this intriguing anticipation caused Toulmin to just happen to be in the territorial capital city of Washington, near Natchez, when Burr surrendered to civil authorities there.[25]

Until formal charges were brought against him, Burr was entertained with balls and parties in Adams County hosted by those generally sympathetic to him. Through his exposure to the local populace, local editorials, and legislative expressions, Burr sensed considerable unrest regarding the Spanish. In fact, Burr met privately with the two representatives to the territorial assembly from the Tombigbee district, James Caller, Judge Toulmin's nemesis, and Lemuel Henry, as well as with Indian agent Col. John McKee, a former associate of Gen. James Wilkinson. Reportedly Burr heartened these representatives by asserting that they had every right to establish their own government due to the neglect of their remote government in the Natchez District. He thus left them with the impression that he would possibly come to their aid in such an enterprise in return for their support of any undertaking he might commence against Spain.[26]

The territory's jurists were reluctant to bring charges against Burr because they were of the opinion that, whatever crimes he had committed elsewhere, no crime had been committed within their jurisdiction. They were perhaps influenced by the fact that the local citizens were sympathetic to Burr's expedition to the extent that it possibly involved wresting Mobile from Spain. Also, Judge Peter Bruin was a personal friend of Burr's, a fact that undoubtedly clouded his judgment. Toulmin, however, did not want to see Burr get away and took it upon himself to bring charges against him and his principal co-conspirators, with the intent of sending them to jurisdictions where their cases could appropriately be tried. In so doing, he set in motion circumstances that would ultimately lead to one of the most celebrated trials in America's history. In the meantime, however, Thomas Rodney, a judge in the western section of the territory, intervened and

---

[24] Welborn, "A Traitor in the Wilderness," 10–19; Joseph Wheelan, *Jefferson's Vendetta: The Pursuit of Aaron Burr and the Judiciary* (New York: Carroll & Graf Publishers, 2005), 131–52; Andro Linklater, *An Artist in Treason: The Extraordinary Double Life of General James Wilkinson* (New York: Walker, 2009), 253.

[25] Welborn, "A Traitor in the Wilderness," 16; Thomas McAdory Owen, ed., "Burr's Conspiracy," *Transactions of the Alabama Historical Society* 3 (1898–99): 168–69; Abernethy, "Aaron Burr in Mississippi," 10–11.

[26] Pickett, *History of Alabama*, 490; Stuart O. Stumpf, ed., "The Arrest of Aaron Burr: A Documentary Record," *Alabama Historical Quarterly* 42 (Fall and Winter, 1980): 116.

arraigned Burr in his own court, asserting that Toulmin had no jurisdiction outside of his eastern Tombigbee district.[27]

Not surprisingly, Burr's friend Judge Bruin objected to Burr's arraignment in his and Rodney's court on the ground that their court was an appellate court and, as such, had no original jurisdiction over any criminal offenses. Rodney overruled Bruin and proceeded with the case against Burr, but would face yet another obstacle from George Poindexter, the territory's attorney general. Poindexter declined to bring charges on the basis that Burr had committed no crime within their territorial jurisdiction. Ignoring the attorney general's refusal to act, Rodney commenced to take depositions which were presented as the only evidence before the assembled grand jury. The grand jury, however, purportedly packed with both Federalists and friends of Burr, exonerated Burr of all charges, including allegations of treason as well as misdemeanors. Showing sympathy for Burr, the grand jury instead charged the territorial administration with irregularities in their treatment of the accused. Although the grand jury was discharged, Rodney refused to release Burr from his bond, instead adding a requirement to the bond that Burr must remain in the neighborhood indefinitely, at the discretion of the judge. He also ordered the jury's verdict to be stricken from the record, with the notation that he disapproved of their "particular impropriety in censuring [the government's] conduct." On February 6, 1807, just two days after the grand jury disbanded, Burr failed to answer a summons to appear before the territorial court. His bond was thus forfeited and territorial governor Robert Williams announced an award of $2,000 for Burr's apprehension.[28]

Burr sent a note to Governor Williams protesting his status as a fugitive and offering to submit to civil authorities if assured that he would be treated as any other citizen and would not be turned over to the military. However, about a week later, fearing the treatment he might receive if turned over to the Army and General Wilkinson, Burr fled the area. He was apprehended on the morning of February 19, 1807, ironically near Judge Toulmin's town of Wakefield in the Tombigbee region. His arrest was well reported by those involved and reads like something out of a spy novel. At approximately eleven o'clock on a cold winter's night in a cabin near Wakefield, a backgammon game between Nicholas Perkins, a lawyer who had been appointed by President Jefferson to serve as a federal land registrar, and Thomas Malone, the clerk of the territorial court, was interrupted by

---

[27] Abernethy, "Aaron Burr in Mississippi," 9–11.

[28] Abernethy, "Aaron Burr in Mississippi," 11–12; Stumpf, "Arrest of Aaron Burr," 117; Roger G. Kennedy, *Burr, Hamilton, and Jefferson: A Study in Character* (Oxford, N.Y.: Oxford University Press, 2000), 328; Hamilton, *Anglo-American Law*, 78–83. The Burr grand jury reported in part: "The grand jury of the Mississippi Territory, on a due investigation of the evidence brought before them, are of the opinion that Aaron Burr has not been guilty of any crime or misdemeanor against the laws of the United States or of this Territory, or given any just occasion for alarm or inquietude to the good people of this Territory. The grand jury present as a grievance, the late military expedition unnecessarily as they conceive, fitted out against the person and property of said Aaron Burr, where no resistance has been made to the ordinary civil authorities...." Walter Flavius McCaleb, *The Aaron Burr Conspiracy* (New York: Wilson-Erickson, 1936), 228.

the sound of horses approaching the cabin. The strangers rode up to the door and asked Perkins and Malone for directions to the local tavern and also to the farm of Col. John Hinson. Based upon the description set forth in the proclamation calling for Burr's arrest, Perkins was convinced that one of the strangers was Burr. He also thought it suspicious that the strangers wanted to press on in the dark of night over unfamiliar and difficult terrain to the Hinson farm. Malone was not so convinced, so Perkins rode fast to the home of Sheriff Theodore Brightwell and got him out of bed to accompany him to the Hinson farm.[29]

Because Perkins feared being recognized by the stranger he believed to be Burr, Perkins remained in the woods while Sheriff Brightwell, a relative of Mrs. Hinson, went up to the Hinson farmhouse to investigate the situation. Tiring of waiting on Brightwell in the cold and convinced that he had the fugitive Burr within his sights, Perkins thought it prudent to go to Fort Stoddert to apprise its commandant Lieut. Edmund P. Gaines of what was going on. As a result, early the next morning, Lieutenant Gaines led a contingent of mounted soldiers to pursue the strangers Perkins had encountered. At approximately nine o'clock they met two travelers on the road to Pensacola roughly two miles from the Hinson farm. Surprisingly, one was Sheriff Brightwell. Gaines stated with confidence to the other traveler that he presumed that he had the honor of addressing Colonel Burr and that, based upon proclamations from both the president and the governor, he was arresting him on behalf of the federal government. Burr challenged his authority to stop a traveler upon the highway and denounced the proclamations ordering his arrest as without justification. Not intimated by Burr's challenges, Lieutenant Gaines told Burr that he must accompany him to Fort Stoddert where he would be treated with the respect due a former vice president so long as he made no attempt to escape.[30]

Burr was detained at Fort Stoddert until March 5, 1807. His period of confinement there was not all that unpleasant as he often competed in games of chess with Lieutenant Gaines' wife, who was Toulmin's daughter. But Gaines quickly became concerned with his ability to keep Burr under lock and key, as he knew that Burr was interacting with his guards to affect an escape, while dangerous sympathizers were eagerly waiting in the wings to help. In the meantime, Maj. Robert Ashley, who had accompanied Burr to Wakefield, was still on the loose telling sympathetic locals that Burr's intention was to throw the Spanish out of West Florida. As a result of this mounting pressure, Lieutenant Gaines decided on his own that it was time to send Burr north to answer the charges of treason pending against him. In

---

[29] Abernethy, "Aaron Burr in Mississippi," 12; Pickett, *History of Alabama*, 490–93; Kennedy, *Burr, Hamilton, and Jefferson*, 333–38. Pickett's account of Burr's arrest is based upon interviews with many of the eyewitnesses, including Thomas Malone, Mrs. Hinson, and George S. Gaines, who was at Fort Stoddert when Burr was incarcerated there. Pickett also obtained a description of events through correspondence with Maj. Gen. Edmund P. Gaines.

[30] Pickett, *History of Alabama*, 490–94. Brightwell professed surprise that it was Burr he was accompanying. Pickett speculated that the sheriff had become intrigued with Burr, regretted that he had sought to arrest him, and was assisting him escape to Pensacola, probably to board a ship to Europe. Kennedy, *Burr, Hamilton, and Jefferson*, 333–37.

this regard, he employed Nicholas Perkins, the man initially responsible for Burr's apprehension, to take Burr approximately a thousand miles through Indian country back east to stand trial for treason.[31]

At the same time he was skirmishing with filibusterers and delving into the Burr conspiracy, Judge Toulmin was in the process of writing the first digest of laws for the Mississippi Territory. The territorial assembly had undoubtedly commissioned him for this project due to his previous experience in Kentucky in this regard. Upon completion of the project, Toulmin forwarded a copy to Governor Williams on January 19, 1807, stating to the governor in an accompanying letter that "I have felt inclined to adopt the opinion that the statute as well as the common law of England, as it stood previously to the settlement of Florida, makes a part of the law of the Mississippi Territory." The laws were categorized as relating to the following subject matters: territorial and county lines; the general assembly; the public revenue; the public force (the militia); courts of justice, their officers, and the regulation of court proceedings; crimes, misdemeanors, and the public police; highways, navigation, commerce, and agriculture; the encouragement for learning; and the relief of the poor and sick. In this submission to the governor, Toulmin suggests that the general assembly "minutely" review his work to see if amendments to existing laws were advisable. He further suggested that a small collection of forms and instructions be added for the use of justices of the peace.[32]

As well as compiling the laws of the territory, Toulmin took interest in the membership requirements of the territorial bar. In a June 1811 letter to Governor David Holmes, Toulmin stated that, although he previously understood that candidates for the bar needed only present a certificate

---

[31] Abernethy, "Aaron Burr in Mississippi," 16–18; Welborn, "A Traitor in the Wilderness," 17. In a letter dated March 3, 1807, William C. C. Claiborne, governor of the Orleans Territory, reported to Secretary of State James Madison that "Lieut. Gaines of Fort Stoddard, has arrested Burr, and forwarded him under escort, to the City of Washington, where the subtle Traitor, will I trust meet the punishments due his crimes." Governor Claiborne further rejoiced that "as an American Citizen, devoted to my Country and Government cannot but express my joy, at the defeat of a Conspiracy, (and not an inconsiderable one) which had for its primary object the dismemberment of the American Union." Owen, "Burr's Conspiracy," 172–73. On August 3, 1807, the young nation's first "trial of the century" began in Richmond as Aaron Burr finally stood trial for treason. The trial was presided over by Chief Justice John Marshall and was prosecuted by John Hay, the United States Attorney for Richmond, former Attorney General Charles Lee, and future presidential candidate William Wirt. Burr's defense was handled by Edmund Randolph and Luther Martin. Chief Justice Marshall employed a strict reading of the Constitution and excluded all evidence not directly related to the act of treason. In this regard, Marshall maintained that it took the testimony of at least two witnesses to the same "overt act" of levying war against the United States committed by the defendant himself, rather than subsequent acts of the defendant or acts of others. In keeping with this narrow definition, he excluded evidence of Burr's conduct subsequent to the activities on Blennerhassett Island. On September 1, 1807, the jury had no choice but to deliver a verdict of not guilty "by any evidence submitted to us." Following his acquittal, Burr sought exile in Europe, returning to America in 1812. Thereafter he lived in relative obscurity, practicing law in New York until his death on September 14, 1836. Wheelan, *Jefferson's Vendetta*, 189–205; Nathan Schachner, *Aaron Burr: A Biography* (1937; repr. New York: A. S. Barnes, 1961), 437–38, 496–515.

[32] Guice, "Cement of Society," 85; Toulmin to Governor Williams, January 19, 1807, Mississippi (Territory), General Correspondence (1795–1815), SG3105–SG3106, ADAH.

from two attorneys attesting to the legal achievement of the applicant, he acknowledged that he now understood the governor also required the party applying for admission to present a certificate from one of the judges he practiced before. Toulmin further observed that, as a judge making such recommendations to him in the future, he would require evidence from an applicant of his possession of what he perceived as necessary characteristics of honesty, honor, sobriety, veracity, and industry. He also recommended that if the attorney came from a distant place, he should bring evidence of these traits from two or more judges of a superior court nearest the applicant's place of residence. Toulmin believed that a uniform rule of admission for attorneys should be adopted by all the judges of the territory, asserting that strict admission requirements were necessary in light of what he described as a "circumscribed power of the court to check or suspend the wayward or profligate practitioner."[33]

In addition to fending off possible filibustering assaults that could lead to war with Spain, Toulmin also walked a fine line in administering justice as related to neighboring Native American tribes. An example of this sensitivity stems from a case where Native Americans within his jurisdiction, "having access to spirituous liquors from local citizens," began fighting amongst themselves, resulting in a man killing his sister's husband. Anticipating retribution from her husband's family if her brother avoided punishment, the widow ordered her teenage son, Illichetubba, to avenge the murder of his stepfather by assassinating his uncle. While Toulmin dutifully committed the teenager to the next term of his court set for July 1810, he also petitioned both Governor Holmes and President Madison to issue a pardon.[34]

Appreciating the deed as one of murder under the common law, Toulmin nevertheless felt the case deserved "executive mercy" due to the fact that the teenage accused was an authorized executioner under Indian law. Failure to act, as Toulmin understood it, could have resulted in the accused's own death or that of his mother's. Further, it would have not entered the young warrior's mind that he was amenable to the white man's laws. Although he requested a pardon, Toulmin also surmised that imprisonment prior to trial would have a serious deterrent effect, serving as a warning to Indians that they would be subject to the white man's law while in American territory.[35]

In a letter the week before, Toulmin had written to Mingo Pooshmataha [Pushmataha] describing this incident as "bad news," and proclaiming that, "liquor, I am afraid, will in time destroy your nation." He went on to tell the Choctaw chief that American law would be applied to everyone entering into the Mississippi Territory, declaring that "our laws do not suffer one man to go kill another man." He thus suggested that the

[33] Toulmin to D. Holmes, June 10, 1811, Mississippi (Territory), Judge of the Superior Court, Correspondence, 1805–1816, SG3111, ADAH.

[34] Toulmin to Holmes, May 27, 1810, 3–5, Mississippi (Territory), Judge of the Superior Court, Correspondence, 1805–1816, SG3111, ADAH.

[35] Ibid.

accused and his mother should have complained to one of the territory's judges, who would have likely condemned the first offender to the gallows. If instead they had wished to exact satisfaction under Indian laws, they should have done so in the territory where American law had no effect. Toulmin emphasized that he must enforce the law since the act occurred within the American jurisdiction. He nevertheless mentioned the possibility of the pardon for which he had already petitioned. Toulmin's entreaty that Illichetubba was perhaps ignorant of American law or was unaware that he was in white man's territory apparently carried the day, because pardons were granted by both Governor Holmes and President Madison.[36]

Judge Toulmin's concern for the territory's relations with surrounding Native American tribes caused him to closely monitor increasing hostility toward white settlers within the territory. After the celebrated visit of Tecumseh, a Shawnee chief from the Ohio River Valley, to rally southern Creeks to defend their tribal lands, the remote white and métis communities of the Tombigbee district began to experience escalating problems with their Native American neighbors. Just a few months after Tecumseh's visit, Toulmin noted an increasing concern among settlers along the Mobile, Alabama, and Tombigbee rivers as he rode the circuit of his local courts. Recounting his observations to a State Department official in a March 10, 1812 report, Toulmin indicated that "a considerable consternation pervades the upper settlements—particularly in the forks of the Tombigbee and Alabama—of an immediate attack upon them by Creek Indians." Toulmin himself was skeptical and suspected that the perceived dangers were blown out of proportion. Although an immediate all-out attack did not occur, the murder of two local citizens by a roaming band of Creeks on March 26 and April 29 naturally increased the settlers' anxiety. Tensions further mounted following a series of Indian raids well to the north in the Tennessee Valley and America's declaration of war against Great Britain.[37]

The advent of the War of 1812 led settlers in the Mississippi Territory to anticipate British instigation of ill will among an already inflamed Indian population, with the Spanish in nearby Pensacola as likely allies. In fact,

---

[36] Toulmin to Mingo Pooshmatahaw, May 18, 1810, 6–7; Toulmin to Holmes, July 7, 1810, 8–9; and Toulmin to Holmes, July 21, 1810; all in Mississippi (Territory), Judge of the the Superior Court, Correspondence, 1805–1816, SG3111, ADAH.

[37] Leland L. Lengel, "The Road to Fort Mims: Judge Harry Toulmin's Observations on the Creek War, 1811–1813," *Alabama Review* 29 (January 1976): 18–21. The circumstances surrounding the killing of Thomas Meredith on March 26, 1812, along Pichona Creek near Pintlala was the subject of much debate due to conflicting accounts of the incident. Despite the fact that Meredith's son was an eyewitness and reported that his father had been murdered, Sam Moniac, a wealthy mixed-blood Creek tavern keeper in the area, described the killing as "accidental." For an extensive discussion of this high-profile case, see Gary Burton, "Pintlala's Cold Murder Case: The Death of Thomas Meredith in 1812," *Alabama Review* 63 (July 2010): 163–91. There was no such debate over the brutal raid in the Tennessee Valley, which involved the murder and scalping of seven settlers (including children) on the Duck River and the celebrated kidnapping of Martha Crawley. This incident enraged local citizens and was widely reported in the frontier press. Crawley eventually eluded her captors and wound up with the family of Indian agent George Strother Gaines in St. Stephens. "Crawley Deposition," in John Spencer Bassett, ed. *Correspondence of Andrew Jackson* (Washington, DC: Carnegie Institution, 1926–1935), 1: 225–226 n.1.

rumor had it that the Spanish were strengthening the old British post at Pensacola and were petitioning the Creek Nation for a minimum of four thousand warrior allies. Toulmin nevertheless supported Indian agent Benjamin Hawkins, who urged patience and the forbearance of governmental action. Toulmin's old adversary Col. James Caller, on the other hand, at that same time sent out a party of militia that Toulmin described as "without any occasion" and "whose avowed design is to murder Indians." Caller's expedition was without any real significant incident, however, and was not followed by an immediate attack on American interests in the area. As a matter of fact, Creek tribal leaders were even influenced by Hawkins to avenge the earlier death of the seven settlers on the Duck River by executing the eight warriors believed responsible. This respite was short lived, however, as the Upper Creek tribes—already enraged over white encroachment onto their lands—erupted into a civil war against the Lower Creek chiefs who put these young Creeks to death in order to placate the Americans. Due to a belief that this civil war was a forewarning of an attack on the settlers themselves, Hawkins moved first his family and then himself to Georgia in the late spring of 1813.[38]

By August 1813 the situation appeared to have worsened, as evidenced by a deposition received by Toulmin from Sam Moniac, a well-known and respected so-called "half-breed" in the Tombigbee district. In this deposition Moniac stated that he had spoken to a rebellious Creek chief who made it clear that they intended to wage war against American settlers. Although some discounted Moniac's deposition because of his unabashed condemnation of Tecumseh, Toulmin nevertheless concluded, based upon all the information available to him, "that war exists between a part of the Creek nation and the people of the United States." His words were prophetic, as the uneasy peace would soon be shattered by a group of militia lead by Colonel Caller, which skirmished with Creek warriors returning from a trip to Spanish Pensacola. This first encounter of the Creek War occurred at the village of Burnt Corn, near present-day Monroeville, Alabama, on July 7, 1813. Caller's troops attacked the Creek party returning from Pensacola, where they had obtained gun powder and supplies from a reluctant Spanish government. The Americans gained the early advantage by a surprise attack on the Creeks as they peacefully lunched. They let their guard down as they ransacked the Indian's pack horses, however, allowing the Indians under Peter McQueen to regroup and launch a surprise attack of their own. This counterattack caused great confusion and sent the Americans into retreat. As the news of this skirmish spread, the Bigbee settlers made their way to hastily constructed forts for protection. Toulmin himself notified Governor Holmes that he was moving his family to Mount Vernon, a new fortification near completion close to Fort Stoddert. On August 30, 1813, Creeks under William Weatherford sought revenge for Burnt Corn by attacking nearby Fort Mims. This bold assault turned into a massacre of some 250 settlers, including women and children, and guaranteed the ultimate removal of the

---

[38] Toulmin to John Graham, August 5, 1812, in Carter, *Territorial Papers of the United States,* 4:306.

Creeks from the territory and a resulting flood of immigrants into the area so great as to be referred to as "Alabama Fever."[39]

Judge Toulmin would survive the Creek War and continue to reign supreme in the Tombigbee district of the Mississippi Territory until it became a part of the Alabama Territory in 1817. In 1819 he took part in Alabama's statehood convention and was subsequently elected to the new Alabama legislature. In 1823, he compiled the first *Digest of the Laws of the State of Alabama*. Toulmin died in December 1824 at the Washington County Courthouse. In his will Toulmin made provision for the emancipation of his loyal slave Tony, directing that he be allowed to go to any state where he could obtain freedom and stating that he felt "towards him almost as one of my family rather than as a slave."[40]

Harry Toulmin's rule of the Tombigbee district earned him the name "the Frontier Justinian." For a period of fourteen years, he brought order and balance to a remote area of the nation that was filled with raucous characters and international intrigue. Fearing no one, whether a former vice president, prominent filibustering local citizens, or rowdy backwoodsmen, Toulmin courageously transformed his remote frontier outpost into a civilized community ready for statehood. Before achieving statehood, however, the Alabama region would be embroiled in a war between the encroaching white settlers and native Creek Indians.

---

[39] Lengel, "Road to Fort Mims," 26–32; Eron Rowland, *Mississippi Territory in the War of 1812* (1921; repr., Baltimore: Genealogical Publishing Company, 1968), 31; Henry S. Halbert and T. H. Ball, *The Creek War of 1813 and 1814* (1895; repr., Tuscaloosa: University of Alabama Press, 1995), 279. On the very day of the Fort Mims massacre, Toulmin wrote to Gen. Thomas Flournoy, passing along a report from a hostage that a Creek war party was seen headed in the direction of Fort Mims. Rogers et al., *Alabama*, 48, 54.

[40] Owen, *History of Alabama*, 4: 1676; Beidler, "Toulmin and Hitchcock," 18–25; Toulmin, "Judge Harry Toulmin—A Sketch."

4

THE CREEK WAR
1813–1814

By the seventeenth century, there were four major Native American tribes occupying what was to become the state of Alabama—Cherokee, Creek, Chickasaw, and Choctaw. The Choctaw within Alabama were principally located on the lower Tombigbee River; the Cherokee occupied sections of northeastern Alabama in present-day Madison, Marshall, DeKalb, Cherokee, and Etowah counties; and the few Chickasaw located within Alabama were in an area south of the Tennessee River in northwest Alabama. The Creek, or Muskogees, the most predominate group, were divided into Upper and Lower Creek within Alabama and Georgia. The Upper Creek primarily occupied the territory along the Coosa, Alabama, and Tallapoosa rivers in Alabama, with the Lower Creek living along the lower Chattahoochee, Ocmulgee, and Flint rivers in southwestern Georgia.[1]

American encroachment into the lower part of the Mississippi Territory bordering Spanish Florida brought settlers increasingly into contact with the Creek Nation. Prior to the American Revolution, French and British traders, known as "Indian countrymen," came to the area and married into Indian families. Many lived with their Indian wives and established farms and ranches in the fork between the Tombigbee and Alabama rivers; some were important cogs in the Creek deerskin trade with the British, and others became Creek political leaders and warriors.[2] European-Native intermarriage produced such offspring as Alexander McGillivray, William McIntosh, and William Weatherford, who all played major roles in the transformation of relations between white frontiersmen and the Creek Nation. Under McGillivray's leadership, the Creeks were able to avoid major hostilities with the Americans in the Mississippi Territory. After McGillivray's death, however, relations among different factions of the Creek Nation, as well as between the Creeks and Americans, deteriorated to the point of war, pitting Weatherford and McIntosh against one another.

Alexander McGillivray, son of a Scottish trader named Lachlan McGillivray and a Creek woman known as Sehoy, was the most influential leader of

---

[1] Rogers et al., *Alabama*, 8–13.

[2] Andrew K. Frank, *Creeks and Southerners: Biculturalism on the Early American Frontier* (Lincoln: University of Nebraska Press, 2005), 26–27; Robbie Ethridge, *Creek Country: The Creek Indians and Their World* (Chapel Hill: University of North Carolina Press, 2003), 77–78. Frank's and Ethridge's works portray a Creek Nation during the seventeenth and early eighteenth centuries that incorporated outsiders and adjusted its social structures to allow increased engagement with both whites and blacks.

the Creeks at the end of the eighteenth century. In 1736 Lachlan McGillivray arrived in Savannah, Georgia, from Scotland as a sixteen-year-old indentured servant. By 1741 he had learned enough of the Creek language to become an interpreter, and three years later obtained a license from South Carolina authorities to commence trade within the Creek Nation. On a trading trip into what is now Alabama, Lachlan met Sehoy, who was the daughter of a Creek woman of the Wind Clan. Sehoy's father was reputed to be a French soldier at Fort Toulouse, Captain Marchand de Courtel.[3] Lachlan took Sehoy as his wife and built a house on the Coosa River at Little Tallassee near present-day Wetumpka. Their son, Alexander, was born in 1750 and grew up in matrilineal Creek society as a member of his mother's Wind Clan. In the native tongue of his mother, Alexander was called Hoboi-Hili-Miko, the Good Child King.[4]

Lachlan McGillivray, a notorious Tory, saw to it that his son was tutored in the classics by his uncle, Reverend Farquhar McGillivray, in Charleston and served an apprenticeship in an accounting firm in Savannah. With the outbreak of the Revolutionary War and a bounty on his head, Lachlan went back to Scotland. Meanwhile, never to see his father again, Alexander returned to the Creek country of his mother and accumulated slaves to run "Apple Grove," the plantation started by his father along the Coosa River at Little Tallassee. The largest slaveholder in the Creek country, Alexander also established a plantation in the Tensaw settlement above Mobile. Due to his mother's position in the powerful Wind Clan, Alexander soon achieved the rank of a lesser chief. About that same time Great Britain commissioned him as a colonel in the British Army so as to maintain the loyalty of the Creeks toward England.[5]

After Britain ceded Florida to Spain at the close of the American Revolution, McGillivray sought Spanish trade and support, offering his services "as an agent for Indian affairs on the part of his most Catholic majesty." By the summer of 1784, McGillivray had negotiated a treaty officially reestablishing relations between the Creeks and Spain. He had decided to avoid a relationship with the United States because of its settlers' encroachment upon Creek territory. Instead, he persuaded Spain that it needed the Creeks as a buffer for its own possessions against American expansionism. Although the British were evacuating the area, he convinced William Panton

---

[3] For a detailed discussion as to whether Sehoy was in fact half French, see Mary Ann Oglesby Neeley, "Lachlan McGillivray: A Scot on the Alabama Frontier," *Alabama Historical Quarterly* 36 (Spring 1974): 5–14.

[4] Rogers et al., *Alabama*, 37–38; Edward J. Cashin, *Lachlan McGillivray, Indian Trader: The Shaping of the Southern Colonial Frontier* (Athens: University of Georgia Press, 1992), 19. So many Carolina traders invaded Indian territory during this period that more than four hundred children would grow up to be "influenced by the capitalistic values of their fathers and bound to their clans by the traditions of their mothers"; John Walton Caughey, *McGillivray of the Creeks* (Norman: University of Oklahoma Press, 1938), 3, 13–16.

[5] Rogers et al., *Alabama*, 39; John Buchanan, *Jackson's Way: Andrew Jackson and the People of the Western Waters* (New York: Wiley, 2001), 81; Claudio Saunt, *A New Order of Things: Property, Power, and the Transformation of the Creek Indians, 1733–1816* (New York: Cambridge University Press, 1999), 70; Braund, *Deerskins & Duffels*, 184; Neeley, "Lachlan McGillivray," 12–13.

to stay and continue the Indian trade through his trading concern, Panton, Leslie, and Company. Panton agreed so long as McGillivray would become a member of the firm, offering him a twenty percent share of profits, and a guarantee of its safeguarding. Panton further persuaded McGillivray to request a trade route through Pensacola and Mobile, giving preference to the Panton firm. Recognizing McGillivray's relationship with William Panton, Spain permitted Panton to continue trading with England with the proviso that his firm pay a Spanish import-export tax.[6]

Panton, Leslie, and Company was thus firmly established as the premier trading company among the southeastern Indian tribes, and McGillivray was aggressive in protecting its status. Following a few violent confrontations instigated by McGillivray, America's pre-constitutional government sought to negotiate a peace between the Creeks and the encroaching Georgians. McGillivray put off the American commissioners in view of the recent hostilities and the continued support of Spanish governor Esteban Rodríguez Miró. After the establishment of America's constitutional government, President Washington sent commissioners to negotiate with McGillivray. Finding the American commissioners inflexible with regard to boundary and sovereignty issues, McGillivray and two thousand of his warriors left without a treaty from a September 1789 convention at Rock Landing on the Oconee River in Georgia. Although an agreement had not been reached, the door had been opened for future negotiations.[7]

The new administration persevered in its pursuit of a treaty by sending Marinus Willett as a special envoy to the Creek Nation. He carried with him a letter from then-Senator Benjamin Hawkins in essence apologizing for the ineptness of the previous commissioners and encouraging McGillivray to accept an invitation to travel to New York to negotiate a solid peace between the nations. Willett urged a council of chiefs to accompany McGillivray to New York to conclude a treaty "as strong as the hills and lasting as the rivers." The chiefs agreed to send a contingent of twenty-six chiefs and warriors to accompany McGillivray, who, although he believed it was to the Creek's advantage to do so, also saw an opportunity to attain prominence. In this regard, he divulged to William Panton that a treaty concluded "at N. York ratified with the signature of Washington and McGillivray would be the bond of Long peace and revered by Americans to a very distant period."[8]

Leaving Creek country by wagon and horseback, McGillivray and his chiefs trekked through the Carolinas, Virginia, and Pennsylvania on their long journey to the political center of the new United States of America. After crossing the Hudson River, they arrived by sloop at Murphy's Wharf

---

[6] Saunt, *New Order of Things,* 75–76 n.40; Caughey, *McGillivray,* 23–24; Rogers et al., *Alabama,* 39.

[7] Saunt, *New Order of Things,* 77–78, 251–54; Caughey, *McGillivray,* 38–39. McGillivray exhibited his aggressiveness in 1787 when he incited approximately five hundred Creek warriors to attack American settlements along the Cumberland River in Tennessee to prevent the establishment of a competitor's trading post there. That same year William Davenport, a Georgia competitor who was working to regain the Chickasaw trade for Augusta merchants, lost his scalp at McGillivray's urging.

[8] Caughey, *McGillivray,* 41–43.

to the crescendo of ships firing their guns in celebratory welcome. They were met by members of the newly organized Society of St. Tammany, a group of former Revolutionary soldiers that would evolve into a powerful political force in New York. Society members were in full Indian regalia similar to that worn by the arriving Creeks, who were bedecked with feathers, beads, earrings, and silver throat armor. McGillivray himself, however, reportedly looked and dressed as a white man. Abigail Adams, wife of Vice President John Adams, observed McGillivray during his sojourn in New York and reported that "he dresses in our own fashion speaks English like a Native, & I should never suspect him to be of that Nation, as he is not very dark." In a ceremony attracting a crowd rivaling that of the inauguration of George Washington, St. Tammany society members and a detachment of soldiers escorted McGillivray and his native Alabamians up Wall Street past Federal Hall, where Congress was in session, to the home of Secretary of War Henry Knox. That evening McGillivray and his chiefs were honored at a dinner at the City Tavern hosted by President Washington, Secretary Knox, Governor Edward Telfair of Georgia, and Governor George Clinton of New York.[9]

On August 7, 1790, the United States of America and the Creek Nation concluded the Treaty of New York. Judith Sargent Murray, sister of future Mississippi territorial governor Winthrop Sargent and an observer on the scene, reported that in celebration of the treaty, Creek chiefs entered Federal Hall with "shrieks and yells" and interlocked their arms with those of President Washington, who was decked out "in rich vestments of purple and satin." Publicly pledging eternal peace and friendship, the final treaty ensured that Creeks enjoyed the protection of the United States to the exclusion of other foreign powers. In return, realizing the impracticality of removing settlers already entrenched on their lands, McGillivray relinquished Creek claims to nearly 2,000 acres in Georgia near the Oconee in return for an annual remuneration of $1,500.[10]

Contributing to McGillivray's reputation among some as duplicitous were certain secret portions of the Treaty of New York, which personally benefited McGillivray and his chiefs and made McGillivray a double agent

---

[9] Ibid., 43; Celia Barnes, *Native American Power in the United States, 1783–1795* (Madison, N.J.: Farleigh Dickinson University Press, 2003), 116; J. L. Wright Jr., "Creek American Treaty of 1790: Alexander McGillivray and the Diplomacy of the Old Southwest," *Georgia Historical Quarterly* 51 (December 1967): 379; Abigail Adams to Mary Adams, August 8, 1790, *Proceedings of the American Antiquarian Society* 55 (1945): 168–69, in Saunt, *New Order of Things*, 75; Joseph J. Ellis, *American Creation: Triumphs and Tragedies at the Founding of the Republic* (New York: A. A. Knopf, 2007), 152.

[10] Other public provisions of the treaty pertained to laws applicable to Creeks and Americans in their respective jurisdictions. There was also a mutual pledge to wait for explanations prior to responding with force to aggressive acts of the other. In hopes of converting Creeks from wandering hunters to established cultivators, the United States pledged to provide them domestic animals and farm implements. Finally, the United States pledged to provide interpreters to promote communication between their peoples. Gordon S. Wood, *Empire of Liberty: A History of the Early Republic, 1789–1815* (New York: Oxford University Press, 2009), 128; Caughey, *McGillivray*, 44; James Lamar Appleton and Robert David Ward, "Albert James Pickett and the Case of the Secret Articles: Historians and the Treaty of New York of 1790," *Alabama Review* 51 (January 1998): 9–11.

of the United States and Spain. The first of the secret articles dealt with convoluted potential trade avenues between the United States and the Creeks, negotiated by the Americans in an effort to make inroads into Spain's stranglehold on Creek trade. Another secret article granted numerous chiefs of the Upper Creek, the Lower Creek, and the Seminole commissions accompanied by stipends of one hundred dollars annually. McGillivray was the sole subject of another secret provision in which he was named as an agent of the United States and given the rank of brigadier general and an annual payment of $1,200. The most unusual of the secret provisions stipulated that the United States would "educate and clothe such of the Creek youth as shall be agreed upon, not exceeding four in number at any one time."[11]

These articles were made secret in an effort to forestall criticism emanating from either the Spanish government or the state of Georgia. Full secrecy was not achieved because Representative James Jackson of Georgia, in denouncing the treaty, asserted that it contained secret articles to which he avowed the people would never agree to be bound. He further alleged that the American government had "given away her [Georgia's] land, invited a savage of the Creek nation to the seat of Government, caressed him in a most extraordinary manner, and sent him home loaded with favors." Not long after this, on September 18, 1790, the *Augusta Chronicle* published a letter from an anonymous source, possibly written by Representative Jackson, which again asserted the existence of the secret articles and correctly stated that McGillivray had been made a brigadier general and was the recipient of an annual pension. The Spaniards likewise began efforts to criticize the treaty. They intimated that McGillivray made concessions out of a selfish motive to recoup his family property and an egotistical fondness for the attention paid to him by the Americans. McGillivray responded to the Spanish by noting Governor Miró's prior entreaties to him to make peace with the Americans and by emphasizing that he did not give up trade with Panton nor renounce Spanish protection.[12]

Despite these criticisms from American and Spanish sources, McGillivray's influence was at its zenith among the Creeks for at least a year following his return from New York. The treaty he had craftily negotiated, however, would soon be renounced primarily due to the conniving of Baron Francisco de Carondelet, Louisiana's new Spanish governor, and William Augustus Bowles, an adventurous former British soldier living among the Creeks who had conned supporters into recognizing him as "Director of Affairs" of the Creek Nation. McGillivray continued the intrigue and double dealing by engineering yet another secret compact, this time with the Spanish, which made him the "Superintendent General" of the Creek

[11] Appleton and Ward, "Albert James Pickett," 25–34. The educational provision also worked to McGillivray's benefit in that David Tait, McGillivray's nephew who had accompanied him to New York, became the first person to take advantage of this unusual scholarship by remaining in New York under the tutelage of Secretary Knox. Other members of McGillivray's family also benefited from this provision, including David Moniac who became the first Native American to graduate from the United States Military Academy at West Point.

[12] Caughey, *McGillivray*, 45–46; Appleton and Ward, "Albert James Pickett," 14–15.

Nation earning an annual salary of $3,500. Noting that McGillivray was still an agent of the United States with a salary of $1,200, the co-partner of Panton, and the self-proclaimed chief of the Creek and Seminole nations, Alabama historian A. J. Pickett asserted that "he was almost unrivalled in intrigue," and yet expressed "doubt that Alabama has ever produced, or ever will produce, a man of greater ability," dubbing him "the Talleyrand of Alabama."[13]

Alexander McGillivray died on February 17, 1793, at Panton's home in Pensacola, leaving a void in the leadership of the Creek Nation. Ironically, the man who would temporarily fill this void was Indian agent Benjamin Hawkins. Hawkins, born in North Carolina in 1754, attended the College of New Jersey (now Princeton University) where he studied French. George Washington chose him to serve on his staff as a translator during the Revolutionary War, after which Hawkins rose up through North Carolina's political ranks; he became its representative in the first United States Senate in 1789. In his role as senator, Hawkins served on several commit-tees investigating matters relating to Indians and served as a commissioner involved in the negotiation of treaties with the Creeks, including the Treaty of New York. Because of Hawkins' keen interest in Indian affairs and his reputation as being fair in his dealings with Indians, in 1796 President Washington appointed him "Principal Temporary Agent for Indian Affairs South of the Ohio River." Washington challenged him, according to one writer, "to sacrifice a few years of your life in making the experiment which you have suggested, and try the effects of civilization among them."[14]

Hawkins embarked upon his mission to the Creek country with the hopes of "civilizing" its inhabitants. Indeed, he was given authority by President Jefferson in 1803 to implement the "plan for civilization," an official governmental policy that had been designed by President George Washington, Secretary of War Henry Knox, and then Secretary of State Thomas Jefferson to entice indigenous Creeks onto small, self-sufficient farms so that whites could settle on their vast ancestral hunting grounds, while at the same time avoiding a policy of forced removal of the native Indians.[15] Upon arriving in Creek country, Hawkins first centered his

---

[13] Rogers et al., *Alabama*, 40; Caughey, *McGillivray*, 46–51; Pickett, *History of Alabama*, 414, 432. At least one later historian, however, opined that McGillivray was "something less than 'the Talleyrand of Alabama,'" citing that Spain in essence forced McGillivray to ultimately choose Spain over the United States as his benefactor and protector. Wright, "Creek American Treaty," 397. Talleyrand's reign as France's foreign minister representing a monarchy, revolutionaries, and Napoleon earned him the reputation of one of the most influential diplomats in European history. For a detailed discussion of the adventures and intrigues of William Augustus Bowles, see Susan E. Reynolds, "William Augustus Bowles: Adventurous Rogue of the Old Southwest," *Alabama Heritage*, no. 103 (Winter 2012): 18–27.

[14] Rogers et al., *Alabama*, 41; Foster, *Collected Works of Benjamin Hawkins*, vii; Ethridge, *Creek Country*, 12; Benjamin W. Griffith Jr., *McIntosh and Weatherford: Creek Indian Leaders* (Tuscaloosa: University of Alabama Press, 1988), 46.

[15] Secretary Knox, recognizing that natives possessed rights that must be respected, wrote President Washington, "Indians being the prior occupants of the rights of the soil . . . To dispossess them . . . would be a gross violation of the fundamental Laws of Nature and of that distributive Justice which is the glory of a nation." Ellis, *American Creation*, 128–29.

efforts in the Creek towns of Tuckabatchee, near present-day Tallassee, Alabama, and Coweta, in western Georgia. Here he sought to bring Creek political organizations under his influence by arranging to have the annual meeting of the Creek National Council meet at his residence in Coweta. Later these meetings alternated between Coweta and Tuckabatchee. During this period of time, Hawkins sought to decentralize the Creek tribal system and infuse more individuality into the Creek Nation. In 1803, when Hawkins was made permanent agent for the southern Indians, he moved the headquarters for his agency to the Flint River near present-day Roberta, Georgia. At this location, he established a teaching farm to train Indian men and women to become self-sufficient farmers. Hawkins' efforts resulted in increased hostility between the submissive Lower Creeks led by William McIntosh, another native Creek of Scottish descent, and the more nativistic Upper Creeks under the influence of chiefs such as Mad Dog, reform leader Peter McQueen, and Prophet Josiah Frances.[16]

Tensions between the two factions eventually erupted into civil war. On one side were the Red Sticks mostly from the Upper Creek towns, so named for the red clubs that they wielded in war.[17] The Red Sticks bitterly opposed any deviation from their traditional ways as advocated by Hawkins. On the other side were most of the tribes from the Lower Creek towns, who sided with the increasing American settlers and were amenable to the new order they brought with them. The Upper Creeks, inspired by the fanaticism of the prophetic movement that advocated a spiritual awakening and a revitalization of Creek society as it existed prior to white encroachment, further increased tensions in the region by senselessly slaughtering white settlers. Upper Creek prophets were led by Josiah Frances who boasted of magical powers, including the ability to see into the future. He and others preached that the Great Spirit would shield their warriors from death in battle and claimed their ability to use lightning against their enemies. They also asserted that Creek towns that refused to aid the prophets would be destroyed by earthquakes.[18]

In response to the violence spawned by increasing fanaticism, and influenced by Hawkins, the Creek National Council established the equivalent of a national police force referred to as the "law menders." This group was headed by William McIntosh, who led several parties on missions to avenge the whites slain in the area. As mentioned previously, of particular brutality was the February 1813 murder of seven settlers along the Duck River in the Tennessee Valley, including a woman and her baby, as well as four other children. Some Creeks also took a woman by the name of Martha Crawley as a prisoner. In response, McIntosh led a party to the Hickory Ground,

---

[16] Ethridge, *Creek Country*, 12–13; Griffith, *McIntosh and Weatherford*, 46–47, 79.

[17] Anthropologist Gregory Waselkov maintains that the Red Stick appellation of these Creeks undoubtedly refers to their wooden war club, or *atássa*, which was painted red. Gregory A. Waselkov, *A Conquering Spirit: Fort Mims and the Redstick War of 1813–1814* (Tuscaloosa: University of Alabama Press, 2006), 88–89.

[18] Griffith, *McIntosh and Weatherford*, 79–80.

the last seat for the National Council of the Creeks located near present-day Wetumpka, Alabama, where five of the murderers were killed. The violence continued when Upper Creeks exacted their own revenge against the Lower Creeks by killing nine members of McIntosh's law menders and setting fire to several villages friendly to Hawkins.[19]

The prophetic movement that inspired the Red Sticks to violence gathered momentum with Tecumseh's celebrated 1811 visit to Alabama. There are conflicting accounts of what transpired during his visit to Tuckabatchee, but Tecumseh, a Shawnee chief from the Ohio River valley, undoubtedly advocated a universal native resistance to further encroachment by white American settlers. He also pushed for a rejection of acculturation (a term denoting an adoption of white culture) and instead advocated adherence to the way of life of their ancestors. Some have attributed Tecumseh's warm reception among the Creeks to the belief that Tecumseh's mother was of Creek origin. However, other historians, including Tecumseh's earliest biographer, believe it more likely that both of his parents were Shawnee. Regardless of Tecumseh's Creek heritage, his message was likely well-received due to the increasing bitterness over the completion of the Federal Road and the arrival of more white settlers onto their ancestral hunting grounds. They were also upset with some of their own leaders who they believed capitulated too much to the encroaching whites and their agents. The Treaty of Washington, concluded on November 14, 1805, had bestowed upon the United States the right to a horse path through the Creek Nation— from the Ocmulgee River in Georgia to Mobile, the precise location of which was left to the discretion of the American government. Earlier in 1805, Congress had authorized the establishment of a post road from Washington by way of Athens, Georgia, to New Orleans. By 1811, a military road had also been opened from Georgia to Fort Stoddert on the Mobile River near present-day Mount Vernon, Alabama, in anticipation of a suspected British attack somewhere along the central Gulf coast. With the openings of these roads and the resulting increased traffic into Creek country, Hawkins reported back to Washington that tribal leaders complained to him that white intruders had begun "building fish traps, driving stock to range on their lands, hunting with dogs, cutting cedar and other

---

[19] Saunt, *New Order of Things*, 249; Griffith, *McIntosh and Weatherford*, 79–86. See also Mary Jane McDaniel, "Tecumseh's Visits to the Creeks," *Alabama Review* 33 (January 1980): 3–14. The horrific violence that was committed by both Americans and Creek warriors was recently addressed by historian Kathryn E. Holland Braund in an article examining the fate of Creek women during wartime. Professor Braund, while recognizing that both sides were guilty of atrocities, posits that excessive violence perpetrated "against women was a departure for Creek warriors, whose usual target was enemy males." As for these atrocities, as well as those committed against children, Braund argues that "Indian men were retaliating against their enemies with a form of violence common to the frontier and practiced by their enemies as well." As Braund relates, Alexander McGillivray had instructed his warriors to perpetrate no cruelty upon women and children during the Revolutionary War, but after the war in continuing fighting with Georgians on the border, Indian women were subjected to atrocities such as partial flaying and children were murdered. As a result, McGillivray contended that it was "such abominable actions as these that has stimulated the Indians to many cruel but just Retaliations." Kathryn E. Holland Braund, "Reflections on 'Shee Coocys' and the Motherless Child: Creek Women in a Time of War," *Alabama Review* 64 (October 2011): 270–72.

timber, and cultivating fields."[20]

Although some Red Sticks were inspired by Tecumseh's fiery oratory, according to the accounts of J. D. Dreisbach and General Thomas Woodward, William Weatherford—later known to Alabamians as Red Eagle—reportedly spoke after Tecumseh, warning that Tecumseh's arguments were against the best interests of the Creek Nation and that to follow them would ultimately lead to its downfall.[21] Weatherford further advised that, should Great Britain and America become embroiled in war, it would be in his people's best interest to remain neutral, but if forced to choose sides, it should join the American cause. Weatherford, the nephew of Alexander McGillivray through his mother, was the son of Charles Weatherford, a Scotch trader and horse breeder, and Princess Sehoy III, the daughter of a Creek chief and reportedly the granddaughter of a French military commander. He was born sometime in 1781 near Coosada, an Upper Creek town on the west bank of the Alabama River a few miles below the site of old Fort Toulouse. From this site, Charles Weatherford tended a trading post and built a track where he could race fine horses that he bred and trained. Although tutored by his uncle to speak English, William Weatherford rejected McGillivray's affinity for white culture and refused to learn how to read and write. Instead of academic pursuits, Weatherford in his youth enjoyed breaking wild horses, frequently engaged in the popular Indian game of stickball, and earned the reputation of being the fastest runner in the Creek Nation.[22]

Although he had rejected the predictions of the prophets and advised against Tecumseh's crusade against encroaching white settlers, Weatherford nevertheless joined with the Red Sticks to share in his people's fate. Weatherford's reluctance to go to war is believed to have been based in part upon the fact that he would be forced to fight the acculturated segment of the Creek Nation supporting the Americans, including members of his own family and close friends. One account claims that Weatherford's reluctance to side with Red Sticks was overcome only after having his life threatened in front of his family by leaders of the prophetic movement. Whatever prompted Weatherford, he was now on a collision course with Andrew

---

[20] Braund, *Deerskins & Duffels*, 185–86; McDaniel, "Tecumseh's Visits to the Creeks," 3–5; Benjamin Drake, *Life of Tecumseh, And His Brother The Prophet, With A Historical Sketch of the Shawanoe Indians* (Cincinnati: E. Morgan & Co., 1841), 61; Henry deLeon Southerland Jr. and Jerry Elijah Brown, *The Federal Road through Georgia, the Creek Nation, and Alabama, 1806–1836* (Tuscaloosa: University of Alabama Press, 1989), 17, 20, 32–33, 36; Lengel, "Road to Fort Mims," 20. Before Tecumseh addressed the Creek Council at Tuckabatchee, Hawkins, in a bad sense of timing, addressed the Creeks to inform them that he had not come to seek their permission to build the road from Georgia to Fort Stoddert, but merely to let them know that it was under construction at that very time.

[21] According to Gregory Waselkov, it is doubtful that Weatherford was known as Red Eagle at the time, as the name did not appear in print until 1855 in A. B. Meek's poem, *The Red Eagle: A Poem of the South*. Waselkov, *Conquering Spirit*, 46–47.

[22] Griffith, *McIntosh and Weatherford*, 3–4, 11, 18, 29–30, 77; Theron A. Nunez Jr., "Creek Nativism and the Creek War of 1813–14 (George Stiggins Manuscript)," *Ethnohistory* 5 (Winter 1958): 7 (hereafter cited as Nunez, "Stiggins Narrative"); see note 3 above and Neeley, "Lachlan McGillivray," 5–14, for a discussion of the great-grandmother's French ancestry.

Jackson and the beginning of the end for the Creek Nation in what was to become the state of Alabama.[23]

As tensions continued to increase following Tecumseh's visit, territorial Governor David Holmes received correspondence in June 1812 from officers of the militia in the Tombigbee region warning that part of the Creek Nation were on a definite path toward war. As seen in the previous chapter, Judge Harry Toulmin was initially leery of these reports, but the Battle of Burnt Corn in July 1813, involving an ambush of Creek warriors returning from Pensacola where they had purchased gun powder and supplies, convinced everyone that a state of war existed in the fork between the Tombigbee and Alabama rivers. The Burnt Corn attack had been carried out by a militia comprised of white settlers and "mixed bloods" led by Col. James Caller, the senior military officer in the area; Sam Dale, soon to gain fame for his heroic "Canoe Fight" with Creek warriors on the Alabama River; and Capt. Dixon Bailey, yet another Creek with Scotch ancestry. As settlers left their farms and scurried for protection in forts along the rivers in the Tensaw District, the Red Sticks were plotting as how to exact revenge against those who had attacked them.[24]

Within a month, the area was to be subjected to one of the most notorious Indian attacks in American history when the Red Sticks attacked Fort Mims—an event, according to battle expert Gregory Waselkov, comparable to other violent turning points in American history including the terrorist attacks of September 11, 2001, and the bombing of Pearl Harbor on December 7, 1941. The Tensaw District that was the object of the initial wrath of the Red Sticks was inhabited largely by persons of mixed Indian and European ancestry, referred to as "mixed bloods" or "métis," the offspring of Creek women and white men. A métis community had begun to emerge along Little River at its juncture with the lower Alabama River in the second half of the eighteenth century, particularly after Alexander McGillivray and his sister Sophia Durant came to the area in 1783 to establish a plantation. Within this small geographic area, métis tended to marry métis, creating a close network of families who utilized slave labor to accumulate wealth on their widely dispersed plantations. Rejecting traditional Creek methods of communal agriculture and trade centering on the declining deerskin market, the Tensaw métis community grew ever more distant

---

[23] Griffith, *McIntosh and Weatherford*, 77, 88–89; Halbert and Ball, *Creek War*, 67; George Cary Eggleston, *Red Eagle and the Wars with the Creek Indians of Alabama* (New York: Dodd, Mead & Co., 1878), 80–81. Eggleston, an early biographer of Weatherford, depicted Red Eagle as extremely biased against whites despite his Scotch ancestry and more openly supportive of war against them. Benjamin Griffith notes that this view of Weatherford was not documented by Eggleston nor confirmed by later historians; Griffith, *McIntosh and Weatherford*, 78. Gregory Waselkov theorizes that Weatherford chose the Red Stick path due to his physical separation from his mixed-blood relatives who lived over 150 miles away from Weatherford's residence on the upper Alabama River, his adherence to traditionalist beliefs, and his relationship with his second wife's father who had joined the Red Sticks; Waselkov, *Conquering Spirit*, 93–94.

[24] Rowland, *Mississippi Territory*, 35–37; Lengel, "Road to Fort Mims," 18–24; Griffith, *McIntosh and Weatherford*, 96–98, 100.

from the towns (*talwas*) and traditions of their ancestors.[25]

Despite the Red Stick determination to kill those among them who rejected their prophets' crusade against acculturation, métis inhabitants such as David Tait, John Weatherford (William's brother), Dixon and James Bailey, and Sam Moniac chose not to give up the entrepreneurial ways of their American neighbors of accumulating property in the form of slaves, plantations, cotton gins, and taverns. The Red Sticks thus carried the civil war south to the métis community on the lower Alabama River in July 1813 by attacking plantations and other property owned by Moniac, James Cornells, and Leonard McGee. As a result, métis families in the area fled their homes to join their American neighbors in makeshift forts hurriedly being built across the border in the Mississippi Territory. One such fort was constructed around the home of Samuel Mims, one of the earliest European settlers in the Tensaw settlement. Mims' house was located about one mile from the Alabama River in present-day Baldwin County, Alabama, about twelve miles north of Stockton and forty miles north of Mobile. He was a former trader among the Upper Creeks; his name first appears on the Spanish census for the Mobile District dated January 1, 1786. After signing an oath of allegiance to the Spanish Crown, Mims married Hannah Raines in a Catholic ceremony in Mobile in 1788. He spent the next twenty-five years speculating in land in the Mobile area and along the Tombigbee River, accumulating wealth from his slave-run plantations and running a ferry across the Alabama River. The stockade built around his frontier residence would soon become the scene of a massacre that put Americans in the Mississippi Territory on the road to a policy of removal of its native inhabitants.[26]

In reaction to the increasing violence along the Southwestern frontier in the spring and summer of 1813, the governors of Tennessee, Georgia, and the Mississippi Territory called up militias commanded by Andrew Jackson, John Floyd, and Ferdinand L. Claiborne, respectively. Governor David Holmes of the Mississippi Territory ordered 550 men of General Claiborne's Territorial Volunteers, mostly from the Natchez District, to shore up the defense of the Tombigbee and Tensaw settlements. Claiborne was a native of Sussex County, Virginia, and a brother of William Charles Cole Claiborne, second governor of the Mississippi Territory, governor of the Territory of Orleans, and governor of Louisiana. In late July 1813 Claiborne's advance troops under Col. Joseph Carson arrived at Fort Stoddert and reported that twenty families had already "forted up" at Mims' house near the Tensaw. Colonel Carson quickly sent sixteen volunteers under Lieut. Spruce McKay Osborne to aid in the construction of a stockade at the residence. When General Claiborne arrived at Fort Stoddert on July 30, he reported that "the inhabitants on Tombigby and Alabama [were] in the state of the utmost confusion and alarm . . . flying from all quarters."

---

[25] Waselkov, *Conquering Spirit*, 1–2, 8–10, 47–48.

[26] Ibid., 20, 91, 97. The Red Sticks were not only determined to expel those who defied the prophets by accumulating wealth and property, but had also begun to abduct métis women away from their white husbands.

Claiborne's troops daily inspected the numerous stockades in the area from their headquarters at Mount Vernon. On August 7, 1813, Claiborne personally inspected Fort Mims and instructed the fort's commander, Maj. Daniel Beasley, to increase the picketing and build at least two other block houses. Claiborne also encouraged him to respect the enemy and send out frequent scouting parties.[27]

Major Beasley proved to be not up to the task of defending the important territory assigned to him. An attorney from the Natchez District who used his political influence to obtain a military commission, Beasley had received no military training, had no experience in Indian warfare, and consistently demonstrated a lack of common sense. Furthermore, he was thought to have a penchant of imbibing too much alcohol, particularly for a man with his responsibility. His lack of common sense was made evident by his failure to follow General Claiborne's instructions for increased vigilance. While Beasley increased pickets, he did not construct the block houses and, incredibly, he kept the gates of the stockade open so that its occupants could go in and out as they desired. Instead of preparing his troops for the attack that was to befall them, Beasley exuded overconfidence and allowed them to pass their days in "fun and frolic" by playing cards, drinking, and horseplay. Perhaps because of the holiday spirit prevailing within the fort, he flippantly ignored reports from slaves tending cattle outside of the fort that Red Sticks were in the area. Instead of heeding their warnings, he ordered the slaves flogged. On the very day of the attack on Fort Mims, Beasley ignored one last chance to ready the fort for what was about to hit them when James Cornells, a métis, rode up to the gate shouting that he had just seen thirteen Red Sticks nearby. Cornells later recalled that Beasley, who appeared drunk, mocked him by saying he must have "only seen a gang of red cattle." Within four hundred yards of where Cornells gave this futile warning, Red Sticks lay in wait for their attack on the fort, just as one of the slaves was ironically being flogged for his "false" report.[28]

Judge Alexander B. Meek, author of the epic poem "Red Eagle," later lamented Major Beasley's incompetence, stating "it is hoped that a man so unfit to command will seldom have five hundred lives committed to his care." Meek also described the dawning of the historic day of the attack poetically: "the sun arose, beautiful and with a dewy coolness, over the forest of needle-leaved pines that extended off to the east, and concealed beneath their high and shafted arcades the grimly painted and the fast approaching warriors of Weatherford and McQueen." But, because of Major

---

[27] Ibid., 96, 104–09; Rowland, *Mississippi Territory*, 6; Peter A. Brannon, "Spruce McCall Osborne: A Mississippi Territorial Volunteer at Fort Mims," *Alabama Historical Quarterly* 5 (Spring 1943): 68. Lieutenant Osborne graduated from the University of North Carolina in 1806 and, according to family records, practiced medicine in the Mississippi Territory prior to his service in the Creek War as an assistant surgeon. Although not listed as a medical officer in territorial records, he was referred to as "Doctor Osborne" in official correspondence from the commander at Fort Mims to General Claiborne. Osborne died in the attack on the fort.

[28] Pickett, *History of Alabama*, 528–32; Rogers et al., *Alabama*, 48; Griffith, *McIntosh and Weatherford,* 102; Halbert and Ball, *Creek War*, 148–50; Rowland, *Mississippi Territory*, 44–45; Waselkov, *Conquering Spirit*, 125–27.

Beasley's unbelievable laxity that bordered on criminal negligence, "in the fort all was confidant and hilarity."[29]

According to family legend, the night before the attack William Weatherford, who foresaw anything but hilarity, entreated with his warriors to spare the women and children who had taken refuge in the fort. In response Weatherford was supposedly accused of having a "white heart" and a desire to save some of his relatives and, according to some, his sweetheart, a young métis woman named Lucy Cornells. Whether true or not, Weatherford nevertheless played an important role in planning the next day's attack, when he took three men on a reconnaissance mission the night before the attack. Major Beasley's security was so careless that Weatherford's party was able to walk right up to the stockade without being detected and peek through the portholes, which were placed four feet high and four feet apart along the entire circumference of the fort. Based upon the casual conversations and conduct heard and observed on this reconnaissance mission, Weatherford was convinced that the fort's inhabitants did not suspect their presence and could easily be taken by surprise the next day.[30]

These unsuspecting inhabitants numbered approximately four hundred on the fateful morning of August 30, 1813. The "Morning Report" for the previous day had tabulated 106 soldiers of the First Regiment, Mississippi Territorial Volunteers, including one major, two captains, one lieutenant, five ensigns, eleven sergeants, six corporals, five musicians, and seventy-five privates. Eleven were considered unfit for duty, including six who were on leave in Mobile. There were also forty-one or forty-two militiamen from the Tensaw area under the leadership of Captain Dixon Bailey. The remainder consisted of about twenty white and métis families along with approximately one hundred slaves who had accompanied them to this assumed safe haven. As the noon hour approached, the fort's occupants went about their business as usual. The east gate, amazingly, remained partially open where a sentry was intently watching two men playing cards while lunch preparations were underway, young people danced, and children played.[31]

Lying in wait just four hundred yards away from the east gate were approximately 750 Red Stick warriors, "every man painted red or black and stripped to the buff." To emphasize their anger for the surprise attack on their brethren at Burnt Corn Creek as they sat eating their midday meal, the Red Sticks waited for the noon hour to unleash their fury on those inside the stockade. When the fort's noon drumbeat sounded, the warriors,

---

[29] Halbert and Ball, *Creek War*, 148–50. Alexander Beaufort Meek was a lawyer, newspaper editor, and poet. He served as editor of the *Tuscaloosa Flag of the Union* and the *Mobile Register*, as Alabama's attorney general, as a probate judge in Mobile County, and as Assistant Secretary of the Treasury under President James K. Polk. Owen and Owen, *History of Alabama*, 4: 1183–84.

[30] Waselkov, *Conquering Spirit*, 113–14; Griffith, *McIntosh and Weatherford*, 101. More than likely, Weatherford and his party noticed the fact that the east gate had been left open, which let them know where to rush the fort the next day; Buchanan, *Jackson's Way*, 221–22.

[31] Waselkov, *Conquering Spirit*, 116; 123–24; Francis F. Beirne, *The War of 1812* (New York: E. P. Dutton, 1949), 235–36; Buchanan, *Jackson's Way*, 222.

fearing that it meant they had been discovered at last, arose as one and charged toward the fort. Upon hearing the war whoops, Major Beasley immediately rushed to close the east gate before the Indians reached it. He was too late; sand had blown against it and made it difficult to close in a hurry. While Beasley struggled to close it, Red Stick warriors overwhelmed him and clubbed him to death. As he fell, the Red Sticks poured through the east gate.[32]

Red Sticks remaining outside the fort fired their weapons through the portholes, causing even more pandemonium. Capt. Dixon Bailey, in command following Major Beasley's death, was able to curb the confusion inside the fort and temporarily rallied the surprised defenders to put up a resistance, with some of the women of the garrison fighting along with the men. By two o'clock that afternoon, the defenders had fought gallantly enough to cause the Red Sticks to withdraw from the fort to assess their situation. They gathered in a council of war about a mile away and debated for almost an hour whether to continue their attack on the fort. Weatherford supposedly urged the warriors to call off the attack, arguing that they had already wreaked enough havoc and "sufficiently humbled" the enemy. A consensus nevertheless emerged in favor of resuming the attack, primarily because the majority believed that the Tensaw métis militia under the command of Captain Bailey had suffered too few losses to avenge the attack at Burnt Corn Creek. With his life reportedly threatened if he intervened and not having the heart to observe the slaughter that he knew was to ensue, Weatherford instead headed north to the plantation of his brother, David Tait.[33]

The Red Sticks resumed their attack about three o'clock, this time unleashing a barrage of fiery arrows that set one of the fort's interior buildings ablaze. The flames quickly spread to the palisade and other buildings where many of the defenders were huddled for safety. As each building caught fire, its inhabitants had to face certain death if they remained or flee and run through a gauntlet of bullets, arrows, and tomahawks. As a result many civilians were killed late in the battle as the Red Sticks gained complete control of the fort. Among those civilians slaughtered was David Mims, Samuel Mims' seventy-six-year-old brother. Likewise was the fate of Dixon Bailey's sister, who, when she identified herself, was unmercifully knocked to the ground, slit open, and disemboweled. Describing the horror facing the inhabitants emerging from the burning buildings, Dr. Thomas G. Holmes, the fort's assistant surgeon and a survivor, said, "The way that

---

[32] Buchanan, *Jackson's Way*, 222–23; George Stiggins, *Creek Indian History: A Historical Narrative of the Genealogy, Traditions and Downfall of the Ispocoga or Creek Indian Tribe of Indians* (Birmingham, Ala.: Birmingham Public Library Press, 1989), 91–93; Beirne, *War of 1812*, 236; Griffith, *McIntosh and Weatherford*, 104–5; Waselkov, *Conquering Spirit*, 115, 127–28.

[33] Beirne, *War of 1812*, 236; Waselkov, *Conquering Spirit*, 129–32; Thomas S. Woodward, *Reminiscences of the Creek, or Muscogee Indians, Contained in Letters to Friends in Georgia and Alabama* (1859; repr., Mobile, Ala: Southern University Press, 1969), 80–81; Nunez, "Stiggins Narrative," 64–65; Buchanan, *Jackson's Way*, 224; Griffith, *McIntosh and Weatherford*, 108.

many of the unfortunate were mangled and cut to pieces is shocking to humanity, for very many of the women who were pregnant had their unborn infants cut from the womb and lay by their bleeding mothers."[34]

At least 247 men, women, and children lost their lives at Fort Mims. This was the number reported interred approximately three weeks after the battle by a burial detail led by Maj. Joseph P. Kennedy and Lieut. Uriah Blue. In addition to the definitive number of bodies counted and buried, an undetermined additional number probably were consumed in the conflagration of the buildings. Waselkov estimates the death toll to have been between 250 and 300. Additionally, approximately one hundred were captured, and a few managed to escape, including ten Mississippi Territorial volunteers, sixteen men from the Tensaw District, two women (one white and one black slave), and one slave girl. Although there are no concrete numbers, George Stiggins, Indian agent and brother-in-law of William Weatherford by his third wife, estimated years later that half of the approximate 750 Red Sticks who participated in the battle were killed, disabled, or wounded.[35]

The Old Southwest would never be the same as word of this tragedy spread across the nation; there were outraged cries for revenge and calls to arms. The news was especially alarming to the citizens of Tennessee, who had been clamoring for revenge ever since the Duck River massacre. The Fort Mims massacre prompted the *Nashville Clarion* to state that the Creeks "have supplied us with a pretext for a dismemberment of their country." Governor Willie Blount, imploring the Tennessee legislature to act, said that "the employment of a competent force at once would teach those barbarous sons of the woods their inferiority." On September 24, 1813, the Tennessee legislature responded by authorizing Blount to call up five thousand men for a three month tour of duty. He in turn ordered Gen. Andrew Jackson to call out two thousand militiamen for a retaliatory invasion of the Creek Nation. Jackson minced no words in his call to "Brave Tennesseans" for volunteers, stating "your frontier is threatened with invasion of the savage foe . . . with scalping knives unsheathed, to butcher your wives, your children, and your babes." Warning that time was of the essence, he declared, "we must hasten to the frontier, or we will find it drenched in the blood of our fellow citizens."[36]

As Jackson's volunteers were mobilizing, Red Stick war parties continued to wreak havoc in the area near Fort Mims in the area between the Alabama and Tombigbee rivers by burning homes, slaughtering livestock, and confiscating property. They even vied with area farmers for the unharvested crops in the ground. On September 1, 1813, just two days after the

---

[34] Waselkov, *Conquering Spirit*, 132–34; Griffith, *McIntosh and Weatherford*, 106; Dr. Thomas G. Holmes, survivor of Fort Mims, interview, in Griffith, *Alabama*, 109; see also Braund, "Reflections on 'Shee Coocys' and the Motherless Child," 270–72, for a discussion of violence perpetrated against Creek women during the Creek War.

[35] Waselkov, *Conquering Spirit*, 134, 137, 149–52, 193; Nunez, "Stiggins Narrative," 66; Griffith, *McIntosh and Weatherford*, 98.

[36] Waselkov, *Conquering Spirit*, 153, 163; Griffith, *McIntosh and Weatherford*, 111–13.

disaster at Fort Mims, a band of Red Sticks led by the Prophet Joseph Francis murdered twelve white women and children at a cabin near Bassett's Creek about a mile from Fort Sinquefield, which was located about five miles east of present-day Grove Hill in Clarke County, Alabama. The victims of what became known as the Kimbell-James Massacre were from two families who had left Fort Sinquefield due to the hot August weather and the overcrowded conditions within the fort to take their chances in the comfort of their own homes. A day later, Fort Sinquefield itself was attacked by the Prophet Francis' warriors, but its defenders were successful in staving off the attack after a fierce fight lasting about two hours. General Claiborne responded to these continuing tensions by establishing bases from which local militia units could launch guerilla-style attacks on the marauding Red Sticks. In November 1813 Capt. Samuel Dale, who was then stationed at Fort Madison, a defensive outpost in present-day Clarke County, obtained permission from its commander to lead such a mission in hopes of bringing stability to the area.[37]

Striking out with thirty Mississippi Territorial volunteers and forty Clarke County militiamen, Dale and his men soon encountered a party of Creek warriors near the mouth of Randon's Creek on the Alabama River. The confrontation that ensued earned its American participants instant fame—the fierce hand-to-hand combat, soon dubbed the "Canoe Fight," was witnessed by soldiers on both sides of the river. Although outnumbered three to one, Dale was determined to engage a canoe full of Red Stick warriors paddling down the Alabama River, a few miles west of present-day Monroeville, Alabama. Accordingly, he ordered an African American man known only as Caesar to paddle a small dugout canoe that could only hold himself, Jeremiah Austill, and James Smith to meet the Creek canoe bearing nine warriors. As Caesar paddled the canoe toward their target, Dale, Austill, and Smith attempted to fire upon the Indians with their weapons. Only one weapon fired, however, as the priming of the other two had been dampened by the water from the river. When the canoes were about to meet prow to prow, the chief recognized Dale, shouting in English, "Now for it, Big Sam," and knocked Austill down with his rifle. After a few minutes of fierce hand-to-hand fighting with rifles and oars being used as clubs, the Americans, although outnumbered three to one, killed all of the Indians remaining in the canoe. To the cheers of their fellow soldiers observing from the sides of the river, the bodies of the dead warriors were cast one by one into the water. Dale's leading role in the Canoe Fight attained him hero status, and he became as legendary to Alabamians as Daniel Boone and Davy Crockett were to Kentuckians and Tennesseans.[38]

---

[37] Waselkov, *Conquering Spirit*, 140, 160–62; Halbert and Ball, *Creek War*, 177–99, 230.

[38] Waselkov, *Conquering Spirit,* 160–66; Halbert and Ball, *Creek War*, 229–40; Herbert J. Lewis, "Canoe Fight," *Encyclopedia of Alabama*, http://www.encyclopediaofalabama.org/face/Article.jsp?id=h-1815 (accessed February 5, 2013); Herbert J. Lewis, "Sam Dale," *Encyclopedia of Alabama*, http://www.encyclopediaofalabama.org/face/Article.jsp?id=h-2460 (accessed February 5, 2013). Dale would later represent Monroe County for several years in the Alabama General Assembly and was conferred the rank of brigadier general in the Alabama militia. Dale eventually moved to Lauderdale County in Mississippi, where he

With these types of skirmishes continuing, General Jackson devised a strategy for deploying the thousands of volunteers responding to his stirring call to arms. As Jackson recovered from a wound received in a gun battle with the brother of future senator Thomas Hart Benton, 1,300 cavalry troops under Brig. Gen. John Coffee set out across the Tennessee border, arriving at Huntsville on October 4, 1813. A few days later, Jackson took control of some 2,500 infantry gathered in Fayetteville, Tennessee, and marched them to Huntsville to join Coffee's troops. The combined forces then crossed the Tennessee River at Ditto's Landing. One detachment was dispatched to establish a supply base named Fort Deposit along the north bank of the Tennessee River, located approximately eight miles north of present-day Guntersville, Alabama. The remainder of the troops crossed rugged terrain over Raccoon Mountain and began construction of Fort Strother on the Coosa River at a spot known locally as the Ten Islands, about thirty miles south of present-day Gadsden, Alabama. Jackson's plan was to launch strikes from this rendezvous point to eradicate Red Stick towns wherever found, to splinter the Creek Nation. His ultimate goal was to construct a military road to Mobile connecting Tennessee to the Gulf of Mexico, with an eye toward eventually invading Florida to seize Pensacola from the Spanish who he believed were aiding the British in their war with the Americans.[39]

Jackson's thrust southward with forces from west Tennessee was just one prong of an overall American plan for the Creek War, in which four armies were to join together at the confluence of the Coosa and Tallapoosa rivers near present-day Wetumpka, Alabama. Another army from East Tennessee was to move south under the command of Gen. John Cocke. Maj. Gen. John Floyd was to lead forces eastward from Georgia. Finally, the Third Regiment of the United States Army regulars along with volunteers of the Mississippi Territory militia was to advance up the Alabama River from the south. While this plan was well-designed, its execution left much to be desired due to command jealousies, continual supply deficiencies, and short-term enlistments.[40]

Deviating from the plan at the outset, General Jackson struck out on his own when General Cocke was slow to start out from east Tennessee with his volunteers. From his base at Fort Strother on the Coosa River, Jackson raced against the clock to deliver a chilling message to those Creek towns

---

died in 1841. Alabama's Dale County was named in his honor. Joel Campbell DuBose, *Sketches of Alabama History* (Philadelphia: Eldredge & Bro., 1901), 42–49; Pearl V. Guyton, "Sam Dale, from J. F. H. Claiborne," *Alabama Historical Quarterly* 7 (Spring 1945): 16–18; Henriosco Austill, "Jeremiah Austill," *Alabama Historical Quarterly* 6 (Spring 1944): 84–86.

[39] Rogers et al., *Alabama*, 50; Griffith, *McIntosh and Weatherford*, 116. After the War of 1812, Coffee settled in north Alabama, where he became a surveyor, land developer, and planter. In March 1818 he joined other influential investors to form the Cypress Land Company and subsequently established the town of Florence at the foot of the Muscle Shoals on the Tennessee River.

[40] Frank Lawrence Owsley Jr., *Struggle for the Gulf Borderlands: The Creek War and the Battle of New Orleans, 1812–1815* (Gainesville: University Presses of Florida, 1981), 43; Griffith, *McIntosh and Weatherford*, 117; Walter R. Borneman, *1812: The War that Forged a Nation* (New York: Harper Collins Publishers, 2004), 146–47.

supporting William Weatherford before the short-term enlistment periods of his volunteers were up. On November 2, 1813, Jackson deployed his right-hand man, Gen. John Coffee, and 900 mounted troops to attack the Upper Creek town of Tallushatchee, just thirteen miles to the east on the south side of the Coosa River. Arriving the next day, Coffee divided his troops into two columns that encircled the village. He then sent two companies into the center of the village to draw the warriors into a trap. When these two companies retreated by design, the warriors pursued them as hoped and were caught in the crossfire of the awaiting columns who had by then completely surrounded them. Literally fighting until the last warrior fell, 186 Red Sticks were killed. This number included all the resisting warriors as well as a number of women and children. However, eighty-four women and children were spared and taken prisoners. By contrast, the Tennesseans suffered only five fatal casualties and forty-one wounded. Legendary frontier hero Davy Crockett, who was among the attacking Tennessee volunteers, reported that forty-six warriors were shot "like dogs" and then consumed by fire when the house they had sought refuge in was set ablaze by Coffee's troops. Sensitive to the killing of Creek women and children, Coffee later asserted that the killing of noncombatants was unintentional, blaming instead the warriors for seeking refuge in houses with their families.[41]

Following the initial battle of his Creek campaign, Jackson reported to Governor Blount that "we have retaliated for the destruction of Fort Mims." The lopsided victory at Tallushatchee also had the desired effect of swaying many Creek towns to side with the Americans even in the face of warnings from William Weatherford that all towns so doing would suffer immediate retaliation from his Red Stick warriors. Talladega was one of the towns that chose to defy these warnings, and, true to his word, Weatherford launched an assault against it with one thousand Red Sticks just as Coffee's men were returning from Tallushatchee. Responding to a cry for help from the besieged friendly Creeks, General Jackson promptly headed south toward Talladega with 1,200 infantry and 800 of Coffee's cavalry and mounted riflemen, leaving a bare minimum of troops to guard the wounded soldiers and dwindling supplies at Fort Strother. Jackson's forces arrived on November 9, 1813, and encircled the besieging Red Sticks surrounding Talladega, hoping to replicate Coffee's successful tactics at Tallushatchee. While they did inflict approximately 300 casualties and were successful in breaking the siege, a gap in Jackson's encircling forces allowed Weatherford and 700 Red Sticks to escape and live to fight another day. Although Jackson characterized this result as the "faux pas of the militia," he never-

---

[41] Borneman, *1812*, 146–47; Owsley, *Struggle for the Gulf Borderlands*, 64–65; Griffith, *McIntosh and Weatherford*, 118–19. The day following the battle, Crockett accompanied a detail to the village, where they found a potato cellar beneath the house they had burned. Crockett grotesquely reported that they were so hungry they ate the potatoes despite the fact that "the oil of the Indians we had burned up on the day before had run down on them, and they looked like they had been stewed with fat meat." Davy Crockett, *A Narrative of the Life of David Crockett of the State of Tennessee* (1834; repr., Lincoln: University of Nebraska Press, 1987), 88–90.

theless lauded the remainder of his troops for their high spirits and gallant-ry. Only fifteen Americans were killed during the battle, with two more dying on the way back to Fort Strother.[42]

As Jackson's forces returned to Fort Strother, General Claiborne's Mississippi militia and General Floyd's Georgia militia set out from the south and east respectively in accordance with the original overall plan for a coordinated four-pronged attack. Like Jackson, neither one reached the confluence of the Coosa and Tallapoosa, but both destroyed important Red Stick towns near the planned rendezvous point. General Floyd, along with 950 Georgia militia and 450 friendly Creeks including William McIntosh, decimated a settlement of twin towns called Auttossee about twenty miles east of the confluence. Their combined forces killed approximately 200 Red Sticks and demolished 400 buildings. Based on the number of white scalps and other items found at Auttossee, members of the regiment were convinced that they had defeated those who had perpetrated the massacre at Fort Mims. Although only nine of Floyd's men were killed in the battle, Floyd himself was seriously wounded when a Red Stick bullet shattered his knee. The successful destruction of the twin towns at Auttossee was tempered by his injury and by the fact that many of the Red Stick warriors managed to escape just as they had at Talladega. Due to serious food shortages, Floyd was unable to pursue the fleeing Red Sticks but instead was forced to temporarily withdraw his forces back to his base at Fort Mitchell.[43]

After recovering from his wound and replenishing his supplies, Floyd led another incursion into Alabama's Creek territory, this time with 1,100 militia and 600 friendly Indians. After arriving at Calabee Creek near the recently destroyed towns of Autossee, Floyd's troops constructed a fortified camp, which they named Camp Defiance. Early in the morning on January 27, 1814, Red Stick leader Paddy Walsh led approximately 1,300 warriors in a surprise attack against Camp Defiance. Gaining the upper hand by their surprise attack, Red Stick warriors almost seized control of two of the Americans' cannons. Reacting quickly, however, Floyd's troops secured the cannons and fired them at point blank range at the attacking warriors. The tide of the battle was thus turned, and Floyd's army dodged a possible total annihilation. The battle left forty-nine Red Sticks dead and Paddy Walsh seriously wounded. Approximately seventeen of Floyd's Georgians were killed and 132 wounded. After the near disaster at Camp Defiance, General Floyd and his army withdrew to Georgia because many of its members' enlistments were soon to expire.[44]

---

[42] Griffith, *McIntosh and Weatherford*, 119–22; Buchanan, *Jackson's Way*, 235–38, 241; Borneman, *1812*, 146–48.

[43] Sean Michael O'Brien, *In Bitterness and in Tears: Andrew Jackson's Destruction of the Creeks and Seminoles* (Westport, Conn.: Praeger, 2003), 96–100; Griffith, *McIntosh and Weatherford*, 123–26; Glenn Tucker, *Poltroons and Patriots: A Popular Account of the War of 1812* (Indianapolis: Bobbs-Merrill, 1954), 2: 458; Borneman, *1812*, 148.

[44] Thomas G. Rodgers, "Night Attack at Calabee Creek," *Journal of the Historical Society of the Georgia National Guard* 4 (Spring 1995): 12.

An attack by east Tennessee forces on a village inhabited by Hillabee Creeks detracted from the modest November 1813 victories attained by Generals Jackson and Floyd at Tallushatchee, Talladega, Calabee, and Auttossee. Unfortunately, the Hillabees were at that very moment in the process of negotiating their surrender to Jackson. Gen. John Cocke, who wished to remain independent of Jackson, was slow to leave Tennessee, did not adhere to his orders, and was unaware of the surrender negotiations. Thus, on November 18, 1813, one thousand men led by Gen. James White under orders from Cocke stormed the peaceful village. The engagement became known as the Hillabee Massacre because, despite the fact that no resistance was offered by the villagers, sixty Hillabees were killed and 250 were wounded. As a result, Jackson lost some of the gains he had made with Creeks in his defense of Talladega—the outraged Hillabees spread word of the treachery inflicted on them by the Americans. Jackson was infuriated because the surviving Hillabees attributed the treachery to him and vowed to fight his forces to the death, determined not to surrender under any circumstances.[45]

As these events were unfolding, General Claiborne's Mississippians were ordered by Gen. Thomas Flournoy of the Seventh Military District to leave their camp at Pine Level in present-day Clarke County ten miles east of St. Stephens, to head northward up the Alabama River. The object of their mission was to establish a depot of supplies to serve as logistical support for Jackson's army. On November 13, 1813, Claiborne set out with a force of about one thousand Americans, made up of volunteers, mounted troops, and militia, along with 135 Choctaws under Lieutenant Colonel Pushmataha. A few days later, they arrived at Weatherford's Bluff (named for William Weatherford's father), about eighty miles upriver, where they constructed a stockade named Fort Claiborne in honor of their commander. Upon completing the stockade, Claiborne's men were joined by Col. Gilbert C. Russell and the U.S. Third Regiment.[46]

Anxious to take the offensive against the Red Sticks despite poor logistical support from General Flournoy, Claiborne provided enough food and munitions at his own expense to support a journey to the Upper Creek settlement at Ikanachaki. Better known as the Holy Ground, Ikanachaki was situated near the Alabama River in Lowndes County, about ten miles from present-day Lowndesboro, Alabama. Prophet Josiah Francis had established this settlement as a safe haven "at a spot made sacred by the great spirit . . . never to be sullied by the footsteps of the real white man." They were convinced that an impenetrable barrier encircled their village across which no white man could cross. Because of this, and in anticipation of a retaliatory strike from the Americans in response to the massacre at

---

[45] Halbert and Ball, *Creek War*, 271–72; Griffith, *McIntosh and Weatherford*, 123.

[46] Owsley, *Struggle for the Gulf Borderlands*, 46–47; Griffith, *McIntosh and Weatherford*, 127. Pushmataha was an influential Choctaw chief recruited by General Claiborne to help replace the militia members whose enlistments were up. Claiborne even gave Pushmataha a fancy uniform costing $300 and made him a lieutenant colonel. Pushmataha proudly wore the uniform that included regimental insignia, gold epaulettes, silver spurs, and a hat topped with a feather.

Fort Mims, many Red Stick families abandoned their old towns to seek the assumed protections afforded by this sacred village.[47]

Although Claiborne secured the approval of General Flournoy to proceed to the Holy Ground, a group of his own officers signed a petition requesting that their commander abandon the proposed mission. They cited several potential reasons for failure: his personal contributions of food and munitions were insufficient in light of the coming winter weather; most men were without warm clothing, shoes, and blankets; there was an absence of roads to transport supplies; and many of the soldiers' enlistments were to expire within days. Claiborne, however, was determined to proceed. He saw this as his best—and maybe only—chance to seek revenge for the embarrassment of his regiment at Fort Mims. Notwithstanding their stated reservations, Claiborne's officers declared that they would "cheerfully obey" a decision of their commander to press forward. Thus, on December 13, 1813, Claiborne's army set out from Fort Claiborne to the strains of "Over the Hills and Far Away." The troops that left with him that day included the U.S. Third Regiment, the Mississippi Territory Volunteers under Joseph Carson, Choctaw chief Pushmataha and his warriors, Major Cassel's Cavalry Battalion, and captains Bailey Heard and Sam Dale. This force arrived within ten miles of the Holy Ground on December 22, 1813, and set up camp in preparation of their impending attack.[48]

Prophet Joseph Frances and his followers at the Holy Ground were quickly warned of Claiborne's arrival in the area by William Weatherford, whose plantation was nearby. As the attack began, Claiborne's forces advanced in three columns—the right consisted of Mississippi Territorial Volunteers under Col. Joseph Carson, the center of Lieutenant Colonel Russell's Third Regiment U.S. Infantry, and the left of assorted militia under Major Benjamin Smoot and Choctaws led by Pushmataha. In hopes of surrounding the Red Sticks and preventing their escape, a battalion of mounted riflemen under Major Cassel were sent further to the right than Carson's volunteers with instructions to block the way to the Alabama River bluff behind the town. Despite the prophets' pronouncement of the town's invincibility, Weatherford nevertheless persuaded them to hide their women and children in the thick woods across the river just in time to avoid

---

[47] Owsley, *Struggle for the Gulf Borderlands*, 47; Waselkov, *Conquering Spirit*, 145; Nunez, "Stiggins Narrative," 66–67. In April 2010 Gregory Waselkov, Director of the Center for Archeological Studies at the University of South Alabama, pinpointed what he believes is the precise location of the Holy Ground battlefield. The site—a half mile up House Creek from the Alabama River—contained artifact clusters of Holy Ground houses. Prior to Waselkov's findings there were two other sites that had been touted as possible locations of the Holy Ground. One, advocated by historians Halbert and Ball in 1895, was on a bluff overlooking the Alabama River where the Holy Ground Creek (now House Creek) emptied into the river. The other was located on Cypress Creek, the next creek upriver. It was at this site that the U.S. Corps of Engineers constructed the Holy Ground Battlefield Park in the 1960s. Gregory Waselkov, "Return to Holy Ground: The Legendary Battle Site Discovered," *Alabama Heritage*, no. 101 (Summer 2011): 35–37.

[48] Waselkov, *Conquering Spirit*, 164–65; Griffith, *McIntosh and Weatherford*, 127–28; Halbert and Ball, *Creek War*, 244–46; Pam Jones, "William Weatherford and the Road to the Holy Ground," *Alabama Heritage*, no. 74 (Fall 2004): 29.

Claiborne's attack on the morning of December 23. Major Cassel's men had become bogged down in swamps and failed to seal off the riverbank allowing not only the women and children to escape before the battle, but opening the way for Weatherford and most of his men to escape as the battle wore to a conclusion.[49]

The prophets and their followers initially held their ground, confident that their mystical powers would protect them. However, when the advancing army did not drop dead as they crossed the supposed impenetrable barrier, Prophet Joseph Frances and his party ran away, escaping through a gap in the American lines to the river. Their hasty exit left Weatherford and a vastly outnumbered group of warriors and Africans—either captured at Fort Mims or runaways—as the remaining defenders of the Holy Ground. Weatherford put up a courageous fight, but began to look for an escape route himself when he saw that most of his men had deserted him. He ultimately cantered away on his horse toward the river. There he saw that his only chance to escape was to jump his horse off a fifteen- to twenty-foot bluff into the river. Weatherford reportedly struck a dramatic pose during this legendary leap, holding his rifle defiantly in the air as he jumped. Although he became separated from his horse during the jump, they both emerged from beneath the water and swam toward the opposite shore to safety.[50]

Simply considering the number of casualties, the Battle of the Holy Ground was not that noteworthy. It is estimated that thirty-three Red Sticks were killed, including twelve escaped slaves who were fighting with them. Only one of Claiborne's men was killed, with an additional twenty wounded. The general was successful in making the Red Sticks abandon their presumed sacred village and seized 1,200 barrels of their corn for his hungry troops, which was of some military significance. America's Choctaw allies were allowed to further loot the village, scalp the dead, and burn down 200 buildings. The minimal military significance of the Holy Ground victory, however, was counterbalanced by the psychological impact it carried, as described by Samuel Dale: "The moral effect of this bold movement into the heart of the nation, upon ground held sacred and impregnable, was great. It taught the savages that they were neither inaccessible nor invulnerable; it destroyed their confidence in their prophets, and it proved what volunteers, even without shoes, clothing, blankets, or provisions would do for their country." Their mission accomplished, Claiborne's

---

[49] Waselkov, "Return to Holy Ground," 31–32; Halbert and Ball, *Creek War*, 249–56; Griffith, *McIntosh and Weatherford*, 129–131; Owsley, *Struggle for the Gulf Borderlands*, 47–48; Jones, "William Weatherford," 30–31.

[50] Halbert and Ball, *Creek War*, 249–56; Griffith, *McIntosh and Weatherford*, 129–131; Owsley, *Struggle for the Gulf Borderlands*, 47–48; Jones, "William Weatherford," 30–31. Halbert and Ball refute Woodward's attempt to discredit the authenticity of the leap while Griffith asserts that the consensus of contemporary accounts is that some sort of leap did occur. According to one account, the prophets later asserted that the ability of whites to capture the Holy Ground, despite the supposed impenetrable barrier established by their spirits, was due to a traitor prophet who unleashed counter charms and incantations. Henry Sale Halbert, "Creek War Incidents," *Transactions of the Alabama Historical Society* 2 (1897–98): 99–100.

men marched back to Fort Claiborne where they mustered out of the service. Their general praised his troops' efforts: "My volunteers are returning to their homes with eight months' pay due them and almost literally naked. They have served the last three months of inclement weather without shoes or blankets, almost without shirts, but are still devoted to their country and properly impressed with the justice and the necessity of the war." Because of their efforts, for all intents and purposes the Red Sticks no longer posed a threat along the lower Alabama River. The war's focus now shifted northward to the Tallapoosa River, where the Red Sticks were seeking refuge.[51]

Following the Battle of Talladega, while Claiborne's forces were laying waste to the Holy Ground, General Jackson was struggling with dwindling supplies, mutinous soldiers, and expiration of enlistments. Indeed, as the end of December 1813 neared, his forces had shrunk to a just a few volunteers and a company consisting for the most part of officers under General Coffee. Fortunately Jackson's troops soon increased to approximately one thousand men with the arrival of a sixty-day volunteer group led by future Tennessee governor Col. William Carroll. With this boost in troop strength, Jackson was ready to make a another foray into the Creek Nation in pursuit of a large contingent of Red Sticks camped in a bend of the Tallapoosa River near the mouth of Emuckfau Creek. Jackson felt compelled to be proactive as it was feared that the British would soon land at Pensacola to provide supplies and ammunition to these Red Stick warriors who were amassing for an attack against the Americans. Thus, on January 15, 1814, Jackson set out with practically his entire command, including eight hundred inadequately trained volunteers, Coffee's officers, and one hundred friendly Creeks and Cherokees.[52]

Jackson's forces reached Talladega on January 18, where they took on a few more Indian allies before proceeding. On January 21 they camped for the evening within three miles of the Red Sticks assembled at Emuckfau. Early the next morning the Red Sticks took the offensive and attacked. After about thirty minutes of fighting, Jackson's left wing under General Coffee charged and ran the Red Sticks from the field. Jackson did not pursue the enemy, however, because he did not have confidence that his army had the wherewithal to capture their town at Emuckfau. As his army was returning to Fort Strother, it was attacked again on the morning of January 24 as it crossed Enitachopco Creek. This time many of Jackson's ill-trained troops lost their nerve and ran. Fortunately for the Americans, Jackson and the more seasoned troops were able to rally the fleeing troops and stop their retreat. Fortunes were then reversed; Jackson sent the Red Sticks scurrying from the field by peppering them with grapeshot from his six-pounder. Having saved his troops from a decimating loss, Jackson continued the march back to Fort Strother without further incident. In all, twenty of Jackson's men were killed and seventy-five were wounded at the

[51] Owsley, *Struggle for the Gulf Borderlands*, 47; Waselkov, *Conquering Spirit*, 165–66; *McIntosh and Weatherford*, 132; Rowland, *Mississippi Territory*, 77.

[52] Owsley, *Struggle for the Gulf Borderlands*, 68–73.

battles of Emuckfau and Enitachopco. Americans eventually discovered 189 Red Stick bodies, but it is believed that actual losses were probably in excess of 200. Although this foray into the Creek Nation did not result in a major victory for the Americans, at the very least it served as a useful reconnaissance of the route Jackson's forces would take for their final showdown with the Red Sticks at Horseshoe Bend on the Tallapoosa River.[53]

Jackson's tenaciousness convinced General Pinckney to rely on him to finish off the Creeks. He therefore assigned Col. John Williams and the 39th Infantry to Jackson and ordered Tennessee's Governor Blount to keep Jackson continually supplied with militia as enlistments expired. In the meantime, 2,000 additional militiamen had been recruited in east Tennessee. With this welcomed troop buildup, Jackson made sure that the quartermasters and food contractors were stockpiling enough provisions for the campaign. As his strength neared 3,500 men, including five hundred Cherokee and one hundred friendly Creeks, Jackson set out on March 24, 1814, to engage the Red Sticks for what he hoped would be the last major offensive against the Creek Nation.[54]

Waiting for Jackson's invasion force were approximately one thousand warriors and another 350 women and children; they had established a temporary village called Tohopeka in a hundred-acre peninsula in the bend of the Tallapoosa River known to Americans as Horseshoe Bend. For the preceding three months, Indians from of the upper Creek towns of Newyaucau, Oakfuskee, Oakchaya, Eufaula, Fishponds, and Hillabee had been gathering there for protection. The only significant leader overseeing their defense was Chief Menawa from the town of Oakfuskee. In the toe of the bend, Menawa and his fellow warriors constructed a village consisting of approximately 300 log houses. In the short neck of the bend they threw up breastworks ranging from five to eight feet high with two rows of portholes to expose any approaching army to a dual crossfire. Their plan was to hold off the Americans long enough to allow the women and children as well as some of the older warriors to escape across the river at the end of peninsula.[55]

On his southward march through Creek country, Jackson's forces had been reinforced by William McIntosh and a force of Creek Indians who had previously served with General Floyd's troops from Georgia. By March 26, Jackson's augmented troops were camped just six miles northwest of Horseshoe Bend at Emuckfau, the scene of only modest success for Jackson a couple of months earlier. The attack on Horseshoe Bend began at 6:30 a.m. on March 27 when Jackson sent General Coffee along with 700 cavalry

---

[53] Ibid., 75–76; Pickett, *Alabama*, 579–87; Buchanan, *Jackson's Way*, 268–70; Griffith, *McIntosh and Weatherford*, 138–43. Jackson's brother-in-law, Maj. Andrew Donelson, was among the dead and Jackson's confidante, Gen. John Coffee, was among the wounded.

[54] Owsley, *Struggle for the Gulf Borderlands*, 76, 79; Griffith, *McIntosh and Weatherford*, 143.

[55] Owsley, *Struggle for the Gulf Borderlands*, 78–79; Rowland, *Mississippi Territory*, 79–81; Griffith, *McIntosh and Weatherford*, 144–49; Waselkov, *Conquering Spirit*, 170.

and mounted riflemen and 600 allied warriors led by William McIntosh across the river to surround the bend from the opposite bank.[56]

As Jackson began his bombardment of the fortifications in the neck of the bend, some of the allied Indians assigned to Coffee swam the river to seize enemy canoes that could be used to escape. They then used the canoes to ferry across troops to capture the village in the toe of the bend. After capturing the village, the troops were then able to move forward to a point where they could begin firing on the breastworks from the rear as Jackson continued his frontal assault. His bombardment of both artillery and small arms lasted for about two hours until he realized that Coffee's men had been successful in their operation in the rear. Believing that the time was now ripe for a final frontal assault on the breastworks, Jackson called upon the Thirty-ninth Infantry, the most disciplined troops in the field, to lead the charge. Maj. Lemuel Purnell Montgomery—for whom Montgomery County, Alabama, was later named—was the first man to mount the breastworks. He was struck down as he was urging his men forward with sword in hand. Major Montgomery's heroic charge was followed by several minutes of ferocious fighting. The Red Sticks, outgunned and outmanned, then retreated to the interior of the bend. Although greatly outnumbered, the Red Sticks continued to take the fight to the Americans for several more hours until darkness fell upon the field. In the interim many tried to escape across the river, but most were shot by Coffee's troops as they swam. Chief Menawa, who had sustained seven gunshot wounds, amazingly managed to escape by canoe that night after lying unconscious all afternoon among a pile of his dead warriors.[57]

More than 800 Red Stick warriors lost their lives during the Battle of Horseshoe Bend, while only forty-nine Americans were killed and 153 wounded. Approximately 350 Indian women and children were taken as prisoners. According to a report from Jackson's officers who had ordered their men to cut off the tip of each dead warrior's nose to assure an accurate accounting, 557 dead warriors were found on the battlefield. Another estimated 250 to 300 warriors were shot in the river trying to escape, causing some to assert that the Americans were guilty of perpetrating a massacre comparable to that which had occurred at Fort Mims. Although as many as 150 to 200 warriors managed to escape from the peninsula, their forces were now scattered, demoralized, and incapable of mounting a counter-attack. This factor is even more important in view of the fact that a few months after the Battle of Horseshoe Bend, the British finally landed along the gulf coast with a massive load of arms and ammunition which would go

---

[56] Griffith, *McIntosh and Weatherford*, 144–48.

[57] Griffith, *McIntosh and Weatherford*, 144–48; Owsley, *Struggle for the Gulf Borderlands*, 79–81; Rowland, *Mississippi Territory*, 80–82. Future Texas hero Sam Houston, who sustained a puncture wound in his thigh from an arrow as he charged through the barricade and later in the day was struck twice by rifle balls in his shoulder, described the brutality of the fighting in the bend as follows: "Arrows and spears and balls were flying; swords and tomahawks were gleaming in the sun; and the whole peninsula rang with the yell of savages and the groans of the dying." Griffith, *McIntosh and Weatherford*, 148.

unused for the most part. Had the British arrived earlier, as Jackson had feared, a totally different outcome may have resulted.[58]

The Battle of Horseshoe Bend in effect ended the Creek War of 1813–1814 and was considered a major victory for the Americans in the War of 1812. Following the battle, General Jackson marched his army down the Tallapoosa to its confluence with the Coosa, where all of the American armies finally converged and built Fort Jackson adjacent to the site of old Fort Toulouse. From there Americans and their Indian allies were sent forth to encourage the surviving warriors from Horseshoe Bend to surrender. As a result, one by one and in groups, starving Indians came into Fort Jackson to surrender. Upon their surrender they were allowed to return to their homes, and, due to their condition, they were given food if at all possible. However, Jackson made a demand on surrendering chiefs to show their good faith by capturing and bringing in William Weatherford, who, although he had not been at Horseshoe Bend, was wanted for his participation in the massacre at Fort Mims. Weatherford relieved his compatriots of this onerous task by turning himself in at Fort Jackson near the end of April 1814. There are many accounts of this event, but there is no question that Weatherford arrived alone without being detected and boldly presented himself to General Jackson, in order to formally surrender. In his statement of surrender he asserted that he had tried to prevent the killing of women and children at Fort Mims; vowed that he would fight no more as all of his warriors were dead, "their bones . . . bleaching on the plains of Tallushatches, Talladega, and Emuckfau"; and sought generous treatment for the Red Stick women and children for which he was responsible. Jackson was impressed by Weatherford's bravery and spared his life despite demands by many that he be executed.[59]

It was inevitable that the Creeks would be defeated at the hands of the Americans. While the Red Sticks had completely annihilated the white and métis defenders of Fort Mims, the enormity and brutality of their attack resulted in a call to arms that almost guaranteed their defeat. After the attack on Fort Mims, there was only a few isolated attacks against white settlements in the Tombigbee and Tensaw districts; for the most part, the Red Sticks assumed a defensive posture within areas which they felt were impregnable due to terrains protected by spiritual powers. In most battles they were clearly outnumbered by the Americans, albeit a large number of whom were ill-trained, ill-fed, and ill-clothed. Furthermore, the Red Sticks did not possess enough fire power because they never attained the weapons and ammunition they had hoped to receive from Great Britain. Had Great Britain made a successful landfall along the gulf coast before the Battle of Horseshoe Bend, the outcome could have been different. The British did

---

[58] Waselkov, *Conquering Spirit*, 171; Halbert and Ball, *Creek War*, 275–77; Owsley, *Struggle for the Gulf Borderlands*, 81.

[59] Halbert and Ball, *Creek War*, 284–85; Owsley, *Struggle for the Gulf Borderlands*, 83–85; Waselkov, *Conquering Spirit*, 171–73; Griffith, *McIntosh and Weatherford*, 150–55. Weatherford, according to one account, was in the Upper Creek town of Hoithlewalee during the Battle of Horseshoe Bend, for some reason not expecting the Americans to attack when they did.

belatedly land in Pensacola in August 1814, with the permission of the
Spanish. The next month they made an attempt to take Fort Bowyer,
located at Mobile Point at the entrance of Mobile Bay, but were staved off
by American defenders led by Maj. William L. Lawrence.[60]

William Weatherford Surrenders to General Andrew Jackson
Courtesy of Alabama Department of Archives and History

After Weatherford's dramatic surrender, Indians who had been in
hiding began surrendering in larger numbers. These surrenders were
accepted with the understanding that a territorial settlement would be
made at a later date. Jackson and his fellow westerners pushed for harsh
terms now that the peaceful coexistence plan originally formulated during
George Washington's administration had been obliterated by the Creek
War. A treaty was finally signed on August 9, 1814, at Fort Jackson, resulting in the cession to the United States of over twenty million acres of Creek

---

[60] The British later successfully captured Fort Bowyer after the Battle of New Orleans in what
would become the last engagement of the War of 1812. On February 12, 1815, Major Williams
surrendered the fort to British forces under the command of Gen. John Lambert. Word came
the very next day of the Treaty of Ghent ending the war. The fort was thus returned to
American control and was eventually replaced by Fort Morgan. William S. Coker, "The Last
Battle of the War of 1812: New Orleans? No. Fort Bowyer!," *Alabama Historical Quarterly* 43
(Spring 1981): 42–63.

lands constituting almost three-fifths of the future state of Alabama. Ironically, the treaty was for the most part only signed by Creek chiefs who had been friendly to the United States during the war. This land cession opened the floodgates. Between 1815 and 1820, more than 100,000 Americans descended upon former Creek lands. This new wave of white settlers would forever change the landscape and lead to statehood for Alabama within a little over five years.[61]

---

[61] Waselkov, *Conquering Spirit*, 204–06; Owsley, *Struggle for the Gulf Borderlands*, 91. The hero status General Jackson attained as a result of his successful prosecution of the Creek War, combined with his subsequent victory over the British at the Battle of New Orleans in January 1815, catapulted him to the presidency in 1828. William Weatherford lived a relatively quiet life after the war, settling down on a farm in present-day Monroe County, Alabama, where he owned approximately 300 slaves and was known for breeding fine horses. Weatherford died in March 1824. William McIntosh went on to fight for the United States in a subsequent war with the Seminoles, and was ultimately executed in April 1825 by Red Sticks led by Chief Menawa in retaliation for his part in relinquishing more Creek lands by signing the 1825 Treaty of Indian Springs. Griffith, *McIntosh and Weatherford*, 232–54.

5

❧

ALABAMA FEVER AND GEORGIANS
BRING ON STATEHOOD

With the cession of millions of acres of Creek lands following the Battle of Horseshoe Bend, the influx of settlers into the future state of Alabama was so great that it was called "Alabama Fever." Many of those settlers were Tennessee veterans of General Jackson's campaign against the Creeks in Alabama and the British in New Orleans, who had become familiar during their military service with the fertile river valleys of the future state. Thousands more came from the piedmont regions of Georgia, South Carolina, North Carolina, and Virginia. Of these, some came on mules and horses pushing or pulling a hogshead containing all of their possessions, some rode in wagons, and others walked with their only possessions on their backs.[1]

Escaping their worn-out fields and a poor economy back East, many of these pioneer settlers were drawn to Alabama by the cheap lands opened up for settlement by the Creek cession, the emergence of high-priced cotton, and the quest for a more affluent lifestyle. The roads and pathways to Alabama were so crowded that an English geographer who came across 1,200 emigrants within just one day "was reminded of a biblical exodus 'except for the decided style of cursing and swearing.'" They came in such numbers in 1816 and 1817 that the few pioneers already there and the local Indian tribes could not furnish enough corn to feed the newly arrived settlers. The situation was so bad that the *Niles' Weekly Register*, a leading weekly national news magazine, reported in April 1817 that "[t]he sudden and very numerous emigrations into the Alabama country threaten many with absolute starvation."[2]

Although there were some wealthy planters accompanied by their slaves among those swarming to the newly opened lands in Alabama, the vast majority were yeoman farmers, or the so-called "plain folk," who toiled to clear the land with their own hands and to provide much needed sustenance to their families and fellow settlers. They cut trees, fenced their fields, built makeshift log cabins, and planted corn. These first settlers lived a demanding and grueling life just scratching out an existence in the wil-

---

[1] The population of Alabama increased more than 1,000 percent between 1810 and 1820, with the biggest increase coming after 1815. Rogers, et al., *Alabama*, 54–55; Thomas Perkins Abernethy, *The Formative Period in Alabama, 1815–1828* (Tuscaloosa: University of Alabama Press, 1995 [1922]), 25.

[2] *Niles' Weekly Register*, April 5, 1817, quoted in Rogers et al., *Alabama*, 57; Virginia Van der Veer Hamilton, *Alabama: A Bicentennial History* (New York: W. W. Norton & Co., 1977), 3; Abernethy, *Formative Period*, 27.

derness abounding in dangerous animals and rowdy neighbors. They had none of the basic services of an orderly society such as medical care, religious instruction, or schools. Law enforcement was basically nonexistent, with order being preserved by individuals themselves or at times by vigilante groups. To relieve the stress of everyday life, many settlers resorted to drinking, gambling, and violence. Drinking was so common that jugs of whiskey became a medium of exchange on the frontier.[3]

Transporting Settlers' Goods by Hogsheads
Courtesy of Alabama Department of Archives and History

Even life in the more populated areas of Alabama's frontier was described as austere by arriving settlers. When Henry Hitchcock, a leading citizen of early Alabama, moved to Mobile from Vermont in 1817, he described it as "a rude place—200 miles from civilization, surrounded by Indians. It was the logical refuge of rogues fleeing from justice." Similarly, in May of 1815, the soon-to-be territorial capital of St. Stephens was described by a resident in a letter to a friend in Boston as "the jumping off place of the world." A correspondent to northern newspapers nevertheless described the Alabama Territory as an "American Canaan" of unlimited opportunities with its "vast bodies of fertile lands," "three noble rivers, of extensive and easy navigation," and "one of the most delightful climates in the world. . . ." Others described the Huntsville area as the "Happy Valley" and the Alabama River basin as the "Acadia of Southern America." The end of the Creek hostilities followed by these types of endorsements ensured Alabama's eventual statehood.[4]

---

[3] Hamilton, *Alabama: A Bicentennial History*, 3–6; Rogers et al., *Alabama*, 54–59; Moore, *History of Alabama*, 128–158.

[4] Herbert J. Lewis, "A Connecticut Yankee in Early Alabama: Henry Wilbourne Stevens and the Founding of Ordered Society, 1814–1823," *Alabama Review* 59 (April 2006): 86–87; Darrell E. Bigham, "From the Green Mountains to the Tombigbee: Henry Hitchcock in Territorial Alabama, 1817–1819," *Alabama Review* 26 (July 1973): 213–15; J.S.W. Parkin to

Even before the onset of "Alabama Fever" at the conclusion of the Creek War, and while the Tombigbee District was consumed with international intrigue and Indian hostilities, a major population center had been quietly, but rapidly, emerging several hundred miles to the north in the Tennessee Valley. Although the area was not permanently occupied by Native Americans, it was within the hunting grounds of the Cherokee and Chickasaw nations. White settlement was further facilitated when the federal government was successful in getting both tribes to relinquish their claims to the area. By treaty dated July 23, 1805, the Chickasaw Nation relinquished all claims they had in lands including what was to become Madison County in return for $20,000, which was to be used in part to pay its debts to merchants and traders, and a $100 annuity to be paid to the head of their nation for the rest of his life. Shortly thereafter, on January 7, 1806, a group of Chickamaugan Cherokees agreed to cede 10 million acres of their hunting grounds in north Alabama between the Tennessee and the Elk rivers to the United States in return for $10,000. The Cherokee cession was not without controversy. A Cherokee chief named Doublehead, who was instrumental in negotiating the 1806 treaty, was later executed for treason by another faction of the Cherokee Nation asserting that the treaty was illegal because it had not been approved by the Cherokee National council.[5]

Just prior to the Chickasaw and Cherokee cessions, the first white settlers began to filter into the great bend area of the Tennessee River in present-day Madison County between 1802 and 1804. James Ditto is believed to have arrived in the area as early as 1802 and established a ferry and trading post on the north bank of the Tennessee River in an area then known as Chickasaw Old Fields, later known as Ditto's Landing or Whitesburg. In 1804, Joseph and Isaac Criner settled on the Flint River just south of today's Tennessee–Alabama border near New Market. John Hunt, a native Virginian and transplanted Tennessee sheriff, settled the area occupying the future city of Huntsville in 1805, building a cabin for his family on a bluff some sixty feet above a natural spring he called "Big Spring."[6]

The Chickasaw and Cherokee land cessions opened the way for more squatters and settlers of moderate means from Virginia, the Carolinas, Tennessee, and Georgia seeking cheap land and fertile soil. They came in

---

Jno. R. Parker, May 15, 1815, J.S.W. Parker Letters, SPR 101, Alabama Department of Archives and History (ADAH), Montgomery, Alabama; "Towns in the Alabama Territory," *Alabama Historical Quarterly* 3 (Spring 1941): 79–80; Lowery, "The Great Migration," 173–78.

[5] Treaty with the Chickasaw, 1805, July 23, 1805, 7 Stat. 89; Treaty with the Cherokee, 1806, Jan. 7, 1806, 7 Stat. 101. Charles J. Kappler, ed., *Indian Affairs: Laws and Treaties,* II, Treaties, (Washington: Government Printing Office, 1904); 79–80, 90–91; Grace Steele Woodward, *The Cherokees* (Norman: University of Oklahoma Press, 1982), 129–30; William Gerald McLoughlin, Walter H. Conser and Virginia Duffy McLoughlin, *The Cherokee Ghost Dance: Essays on the Southeastern Indians, 1789–1861* (Macon, Ga.: Mercer University Press, 1984), 57, 63.

[6] Frank Alex Luttrell, III, ed., *Historical Markers of Madison County, Alabama* (Huntsville–Madison County Historical Society, 50th Anniversary, 1951–2001), 3; Thomas Jones Taylor, "Early History of Madison County And, Incidentally of North Alabama," *Alabama Historical Quarterly* 1 (Spring 1930): 110.

enough numbers that Mississippi territorial Governor Robert Williams created Madison County, named in honor of President James Madison, by executive order dated December 13, 1808. In order to encourage the development of this new county, the federal government ordered sales of the recently ceded lands in the Tennessee Valley of northern Alabama. The first sale of public land was held on August 7, 1809, at the Public Land Office then located in Nashville. The sales were so brisk that by October 1809, some 24,000 acres had been purchased, including acreage surrounding "Big Spring" bought up by a group of settlers led by Leroy Pope with the hopes of it becoming the county seat for the newly created Madison County.[7]

Before the creation of Madison County in 1808, there was no organized government to protect its settlers from the rogue element that inevitably inhabit frontier areas as had been the case in the Tombigbee District. The situation was such that Governor Williams reported that the county's squatters had even formed informal militia units to maintain law and order. Legend has it that one of these units, Captain Slick's Company, was more of a vigilante group that warned those mixed up in nefarious criminal activities to leave the county by a certain date or face corporal punishments such as whipping, branding, or cropping of the ears. In any event, squatters saw the need to demand official protection from the territorial government and implored Governor Williams to appoint military and civil officers to enforce the law. In response, Williams obtained authorization from President Thomas Jefferson to appoint civil officers for the area in November 1808, a month prior to the creation of Madison County, and some three months prior to the formal extension of the laws of the Mississippi Territory to the new county.[8]

An act passed by the Mississippi territorial legislature on February 27, 1809, extended the territory's laws pertaining to the judiciary and militia to Madison County and directed the immediate establishment of circuit and county courts. For a few months, until these courts could be organized, the county's laws were enforced and justice meted out by the Supreme Court of the Mississippi Territory. Then on December 22, 1809, the county was authorized to establish its own court to be known as the "Superior court of law and equity," which could dispense justice with a more local flavor. By the end of 1810, all requisite courts had been established and the officers needed to run them appointed by the territorial governor. In 1809, Governor Williams, who was some four hundred miles away in the territorial capital of Washington near the Mississippi River, sent Captain Stephen Neal to serve as the new county's sheriff and justice of the peace, as well as

---

[7] Edward Chambers Betts, *Early History of Huntsville, Alabama, 1804–1870*, rev. ed. (Montgomery, Ala.: The Brown Printing Co., 1916), 6–11; Lutrell, *Historical Markers of Madison County*, 3; Thomas Jones Taylor, "Early History of Madison County and, Incidentally of North Alabama" (second installment), *Alabama Historical Quarterly* 2 (summer 1930): 164; Carter, *The Territorial Papers of the United States*, 5: 724–25.

[8] Daniel S. Dupre, *Transforming the Cotton Frontier: Madison County, Alabama, 1800–1840* (Baton Rouge: Louisiana State University Press, 1997), 23–24; Betts, *Early History of Huntsville*, 14–18; Taylor, "Early History of Madison County" (second installment), 159.

to help him select officers of good character. Neal, with the help of Thomas Freeman, who had been sent to the area as a surveyor, made recommendations to the governor of persons to serve as militia officers, justices of the peace, and justices of the quorum to make up the county's inferior court. The inferior court is believed to be the first court to ever convene in Madison County, holding its first session on the first Monday in January, 1810. Leroy Pope presided as chief justice of the quorum with four associate justices, including Edward Ward, William Dickson, John Withers, and future governor Thomas Bibb. William Winston served as the inferior court's clerk. The Superior Court of Law and Equity did not hold its first session until October 1, 1810, with Obidiah Jones presiding as its judge and Peter Perkins as its clerk.[9]

The same legislation that extended the territory's laws to the county and directed the establishments of its courts, appointed a commission to select a site to house the public buildings of the county. On July 5, 1810, upon recommendation of this commission, the area surrounding Big Spring was designated as the county seat of Madison and, pursuant to the authorizing statute, was given the name of Twickenham. Leroy Pope, part of an emerging wealthy group of settlers from the Broad River region of Georgia, became the principal owner of the acreage around the town after ousting older squatters from the land. He then used his influence in having the legislature mandate the town's name in honor of the estate of the English poet, Alexander Pope, whom he greatly admired. The older settlers of more moderate means were so outraged at what they perceived as aristocratic arrogance that they made the town's name an issue in the next year's election to the Mississippi territorial legislature and were successful in defeating two out of the three candidates put up by Pope's Georgia faction. One of the defeated Georgians was John W. Walker, a Princeton-educated lawyer who would later serve as Speaker of the Alabama House of Representatives, as president of Alabama's constitutional convention in 1819, and as one of the state of Alabama's first U.S. Senators. In the meanwhile, the first action of the county's new legislative delegation was having the town's name changed to Huntsville, this time in honor of John Hunt, one of the original yeoman settlers in the Big Spring area. The new town of Huntsville was incorporated on December 9, 1811.[10]

Prior to the 1809 land sale, Madison County had primarily been settled by yeoman farmers who were squatting on the land in anticipation of it being made available for purchase. When the land sale occurred in Nashville, however, quite a few wealthy planters from Georgia joined Leroy Pope

---

[9] *Statutes of Mississippi Territory* (1816), 177–78, cited in Betts, *Early History of Huntsville*, 14, 19–21. The first session of the Superior Court was filled with much solemnity as attorneys presented their credentials to be admitted to the bar of the court. The new court's bar included John W. Walker, Gabriel Moore, and Marmaduke Williams, all of whom would play significant roles in future Alabama politics. Other members included J.C. Hamilton, George Cotter, James Rogers, and Lewis Winston.

[10] *Statutes of Mississippi Territory* (1816), 98, cited in Betts, *Early History of Huntsville*, 14–15; Dupre, *Transforming the Cotton Frontier*, 37; Luttrell, *Historical Markers of Madison County*, 3.

in the purchase of land in the area surrounding Huntsville. Although many of the original squatters were unable to purchase the land they had toiled to clear, an overwhelming majority of the land was still held by small home-steading farmers. Nevertheless, the best land, most fertile and suitable for growing cotton, was snatched up by the wealthy Georgians. This Georgia contingent, termed the "Broad River Group" by historian J. Mills Thornton, III, had originally emigrated from an area near Charlottesville, Virginia, to Georgia in 1784, in response to an offer of homesteads on state-owned lands. Gen. George Mathews led the group, made up primarily of veterans of the Revolutionary War, to settle on the banks of the Broad River in northeastern Georgia near Petersburg. There they established tobacco farms, married into the local planter families, and acquired great social standing within their close knit community. Before members of this group moved to Alabama, they had become politically powerful in Georgia, pro-ducing a governor, three senators, and a number of congressmen and state legislators. Of these, several would play a major role in Alabama's road to statehood, including senators William Wyatt Bibb and Charles Tait, as well as U.S. Secretary of the Treasury William H. Crawford.[11]

The migration of the Broad River Group into Alabama took part in two stages, with the main thrust not coming until 1816 when a group of their investors bought significant acreage surrounding the future towns of Montgomery and Cahaba when the Black Belt region came open for pur-chase. As we have seen, however, very influential members of the group, including Leroy Pope, had already migrated to Madison County in 1809 after buying up the best land surrounding Huntsville in the Tennessee Valley for $2.00 per acre. Other Georgians migrating at that time included Pope's cousin and future governor, Thomas Bibb, as well as Pope's son-in-law, John W. Walker, future president of Alabama's Constitutional Conven-tion of 1819 and one of Alabama's first U.S. Senators. As demonstrated by the resentment over the naming of Huntsville, those representing the small yeomen farmers such as future governors Hugh McVay and Gabriel Moore would often clash with the wealthy Georgia investors for political domina-tion of the county. The Broad River settlers nevertheless maintained social and economic dominance within the county, and—along with the Broad River settlers who later settled the Black Belt—would become instrumental in attaining eventual statehood for Alabama.[12]

The brisk emigration to the Tennessee Valley resulting from the 1809 land sale was soon interrupted by Indian hostilities to the south and the resulting advent of the Creek War of 1813–1814. With the defeat of the Creeks at Horseshoe Bend and the ensuing Alabama fever as discussed in

[11] J. Mills Thornton, III, *Politics and Power in a Slave Society: Alabama, 1800–1860* (Baton Rouge: Louisiana State University Press, 1978), 7–9.

[12] Ibid.; Hugh C. Bailey, "John W. Walker and the 'Georgia Machine' in Early Alabama Politics," *Alabama Review* 8 (July 1955): 179, 181; Hugh C. Bailey, *John Williams Walker: A Study in the Political, Social, and Cultural Life of the Old Southwest* (Tuscaloosa: University of Alabama Press, 1964), 68; Stanley Elkins and Eric McKitrick, "A Meaning of Turner's Frontier: Part II: The Southwest Frontier and New England," *Political Science Quarterly* 69 (December 1954): 570.

the previous chapter, those within the Alabama portion of the Mississippi Territory were ready to control their own destiny. As early as 1803, over one hundred settlers within the Alabama sector petitioned Congress to separate them from the Mississippi River settlements, complaining that difficulty of transportation and communication isolated them from the seat of the territorial government approximately three hundred miles away, "all of which distance is a howling wilderness with its usual inhabitants of Savages and beasts of prey." They also cited differences in customs, manners, and interests. Heading the list of signers was Nicholas Perkins, a lawyer who is believed to have authored the petition. As previously discussed, Perkins was later involved in the identification and arrest of former Vice President Aaron Burr in Washington County.[13]

In May 1809, nearly three hundred more settlers, citing similar concerns, added their objection to having to pay taxes to help sustain a government from which they received no benefits in return, particularly with regard to the administration of justice. Another petition just a few months later, dated November 11, 1809, boldly proclaimed, "Representatives of the American People! We have Petitioned for a Government.—At Present we have only the name of one. We know nothing of our Executive Officers:— we know nothing of our Delegates in Congress.—They know nothing of us." The petition also focused upon their "frequent collisions with the Indians and Spaniards," and complained of continuing Spanish control of Mobile and the resulting high tariffs paid to the Spanish government, despite the fact that "our runaway Negroes find protection under it." The petition then posed the question, "Are we Americans or Spaniards?—Shall we support the Republic of the United States or the Spanish Monarchy?"[14]

The push for territorial division and ultimate statehood waxed and waned and involved shifting opinions on the subject. Most settlers in the more populous Mississippi section of the territory were opposed to these calls for division, at least for the time. The statehood question quickly became embroiled in the political maneuverings related to the nation's division over the slavery issue. As early as 1812, the U.S. House of Representatives passed an enabling act allowing the entire Mississippi Territory to be admitted as one state. Southern senators, on the other hand, pushed to carve as many states as possible out of the southern territories so as to keep pace with the admission of non-slave states. These southern senators were successful in convincing the Senate committee to which the House bill had been assigned to recommend that the territory be divided, thus allow-

---

[13] McMillan, *Constitutional Development in Alabama*, 16–17; Petition to Congress by Inhabitants of Washington District, November 25, 1803, Carter, *Territorial Papers of the United States*, 5: 290–292; William H. Brantley, Jr., *Three Capitals, A Book About the First Three Capitals of Alabama: St. Stephens, Huntsville & Cahawba, 1818–1826* (1947; repr., Tuscaloosa: University of Alabama Press, 1976), 13.

[14] McMillan, *Constitutional Development in Alabama*, 16–18; and see Petition to Congress by Inhabitants East of the Pearl River, May, 1809; Petition to Congress by a Convention East of the Pearl River November 11, 1809; and Memorial to Congress by a Convention East of the Pearl River, December 26, 1809 (all in Carter, *Territorial Papers of the United States*, 5: 733–37; 6: 26–31, 36–39).

ing the admission of two states. The same committee, however, went on to propose that the question be deferred until the next session because of the complicated title questions in the territory and the split of opinion of the inhabitants as to whether they wanted to be admitted as a state. These questions would remain unresolved and would not come to a head during the Creek hostilities.[15]

Campaigning for and against statehood resumed after the Creek War, but this time the positions were reversed—the eastern Alabama section now seeking admission of the whole territory as one state, while the western Mississippi section supported division. This shift in positions was for the most part due to the increasing population in the east brought about by the acquisition of Mobile in 1813 and the cession of millions of acres of Creek lands. With this increase in population, easterners anticipated that they would gain control of the territorial legislature and perhaps even have the capital moved to St. Stephens in present-day Alabama. For a while, however, a significant number of settlers in both sections of the territory were opposed to admission to the union at all due to concerns that federal courts, which would assume jurisdiction upon statehood, would not honor the titles to the lands they had acquired due to the confusion brought about by the granting of titles by three different European nations—France, Great Britain, and Spain—and by the fraudulent granting of large areas of land by the state of Georgia to the Yazoo land companies. Much of this opposition was eliminated in 1814 when the federal government cleared the title to the Yazoo lands by authorizing the issuance of script to Yazoo claimants redeemable in land.[16]

In October 1816, a convention of eastern citizens in favor of admission of the entire territory as one state selected Judge Toulmin to take its resolutions opposing division to Washington and appropriated five hundred dollars to cover his travel expenses. Judge Toulmin, however, was unable to overcome Congressional sentiment for division of the territory mandated by their desire for a balance of power between slave and non–slave states. On March 1, 1817, the House and the Senate finally came to an agreement and passed an enabling act for the admission of the western part of the territory into the Union as the state of Mississippi.[17]

Having lost this battle, Judge Toulmin next attempted to include the western Mississippi counties of Wayne, Green, and Jefferson within the new Alabama Territory. While he fell short in this regard, a compromise line was agreed upon running from the Gulf due north to the northwestern corner of Washington County and directly northward to where Bear Creek empties into the Tennessee River. This compromise paved the way for

---

[15] McMillan, *Constitutional Development in Alabama*, 19–22; Richard A. McLemore, "Division of the Mississippi Territory," *Journal of Mississippi History* 5 (1943): 79–82; Moore, *History of Alabama*, 93–95.

[16] McMillan, *Constitutional Development in Alabama*, 20–22; McLemore, "Division of the Mississippi Territory," 80; Moore, *History of Alabama*, 94–95.

[17] Moore, *History of Alabama*, 95; McMillan, *Constitutional Development in Alabama*, 22–23; McLemore, "Division of the Mississippi Territory," 81; Brantley, *Three Capitals*, 21.

Alabama to achieve its own territorial status with Congressional passage of the Alabama Territorial Act of March 3, 1817. In addition to setting the territory's boundaries, this act made applicable the laws of the old Mississippi Territory until overridden by the new Alabama territorial legislature, established St. Stephens as the territorial capital, supplied an additional judge so as to allow the creation of a territorial court of three members, and formed a House of Representatives and a Council (Senate) to be composed of all the previous members of the Mississippi territorial legislature who had represented counties located in the Alabama portion of the old territory. The act further provided that the territory's governor and secretary were to be appointed by the president and would possess the same powers, perform the same duties, and be paid the same as the governor and secretary of the Mississippi Territory. On December 10, 1817, the Alabama Territory officially came into existence on the same day that Mississippi was admitted into the Union as a state.[18]

William Wyatt Bibb, ex-Senator of Georgia, was appointed by President James Monroe as governor of the new Alabama Territory. Alabama's first chief magistrate was born in Amelia County, Virginia, on October 2, 1781, in the midst of America's struggle for independence. His parents were William Bibb, an officer in the Revolutionary army and a member of the Virginia legislature, and Sally Wyatt Bibb. In 1789, the Bibb family relocated to Elbert County, Georgia, to join other Virginia families in the Broad River region. Although his mother was left to care for eight children upon his father's death in 1796, Bibb was nonetheless able to attend the College of William & Mary in Williamsburg, Virginia. Upon completion of his studies there, Bibb entered the medical school at the University of Pennsylvania where he obtained a Doctor of Medicine degree in 1801. He then returned to the Broad River region where he began his medical practice in Petersburg and married Mary Freeman of Wilkes County, Georgia. He was very successful as a physician, building up a practice consisting of numerous clients prior to diverting his attention to politics.[19]

Bibb's political career began when he was elected to the Georgia House of Representatives in 1802. There he served two terms before election to the Georgia State Senate. In 1807, his popularity was such that he convincingly won a seat in the U.S. House of Representatives where he served for six years and gained the confidence of President James Monroe by consistently supporting his policies. Bibb's political career continued to soar when he was selected in the fall of 1813 to fill the U.S. Senate seat held by William H. Crawford—also hailing from the Broad River region—because of Crawford's appointment by President Madison as U.S. minister to France. At the height of his popularity, it looked as if Bibb would be able to exert political

---

[18] McLemore, "Division of the Mississippi Territory," 82; McMillan, *Constitutional Development in Alabama*, 23–24; *U.S. Statutes at Large*, III, 371–73.

[19] Charles Edgeworth Jones, "Governor William Wyatt Bibb," *Transactions of the Alabama Historical Society* 3 (1898–99): 128–30; Daniel S. Dupre, "William Wyatt Bibb and Thomas Bibb," in Samuel L. Webb and Margaret E. Armbrester, eds., *Alabama Governors: A Political History of the State* (Tuscaloosa: University of Alabama Press, 2001), 13–17.

power from his Georgia senatorial seat for as long as he desired. In the spring of 1816, however, Bibb quickly lost favor with his constituents by joining the majority in voting to pass an act that effectively doubled the pay of all congressmen. Most of those voting for this act were forced to resign or were not reelected by their enraged constituents. Bibb was no exception, losing his bid for reelection to George M. Troup and resigning his seat in the Senate in the fall of 1816.[20]

Bibb's fall from grace in Georgia did not end his career. Instead, his ties to the powerful Broad River Group, by then wielding power in both Georgia and Alabama, and his consistent support for President Monroe earned him appointment as the Alabama Territory's governor in 1817. According to historian Mills Thornton, the Broad River faction's support for Alabama's forthcoming bid for statehood was based upon a political *quid pro quo*, by which they would support Alabama statehood in return for important political appointments in the future state. Bibb obviously welcomed appointment as the Alabama Territory's governor in light of his sudden unpopularity in Georgia. Obviously, his friendship with Treasury Secretary William H. Crawford, as well as his solid support of President Monroe, did not fail him. Ensconced as Alabama's territorial governor, Bibb began to push for statehood as expected. Charles Tait—another close friend of Bibb's and Georgia's other senator who supported the congressional pay increases—wanted to join Bibb in Alabama to escape the storm of protest created by their pay increase votes. However, addressing Tait as the "Patron of Alabama," John W. Walker, another member of the Georgia faction now serving in the new Alabama territorial legislature, persuaded him to retain his Georgia senatorial seat long enough to shepherd the Alabama admission bill through Congress.[21]

Alabama would not remain a territory long, as Bibb and his Georgia allies became immediately engaged in pressing for statehood and preparing a petition for that purpose. In the interim, as directed by the act creating the new Alabama Territory, Governor Bibb called for the first territorial legislature to meet in St. Stephens on January 19, 1818. Seven counties previously existing in the Alabama portion of the former Mississippi Territory sent twelve Representatives to the lower house of the Alabama Territorial General Assembly: Washington (A.S. Lipscomb and John F. Everitt), Madison (Gabriel Moore, Hugh McVay, John W. Walker, and Clement C. Clay), Clarke (John McGrew and Neil Smith), Baldwin (Henry B. Slade), Mobile (Alvan Robishow), Monroe (Samuel Dale), and Montgomery (Phillip Fitzpatrick). These members elected Gabriel Moore as first Speaker of the House. The Council, or Senate, was initially to have three members, but only convened with one—James Titus of Madison County—due to the resignation of Robert Beatty also of Madison County and the death of Joseph Carson of Washington County. In accordance with the act creating the

---

[20] Jones, "Governor William Wyatt Bibb," 128–130; Dupre, "William Wyatt and Thomas Bibb," 13–17.

[21] McMillan, *Constitutional Development in Alabama*, 24; Thornton, *Politics and Power*, 10–11; Abernethy, *Formative Period*, 38; Bailey, *John Williams Walker*, 87.

territory, an additional three councilors were to be chosen from a list of six persons nominated to the President by the Alabama Territorial General Assembly. The first nominees sent to the president were George Phillips, Joseph Howard, Mathew Wilson, Joseph P. Kennedy, John Gayle, and Reuben Saffold. Of these, Philips, Wilson, and Gayle were chosen by the president to serve in the second session of the General Assembly. Finally, the first joint assembly elected John Crowell, a former Indian agent who had settled in St. Stephens, as the Alabama Territory's first delegate to the U.S. Congress.[22]

St. Stephens, site of the Territory's temporary capital, was situated high atop a limestone bluff overlooking the Tombigbee River, approximately sixty-seven miles north of Mobile. Although the British never took advantage of this site during their rule of the region prior to the American Revolution, the site's strategic importance was recognized by Spain when it assumed control of the area after the Revolution. Accordingly, in 1789, Spain built a fort on the bluff above the Tombigbee. It was named Fort San Esteban, presumably in honor of Spanish Governor Esteban Miro. But Spain's stay was anything but permanent: its fort soon fell into the hands of the United States as a result of the 1795 Treaty of San Lorenzo and the resetting of the boundary between the United States and neighboring Spanish territory at the 31st parallel. Deciding not to challenge the survey of Andrew Ellicott, which put Fort San Esteban just north of the boundary line and within American territory, Spain abandoned the fort, allowing American Lieutenant John McLary to assume control and raise the American flag on May 5, 1799.[23]

By 1803, the United States had opened a "factory" or trading post at the site which was now known as St. Stephens. This post established a brisk trade with the Choctaw Indians and was known as the Choctaw Trading House. George Strother Gaines became head of the Choctaw agency in 1805 and continued to use the old Spanish blockhouse as the agency's store. A building formerly used by the Spanish as a warehouse became a land office and a post office was established in January 1805. In recognition of St. Stephens having quickly become the population center of the Alabama portion of the Mississippi Territory, the territorial government created a new court district for Washington County in which it was located.[24]

In its heyday as the territorial capital, St. Stephens had over 500

---

[22] Brantley, *Three Capitals*, 24–25, 229; Joel C. Dubose, ed., *Notable Men of Alabama: Personal and Genealogical with Portraits*, vol. 1 (Atlanta, Ga.: Southern Historical Association, 1904), 395.

[23] Brantley, *Three Capitals*, 2–42; John Sledge, *St. Stephens Historical Overview*, The American Center for Artists, http://www.americanartists.org/art/article_st_stephens_historical_overview.htm (accessed June 22, 2010); Abernethy, *Formative Period*, 18, 50; Herbert J. Lewis, "Old St. Stephens," *Encyclopedia of Alabama*, http://www. encyclopediaofalabama .org/face/Article.jsp?id=h-1674 (accessed January 9, 2013); "History of Old St. Stephens," http://www.oldststephens.com/history_of_old_st_stephens.htm (accessed January 5, 2013); *Old St. Stephens: Historical Records Survey*, compiled by Jacqueline A. Matte, Doris Brown, and Barbara Waddell (St. Stephens Historical Commission, 1997).

[24] Lewis, "Old St. Stephens."

homes—nearly ten times than the number it had just three years before—and a population of several thousand. There were also approximately twenty stores and commercial establishments, including two hotels, lawyers' and doctors' offices, a theater, and the Tombeckbe Bank, Alabama's first chartered bank. The capital city attracted a number of prominent citizens, including Henry Hitchcock, the state's first attorney general and later a chief justice of the Alabama Supreme Court; Thomas Eastin, the publisher of *The Halcyon and Tombeckbe Advertiser*; Lewis Sewall, Alabama's first poet; Reuben S. Saffold, another chief justice of the Alabama Supreme Court; and Israel Pickens, a member of the state Constitutional Convention and the third governor of Alabama.[25]

On January 20, 1818, Governor Bibb delivered a written message to the members of the new territorial legislature, who had assembled in the Douglas Hotel in St. Stephens because government buildings had yet to be built in this frontier town. He congratulated the members on their first session and extolled the virtues of the new Territory as "ample in extent, abounding in navigable waters, and rich in the advantages of soil and climate. . . ." He predicted rapid development of the territory, stating that it would not be long before "the haunts of the savage will become the dwelling place of civilized man, and the forests of the wilderness be converted into fruitful fields." He then urged the legislature to direct its attention to education and internal improvements—such as roads, ferries, and bridges. Acknowledging that the new legislature might change boundaries of the existing counties by creating new ones, Bibb indicated that he would await their action before filling civil and military posts within the counties. He also informed the assembled delegates that he had deployed two companies of the territorial militia to Fort Crawford in Escambia County for a period of two months to participate in the defense of the southern frontier at the request of Maj. Gen. Edmund Pendelton Gaines, commander of the U.S. Army's southern military district. Another point of emphasis concerned the State of Mississippi's petition to Congress requesting an enlargement of that state by limiting the boundary of the Alabama Territory to the Tombigbee River. As far as Bibb was concerned it was indisputable that the boundary had already been established by competent authorities and that there were no just grounds to reverse what the inhabitants of Mississippi had previously agreed. Finally, the governor, with an eye toward justifying a petition for statehood, urged the delegates to pass during their present session an act authorizing a census to be taken prior to the next meeting of the General Assembly.[26]

The legislature quickly took action in response to the message from Governor Bibb. In its first session consisting of just twenty-four days in January and February of 1818, the legislature ambitiously enacted over fifty laws and resolutions designed to transition the new territory into a func-

---

[25] Ibid.

[26] *Journal of the Legislative Council of the Alabama Territory at the First Session of the General Assembly in the Forty-Third Year of American Independence* (St. Stephens: Thomas Eaton, 1818), 1–12.

tioning government ready for statehood. Many of these laws involved either the modification of existing county boundaries or the creation of entirely new counties. In all, the legislature created thirteen new counties, including Cotaco (renamed Morgan in 1821), Lawrence, Franklin, Limestone, Lauderdale, Blount, Tuscaloosa, Marengo, Shelby, Cahawba (renamed Bibb in 1820), Dallas, Marion, and Conecuh. The acts establishing these counties also required that a Superior Court of Law and Equity, a County Court, and an Intermediate Court meet for a specified number of sessions in each county and designated primarily private residences in each county as the temporary location for the sessions of these courts. Additionally, an act was passed dividing all of the territory's counties into three judicial districts, each to be served by an Attorney General, the equivalent of today's District Attorney.[27]

The territory's first legislature also focused on education and internal improvements as urged by Governor Bibb. With respect to education, the delegates chartered the St. Stephens Academy and authorized its trustees to raise four thousand dollars by way of a lottery, or lotteries (a method that present-day voters have refused to adopt). In an effort to improve transportation and to promote internal improvements in the new territory, the legislature chartered the St. Stephens Steam Boat Company, authorized the building of bridges over two creeks in Washington County, and appointed commissioners to select the most suitable and practicable routes for roads from the Falls of Tuscaloosa to the Tennessee River in the northern part of the territory and from the town of Blakeley to Fort Claiborne in the southern part of the territory. In other significant actions, the legislature provided for the regulation of judicial proceedings, gave the governor authority to organize the militia and to call it into service of the United States, authorized the taking of a census as requested by Governor Bibb, repealed the law against usury, chartered the Tombeckbe Bank at St. Stephens, chartered the towns of Blakeley and Rodney, granted two divorces, and authorized the emancipation of two slaves.[28]

Two of the laws passed in the territorial legislature's first session had a significant impact on the future course of politics in Alabama by further fueling the "popular" opposition to the Georgia faction, later derisively dubbed the "Royal Party" because of the privilege and power it represented.[29] As we have seen, yeoman farmers and frontiersmen had successfully challenged the wealthy Georgia planters as early as 1811 in reaction to perceived arrogance in their giving the future site of Huntsville the name of the estate of an English poet. As a result, two out of three of the Georgia

---

[27] *Acts Passed at the First Session of the First General Assembly of the Alabama Territory in the Forty-Second Year of American Independence* (St. Stephens: Thomas Easton, 1818), 8–21, 29–32, 47–48, 96–100 (hereafter *Ala. Acts,* 1 Sess., 1818).

[28] Ibid., 3–116.

[29] Ruth Ketring Nuermberger, "The 'Royal Party' in Early Alabama Politics," *Alabama Review* 6 (April and July 1953): 81–98, 198–212. According to Nuermberger, the Georgians were named by their opponents as "the 'Georgians,' 'Bank,' or 'Royal Party,'" and were condemned as "representing conservatism, wealth, tyranny and oppression."

faction's candidates for the Mississippi Territorial legislature were defeated and the town's name was changed to Huntsville. In the first session of the Alabama Territorial General Assembly, however, John W. Walker, one of those earlier defeated by the populists, now possessed tremendous influence which he used to win passage of two bills beneficial to his fellow Georgians' financial interests. One of these pertained to the Planters and Merchants Bank of Huntsville and the other repealed the laws against usury.[30]

The Planters and Merchants Bank had originally been known as the Planters and Mechanics Bank when it was created by the Mississippi Territorial legislature in 1816. There was much opposition to the bank when it opened in March 1817 with leadership being provided by Georgian Leroy Pope as its president. Notably, John W. Walker was one of the nine directors of the bank. More importantly than the renaming of the bank, the bill sponsored by Walker authorized the Alabama Territory to purchase two-thirds of the bank's stock. Oddly enough, Governor Bibb, exercising the first veto in Alabama legislative history, did not lend his support to the financial interests of his fellow Georgians. Bibb's veto message instead expressed fear that the territory would not have sufficient control over the bank and would be forced to accept the bank's notes at face value for all obligations due it. He also frowned upon giving power to a private bank to decide where to open branches throughout the territory. Despite these arguments, Walker nevertheless secured the passage of a very similar bill over the governor's veto.[31]

Just as offensive to the popular party was the repeal of the Mississippi Territorial Act against usury. Enacted to limit the interest rate that could be charged on loans, the law had the unfortunate effect of making it extremely difficult to borrow money even during the then robust economy. As a result, legislation was introduced by Abner S. Lipscomb of Washington County, allowing individuals to charge an unlimited rate of interest with the proviso that such interest rate agreement be reduced to writing. Walker used his influence to steer the measure through the Ways and Means Committee and aided in its ultimate passage by the legislature. Despite provisions setting a ceiling of six per cent on bank loans and discounts and eight per cent on personal loans where no interest rate was specified in the note, the popular party, or "Champions of the People," viewed the act as hostile to debtors and providing too much protection to the moneyed interests. The unpopularity of the amendment to the usury law increased with the onset of the Panic of 1819, America's first great economic crisis, so much so that the first legislature of the new State of Alabama repealed it.[32]

The Planters and Merchants Bank of Huntsville fared no better in the long run. It withstood accusations of deceitfulness and abuse of the lower classes in favor of the rich until eventually forced to close its doors in 1825

---

[30] Bailey, *John Williams Walker*, 83–86.

[31] Ibid.

[32] Bailey, *John Williams Walker*, 83–86; Nuermberger, "Royal Party," 84–95.

as a result of its inability to resume specie payment after a period of suspension. Although the Georgians bore the brunt of the criticism voiced against these two unpopular measures, Representative Walker managed to avert significant criticism due to the fact that he was highly regarded by his colleagues, as well as the electorate. In fact, Madison County rewarded Walker by sending him back to the second session of the Territorial General Assembly.[33]

The General Assembly's second session in November 1818 was its last before Alabama became a state. Early in that session, the Assembly was shaken when Mary Parham Moore, the wife of the Assembly's first Speaker of the House, Gabriel Moore, petitioned it for a divorce as well as for permission to revert to her maiden name, Mary Parham Caller. Her petition for divorce followed a marriage doomed from the outset as a result of meddling by Mary's father, militia colonel James Caller of Washington County, who had encouraged the union with the hopes of uniting his family—politically influential in the southern part of the territory—with that of an emerging prominent politician residing in the northern portion of the territory. But the marriage quickly failed, due to the fact that Mary evidently had only married Moore to satisfy her father's wishes even though she was in love with someone else. The circumstances of Alabama's first highly publicized divorce caused Gabriel Moore to temporarily withdraw from politics. Adding to his troubles, Moore later engaged in a duel with his ex-wife's brother, fortunately resulting in no serious injuries to either man. Neither the divorce nor the duel, however, put a permanent end to Moore's political career. Far from it: Moore subsequently served as a representative to the 1819 constitutional convention, in the state Senate in 1819 and 1820, in the United States Congress from 1821 to 1829, as Alabama's fifth governor from 1829 until 1831, and in the United States Senate from 1831 to 1836. Nevertheless, the interruption in Moore's career due to the notoriety of his divorce opened the way for John W. Walker to succeed Moore as the Speaker of the House.[34]

In his role as Speaker, Walker was relieved of committee assignments, giving him more time to focus on securing statehood for Alabama. Anticipating a qualifying population very soon, on November 10, 1818, the houses of the second General Assembly passed a joint memorial formally petitioning Congress for statehood. Speaker Walker immediately sent the petition to Senator Tait of Georgia so he could begin the process to pass an Enabling Act for the proposed State of Alabama. Meanwhile, the General Assembly managed to create two new counties (Autauga and St. Clair), incorporate two new towns (Mooresville and Athens), charter a bank in Mobile, allow existing banks in Huntsville and St. Stephens to increase their capital stock, and impose a license fee on "hawkers and pedlars." In addition to the high

---

[33] Bailey, *John Williams Walker*, 85–86.

[34] *Acts Passed at the Second Session of the First General Assembly of the Alabama Territory in the Forty-Third Year of American Independence* (St. Stephens: Thomas Easton, 1818), 10 (hereafter *Ala. Acts (2 Sess. 1818)*); Harriet Amos Doss, "Rise and Fall of an Alabama Founding Father," *Alabama Review* 52 (July 2000): 163–71.

profile divorce of one of its own former members, the Assembly granted four additional divorces and one slave manumission.[35]

Perhaps the most important action taken by the territorial Assembly in its second and final session was its apportionment of representation based upon the census authorized in the Assembly's first session. This had become a burning issue because it was known that Congress would use the results of their apportionment to allocate representation in the upcoming constitutional convention. As a result, a power struggle developed between the northern and southern counties as to how to apportion the legislature. The northern counties, led by Madison County, pushed for counting white population only, which would give it, double the representation of the next most populous county. The southern counties fought back by attempting to place a limit as to the number of representatives any one county could have. The representatives of the southern counties only backed off this attempt when a rider was added to the apportionment bill designating Cahaba, located at the confluence of the Cahaba and Alabama rivers in Dallas County, as the capital of the territory. In exchange, however, the northern representatives were successful in having Huntsville selected as temporary site of the capital until the town of Cahaba could be laid out.[36]

The action of the territorial Assembly with respect to Cahaba came about as the result of Governor Bibb outmaneuvering the commission appointed by the Assembly's first session to make recommendations concerning the location of a permanent seat of government. The commissioners who had been chosen for this important task were Clement C. Clay, Samuel Taylor, Samuel Dale, James Titus, and William L. Adams. Specifically, the commission had been tasked to recommend "the most eligible site for the Territorial Government, as near the center of the Territory as may be, having due regard to commercial advantages, and the nature and situation of the country. . . ." According to William H. Brantley's extensive coverage of this issue in his history of Alabama's first three capitals, two major factions lobbied the commission to recommend a site in their part of the state—the Alabama/Cahaba River basin group and the Warrior/Tombigbee system group. Because of its distance from the geographic center of the territory, the Tennessee Valley section, the territory's most populous area, did not itself compete for the capital site, but instead lent its powerful political support to the Warrior/Tombigbee group. As a result, Tuscaloosa, located on the banks of the Black Warrior River, was the commission's choice for the permanent seat of government.[37]

In the interim, however, Governor Bibb had become a strong proponent

---

[35] *Ala. Acts* (*2 Sess. 1818*), 6–7, 10–11, 12–13, 16–17, 19–21, 22–32, 33–34, 40–42, 50–52, and 56–57; *Journal of the House of Representatives of the Alabama Territory at the Second Session of the First General Assembly in the Forty-Third Year of American Independence* (St. Stephens: Thomas Easton, 1818), 38.

[36] Bailey, *John Williams Walker*, 88; McMillan, *Constitutional Development in Alabama*, 25–26; Moore, *History of Alabama*, 98–99.

[37] *Ala. Acts* (*1 Sess. 1818*), 94–95; Bailey, *John Williams Walker*, 88–91; Brantley, *Three Capitals*, 27, 31–39; Sam Earle Hobbs, "History of Early Cahaba, Alabama's First State Capital," *Alabama Historical Quarterly* 31 (Fall and Winter 1969): 155–63.

of the Alabama–Cahaba basin due to the purchase of land within its confines by fellow Georgians. Bibb himself had purchased a plantation abutting the Alabama River near Coosada in what was then Autauga County. Anticipating that the commission was stacked in favor of the Warrior/Tombigbee group, Bibb began an end run around the commission using his connections with Secretary Crawford and Senator Tait to obtain passage of an act whereby the federal government granted a free section of land for use as the territory's seat of government and gave the governor the prerogative to select the site for such purpose. Bibb's decision to choose a site at the confluence of the Alabama and Cahaba rivers in contravention of the commission's report was not made known until he addressed the second session of the General Assembly in November 1818.

With this surprise announcement, Bibb was able to ram through the Assembly the rider to the apportionment bill to establish Cahaba as the permanent capital instead of the commission's choice of Tuscaloosa. Brantley's study of the issue led him to conclude that the two most important weapons in Bibb's arsenal to win approval for the Cahaba site was the state's empty coffers that made free land very enticing and the veto power held by Bibb over the apportionment bill desired by north Alabamians. Also, while most of those in the north supported Tuscaloosa, Speaker of the House Walker and his followers reluctantly supported Cahaba due to his friendship with Bibb. Walker nevertheless voiced his displeasure at the high handed manner in which Bibb had handled the matter. Although Governor Bibb had won the day, the issue would resurface again in a few years with the Tuscaloosa supporters gaining the upper hand.[38]

The General Assembly appointed Bibb as commissioner with the authorization to lay out the town of Cahaba in any manner deemed suitable by him. He was then to survey the lots and sell them to the highest bidders after giving a minimum notice to potential buyers through advertisements in all newspapers published within the territory, as well as those newspapers in other states considered appropriate by Bibb. From the proceeds of the sale of these lots, in an amount not to exceed ten thousand dollars, the governor was authorized to contract for the construction of "a building suitable for the temporary accommodation of the General Assembly of the territory or [anticipated] state."[39]

While Governor Bibb was very adept at the governance of the territory, he was also fortunate to be supported by Secretary of State, Henry Hitchcock. A native of Burlington, Vermont, Hitchcock was the grandson of General Ethan Allen, Revolutionary War folk hero and leader of the famed Green Mountain Boys. Hitchcock immigrated to Mobile by way of Natchez in January 1817. Previously admitted to the bar of Vermont in 1815, Hitchcock became one of Alabama's first lawyers. To take advantage of the opportunities presented for attorneys in the new territory, Hitchcock moved from Mobile to the territorial capital of St. Stephens in August 1817.

---

[38]Bailey, *John Williams Walker*, 88–91; Brantley, *Three* Capitals, 27, 31–39; Sam Earle Hobbs, "History of Early Cahaba," 155–63.

[39] *Ala. Acts (2 Sess. 1818)*, 46–49.

There he opened a law office with William Crawford (not to be confused with U.S. Secretary of the Treasury William H. Crawford) who was also then serving as the territory's United States district attorney. Based upon the recommendation of the politically influential Secretary Crawford, President James Madison appointed Hitchcock as Secretary of State of the Alabama Territory in April of 1818. This position paid $1,200 per year and required Hitchcock to serve as acting governor in the absence of Bibb. In the summer of 1818, Hitchcock assumed the duties of governor when Bibb temporarily left the area at a time when trouble was brewing among neighboring Creeks and Seminoles. Hitchcock then enlisted the territorial militia to keep the peace along Alabama's eastern border with the Creeks. As acting governor, Hitchcock was also able to dispense some political patronage when he filled a number of county offices in the governor's absence.[40]

Both Hitchcock and Bibb were faced with the problem of finding the right persons to help them bring order to the Alabama frontier. The need for law enforcement and military officers was critical and it was difficult to keep these positions filled. For example, Henry W. Stevens, a justice of the peace and of the quorum in Cahawba County (now known as Bibb County) addressed the pressing need for law enforcement officers in his county in a letter dated October 27, 1818, to Governor Bibb. Stevens had migrated to Alabama in 1814 from Connecticut where he had graduated from Litchfield Law School in 1811. In his letter to the governor, Stevens expressed concern that "William W. Capshaw is not yet recommissioned as a Justice of the Peace—which leaves our part of the country in the same situation as when I last saw you, one Justice only and him a sot of a Dutchman, altho' we have half the population of the county." Stevens complained further that "our Military company has no other officer than Captain." Thomas C. Hunter of Tuscaloosa County similarly urged the governor to appoint military officers for his county as soon as possible because of "our frontier situation and the hostility of neighbouring Indians." A letter dated April 16, 1818, to Governor Bibb from William Johnston, the justice of the quorum of Blount County, provides an example of the difficulty of retaining competent judicial officers. Johnston sought to give up his judgeship in exchange for a military position, lamenting that he had only accepted the judgeship "in abrupt that we might have law among [us] as early as practicable," noting that "civil offices are not "conguneal [sic] with the bent of my inclination."[41]

While Alabama's territorial officers were grappling with the basics of establishing a government and trying to bring order to their frontier society, the territory's population had continued to grow at a rapid pace causing land booms in several areas. The Tennessee Valley led the way with seven

---

[40] William H. Brantley, Jr., "Henry Hitchcock of Mobile: 1816–1839," *Alabama Review* 5 (January 1952): 4–6; Bigham, "From the Green Mountains," 209–22.

[41] Lewis, "A Connecticut Yankee in Early Alabama," 94; Henry W. Stevens to Gov. William Wyatt Bibb, October 27, 1818, in Carter, *Territorial Papers of the United States*, 2:446–47; Thomas C. Hunter to Gov. William Wyatt Bibb, March 29, 1818 and William Johnston to Gov. William Wyatt Bibb, April 16, 1818, Records of Gov. William Wyatt Bibb concerning Appointments, Commissions, and Resignations, 1817–1819, SG24709, reel 22, Alabama Department of Archives and History (ADAH), Montgomery, Alabama.

million dollars' worth of land being sold west of Madison County on both sides of the Tennessee River in 1818. Land companies quickly sprang up to compete for the business of settlers and speculators who began flocking to the area from all over the country to purchase these newly opened lands. Land sales were particularly lucrative at this time as evidenced by land purchased in 1809 at two dollars per acre selling from ten to twenty dollars an acre. These prices quickly caught the eyes of investors, both within the territory and without, who formed the influential Cypress Land Company. James Jackson and John Coffee, protégés of Gen. Andrew Jackson from Tennessee, were the principal organizers of this powerful company whose most prominent investors included General Jackson, Thomas Bibb, Leroy Pope, and John McKinley. James Jackson, although no kin to the General, had been his business agent, and Coffee, who was married to a niece of the General's wife, had ably served as the leader of General Jackson's cavalry in the Creek War and later commanded the defense of Jackson's left flank during the Battle of New Orleans. In 1817, Coffee received appointments as surveyor of the Creek boundary lines, as well as for the lands in the northern part of the Mississippi Territory, including the Tennessee Valley. These appointments were bestowed upon Coffee primarily due to the efforts of Huntsville's John W. Walker with whom Coffee had forged a friendship when he and Jackson visited Walker on their way south to engage the Creeks.[42]

Under Coffee's leadership the Cypress Land Company was successful in obtaining a tract of land consisting of 5,515 acres at the foot of Muscle Shoals for $85,235.24. This desirable tract was located on the north bank of the Tennessee River at the head of clear navigation and became the site of the town of Florence. Ferdinand Sannoner, a young Italian engineer who had served with Napoleon as a surveyor, laid out the new town under Coffee's supervision and was allowed to name it Florence in honor of the city of that same name previously surveyed by him in his native Italy. With this European influence, the town's lots, unlike other frontier settlements, were laid out amongst wide boulevards and a public park. These lots were offered for sale on July 22, 1818, and after only several days on the market brought in $223,580. The new town's rapid development led Coffee to move the federal land office from Huntsville to Florence in 1823, and, in the absence of modern-day ethical standards, the Cypress Land Company was given office space in the new land office.[43]

Similarly, an absence of ethical standards had allowed nationally prominent public men such as future president Andrew Jackson, joined by those locally influential such as Thomas Bibb, Leroy Pope, and John McKinley, to openly take part in land speculation schemes as evidenced by their invest-

---

[42] Moore, *History of Alabama*, 81–83; Thomas Perkins Abernethy, *From Frontier to Plantation in Tennessee—A Study in Frontier Democracy* (Chapel Hill: University of North Carolina Press, 1932), 271–72; Bailey, *John Williams Walker*, 76–77.

[43] William Lindsey McDonald, *A Walk Through the Past: People and Places of Florence and Lauderdale County, Alabama* (Florence, Ala.: Bluewater Publications, 2003), 17–19; Moore, *History of Alabama*, 84–85.

ment in the Cypress Land Company. The returns from their investments were sometimes very profitable, often unapologetically simply due to their office or station in life. As an example, General Jackson owned a few shares of stock in the Cypress Land Company's Florence venture and purchased some cotton land from the company at two dollars per acre as opposed to the going rate of eighty dollars per acre. Other bidders, understanding Jackson's prominence, remained silent and did not bid against him thereby allowing the General to acquire valuable cotton lands located at the head of the Elk River shoals in present-day Lawrence County, at rock-bottom prices. Now, in addition to the Hermitage near Nashville, Jackson, with the aid of an overseer and over sixty slaves, operated a full scale cotton plantation at Melton's Bluff near Florence next to that of his good friend John Coffee. Jackson had other interests in Alabama during that time that brought him there regularly. In addition to visiting the plantation that he had set up for an orphan of a business partner, he would also quite often stop at the Old Green Bottom Inn in Huntsville where he reportedly brought his horses to race and his cocks to fight. These early business connections would benefit Jackson politically within the state when he later sought national office.[44]

Another land boom further to the south, somewhat more modest in scope, was occurring about the same time as that in the Tennessee Valley. In 1817 and 1818, valuable lands abutting the Alabama River in present-day Montgomery County were offered for sale by the U.S. land office at Milledgeville, Georgia. Total land sales from this offering totaled almost two million dollars. Two groups of speculators succeeded in acquiring the most lucrative portions of this tract located in the bend of the Alabama River that soon would become the city of Montgomery. Early white traders had discovered a convenient landing spot on the river at the foot of what was known to local Indians as Chunnanugga Chatty or "high red bluff." Two villages of the Alibamu tribe—Towasa and Ikantchati—once were located at the top this buff, which was the hub of many well-worn trails crisscrossing the region. By the middle of the eighteenth century the British took advantage of the location's benefits by making it the center of their trade with the Alibamu. The Alibamu maintained their villages at the site until they were forced out when the Creeks surrendered to Andrew Jackson at Fort Jackson in 1814. The area was ready for extensive white settlement after the Mississippi territorial legislature created Montgomery County in 1816.[45]

Two groups of investors purchased the lands surrounding Chunnanugga Chatty when they were put up for sale in August 1818. Thomas Bibb, Alabama's second governor, was a member of a group of wealthy Georgians, including Major General John Baytop Scott and Dr. Charles Williamson, who established the Town of Alabama out of the lands they

[44] Moore, *History of Alabama*, 82–83; Marquis James, *The Life of Andrew Jackson* (New York: Bobbs Merrill Company, 1938), 277, 306, 336, 348–349, and 450; Betts, *Early History of Huntsville*, 33.

[45] Clanton W. Williams, "Early Antebellum Montgomery: A Black Belt Constituency," *The Journal of Southern History* (November 1941): 495–97.

purchased located in the west end section of the current city of Montgomery. Rival northern investors led by Andrew Dexter, a member of the bar of
Massachusetts, and John Falconer, a businessman from Delaware, purchased land east of Court Street and established a rival town called Philadelphia. With the establishment of Philadelphia, referred to by some as
"Yankee Town," the Georgia group deserted the Town of Alabama and
established a new town called East Alabama to compete with nearby Philadelphia. These groups bitterly battled each other before finally agreeing to
consolidate the two towns. On December 3, 1819, the consolidated group
won approval from the legislature for the incorporation of the city of Montgomery, just eleven days before Alabama became a state. At the time of its
incorporation, Montgomery, named for Revolutionary War hero General
Richard Montgomery, had only 401 persons, approximately forty per cent
of which were slaves. The new town consisted of only five two-story and
twenty-one one-story frame houses, as well as thirty-eight log cabins. In
less than three decades, however, Montgomery would become Alabama's
fifth capital.[46]

Just a few days after Montgomery's incorporation, the legislature authorized the incorporation of Tuscaloosa on December 13, 1819. Tuscaloosa,
named for chief Tascaluza who had fought against Hernando de Soto, was
established at the fall line of the Black Warrior River which had been the
home of various Native American tribes dating back to as early as 1580.
Like Montgomery, old Indian trails converged upon the site where Tuscaloosa was to be located. In 1816, Thomas York was the first white settler to
arrive in the area, and by 1817 the old "Black Warrior Village" consisted of
200 people. As other settlers began to arrive via the Indian trails, Tuscaloosa's population expanded briskly over the next three years. In 1820, the
population for Tuscaloosa and the county consisted of 5,894 whites and
2,335 slaves. In 1826, the capital was relocated from Cahaba to Tuscaloosa
where it remained until being moved a final time to Montgomery in 1846.[47]

As Montgomery and Tuscaloosa emerged, the older cities of Huntsville
and Mobile became more established. In 1816, a brick courthouse was
completed in Huntsville and stood in the center of a city square bordered by
a market house, the Planters and Merchants Bank, a wooden jail, approximately twelve brick stores, and several lawyers' offices. In 1818, there were
estimated to be 260 houses, most of which were brick. By 1820, Huntsville's population consisted of 732 whites, 570 slaves, and 22 free blacks. In
1812, the year before Mobile was seized from Spain by the United States, an
early resident reported that there were only 90 residences in Mobile, all
wooden structures. At that time the population was declining, with its
citizens only numbering approximately 500 (about half of which were

[46] Moore, *History of Alabama*, 81–82; Clanton W. Williams, "Conservatism in Old Mont-
gomery, 1817–1861," *Alabama Review* 10 (April 1957): 96–97; Williams, *The Early History of
Montgomery* 27–47; Harvey H. Jackson III, *Rivers of History: Life on the Coosa, Tallapoosa,
Cahaba, and Alabama* (Tuscaloosa: University of Alabama Press, 1995), 49–50.

[47] Thomas P. Clinton, "Early History of Tuscaloosa," *Alabama Historical Quarterly* 1
(Summer 1930): 174; Herbert J. Lewis, "Tuscaloosa," *Encyclopedia of Alabama*, http://www.
encyclopediaofalabama.org/face/Article.jsp?id=h-1654 (accessed January 4, 2013).

slaves), down from 810 persons in 1803. A decade later, however, the population increased fivefold to 2,672. The *Mobile Register* reported that by 1822, Mobile consisted of "240 dwellings, 110 stores and warehouses, one Catholic and one Protestant Church, two Seminaries, two printing offices," a post office, a customs house, a bank, and three hotels.[48]

Mobile competed for a while with the nearby town of Blakeley to become Alabama's predominant seaport. Located across Mobile Bay and approximately six miles up the Tensaw River, Blakeley was founded by Josiah Blakeley who had emigrated from Connecticut. Originally chartered by the Mississippi Territorial legislature in 1814, Blakeley flourished temporarily as a separate port of entry and also served as the county seat for Baldwin County. At its zenith, Blakeley's population approached 4,000 and the town underwent a building boom, which adorned it with hotels, churches, stores, and Baldwin County's first courthouse. The *Blakeley Sun* became one of Alabama's first newspapers. By the mid-1820s, however, Blakeley quickly began to fade as a serious competitor with Mobile due to land speculation which drove its merchants to the lower prices across the bay. The town slowly deteriorated, but was temporarily resurrected during the Civil War to serve as home to the Confederacy's Fort Blakeley, which would be the scene of the last major battle of the war.[49]

Another settlement begun prior to statehood quickly captured the attention not only of the territory's local inhabitants, but that of the nation as well. Having international ramifications, the Vine and Olive Colony located in present-day Marengo County was created by an act of Congress at the request of a group of exiles who had fled a bloody slave insurrection in the French colony of Saint-Domingue (modern Haiti). They were joined by a much smaller group of French military veterans who had served with the recently deposed Napoleon. The act, which became law on March 3, 1817, conveyed to these emigrés four entire townships consisting of 144 square miles near the confluence of the Tombigbee and Black Warrior rivers. In return, the French colonists were to cultivate the donated lands with grape vines and olive trees, presumably with the hopes of making America competitive in the wine industry. Congress, many members of which were very sympathetic to the French exiles who they viewed as fellow Republicans, was very generous in its terms, allowing colonists fourteen years to begin cultivation of the grapes and olives and to begin payment on their land at a very favorable price of $2.00 per acre.[50]

Most of these expatriates had congregated in Philadelphia where they formed a society to receive the donated lands. The company, which consist-

---

[48] Dupre, *Transforming the Cotton Frontier*, 38; Charles Grayson Summersell, *Mobile: History of a Seaport Town* (Tuscaloosa, Ala.: University of Alabama Press, 1949), 10–12.

[49] James C. Parker, "Blakeley: A Frontier Seaport," *Alabama Review* 27 (January 1974): 39–51; "History: The Town of Blakeley," http://www.blakeleypark.com/history.asp (accessed January 8, 2013).

[50] Gaius Whitfield, Jr., "The French Grant in Alabama," *Transactions of the Alabama Historical Society* 4 (1899–1903): 325–38; O.B. Emerson, "The Bonapartist Exiles In Alabama," *Alabama Review* 11 (April 1958): 135–36.

ed of approximately 347 associates, was named the Colonial Society (later renamed the Society for the Cultivation of the Vine and Olive). The president of the society was General Count Lefebvre-Desnouettes, a former aide to Napoleon. In April 1817, an advance party of this group set sail for Mobile on the schooner *Macdonough*, reaching Mobile Bay three weeks later. After a brief stop in Mobile, Addin Lewis, customs agent for the Port of Mobile, sent the French colonists on their way up river on a loaned United States revenue cutter. They then made stops at Fort Stoddert, Fort Montgomery, and St. Stephens before taking a barge for their destination much further up river at White Bluff (*Ecor Blanc*).[51]

In 1817 members of the society commenced the colony by building cabins at a town they named Demopolis—meaning "City of the People." According to earlier histories, these cabins were occupied primarily by aristocratic Napoleonic officers and their stylish ladies. These accounts painted a picture of inept aristocrats tackling an unrelenting Alabama wilderness and failing to succeed in cultivating the promised grapes and olives. For example, Anne Bozeman Lyon romantically chronicled that these aristocrats did not even have good judgment as how to dress for the enormous tasks before them, reporting that "the women milked and sowed corn in the velvet gowns and satin slippers they had danced in at court balls; the men ploughed and dug and sawed wood in their finest military clothes." She also depicted their crude wooden cabins being adorned with fine paintings, china, glassware, books, and musical instruments.[52]

Quite a different view of this enterprise was set forth recently by historian Rafe Blaufarb who examined in detail the formation and operation of the Vine and Olive Colony and placed it in a much broader historical context. Contrary to the popular earlier accounts that portrayed the colonists as members of the French aristocracy who were not cut out to cultivate the required grapes and olives, Blaufarb maintains that the majority of the colonists were middle class refugees from the slave rebellion in Saint-Domingue. He further notes that most of the military officers settling in the colony were not aristocrats, but rather were lower ranking officers who had been born in "modest circumstances." Also, only one so-called "aristocrat," General Count Charles Lefebvre-Desnouettes, ever settled in the colony. He further emphasizes that many of the Saint-Domingue refugees were successful at adapting to the soil of the area by diverting their attention from the vine and the olive to planting cotton.[53]

---

[51] Emerson, "The Bonapartist Exiles," 137–78; Anne Bozeman Lyon, "The Bonapartists in Alabama," *Alabama Historical Quarterly* 25 (1963): 227–32.

[52] Lyon, "The Bonapartists in Alabama," 233. See also Pickett, *Alabama*, 622–33, and Abernethy, *Formative Period*, 51, for traditionalist recounts of the Vine and Olive Colony.

[53] Rafe Blaufarb, *Bonapartists in the Borderlands: French Exiles and Refugees on the Gulf Coast, 1815–1835* (Tuscaloosa: University of Alabama Press, 2005), xi–xiv; Rafe Blaufarb, "Alabama's Vine and Olive Colony," *Alabama Heritage*, no. 81 (Summer 2006): 26–34. Lefebvre-Desnouettes was a lieutenant general and an aide-de-camp to Napoleon. He served with distinction against the Austrians in the Battle of Marengo, for which Marengo County was named. He was hardly from aristocratic origins as he was the son of a cloth merchant. His noble title was bestowed upon him by Napoleon as part of an attempt to set up a hereditary class supporting his reign.

Ironically, most of the French grantees never settled in the colony at all, instead many selling their allotments to a group of French speculators for $1.00 an acre. This was part and parcel of a scheme hatched by General Charles Lallemand, who succeeded Lefebvre-Desnouettes as president of the Colonial Society, to fund a mission to colonize Texas, whose possession was disputed at the time by the United States and Spain. Lallemand succeeded in convincing sixty of his loyalists to sell their lands, resulting in the merchants acquiring over 11,000 acres of land. Many of these merchants sold their lands for significant profits, but at least some actually settled in the Colony and became prominent residents. By January 1818, however, there were only sixty-nine settlers inhabiting the Colony. In all, only 150 or so of the original grantees ever even visited the Colony, much less settled there.[54]

Lallemand's scheme fueled the fires of those who had already begun to complain that the Vine and Olive Colony was an unfair privilege bestowed upon foreigners at the expense of yeoman settlers in the Alabama Territory. One irate citizen of the territory wrote the editor of the *Huntsville Republican* on October 28, 1817, complaining of the "special and peculiar privileges" bestowed on these "foreign capitalists of immense wealth" by Congress. This same detractor followed up with another letter to the *Alabama Republican*, appearing in its April 4, 1818, edition outlining in detail the excessive advantages that Congress had given away by granting to the colonists 92,000 acres of "the choicest selections," worth in excess of $1 million. Even more damaging was the fact that the site they chose was the best location for a town on the Tombigbee waterway. He concluded by predicting that the French would fail to live up to the agricultural conditions of the grant, but would nevertheless benefit by selling their land to Americans "at an incredible price." Just a few months later, the influential *Niles' Weekly Register* echoed the Alabama critic, calling the colony one of the most "splendid fooleries" ever perpetuated on the American public. Niles further voiced concern that a colony of foreigners who introduced "manners and prejudices . . . repugnant to our rules and notions of right" threatened the "national character" of the United States.[55]

Despite this growing criticism, the colony continued to develop. But those who had initially settled in Demopolis were soon disrupted when it was discovered from a survey that the newly created town itself lay outside of the lands granted to them. The Demopolis colonists were thus forced to pull up stakes and move approximately five miles further to the northeast where they laid out a new town on French Creek named Aigleville— meaning Eagle City. Later a second town was laid out just across the creek when it was discovered that Aigleville was also outside the boundaries of the grant. Other colonists relocated instead to settlements such as Linden and Greensboro, where they took their slaves to cultivate cotton rather than

---

[54] Blaufarb, "Alabama's Vine and Olive Colony," 30–32; see also Rafe Blaufarb, "Vine and Olive Colony," *Encyclopedia of Alabama*, http://www.encyclopediaofalabama.org/face/Article.jsp?id=h-1539 (accessed January 8, 2013).

[55] Blaufarb, *Bonapartists in the Borderlands*, 50–51.

grapes and olives. Others left the area entirely to unite with French compatriots who had preceded them to Mobile and New Orleans.[56]

While the Vine and Olive Colony ultimately did not succeed in producing the objects of its charter, the General Assembly of the Alabama Territory nevertheless created Marengo County by an act passed on February 6, 1818, in anticipation of more settlers coming into the colony. Those Saint-Domingue refugees who remained in the area took advantage of the area's rich soil to contribute to the cotton production of the emerging Black Belt of Alabama. According to Blaufarb, of more significance was the fact that the colony fulfilled a Congressional desire to bring settlers into the borderlands of Alabama to act as a barrier against Spanish inspired attacks perpetrated by Indians and runaway slaves emanating from Spanish-held Florida. The colony also was considered to be instrumental in helping to ensure that the interior of the country would continue to have access to the Gulf of Mexico even in the advent of another war with Great Britain.[57]

Meanwhile, the territory's land booms and increasing population had ensured Alabama's admission into the Union. In January 1819, a copy of Senator Tait's proposed Enabling Act for Alabama's entry into the Union was received by his Georgia brethren in Alabama who were generally pleased with its provisions. One favorable provision reserved seventy-two sections of land, or two entire townships, for the purpose of financing "a seminary of learning," or state university, while another reserved the sixteenth section of each township for the use of public schools. Additionally, the new state was granted all of the salt springs within its borders; and five per cent of the net proceeds of the sale of lands by the United States within the new state were reserved for the construction of public roads and canals, as well as for the improvement of the navigation of rivers. The state was also granted 1,620 acres of land for the location of its permanent seat of government at the junction of the Cahaba and Alabama rivers. Another particularly favorable provision left Alabama's western boundary intact, giving it most of the Tombigbee River to the chagrin of neighboring Mississippians. Governor Bibb would have preferred to eliminate the Enabling Act's provision requiring minimal residence requirements—albeit only

---

[56] Emerson, "Bonapartist Exiles," 140.

[57] Blaufarb, *Bonapartists in the Borderlands*, 49–55. In a recent extensive study of the Vine and Olive Colony, French author Eric Saugera rejects Blaufarb's theory that the United States was using the colony for internal security purposes. He likewise rejects the theory that the French were using the colony as a base from which to hopefully establish a Bonapartist Empire in the western hemisphere, possibly in Mexico with Napoleon at the helm. Instead Saugera posits that America granted a colony to the French because of "the country's natural duty of hospitality and its solicitude for exiles touched with Napoleonic radiance" and also because of its hopes for "the development of new crops profitable to the national economy." Sauguera argues that the two countries "committed to each other in an equitable exchange: work in exchange for land and the promise of riches to be shared." Saugera, *Reborn in America: French Exiles and Refugees in the United States and the Vine and Olive Colony Adventure, 1815–1865* (Tuscaloosa: University of Alabama Press, 2011), 165–74.

three months—for voters of delegates to the upcoming Constitutional Convention.[58]

The most important provision of the enabling act authorized the inhabitants of the Alabama Territory "to form for themselves a constitution and State government, and to assume such name as they may deem proper; and that the said territory, when formed into a state, shall be admitted into the Union, upon the same footing with the original states, in all respects whatsoever." Further, all white male citizens twenty-one years of age or older who had resided in the Territory for at least three months and who were otherwise eligible to vote for representatives in the General Assembly were made eligible to "choose delegates to form a constitution." The number of delegates was apportioned among the territory's twenty-two counties, with Madison County leading with eight; Monroe County was allocated four; Blount and Limestone counties were allocated three; and the remainder was allocated either one or two. The election of delegates was to take place on the first Monday and Tuesday of May 1819. The delegates so elected were then directed to convene in Huntsville on the first Monday in July 1819.[59]

When Alabama's Enabling Act became law on March 2, 1819, the stage was finally set for Alabama to become a state once a constitution was adopted by a duly elected convention and submitted to Congress for approval. Yet just one month before delegates were to convene in Huntsville to create a state government, excitement surrounding the upcoming convention was briefly overshadowed by President James Monroe's unexpected arrival in Huntsville on June 1, 1819. The unannounced visit was part of a tour of the South made by the president to examine southern military fortifications, to view possible sites for future defensive posts, to gauge improvements in agricultural and manufacturing pursuits, and to examine the condition of Indian tribes in the area. As soon as the president's presence in the city was known, local citizens quickly formed a committee led by Clement Comer Clay to invite him to a public dinner in his honor. The invitation delivered by Clay was accepted, and on June 2, 1819, at 4:00 p.m. approximately one hundred of the leading citizens of Huntsville assembled to pay tribute to President Monroe. Col. Leroy Pope served as president of the dinner, assisted by Clay and Henry Minor as vice presidents. During the course of the dinner over twenty toasts were made by various participants, including toasts to the country, the Constitution, the memory of George Washington, the heroes of the American Revolution, President Monroe, the victory at the Battle of New Orleans, Maj. Gen. Andrew Jackson, Gen. John Coffee, the Armed Forces of the United States,

---

[58] Bailey, *John Williams Walker*, 91–92; "An Act to Enable the People of the Alabama Territory to Form a Constitution and State Government," 1819, 3 *Stat.* 489–492 (hereinafter "Enabling Act"). It is also found at http://www.legislature.state.al.us/misc/history/constitutions/1819/1819enablinginst.html (accessed February 4, 2013). A territory with a minimum of 65,000 free inhabitants was entitled to admission to the Union. One with less than 65,000 could be admitted when "deemed consistent with the general interest of the confederacy." Art. 5, Northwest Ordinance.

[59] Enabling Act, §§ 1, 4, and 5.

and Thomas Jefferson, among others. Perhaps the most fitting toast in view of what was about to happen in Huntsville was the one from President Monroe to the Territory of Alabama — "May her speedy admission into the Union advance her happiness, and augment the national strength and prosperity."[60]

With the departure of President Monroe from Huntsville, the citizens of the Territory turned their attention back to the Constitutional Convention which was set to convene in Huntsville on July 5, 1819, for the distinctive purpose of creating the young nation's twenty-second state.

---

[60] Thomas McAdory Owen, ed., "The Visit of President James Monroe to Alabama Territory, June 1, 1819," *Transactions of the Alabama Historical Society* 3 (1898–99): 128–30 (based upon article published in the St. Stephens *Halcyon*, June 28, 1819, reprinted from the *Alabama Republican*, Saturday, June 5, 1819).

Governor Bibb Addressing the Constitutional Convention
Huntsville, 1819

Courtesy of Alabama Department of Archives and History

6

CONSTITUTIONAL CONVENTION OF 1819

Clement Comer Clay
Delegate, and later Governor and U.S. Senator

On July 5, 1819—forty-three years and one day after the signing of the Declaration of Independence, thirty-one years after the adoption of the United States Constitution, twenty years after the creation of the Mississippi Territory, and less than a year and a half after the emergence of territorial Alabama from the Mississippi Territory—the convention to bring Alabama into the Union as a state assembled in Huntsville for its historic function. Forty-four delegates had been elected to represent their respective counties in adopting a constitution for the new state. In most counties there had not been much of a contest for these delegate positions as there was usually an informal consensus amongst the electorate to give their support to the counties' most prominent citizen or citizens, more often than not well-educated and politically experienced. However, there were more spirited elections for delegates in the counties of the Tennessee Valley. Madison County led the way with twenty-two candidates vying for eight positions; Limestone County was next with seven candidates for three places; and Cotaco (later Morgan) County had four candidates for two positions.[1]

Not surprisingly, a number of delegates to the convention had previous governmental experience, either in the Alabama Territory (nine) or the states from which they had migrated (five). Sixteen—slightly more than a third—of the forty-four delegates were lawyers. Four were planters, four

---

[1] McMillan, *Constitutional Development in Alabama*, 30–31; Moore, *History of Alabama*, 99–100.

were physicians, two were ministers, one was a merchant, and the remainder unknown. Only one delegate had arrived in what is now Alabama prior to 1800, with the majority arriving after the Creek surrender to General Jackson in 1814. Of the twenty-eight members whose place of birth is known, fifteen were from Virginia; five from North Carolina; two from South Carolina; two from Georgia; one each from Vermont, Delaware, and Pennsylvania; and one from England.[2]

Among the lawyers were quite a few of those who had been leaders in the Alabama Territory and in other states, as well as those who would become distinguished leaders in their new state. Judge Harry Toulmin of Washington County had been a territorial judge since 1804, and had previously served as President of Transylvania University and as Kentucky's Secretary of State. William Rufus King of Dallas County had served in the North Carolina state senate, in the U.S. Congress, and as the Secretary of the American Legation to St. Petersburg in Russia. After statehood, King would serve as one of Alabama's first U.S. Senators and later was sworn in as Vice President to President Franklin Pierce shortly before his death in April 1853. Marmaduke Williams had served in the North Carolina state legislature and had represented that state in the U.S. Congress from 1803 to 1817. John Leigh Townes served in the Virginia legislature in 1815 and 1816. Seven of the lawyers had served in the Alabama Territorial Legislature—Clement Comer Clay, Henry Hitchcock, Hugh McVay, James McCoffin, Gabriel Moore, Reuben Saffold, and John W. Walker. Significantly, six delegates would become governor of Alabama (Thomas Bibb, Israel Pickens, John Murphy, Gabriel Moore, Clement C. Clay, and Hugh McVay); six represented Alabama in the U.S. Senate (William Rufus King, John W. Walker, Clement Comer Clay, Israel Pickens, Gabriel Moore, and Henry Chambers); and six became justices of the Alabama Supreme Court (Reuben Saffold, Clement Comer Clay, Henry Hitchcock, Arthur Francis Hopkins, Henry Minor, and John M. Taylor).[3]

The Huntsville that these distinguished delegates converged upon in July 1819 was the seat of the Alabama Territory's most populous county and was perhaps the most important burgeoning city in the frontier of the Old Southwest. As previously noted, Huntsville's growing importance had recently garnered a visit by President Monroe during his tour of America's frontier fortifications. Approximately a year and a half prior to the constitutional convention, Anne Royall, a journalist touring the South, visited Huntsville and other areas of north Alabama. She described the land in and around Huntsville as "rich and beautiful as you can imagine; and the appearance of wealth would baffle belief." As for Huntsville itself, she said it "stands on elevated ground, and enjoys a beautiful prospect." She described the buildings and residences in Huntsville, most of which were built

---

[2] Peter A. Brannon, "Interesting Characters of the Constitutional Convention of Alabama of 1819," *Alabama Lawyer* 8 (October 1947): 388–89; Malcolm Cook McMillan, "The Alabama Constitution of 1819: A Study of Constitution-Making on the Frontier," *Alabama Lawyer* 12 (January 1951): 74–77.

[3] McMillan, *Constitutional Development in Alabama*, 32–33.

of brick, and indicated that "the workmanship is the best I have seen in all of the states; and several of the houses are three stories high, and very large." As for Huntsville's citizens, she observed that "they are gay, polite, and hospitable, and live in great splendor. Nothing like it in our country."[4]

Upon their arrival in this impressive frontier capital, the first act of the delegates was to elect a president to preside over the constitutional convention. In a unanimous vote, John W. Walker of Madison County, who had been Speaker of the House of the last session of the Alabama Territory's General Assembly, was bestowed this honor. The fact that northern county delegates outnumbered those from the south 28–16 obviously worked in Walker's favor; yet, as observed by historian Malcolm Cook McMillan, the fact that Walker received a unanimous affirmation as president reveals that he was well liked statewide. In a short address to the convention upon his election, Walker expressed his desire that "our deliberations may terminate in the adoption of a constitution which will secure to [Alabama's] sons, to the remotest generations, the full enjoyment of the great blessings of life, liberty, and property." The other two convention officers were likewise filled by Madison Countians with the election of John Campbell as secretary and Daniel Rather as doorkeeper. Surprisingly, in view of Walker's excellent reputation, John Campbell wrote to his brother in Tennessee that Walker "knew little more of parliamentary proceedings than your boy Richard, although an accomplished scholar and a man of some smartness." He went on to state that Walker was "amazingly spoilt by the flattery which is lavished upon him in our new country." Campbell was more positive in his overall assessment of the convention in a letter written to his father in Virginia in which he stated that "the convention is composed of 44 members and I have never seen in any deliberative body for the numbers more urbanity and intelligence."[5]

With its officers in place, the convention settled down to the business of writing Alabama's constitution. In this regard, the constitutional convention appointed a Committee of Fifteen to write an original draft. Clement Comer Clay was appointed as chairman of the committee further consisting of John M. Taylor and Henry Chambers of Madison county, Israel Pickens and Henry Hitchcock of Washington County, John Murphy and John Watkins of Monroe County, Thomas Bibb and Beverly Hughes of Limestone County, William Rufus King of Dallas County, Arthur F. Hopkins of Lawrence County, Reuben Saffold of Clarke County, John D. Bibb of Montgom-

---

[4] Anne Royall to Matthew Dunbar, Huntsville, January 1, 1818, in Anne Newport Royall, *Letters from Alabama on Various Subjects*, ed., Lucille Griffith (Tuscaloosa: University of Alabama Press, 1969), 10, 118–19.

[5] McMillan, *Constitutional Development in* Alabama, 33–34; "Journal of the Constitution, 1819, as reported in the *Alabama Republican*," *Alabama Historical Quarterly* 31 (Spring and Summer 1969): 131. Campbell was no doubt a gossip as evidenced by his assertion in another letter to his brother that Thomas Bibb, soon to be Alabama's second governor, "gets sometimes in his cups," and in that condition "would keep the house in a roar for an hour at the time." Campbell to David Campbell, August 11, 1819, and October 27, 1819, and David Campbell to John Campbell, Sr., July 10, 1819, in Campbell Collection (Duke University Library, Durham), all quoted in McMillan, "Alabama Constitution of 1819," 78.

ery County, Richard Ellis of Franklin County, and George Phillips of Shelby County. Representatives from planter counties bordering the Tennessee, Tombigbee, and Alabama rivers controlled the committee. Mobile County was conspicuously without representation on the committee.[6]

A subcommittee of just three delegates—William Rufus King of Dallas County, Judge John M. Taylor of Madison County, and Henry Hitchcock of Washington County—was given the task of reducing the rough draft of the entire committee to a form suitable for presentation to the convention as a whole for debate and adoption. The Committee of Fifteen's final draft, reported to the convention on July 13, 1819, was eventually adopted by the convention with minimal modifications after less than a month of deliberations on August 2, 1819. The delegates were obviously not working in a vacuum and had the benefit of reviewing constitutions written by states previously admitted to the union, as well as the federal Constitution. Like the federal Constitution, it contained a Bill of Rights and apportioned powers among three branches of government—legislative, executive, and judicial. Unlike the federal Constitution, however, and most other state constitutions, Alabama's constitution allocated the legislative branch considerably more power than the other two branches.[7]

The preamble of the Alabama Constitution of 1819 contained language similar to that contained in the preamble to the United States Constitution, e.g., "in order to establish justice, insure [domestic] tranquility, provide for the common defense, promote the general welfare. . . ." In addition to the preamble, Alabama's constitution consisted of six substantive articles, the first of which set forth Alabama's declaration of basic rights for its citizens. The remaining five articles outlined the shape of government for the new state. Article II provided for the separation of powers between the three branches of government; Article III set forth the powers of the Legislative branch; Article IV set forth the powers of the Executive branch and the state's Militia; Article V provided for the Judicial branch and the rules for impeachment; and Article VI contained general provisions; provisions pertaining to education, banks, and slaves; a mode for amending and revising the constitution; and a schedule for transitioning from territorial status to statehood.[8]

Generally considered liberal for its time, the constitution had conservative features also. The liberal provisions were the product of those delegates who came from the "white counties" consisting of small farmers who generally owned very few slaves, if any. Although few changes were made to the Committee of Fifteen's draft, those that were made brought more democratic features to Alabama's constitution, the chief of which was universal suffrage for all white males at least twenty-one years of age who had been in Alabama for at least a year. The convention rejected restrictive

---

[6] McMillan, "Alabama Constitution of 1819," 79.

[7] Moore, *History of Alabama*, 100–102; McMillan, *Constitutional Development in Alabama*, 34, 44–45; Abernethy, *Formative Period*, 54.

[8] *The Constitution of the State of Alabama*, adopted August 2, 1819 (hereafter *Ala. Const. of 1819*).

voter and office qualifications such as property ownership, taxpayer status, or membership in the state militia. Also of significance was the failure of the slave-owning, planter-lawyer delegates to impose the federal three-fifths ratio, which allowed slaves to be counted as three-fifths of a person for representation purposes in the state legislature. Although the Committee of Fifteen recommended this ratio, the convention as a whole, in which the yeoman farmers had a greater representation, rejected it in favor of counting white population only. Likewise, the apportionment of state senators was limited to one based upon the overall white population. Of similar liberality was the fact that the state's governor and the counties' sheriffs and clerks of court were to be directly elected by the people (as opposed to by the legislature in the case of governor, and county courts in the case of sheriffs and court clerks). Other liberal provisions included direct voter participation in a complicated amendment process, as well as a specification of basic rights for slaves, including an affirmative requirement for their humane treatment.[9]

Conservative influence was evidenced by the disproportionate powers placed in the legislative branch at the expense of the other two branches of government, as well as the people. Of particular note, the legislature was given power to appoint most state officials, including secretary of state, state treasurer, comptroller, supreme court justices, circuit court judges, and inferior court justices. This had the dual effect of undermining democracy by depriving the people the right to vote for such important positions, while at the same time weakening the executive branch by depriving the governor this power. The executive was further weakened by giving the legislature the power to overcome the governor's veto by a simple majority vote, rather than a two-thirds as originally proposed by the Committee of Fifteen. Although the representatives from the white counties were successful in weakening the governor's veto power, they failed in their attempt to reduce the life tenure given to judges to a term limit of six years, allowing conservatism to prevail in the judicial department. The only democratic aspect of the court system was the requirement that county court clerks be elected by the people. As previously seen, all judges, including those of the inferior courts, were to be appointed by the legislature and were to serve for life, or "during good behavior." The members of the judiciary were, however, subject to impeachment for "willful neglect, or other reasonable cause," upon a two-thirds vote of each house of the General Assembly.[10]

Included within the article pertaining to the legislative branch was a provision with respect to the location of the capital of the state that would have future political ramifications. As previously seen, territorial governor Bibb had skillfully ensured that the "permanent" capital would be located at

---

[9] McMillan, *Constitutional Development in Alabama*, 36–37, 45; *Ala. Const. of 1819*, Art. III, Secs. 5, 8–10; Art. IV, Secs. 2, 24; and Art. VI (Slaves) Secs. 1–3.

[10] McMillan, *Constitutional Development in Alabama*, 38, 44–45; *Ala. Const. of 1819*, Art. IV, Secs. 14, 23; Art. V, Secs. 12–13. Historian Mills Thornton asserts that the constitution "was the most liberal of any state's at the time," and he is of the view that the provision setting a life tenure for judges was its only "even vaguely conservative" provision. Thornton, *Politics and Power*, 12.

Cahaba, rather than Tuscaloosa as had been recommended by a special commission appointed by the first session of the territorial legislature. Although Bibb was not a delegate to the convention, he attended the deliberations and, as the state's most influential public figure, he undoubtedly informally helped shaped the constitution's provisions to a certain extent. His influence was not enough, however, to stop the northern delegates, led by Clement Comer Clay, from adopting a provision to begin a process that would ultimately unravel Governor Bibb's earlier end run around Tennessee Valley and Tombigbee-Warrior basin delegates with respect to the location of the capital. The constitution provided that the first session of the General Assembly would meet in Huntsville and thereafter in Cahaba until 1825. However, after the legislature's first session in 1825, the members were then authorized to declare a new "permanent" seat of government, without the concurrence of the governor. This was no guarantee for the supporters of Tuscaloosa because they would have to have a majority in both the House and the Senate in 1825 to achieve their goal. If they did obtain these majorities, however, the governor lacked the power to veto any measure to establish a permanent seat of government. If a majority did not declare a new seat of government in 1825, the constitution provided that Cahaba would become the permanent capital by default.[11]

The exclusion of the governor from participation in the possible relocation of the capital, along with denying him appointive power for state offices and seriously weakening his general veto power, is evidence of a popular distrust for the office of governor. This distrust—and the resulting weakness of the executive branch—was in part reflective of the ill will that had existed between the people and Governor Winthrop Sargent of the former Mississippi Territory, as well as the friction between Governor Robert Williams and the territorial legislature. The territorial governors had possessed much stronger powers and were not adept at ingratiating themselves with their frontier citizens. The feelings of some were reflected by a south Alabama newspaper that went so far as to propose that the convention provide for no governor at all "lest he trans-magnify himself into a king."[12]

Under the proposed constitution, the militia was a sub-branch of the Executive Department and, although commanded by the governor, its organization and modes of discipline were to be legislated by the General Assembly. Methods of elections or appointments of officers were also left to the Assembly's discretion, with a proviso that it could make no appointments other than those of Adjutant Generals and Quartermaster Generals. The governor was given the authority to call the militia into service "to execute the laws of the state, to suppress insurrections, and repel invasions." Interestingly, the delegates made sure that those with conscientious

---

[11] *Ala. Const. of 1819*, Art. III, Sec. 29; Brantley, *Three Capitals*, 46.

[12] McMillan, *Constitutional Development in Alabama*, 40 (newspaper quoted in correspondence from John W. Walker to Charles Tait, June 17, 1819).

objections could not be compelled into military service, provided those so objecting paid "an equivalent for personal service."[13]

In addition to articles providing for the basic structure of Alabama's government, Article VI of the constitution contained general provisions, several of which were reflective of the frontier society in which they were to be applied. Included in this category were provisions authorizing the General Assembly "to pass such penal laws, to suppress the evil practice of Duelling, extending to disqualification from office"; assuring that an absence from the state on governmental or personal business "shall not cause a forfeiture of a residence once obtained"; and urgently directing the General Assembly "to form a penal code, founded on principles of reformation, and not of vindictive justice." More extensive provisions in Article VI further reflected the needs of an emerging frontier society by ensuring the promotion of public education and preservation of the lands dedicated for that purpose; placing restrictions on the establishment of banks; and providing a code for the governance and protection of its slave population.[14]

The constitution's section pertaining to education was basically a mandate to the General Assembly to ensure that the Enabling Act's provisions setting aside lands for public schools in every township and giving two sections of land to support a state university were carried out in accordance with the purposes specified and that said lands be improved and protected from "unnecessary waste and damage." The establishment of banks next garnered the attention of the delegates, particularly in light of the ongoing Panic of 1819. Rampant land speculation had contributed to the panic and caused the collapse of many banks in the nation that had relied principally upon land as collateral. With these harsh results in mind, the convention delegates chose to closely regulate the establishment of banks within the new state. As a consequence, the legislature was authorized to establish just one bank and was also limited to establishing only one branch per session, and then only by a two-thirds vote. A chartered bank was not allowed to commence operation until it had $50,000 worth of specie in hand, representing at least half of a minimum capitalization of $100,000. Furthermore, the state was given a proportionate role in control of the bank, and was guaranteed a minimum of two-fifths of capital stock. Finally, if a bank suspended specie payments, it was required to pay 12 per cent interest to the holder of its notes unless excused by the General Assembly.[15]

The final special emphasis section of Article VI addressed the status of slaves within the new state by guaranteeing its citizens the right to own slaves, while also guaranteeing certain basic rights to the slaves themselves. To keep state government from interfering with the right to own slaves, the General Assembly was prohibited from passing laws to emancipate slaves without the consent of their owners. The legislature was also denied the power to prohibit immigrants from bringing with them persons deemed

---

[13] *Ala. Const. of 1819*, Art. IV.

[14] Ibid.

[15] McMillan, *Constitutional Development in Alabama*, 42; *Ala. Const. of 1819*, Art. VI.

slaves according to the laws of any of the other states. The legislature was granted the power, however, to prevent slaves from being brought into the state as commodities to be sold and was given the authority to pass laws to prevent the importation of slaves who had committed serious crimes in other states or territories. While the legislature could not free slaves without their owners' consent, it was given the power to establish the conditions under which their lawful owners could emancipate them, with an emphasis on protecting the rights of creditors and ensuring that any slaves freed did not become "a public charge."[16]

The legislature was also given the authority to provide protection for slaves by requiring owners to treat their slaves "with humanity, to provide for them necessary food and clothing, to abstain from all injuries to them extending to life or limb, and, in case of their neglect, or refusal to comply with the directions of such laws, to have such slave or slaves sold for the benefit of the owner or owners." Furthermore, any person who maliciously dismembered or killed a slave would be subjected to "suffer such punishment as would be inflicted in case the like offence had been committed on a free white person." The only exception was if such injury or death occurred during an insurrection. The original draft of this section also provided for an exception if the slave was determined to be accidentally killed during punishment, but this portion was stricken out. Finally, slaves were accorded the right to a trial by jury for any crimes higher than that of petty larceny. However, they were obviously not allowed a jury of their peers.[17]

The constitution's final provisions provided a process for its amendment, as well as providing an orderly schedule for the transfer of functions from the territorial government to that of the new state. Changing the constitution was not made easy as the delegates set forth a rather convoluted amendment scheme. First, a proposed amendment must receive a two-thirds vote in the General Assembly. The proposed amendment then was to be submitted to a vote of the people in the next general election. If the amendment received a majority of the votes in the general election, it was presented to the next session of the Assembly, where it must again receive a two-thirds vote of the representatives to finally be approved. Even this cumbersome process was considered a liberal provision at the time because, according to McMillan, it was one of the first in the nation to give the people any active participatory role in the amendment process. Although amending the constitution included direct participation by the electorate, its original ratification was never submitted to the electorate for approval since the Enabling Act did not require such approval and none of the previously admitted states had done so.[18]

The delegates lastly set forth a schedule which basically ensured a smooth transition for Alabama's transition from territorial status to statehood. For example, to avoid interruption or inconvenience "it is declared

---

[16] *Ala. Const. of 1819,* Art. VI.

[17] Ibid.

[18] McMillan, *Constitutional Development in Alabama,* 42–44; Rogers, et al., *Alabama,* 70.

that all rights, actions, prosecutions, claims, and contracts, as well of individuals as of bodies corporate, shall continue as if no such change had taken place," and "[a]ll fines, penalties, forfeitures, and escheats accruing to the Alabama Territory, shall accrue to the use of the State." All civil and military officers of the Alabama Territory would keep their office and the same rate of pay until superseded under the authority of the new Constitution. Similarly, "all laws and parts of laws, now in force in the Alabama Territory, which are not repugnant to the provisions of this Constitution, shall continue and remain in force as the laws of this State, until they expire by their own limitation, or shall be altered, or repealed by the Legislature thereof."[19]

The proposed constitution deemed all white males at least twenty-one years of age, who were citizens of the United States and residing in the state at the time of the adoption of the constitution, qualified to vote in the state's first election and also eligible to hold office. The president of the constitutional convention was directed to issue writs of election to the county sheriffs requiring them to hold elections in their respective counties for the offices of governor, representative to the United States Congress, members of the General Assembly, clerks of the various courts, and for their own office of sheriff. These elections were directed to be held in less than two months, on the third Monday and the following day in September 1819.[20]

Shortly prior to the adoption of the constitution, on July 30, 1819, in an action which has received relatively little attention, the delegates sought to expand the soon-to-be state's borders by sending a memorial to Congress seeking permission to annex that portion of Florida west of the Apalachicola River as soon as the Adams–Onis Treaty of 1819 between Spain and the United States resulted in America's anticipated acquisition of East and West Florida. The matter was pressed by John W. Walker, one of Alabama's first U.S. Senators, when the treaty was ratified. Charles Tait, Alabama's first federal judge and former Georgia senator who was the architect of Alabama's admission into the Union, expressed the sentiments of the new state when he said, "Our Geographical symmetry will be marred unless this annexation takes place." Despite these sentiments and Walker's efforts, Alabama's request for annexation never received much support in Congress and ultimately died on the vine.[21]

On August 2, 1819, their work finally completed, all forty-four delegates signed Alabama's first constitution less than a month after their assembly as a constitutional convention. After the Constitution's adoption, the delegates resolved to commend the "dignity, ability, and impartiality" with which President John W. Walker had discharged his duties in chairing the convention. Included within his response to their laudatory resolution, Walker said, "We have given the State of Alabama a Constitution—not

---

[19] *Ala. Const. of 1819*, Schedule.

[20] Ibid.

[21] *Journal of the Constitutional Convention, 1819*, 37 (hereafter *Official Journal*); Bailey, *John Williams Walker*, 133–36.

indeed perfect—Yet emphatically republican and such as gives us a clear and indisputable title, to admission into the great family of the Union." In addition to the closing accolades, the delegates made arrangements for the enrollment of the Constitution and its deposit with the Secretary of State. A copy was then transmitted to the U.S. Congress where it was accepted by the passage of a resolution of admission on the first Monday in December. On December 14, 1819, President Monroe signed the resolution and Alabama became the nation's twenty-second state.[22]

Upon acceptance of the office of convention president, John W. Walker had expressed to his fellow delegates a hope "that party views, local feelings, and sectional jealousies, may find no entrance within these walls; that we may look only to the true and permanent interest, the future character, dignity, and prosperity of the state of Alabama." Such sentiments were laudatory, but obviously unrealistic as demonstrated by the practical give and take by the planter-lawyer delegates and those who represented the so-called "plain men" or yeomen farmers in crafting a constitution with both liberal and conservative aspects. At the conclusion of the convention, Walker in essence acknowledged this when he stated that the convention had crafted a constitution "not precisely such as any one member of this body or perhaps of any one individual of this community, would, unassisted, have framed in his closet." Walker went on to say that the document had its faults as well as its merits, but that "for all of its defects it carries with itself the grand corrective of amendment." Alabama's Constitution of 1819 would remain in effect until replaced by a secessionist constitution in 1861 when Alabama left the Union on the eve of the Civil War. Notably, it was amended only three times in its forty-one year history.[23]

With the adoption of Alabama's Constitution, it would be up to Alabama's newly elected officers to implement a government in accordance with its terms.

---

[22] McMillan, *Constitutional Development in Alabama*, 45; *Official Journal, 1819*, 39–40.

[23] McMillan, *Constitutional Development in Alabama*, 45; *Journal of the Constitutional Convention, 1819*, as reported in the *Alabama Republican*, 130–31.

7

❧

GOVERNOR WILLIAM WYATT BIBB AND
THE ADVENT OF STATE GOVERNMENT

Alabama's admission into the Union occurred in close proximity with two significant national events, one of which would have an immediate effect and one of which would have a profound long term effect. Of immediate economic effect was the Panic of 1819, which was the nation's first serious economic depression. The excitement over Alabama's entry into the Union was certainly tempered by the effects of the depression that had begun to take hold. Times had certainly been better in the years leading up to Alabama's statehood. Indeed, the area to become Alabama had been one of the major benefactors of a post-War of 1812 economic boom, which was accompanied by a rise in cotton prices and a tremendous influx of emigrants. The Alabama country also had the dubious distinction, however, of being at the center of the young nation's speculation in public land purchases. As a result, by 1820, the year after Alabama had achieved statehood, it was responsible for half of the nation's $22 million public land debt.[1]

The Panic of 1819 that paralleled Alabama's admission into the Union caused bank failures, foreclosures, and unemployment, which in turn forced people out of their homes and off their farms. The effects in Alabama were particularly felt in the Tennessee Valley where traders used Tennessee bank notes. Huntsville's Planters and Merchants Bank took a beating as a result of the suspensions of specie payment of the neighboring Tennessee banks and doomed its own ultimate failure by suspending specie payments in 1820.[2]

The event that would have a more long term effect on the new state was the passage of the Missouri Compromise of 1820. This agreement was passed on March 3, 1820, a little over two months after Alabama achieved statehood. Alabama's admission had once again created an even balance with eleven slave states and eleven free states. Because Missouri was seeking admission as a slave state right after Alabama, the free states opposed Missouri's admission since it would throw the balance of power in favor of the slave states. Nevertheless, the pro-slavery and anti-slavery parties reached a compromise through the efforts of Speaker of the U.S. House Henry Clay whereby Missouri was admitted as a slave state and Maine as a free state. Furthermore, with the exception of Missouri, this law prohibited slavery in the Louisiana Territory north of the 36° 30′ latitude line. Even in his declining years, Thomas Jefferson lived up to his name as

---

[1] Murray N. Rothbard, *Panic of 1819* (New York: Columbia University Press, 1962), 46, 81–85.

[2] Ibid.

the "Sage of Monticello" when he likened the compromise as "a fire bell in the night, [which] awakened and filled me with terror. I considered it at once as the knell of the Union. It is hushed indeed for the moment, but this is a reprieve only, not a final sentence. . . . We have the wolf by the ears, and we can neither hold him nor safely let him go." While this compromise did set a pattern of states being admitted in tandems of one slave state and one free state for the next thirty-four years, the compromise eventually broke down in 1850s, as Jefferson had feared, giving impetus to a further division between the North and South that led the nation into the Civil War. As a result, Alabama, like the rest of the South, from its very inception as a state was set on a fateful course of pro-slavery politics, which would ultimately devastate it and its people for many years.[3]

In the interim, Alabamians went about the business of forging a state government in accordance with the constitution it had adopted. As soon as the constitutional convention had adjourned *sine die* on August 2, 1819, campaigning began for representatives in both houses of the General Assembly and for the office of governor. On the third Monday and Tuesday of September 1819, twenty-two senators and fifty representatives were elected to the state of Alabama's first General Assembly. Each county was allotted one senator and a fixed number of representatives based upon the census. Once again, Madison County led the way with eight representatives; Monroe was next with five; Blount, Limestone, Montgomery, and Tuscaloosa each had three; Clarke, Conecuh, Cataco (later Morgan), Dallas, Franklin, Lauderdale, Lawrence, Shelby, and Washington each had two; and Baldwin, Marion, Mobile, and St. Clair each had just one.[4]

Alabama's first gubernatorial election pitted William Wyatt Bibb, just finishing up his term as the governor of the Alabama Territory, against Marmaduke Williams, a former Congressman from North Carolina. Williams, also a member of the North Carolina bar, had moved to the Mississippi Territory in 1810, first living in Huntsville before settling in Tuscaloosa. Although Bibb was extremely popular, Williams ran a fairly competitive campaign by attracting voters who were opposed to the Georgia faction and who also resented the high-handed manner in which Bibb maneuvered to have the capital located at Cahaba. When the votes were finally tallied, Bibb hung on to win with 8,342 votes to Williams' 7,140 votes. However, Bibb's election would turn out to be the high water mark of the Georgia faction's success in Alabama politics. As a matter of fact, the results of the 1819 elections contained plenty of evidence of a beginning decline in the influence wielded by this powerful group. For example, in the northern part of the state, Williams outpolled Bibb by commanding majorities in all but two counties. Not surprisingly, in Tuscaloosa County, whose citizens were

---

[3] Bailey, *John Williams* Walker, 118–19. Unlike former President Jefferson, Senator John W. Walker expressed his "satisfaction with the compromise and stated that it 'has saved the Republic.'" Thomas Jefferson to John Holmes, April 22, 1820, Manuscript Division, Library of Congress Internet site, http://www.loc.gov/exhibits/jefferson/159.html (accessed December 28, 2012).

[4] Brantley, *Three Capitals*, 47, 230–31.

miffed about losing the state capital to Cahaba, the vote was overwhelmingly in favor of Williams 824 to 123. Williams also achieved significant majorities in Lauderdale, Blount Cotaco (later Morgan), Marengo, Franklin, and
Marion counties. The most interesting returns came from Madison County,
which although home to many influential members of the Georgia faction,
was also carried by Williams, albeit in a squeaker, 1,244 votes to 1,225
votes. Even more significantly, all of the Georgia faction's representatives in
Madison County who had sat in the territorial Assembly lost their bids for
election to the state's General Assembly. Moreover, Gabriel Moore outdis-
tanced Georgian Leroy Pope by a large majority in the race for the county's
single senate seat.[5]

Alabama's First Governor William Wyatt Bibb

Courtesy of Alabama Department of Archives and History

Upon the election of the members of its legislature and its governor in
the fall of 1819, Alabama got a jump start on governance by commencing
the first session of its General Assembly in Huntsville on October 25, 1819,

---

[5] Ibid., 47–48, 52–53; Thornton, *Politics and Power*, 14.

approximately six weeks before it was formally admitted into the Union. The legislature apparently went ahead and convened based upon the assumption that the approval of Alabama's statehood was a foregone conclusion. This first session met for forty-four days, only the last three of which were after Alabama officially became a state. Even during those last three days, none of the representatives had received word of President Monroe's signature making Alabama's entry into the Union official. The organization of the state nevertheless began in earnest with the first order of business for each house to elect their leadership. The House of Representatives elected James Dellet of Monroe County as Speaker of the House, Jonas J. Bell as clerk, and Daniel Rather as door-keeper. The Senate elected Thomas Bibb, the brother of the governor, as president of the Senate. According to the new constitution, this position put Bibb next in line to succession to the governor's office should the governor be removed from office as a result of impeachment, a refusal to qualify, death, resignation, or absence from the state. Additionally, the Senate elected Thomas A. Rogers as Secretary and John K. Dunn as door-keeper.[6]

Governor Bibb, just as in the first session of the Alabama territorial legislature, had the distinction of addressing the state of Alabama's first General Assembly. Instead of personally addressing this historic assemblage, however, he sent a written message which was read to the elected representatives. He commenced this momentous address by stating to the assembly's members that "your present meeting will form a memorable epoch in our history; chosen to perform the first acts of legislation, for the state of Alabama, you cannot estimate too highly the great interests committed to your charge, or the important consequences which may flow from your deliberations." As he had in his address to the territorial legislature, he once again stressed the importance of education and internal improvements. Of particular personal importance to himself, he reported that in May 1819, one hundred and eighty-two lots had been sold in Cahaba, the site he had finagled for the new state's capital, for a total of $123,856. Of that amount, $10,000, the full extent of the amount appropriated by the previous territorial assembly, was deposited in the Planters and Merchants Bank of Huntsville to "be expended in the erection of a temporary State House at the town of Cahawba." On a practical political level, in order for the new state to be represented in the U.S. Senate, he urged that "at an early period of their session, it is desirable that the Senators should be elected as soon as your deliberations will permit."[7]

Following the governor's advice, the House and Senate immediately began to assess the candidates for the U.S. Senate who had been jockeying for position ever since the constitutional convention. Not surprisingly, the

---

[6] *Journal of the House of Representatives of the General Assembly of the State of Alabama, 1819* (Cahawba: Charles A. Henry Press, 1820), 4 (cited hereafter *Ala. House Journal (1819)*); *Journal of the Senate at the First Session of the First General Assembly of the State of Alabama* (Cahawba: Charles A. Henry Press, 1820), 4 (hereinafter *Ala. Senate Journal (1819)*); Leah Atkins, "The First Legislative Session: The General Assembly of Alabama, Huntsville, 1819," *Alabama Review* 23 (January 1970): 30–31.

[7] *Ala. House Journal (1819)*, 8–16.

political maneuvering involved in the naming of Alabama's first two senators centered on the north versus south sectional jealousies, as well as a growing opposition to the Broad River group from Georgia. Charles Tait, the former Georgia senator who was instrumental in shepherding Alabama's statehood bill through Congress, fully expected to be rewarded for his efforts and let it be known that he was available to serve as one of Alabama's first senators. In an effort to accommodate him, the Georgia faction put together a proposal that recognized the balance needed between north and south Alabama, yet at the same time ensured that members of their group would fill both senatorial seats. In accordance with this plan, they proposed John W. Walker of Madison County representing the northern part of the state and Charles Tait of Monroe County representing the southern part. Walker met little opposition, but the representatives from the southern part of the state who were opposed to the Georgia group supported the candidacy of William Rufus King, a former Congressman from North Carolina. The earnestness of this opposition led Tait to withdraw his candidacy, stating "I came to bring peace, not a sword." This result was just another example of the Georgia faction's declining power. Regardless, on October 28, 1819, just three days after Governor Bibb's urging, the combined houses of the General Assembly elected John W. Walker and William Rufus King as Alabama's first U.S. Senators.[8]

Now that the General Assembly had been organized and Alabama's U.S. Senators had been chosen, the Assembly was ready to settle down to the business of enacting legislation to implement the state's constitution. Before it could do so in earnest, however, the members' attention was briefly diverted by a visit of General Andrew Jackson to Huntsville. Jackson was ostensibly surveying his north Alabama plantation interests. He was staying at the Old Green Bottom Inn just north of Huntsville where he had brought his horses to race once again. Undoubtedly, however, his visit was also politically motivated to shore up his support in north Alabama and to counterbalance the influence of the Georgia faction in the region, whose members were among those trying to deflate Jackson's popularity as a war hero in hopes of dimming his rising star status as a presidential hopeful. Secretary of the Treasury William H. Crawford, the Georgia faction's major benefactor on the national level, was definitely in the group opposing Jackson and was himself to be a candidate for president against Jackson in the election of 1824. Despite his strong support in Alabama, Jackson lost his first run for the presidency to John Quincy Adams in an election that was decided in the House of Representatives when no candidate garnered a majority of the vote.[9]

---

[8] On May 13, 1820, Charles Tait was finally rewarded for his efforts on behalf of Alabama's statehood when, at the urging of Senator John W. Walker and U.S. Secretary of the Treasury William H. Crawford, he was appointed by President Monroe as Alabama's first, and at the time, only federal judge. Charles H. Moffat, "Charles Tait: Planter, Politician, and Scientist of the Old South," *Journal of Southern History* 14 (May 1948): 221–22; Atkins, "The First Legislative Session," 33–34; *Ala. House Journal (1819)*, 28–29.

[9] Brantley, *Three Capitals*, 54–57; Atkins, "The First Legislative Session," 35–36. Jackson dubbed Clay "The *Judas* of the West," and would forever accuse Adams and Clay of a "Corrupt

As demonstrated by the 1819 elections in Alabama, there was a growing opposition to the Georgia faction, also known as the Broad River Group or the Royalist Party. Original opposition to the Georgia faction had been commenced by a less organized group of settlers from Tennessee and North Carolina. This group would eventually become supporters of Andrew Jackson on the national level, but at its outset was strictly anti-Georgia rather than pro-Jackson. For example, Marmaduke Williams of Tuscaloosa opposed Bibb for governor because of the high handed manner in which Bibb had handled the location of the state capital at Tuscaloosa's expense. Gabriel Moore, another opposition leader of the so-called "champions of the people," stated on the stump that he was not from the "Royal Party," but from the poor. Ironically, Moore and Williams were both far from poor, but instead well-educated and well-to-do lawyers. While the anti-Georgia group was gaining strength and welcomed Jackson's visit to the state, the visit caused uneasiness among those still loyal to the Georgians who were well aware of Jackson's popularity within the state.[10]

The Georgians nevertheless understood that Jackson's hero status clearly warranted him an invitation by the General Assembly "to take a seat within the bar of this house." This invitation was extended as a result of a resolution unanimously adopted by the Senate without discussion on November 1, 1819. A controversy ensued, however, the next day when Senator Howell Rose of Autauga County, an ardent Jackson supporter, offered a resolution praising General Jackson's recent military successes, including his "meritorious conduct" in the late war against the Seminoles, during which Jackson had taken it upon himself to occupy Spanish-held Pensacola. Jackson's critics seized upon this incidence to discredit him, claiming he had exceeded his orders in taking Pensacola. There resulted a Congressional attempt to censure Jackson for his conduct. Because of this, Senator Joseph Farmer of Lauderdale County did not believe the resolution was strong enough in Jackson's favor and offered an amendment resolving that "this General Assembly do highly disapprove" of the attempted censure by some members of Congress from other than patriotic motives. This amendment was adopted by the Senate and the resolution as amended was sent to the House for concurrence.[11]

The House first approved the resolution, but upon reconsideration the next day, rejected that part of the resolution containing Senator Farmer's amendment condemning Congress. The House then tempered the language of the Senate's condemnation of Congress by changing its declaration that the General Assembly "disapprove[s]" the Congressional attempted censure, to the General Assembly "sincerely regret[s]" such attempt. The Sen-

Bargain," alleging that Adams won the presidency by promising to appoint Henry Clay as Secretary of State in return for Kentucky's electors who had not initially supported Adams. See Brands, *Andrew Jackson*, 388–91.

[10] Moffatt, *Charles Tait*, 221; Thornton, *Politics and Power*, 15–18; Doss, "The Rise and Fall of an Alabama Founding Father," 163–76.

[11] *Ala. Senate Journal (1819)*, 38, 42–43; Brantley, *Three Capitals*, 54–55; Atkins, "The First Legislative Session," 35–36; Pickett, *Alabama*, 661–62.

ate voted this proposed change down and counter-proposed a protracted complimentary resolution that made no mention of the attempted Congressional censure, but instead included the statement "that his [Jackson's] whole conduct during his military career receives our entire approbation." This proposal met with the House's approval and a suitable resolution was finally passed by the Assembly, which then appointed a committee to deliver the resolution to General Jackson. Despite these verbal gymnastics, General Jackson was very appreciative of the resolution finally delivered to him. In a grateful response, Jackson stated, "I have received with the highest satisfaction the resolutions of the General Assembly of the State of Alabama; the honor conferred on me by that body is accepted with feelings of warmest sensibility." It is not recorded whether Jackson actually ever took a seat in the Assembly to watch the see-saw debates concerning the appropriateness of Congressional criticism of his military excursion into Spanish Florida. However, it would soon be evident that those who had voted against the resolution praising Jackson would be targeted for revenge by an Alabama electorate that would be very supportive of Jackson's future campaigns for the presidency.[12]

As the hubbub concerning General Jackson died down, the General Assembly was dealing with the practical matter of where it would hold its sessions since Huntsville was just a temporary site for the seat of government. During the first few sessions the houses met in separate locations, with the House convening in the private residence of Irby Jones and the Senate believed to be convening in the private residence of its door-keeper, John K. Dunn. They both were compensated approximately $150 for use of their residences. The House soon moved to the lower floor of the Madison County courthouse; the Senate remained where it was. When joint sessions were necessary, the Assembly convened in the courthouse where the House was quartered.[13]

The most important of the Assembly's joint sessions occurred on November 9, 1819, when the members convened to officially publish the vote for the state's new governor. Upon the publication of the official tally, Governor Bibb entered the hall of the House of Representatives where the Speaker of the House administered the oath of office to the governor. Upon receipt of the oath, Governor Bibb delivered a very brief inaugural address. The governor had previously addressed the Assembly when it first convened by way of a written statement. This was his first and only personal appearance before the Assembly. His inaugural address, unlike his detailed written address in which he outlined specific proposals, was mainly an expression of appreciation for the confidence placed in him and a pledge

---

[12] *Ala. House Journal (1819)*, 50, 59; *Ala. Senate Journal (1819)*, 47–51; Brantley, *Three Capitals*, 55–57; Atkins, "The First Legislative Session," 36–37. Governor Bibb privately expressed his condemnation of General Jackson's conduct in Florida in a letter to Charles Tait wherein he stated, "Not a moment should have been lost in arresting the Genl. and thereby showing a just regard to the preservation of our constitution." Abernethy, *Formative Period*, 61–63.

[13] *Acts of the General Assembly of the State of Alabama, 1819* (Huntsville, 1820), 136 (hereafter all references to acts passed by Alabama's General Assembly will be cited as "*Ala. Acts*, (appropriate year), followed by the page number"); Brantley, *Three Capitals*, 49–52.

full of platitudes to diligently advance "virtue and intelligence," to promote "obedience to the law," to cultivate "harmony, and good will among ourselves, and with the public functionaries of our sister states, and of the United States," to develop "those natural advantages with which we are so bountifully supplied," and to carry out "every object which . . . may tend to elevate the character of our State and to establish its true and permanent interests."[14]

The first few days of the state's new General Assembly had seen a whirlwind of historic activity, commencing with the verbal machinations surrounding General Jackson's visit and concluding with the inaugural address of Governor Bibb. After Bibb's address, the Assembly resumed in earnest the important task of filling in the framework provided by the Constitution for the state's government. The ensuing ambitious work of the Assembly resulted in the passage of a total of seventy-eight acts and eight resolutions in a session lasting just forty-four days. The members did yeomen-like work in filling in the details of the outline of government as had been set forth in the Constitution. Two of their most important tasks, particularly as relating to the peace and security of Alabama's citizens, was providing for the regulation of the courts within the state and providing for the organization of the state militia. With regard to the judicial system, an act was passed that required the establishment of an Inferior Court in each county, consisting of five justices who were to meet quarterly within their respective counties. This court, in addition to its general civil jurisdiction, was also to have the jurisdiction previously accorded to the Orphan's Court in the territorial government. (Orphans Courts were essentially tribunals responsible for the probate of wills and the estates of minor children.) The state was also divided into five Judicial Circuits, each with just one Circuit (Superior) Court judge. The circuit judges were to hold court twice annually in each of the counties composing their circuit. These same judges would all convene twice annually in the capital at Cahaba where they would together perform the function of the state's Supreme Court. The judicial act provided further that, at their first session, the circuit judges were to appoint one of their own as Chief Justice of the Supreme Court. Finally, as an alternative method for resolving lawsuits and controversies, the Assembly provided for voluntary binding arbitration. Persons appointed as arbitrators were administered an oath by a judge or justice of the peace affirming their impartiality and were empowered to subpoena witnesses. An arbitrator's award could not be set aside absent a showing that it was "obtained by corruption, evident partiality, or other undue means."[15]

As for the state militia, the Assembly adopted detailed rules concerning its organization and discipline. In recognizing the need for the protection of its citizenry still apprehensive as result of the recent Creek War, all free white men and indentured servants between eighteen and forty-five years of age were obliged to serve in the state militia. Exempted from service, except in times of "imminent danger, insurrection, or invasion," were

---

[14] *Ala. Senate Journal (1819)*, 55–56.

[15] *Ala. Acts (1819)*, 3–16, 58–60.

judges, state officials, licensed members of the clergy, ferrymen, postmasters, and post riders. Persons "conscientiously scrupulous of bearing arms" could also be exempted from service by giving an oath of affirmation of such belief before the court martial of the regiment to which they belonged. Power was vested in regimental courts martial to exempt anyone taking this oath from military duty provided, however, that in times of war or insurrection, the person so exempted would be required to pay a sum equal to the value of his military services. No equivalent payment was required in times of peace.[16]

The governor served as commander-in-chief of the militia, which was divided into four major divisions. Each division was commanded by a brigadier general and consisted of between two and five regiments. The act further detailed the organization down the chain to battalions and companies. Companies were to consist of between forty and one hundred twenty privates who were to be commanded by "a Captain, First and Second Lieutenants, one Ensign, five Sergeants, four Corporals and two Musicians." Field officers were to be elected by all persons liable to do militia duty in their respective companies. Noncommissioned officers were to be appointed by officers of their respective companies. The governor, as commander-in-chief, was obliged to order all commissioned officers of the several brigades to drill their troops not less than four, nor more than six days, each year. The governor was also authorized to aid local citizens by erecting temporary works and redoubts and establishing such military posts deemed necessary for the common defense. Additionally, the militia act created a thorough court-martial system that promoted a strict discipline amongst the officers and their soldiers.[17]

The military value of Alabama's militia system, which was first codified by the territorial legislature, is debatable. During the territorial period, we have already seen that a significant number of male citizens frequently ignored call-up orders because of their resentment over not being allowed to elect their own officers. Although the source of this resentment was removed in 1819 when the new state legislature allowed militia members to elect their own field officers, the question remained as to their military effectiveness.[18]

In an in-depth examination of a militia unit in antebellum Greensboro, Alabama, G. Ward Hubbs noted that the first militia companies in Greensboro, not unlike those throughout the nation, were "notoriously amateurish" and were "[o]ften led by incompetent hacks" in drills that "might be conducted with brooms and umbrellas rather than muskets." He further noted that some of these units would vanish for years, to reappear only when the citizenry sensed a specific threat to their safety from Indians or potentially rebellious slaves.[19]

---

[16] Ibid., 17–34.

[17] Ibid., 18–34.

[18] Wunder, "American Law and Order," 147–48; *Ala. Acts (1819)*, 19.

[19] Ward G. Hubbs, *Guarding Greensboro: A Confederate Company in the Making of a Southern Community* (Athens: University of Georgia Press, 2003), 49. Harry S. Laver, in his

In 1828, militia leaders in Greensboro reported to Governor Murphy that retention of good officers was a growing problem. They also expressed displeasure over the legislature cutting the number of required musters in half, the failure of the legislature to require that members carry weapons, and the fact that company captains were not even required to wear uniforms. Because not one man in twenty was armed and due to a significantly reduced attendance because of the exemption of noncommissioned officers from regimental drills, the unit's leaders stressed to the governor that drills had an "awkward and unnatural appearance."[20]

In response to repeated deficiencies such as these, the Alabama General Assembly reorganized the state militia in 1837 by turning over the duty of primary defense from the general militia to volunteer companies that had been springing up throughout the state. The legislature also formally incorporated many more of these volunteer units, which, although attached to the general militia, were accorded substantial autonomy. These volunteer units generally exhibited more enthusiasm and passion and, with time, more precision in their drills.[21]

The militia units of antebellum Alabama, whether of the general militia or a volunteer unit, were primarily utilized to patrol for hostile Indians and potentially mutinous slaves. No militia units were officially called up by the state, however, until Governor Clay did so at the outbreak of the Creek War of 1836. Clay then selected the "Montgomery Huzzars," otherwise known as "Henry's Horse Company," to be under his personal command. Other events that caused Alabama units to volunteer for service in fits and starts between the Creek War and the Civil War included the Seminole War in Florida, the Texas War for Independence, and the Mexican War. While most of Alabama's volunteers saw limited military action, if at any all, in these engagements, a company of sixteen volunteers from Montgomery led by Isaac Ticknor paid the ultimate sacrifice when they were among 365 Americans prisoners of war who were shot in cold blood at Goliad during the War for Texas Independence.[22]

Despite their questionable military value, antebellum militia units in Alabama, as elsewhere, provided a positive social and cultural force in the communities in which its members mustered. In his study of the early

study of the early Kentucky militia, confirmed that early American militias were perceived as "[i]ncompetent at best, dangerous at worst" and its members were "depicted as drunken buffoons who stumbled into a crooked line, poked each other with corn-stalk weapons, and inevitably shot their commander in the backside with a rusty, antiquated musket." Harry S. Laver, *Citizens More Than Soldiers: The Kentucky Militia and Society in the Early Republic* (Lincoln: University of Nebraska Press, 2007), 1, 144.

[20] The Greensboro Volunteer Artillery Company's incorporation by the General Assembly in 1834 provides an example of the advantages of formal incorporation. The articles of their incorporation required them to muster at least six times per year and to serve on slave patrols at least twenty-four nights. On the other hand, however, they were exempted from jury and road duties, could choose their own uniforms, and were answerable to no one within the State militia except when called into active service. Hubbs, *Guarding Greensboro,* 50–53.

[21] Hubbs, *Guarding Greensboro,* 51.

[22] John Napier, "Martial Montgomery: Ante Bellum Military Activity," *Alabama Historical Quarterly* 29 (Fall and Winter 1967): 111–15, 121–22.

Kentucky militia, Harry Laver concluded that its "influence reached beyond the narrow responsibilities of a purely martial institution as they made significant contributions to the social, political, and cultural maturation of the public sphere." Similarly, G. Ward Hubbs, in his examination of a Greensboro militia unit, concluded that it was a "community-building" force within the Canebrake of west Alabama's Black Belt.[23]

Militia musters in Alabama, as elsewhere, resulted in large gatherings of people in frontier communities, even more so than court days or log-rollings. Frequently militia members, in addition to drilling, would later become involved in horse play and fighting after a day of barbequing and drinking. The excitement generated by these musters attracted scores of people other than militiamen, including "office-seeking candidates, exhort-ing preachers, quacks peddling their noxious nostrums, gamblers fleecing bumpkins, [and] horse traders bickering. Ladies, both sullied and un-sullied, came to witness the gallantries of the day." On these days important business was often transacted, important issues of the day were debated, and news and views were exchanged.[24]

In addition to providing an opportunity for frontier communities to come together for social interaction on muster days, militia units also promoted patriotism and community pride by turning out at other times to escort distinguished visitors, mourn the deaths of important personages, and celebrate holidays and significant community events. For example, in 1830 the Greensboro Guards marched in a procession carrying the body of former Governor Israel Pickens to the Greensboro cemetery for interment. As we have previously seen, militia units from Montgomery and Claiborne under the command of Brigadier General Thomas S. Woodward escorted Revolutionary War hero, the Marquis de Lafayette, through the Creek Nation during his celebrated visit to Alabama in 1825. Holiday celebrations included the Fourth of July, Washington's Birthday, and the anniversary of the Battle of New Orleans. Many of these celebrations began with the firing of the militia's cannon at sunrise, followed by a dinner with patriotic toasts, and later a military ball.[25]

As civil war appeared inevitable by 1860, incorporation of militia units in Alabama increased and the legislature called for an additional 8,000 men to serve in the Voluntary Corps of the State of Alabama comprised of forty-four companies of 80 men each. These units, unlike their predeces-sors, would not be around to frolic at musters or lead holiday celebrations; instead most would become engaged in extensive combat throughout the bloodiest war in American history. Many of their members would never return to the communities that had been solidified by the early militias. While antebellum militia units were not as militarily significant as those

---

[23] Laver, *Citizens More Than Soldiers*, 144; Hubbs, *Guarding Greensboro*, 49–57.

[24] Napier, "Martial Montgomery," 115; Laver, *Citizens More Than Soldiers*, 2.

[25] Laver, *Citizens More Than Soldiers*,3–4, 6; Hubbs, *Guarding Greensboro*, 52; Napier, "Martial Montgomery," 110, 117–18.

that were thrust into battle during the Civil War, they nevertheless played an important role in the transformation of their frontier communities.[26]

After creating judicial and militia systems to provide for the peace and security of its citizens, the Assembly next provided support for educational and internal improvement measures as had been urged by Governor Bibb in his written address. With regard to education, the Assembly required each county to hold an election for three agents who would be authorized to rent or lease the sections of land donated by Congress for the support of schools within each township of their respective counties. Lands subject to this provision could be leased in lots, not exceeding eighty acres, for a term of no more than four years. Lessees of such lands could clear no more than half of their lot and were bound by a suitable penalty not to commit waste on the premises, such as cutting timber or removing stones, and were required to make such improvements to the premises as deemed proper by the leasing agents. In addition to leasing lands reserved for schools, the county agents were tasked with contracting with teachers and for a school house or houses. They were also to serve as the trustees for the schools within their counties and were vested with all powers necessary to provide their schools with general "superintendence, due organization, and wellbeing." With respect to higher education, the act provided for the election of five commissioners by a joint vote of both houses of the Assembly to examine "the most eligible site for a state university." They were to report their findings to the next session of the General Assembly. Although this commenced the process of establishing a state university, the state's "Seminary of Learning" would not come into fruition until the University of Alabama first opened its doors in 1831.[27]

With regard to internal improvements, the Assembly passed several acts with respect to public roadways and navigable waterways. Responding to Governor Bibb's request, the Assembly appropriated four thousand dollars to employ an engineer to study the rivers in Alabama and to report "to what extent, in what manner, and at what expense, the navigation of each may be improved." The engineer was also tasked with locating "the nearest and most eligible approaches" between the Mobile and Tennessee river systems "for facilitating the commercial intercourse of this State," apparently seeking a recommendation for a canal between the two. Such a complex engineering feat, however, would not be realized for another one hundred and sixty-five years with the completion of the Tennessee-Tombigbee Waterway in December 1984. Of more immediate practicality, the Assembly made it illegal to obstruct the existing navigable waters within the state, with a fine of ten dollars per day for so long as an obstruction remained in place. To encourage navigation of the Tennessee River through Muscle Shoals, the Assembly directed Lawrence County officials to license pilots to steer boats safely through the shoals. Additionally, all county courts were authorized to license public ferries within their jurisdiction for those who posted a bond with the condition that they continuously

---

[26] Napier, "Martial Montgomery," 125–26.

[27] *Ala. Acts (1819)*, 60–64; Atkins, "The First Legislative Session," 37–38.

provide a sufficient number of boats and hands to attend to them, as well as to "keep in good order the banks on either side of the water-course."[28]

The first legislature also ambitiously authorized the construction of a series of public roads throughout the state. One road was to run from the old Military Road in Lauderdale County to Tuscaloosa. Those who constructed this road were authorized to put up a turnpike gate upon the road's completion and charge a toll of 75 cents for four wheel carriages, 50 cents for two wheel carriages, 12½ cents for one man and a horse, 6¼ cents on each pack horse or loose horse, 1 cent for each head of cattle, and a half cent for each head of hog and sheep. The act creating this road also provided for a forfeiture of three times the total toll that would have been due by any person who broke through or went around the turnpike gate with the intent to avoid payment of the toll. Other major projects included a road to run from the falls of the Black Warrior at Tuscaloosa by way of Cahawba and Claiborne to Blakeley located across Mobile Bay from Mobile, as well as one from Cahawba via Coffeeville to the Washington County courthouse thence to the post road leading from St. Stephens to Natchez. Each county through which these roads passed were to appoint three commissioners to direct the construction efforts within their respective counties. In addition to the above definitive projects, the legislature also appointed commissioners to study the feasibility of a road from Cahawba to connect with the Old Federal Road coming out of the Creek Nation.[29]

Alabama's "peculiar institution" of slavery also received much attention from the General Assembly's first session. The most detailed legislation in this regard was that which created a patrol system for policing the state's slave population. This act required every male owner of slaves, and all other persons below the rank of ensign liable to perform military duty to perform patrol duty. However, there was a proviso that any such person could send a substitute to perform the duty in his stead. It was the responsibility of each patrol detachment "to visit all negro quarters, [and] all places suspected of entertaining unlawful assemblies of slaves or other disorderly persons unlawfully assembled." The detachment was authorized to bring such disorderly persons to the nearest justice of the peace. Further, if slaves were found traveling without a pass or token from his or her owner, the patrols were empowered to administer corporeal punishment on the spot of no more than fifteen lashes and were to be paid a sum of ten dollars by their owners for each runaway slave captured. The legislature did afford slaves charged with any crime in excess of petit larceny the right to a trial by a jury, from which the master or anyone related to the master or the prosecu-

---

[28] *Ala. Acts (1819),* 69–70, 73–75, 93–95.

[29] *Ala. Acts (1819),* 76–78, 80–81, 92–93. All free white male persons between ages 18 and 45, and all male slaves, and other persons of color over 18 and under 45, were required to perform road work for at least 10 days per year. They were subject to a fine of ten dollars for each day they refused to work. Certain persons such as ministers, school teachers and various public officials were exempted from this service. *Ala. Acts (1818),* 4–6; *Ala. Acts (1819),* 95; Henry Hitchcock, *The Alabama Justice of the Peace: Containing all the Duties, Powers and Authorities of that Office as Regulated by the Laws Now in Effect in this State* (Cahawba: William B. Allen Press, 1822), 398–406.

tor were excluded. The legislature also exercised its discretion in authorizing the manumission of seventeen slaves during its first session.[30]

In terms of fiscal issues, the first legislature dealt with a variety of subjects, one of which involved the repeal of the controversial act of the Alabama Territorial General Assembly that had removed all restrictions on interest rates if provided for in a written agreement. High interest rates became particularly unpopular as a result of the onset of the Panic of 1819. Their continued viability became even more vulnerable due to the decline of the influence and power of the Georgia faction. As a result, the territorial act was repealed by the state's first legislature and replaced by an act setting the maximum rate of interest at eight per cent per annum. Any persons convicted of violating this act were to be barred forever from being a director of a bank within the state, and all persons becoming bank directors after the passage of this act were required to take an oath affirming that he had not violated this provision and pledging that he would not do so in the future.[31]

Another monetary issue involved the important matter of setting the salaries of state officials. The Governor was to be paid the most with an annual salary of $2,500; the Circuit Court judges received the second highest salaries of $1,750 each. The Secretary of State, Treasurer, and Comptroller were paid one thousand dollars annually. The Attorney General's salary was set at $650 dollars, while the Solicitors (District Attorneys) were paid only $250. Thus, the entire official payroll for the new state of Alabama, excluding legislators, was approximately $22,375—or less than an entry-level salary for many ordinary state employees at the present time. As for legislators, they fixed their own compensation at five dollars per day of attendance at the Assembly together with an allowance of five dollars per twenty miles of travel to the seat of government.[32]

Of all the fiscal measures passed in the first Assembly, perhaps the most important in the eyes of the citizenry was an act creating a tax structure, which relied on an all-embracing property tax as the state's principal revenue raiser. The most lucrative property for tax purposes was land. The state's lands were classified according to quality—the highest quality valued at six dollars per acre, an intermediate quality valued at four dollars per acre, and the lowest quality valued at two dollars per acre. The land was then assessed taxes at twenty-five cents per one hundred dollars valuation. Although lands were a prime revenue producer, the legislature left no stone unturned in taxing all forms of property from slaves to billiard tables. Slaves over ten years old were taxed at seventy-five cents each and all free males between twenty-one and forty-five years of age were taxed at twenty-five cents each. Every billiard table "kept for play" was taxed $150. Merchants were taxed thirty cents for every one hundred dollars of sales and auction goods were taxed two per cent of the amount of sales. Pleasure

---

[30] *Ala. Acts (1819)*, 35–38, 88–89, 144–46.

[31] Ibid., 48–50.

[32] Ibid., 86–87, 96.

carriages were taxed two per cent on every one hundred dollars of their estimated value. Other taxes included one dollar on pleasure horses, gold watches, and clocks; fifty cents on silver watches; and five dollars on race horses. The legislature also derived revenue from business licenses—fifteen dollars for public racetracks; twenty dollars for taverns, or places retailing "spirituous liquors"; fifty dollars for "hawkers and pedlars"; and five dollars for attorneys and physicians. In another effort to raise revenue, the General Assembly authorized the governor to appoint a person to lease the "Salt Lands" and other lands that had been donated by the United States in the act authorizing Alabama's entry into the Union. Also, at Governor Bibb's request the Assembly authorized him to sell two hundred additional lots in Cahawba, so long as property was set aside for an educational academy, a court house and other public buildings, churches, and the executive department.[33]

The General Assembly also began the all-important process of the political subdivision of the state by creating more new counties and towns. The new counties included Butler, Henry, Greene, Jackson, Jefferson, Perry, and Wilcox. The new towns included Sommerville in Catoca (later Morgan) County, Triana in Madison County, Russellville in Franklin County, and Courtland in Lawrence County. Laws were further enacted to incorporate the existing towns of Claiborne, Mobile, Montgomery, Moulton, and Tuscaloosa. In addition provisions were made for the establishment of seats of government for Cahawba (later Bibb), Franklin, Lawrence, Autauga, Dallas, and Limestone counties.[34]

The frontier temperament of the new state was dealt with in other legislation passed by the first General Assembly. Notwithstanding the establishment of several new towns, the state was still primarily composed of wild undeveloped lands. So much so, that the legislature offered bounties to encourage the killing and destruction of wolves and panthers within the state. Upon production of the scalp of each animal killed to a local justice of the peace, a person was awarded three dollars for every wolf or panther less than six months of age, and five dollars for those over six months old.[35]

The backwoods containing such wild animals were peopled by equally wild frontiersmen who were not used to the imposition of law and order by an organized government, but were thoroughly familiar with the *code duello* still prevalent on the southwestern frontier. In an effort of promoting cooler heads to prevail within its borders, the General Assembly passed an act to "suppress dueling." The legislature, however, gave fair warning of their action by delaying until April 1, 1820, the prohibition against fighting or challenging to fight a duel. After an apparent open-season until that date, any persons engaging as either principals or seconds in fighting a duel, or conveying a challenge to do so, would be imprisoned for three months and fined up two thousand dollars. Also, circuit court and county

---

[33] Ibid., 80, 84–85, and 89–90.

[34] Ibid., 50–57, 101–102, 104–108, 110–118, 121–125, and 134.

[35] Ibid., 101–02.

court judges, as well as justices of the peace, were authorized to have any person arrested who they had reasonable suspicion to believe were about to engage in a duel, and have them brought before them to be bound with peace recognizances upon a finding that they in fact did intend to participate in a duel. Another measure directed at suppressing duels included one requiring all public officials and attorneys to take an oath affirming that they had not participated in a duel since January 1, 1820, nor would they do so during their term of office, or for as long as they practiced law, in the case of attorneys. Furthermore, anyone guilty of proclaiming in a newspaper or hand bill "any other person or persons, as a coward, or use any opprobrious and abusive language," for not accepting a challenge or fighting a duel were subject to a fine of up to five hundred dollars.[36]

Other legislation of the first General Assembly include acts setting forth regulations for the admission of attorneys to practice law, with grandfather clauses for those admitted to practice in the old Mississippi and Alabama territories; directing that the laws of the General Assembly be compiled in a digest of laws; preventing fraud in the sale of public lands; and empowering religions of all denominations to hold real estate within the state. In addition the Assembly passed nine private bills pertaining to the administration of estates and the granting of relief to females to contract and hold property. Finally eight resolutions were passed, including one praising President Monroe, who had just recently visited Huntsville, "for the dignified and useful course he has pursued as Chief Magistrate of the Union."[37]

In addition to a thorough initial structuring of a state government in accordance with the dictates of the 1819 Constitution, the Assembly's rapid first session made important personnel decisions for the new state when votes were taken for the office of Attorney General and for Circuit Court judges. Henry Hitchcock, who had served as the Secretary of the Alabama Territory, was overwhelmingly elected as the state's first Attorney General, receiving forty-five votes over Dunklin Sullivan who received fourteen votes and John N. S. Jones who received ten votes. The vote for the state's first five circuit judges determined the composition of Alabama's first Supreme Court. Abner S. Lipscomb, who had studied law under John C. Calhoun and would later serve as the Secretary of State for the Republic of Texas, was elected as circuit judge for the state's First Circuit. Surprisingly, he trounced Judge Harry Toulmin who had been a federal judge during Alabama's territorial days, by a vote of sixty-three to five. Henry Y. Webb, who had served as a territorial judge and Reuben Saffold, who had fought in the Creek Indian wars of 1813–14 and had served in the territorial legislature, were elected without opposition in the Second and Third Circuits, respectively. After four ballots in a very close election for circuit judge in the Fourth Circuit, Richard Ellis finally defeated John McKinley, who later became an Associate Justice of the United States Supreme Court, by a vote of thirty-seven to thirty-one. Ellis, like Lipscomb would go on to the Republic of Texas where he became the president of the Convention of 1836,

---

[36] Ibid., 64–67.

[37] Ibid., 68–69, 71–73, 100–01, 133–34, 137–44, and 146–50.

which declared Texas' independence from Mexico. Clement Comer Clay rounded out the members of the first Supreme Court, becoming the circuit judge for the Fifth Circuit without opposition. Clay, who would later serve as governor and U.S. senator, was elected by his colleagues to serve as the Supreme Court's first chief justice.[38]

The final matters of business for the first session of the General Assembly were to pay for the goods and services that had been provided it while in Huntsville and to prepare for its move southward to Cahawba (now Cahaba). The committee of accounts reported a number of bills to be paid for an assortment of items such as printing services, railings for the lobby of the House, stationary, two sheet iron stoves and pipes, tables, benches, fifty chairs, and the hire of a stove. With respect to the majority of accounts submitted for payment, the accounts committee declared them as unreasonable and recommended that they be paid at a rate deemed more reasonable. The Assembly also passed a resolution authorizing the doorkeeper of the House, Daniel Rather, to auction off tables, stoves, and other furniture, and, after deducting the costs of the sales, to deposit the proceeds in the state treasury.[39]

Their business completed, the General Assembly adjourned on December 17, 1819, and three days after President Monroe signed the resolution formally admitting Alabama as the nation's twenty-second state. The state government then packed up and moved to Cahaba to establish the state's "permanent" seat of government. The trip was not an easy task. Setting out overland from Huntsville travelers went down the Tuscaloosa Road through Elyton in Jefferson County and then on to the falls of the Black Warrior River at Tuscaloosa. They then either went down the Warrior and Tombigbee Rivers to St. Stephens, where they changed boats and headed up the Alabama River to finally reach Cahaba; or, they went overland from Tuscaloosa to Wilson's Hill (later Montevallo) and then on to the falls of the Cahaba at Centreville, where they could take a flat-bottomed boat down the Cahaba River to the site of the new capital. Either way subjected travelers from the old capital to a rugged and time consuming journey.[40]

The frontier residents of Cahaba were eagerly awaiting the arrival of the state government to their town. Even before Alabama had become a state, Governor Bibb had succeeded in increasing the original federal land grant for the new capital from 640 acres to 1,620 acres. In May 1819, Cahaba's town lots were first opened up for sale. The sales occurred about the same time that the land office in Milledgeville, Georgia, was relocated to Cahaba. An early settler said of these auction sales, "it was a perfect harvest for the tavern keepers, merchants and liquor sellers" because as soon as the surrounding settlers learned that the state's capital was to be located in Cahaba, they "poured in like bees setting on a limb where they could find the

---

[38] Brantley, *Three Capitals*, 57–58; *Ala. Senate Journal (1819)*, 166–170; see also Daniel J. Meador, "The Supreme Court of Alabama—Its Cahaba Beginning, 1820–1825," *Alabama Law Review* 61 (2010): 896–97.

[39] *Ala. House Journal (1819)*, 175; *Ala. Acts (1819)*, 150.

[40] Rogers et al., *Alabama*, 82.

queen had pitched her quarters." As a result of these auctions, attended by Governor Bibb himself, eighty-two lots were sold for a sum total of $123,856, with two of the choicest lots going for approximately $5,000 each. Those purchasing lots constituted a virtual who's who of early Alabama, including such prominent leaders as Reuben Saffold, Uriah J. Mitchell, Samuel Dale, Jesse Beene, William Rufus King, John Crowell, Thomas Bibb, Israel Pickens, Gabriel Moore, Clement C. Clay, and Henry Hitchcock.[41]

The federal land from which these lots were carved was situated at the point where the Cahaba River flows into the Alabama River. This site had been inhabited as early as the Mississippian Period. Its name was derived from two Choctaw words meaning "water above." Unsubstantiated reports place Hernando de Soto and his conquistadors at the site of Alabama's capital-to-be during their 1540 journey through Alabama. Much earlier it was the site of a large village of mound builders during the Mississippian Period (AD 1000–1550). Although the Mississippian culture eventually vanished, many of its members were assimilated by future tribes inhabiting Alabama, including Creek, Choctaw, Chickasaw, and Cherokee. In fact, a Choctaw town of considerable size is believed to have existed at the site in the early eighteenth century, but was abandoned well before Alabama became a territory. Soon after the Alabama River valley became open to white settlement as a result of the end of the Creek War of 1813–1814, the location was called "White's Bluff" for a while in honor of a settler by the name of James White, who is believed to have squatted at the location in 1816. Two years later the first session of the Alabama Territorial General Assembly created Dallas County and designated the "mouth of the Cahawba" as its county seat.[42]

As previously seen, Governor Bibb out-maneuvered the Tombigbee-Warrior faction who had wanted the capital located in Tuscaloosa by using his Washington connections to get the federal government to grant a free section of land at the "mouth of the Cahawba." Having purchased land near Coosada on the Alabama River, Bibb was an advocate for the central part of the state for the capital's location. Bibb had great vision for the Cahaba location, so much so that he asserted that the river's capability of being "navigated by boats of great burthen" combined with the area's "abundant production of an extensive and fertile back Country," assured that the town of Cahawba "promises to vie the largest inland towns in the Country."[43]

Unfortunately, Governor Bibb would not live to see the completion of Cahaba's temporary capitol building nor would Cahaba itself blossom into a

[41] Hobbs, "Early Cahaba," 164–65; Walter M. Jackson, *The Story of Selma* (Birmingham, Ala.: The Birmingham Printing Company, 1954), 6–7; Brantley, *Three Capitals*, 63.

[42] Hobbs, "Early Cahaba," 155–57; Todd Kieth, *Old Cahawba* (Brierfield, Ala.: Cahaba Trace Commission, 2003), 2; Herbert J. Lewis, "Old Cahaba," *Encyclopedia of Alabama*, http://www. encyclopediaofalabama.org/face/Article.jsp?id=h-1543 (accessed January 29, 2013).

[43] Hobbs, "Early Cahaba," 158–59; Brantley, *Three Capitals*, 32–35 (setting forth in its entirety Governor Bibb's address to Alabama's first Territorial Assembly in which he justified his choice of Cahaba as the state's capital).

metropolis. However, at least for a short while, Cahaba reigned supreme in the middle of the wilderness as Alabama's frontier capital. Governor Bibb's grandiose visions concerning Cahaba's future were reflected in the layout of the town said to be modeled after the city of Philadelphia. Its streets bore the same names as those in the nation's former capital, including Walnut, Oak, Mulberry, Chestnut, Ash, Peach, and Pine. On April 5, 1819, even before the sale of the town's lots, Bibb had placed a notice in St. Stephens' *Halcyon and Tombeckbe Advertiser*, inviting bids for the construction of the first State House. The notice set forth detailed specifications for the building's construction, calling for a two-story building, fifty-eight feet long and forty-three feet wide; an interior passage fourteen feet wide on both floors separating one long room on one side from two rooms on the other side; two chimneys and eight windows on each end of the building and twelve windows on the front and back of the building; outer walls to be two feet below the surface thence upward to the first floor two and a half bricks thick and on to the second floor two bricks thick; dividing walls inside were to be one brick and a half, with rooms being plastered and white-washed; the roof's shingles were to be of cypress or heart pine; and doors and stairs to be included.[44]

In May 1819, David and Nicholas Crocheron of Dallas County were awarded the contract to build the State House at Cahaba. The contract was in the amount of $9,000 and required that the principal part of the building be completed by August 1, 1820. The precise time that construction commenced is unknown, but work was definitely in progress when the state's first General Assembly met in Huntsville in October 1819. When finished, offices for the governor and the executive branch were located on the first floor and separate chambers for the Senate and House were housed in two large rooms on the second floor. The completed structure, capped by a shiny copper dome, arising suddenly in the midst of Alabama's back-woods was undoubtedly an imposing sight to the area's frontier settlers.[45]

When those who were to run the state government arrived in Cahaba in November 1820, they found a town not yet completed, but yet full of life on the way to becoming the state's seat of government, as well as the center of its business and social activity. Already there were several taverns, inns, and boarding houses eagerly awaiting the arrival of the members of the General Assembly and other governmental officials coming from all over the state. Merchants were rapidly building stores to accommodate the needs of the town's new citizens. Blacksmiths, carpenters, hostlers, and hatters were opening up shops along with several physicians and a handful of lawyers. Two weekly newspapers, the *Alabama Watchman* and *the Cahawba Press and State Intelligencer* were already in circulation. An advertisement for the Arch Street Hotel located across the street from the State House, appearing in the September 29, 1820, edition of the *Alabama Watchman*, demonstrates the eagerness of local businesses to cater to the

---

[44] Brantley, *Three Capitals*, 63–64.

[45] Ibid., 64; Bert Neville, *A Glance at Old Cahawba, Alabama's Early Capital*, (Selma, Ala.: Coffee Printing Co., 1961), unnumbered pages.

needs of the members of the legislature. This ad stressed that the owner's "utmost exertions will be used to render their customers comfortable," by furnishing their tables with the finest foods available in the market, keeping their rooms neat, and stocking their bar with "genuine liquors." Finally the ad emphasized that the owner was "prepared to accommodate a great many members of the Legislature, having a number of rooms with fire-places," and that "boarders could be accommodated by the week, month, or year."[46]

Even before the completion of the State House and the arrival of the members of the legislature, the judicial branch of the new government met in Cahaba on the second Monday in May 1820 to organize Alabama's first Supreme Court and to hold its first session. Abner S. Lipscomb, Reuben Saffold, Henry Y. Webb, Richard Ellis, and Clement Comer Clay, the justices of the first court, held the court's organizational meeting and first session in the private home of William Pye, who was awarded the sum of $20 for his inconvenience. Before settling down to deciding cases, the justices' first acts of business were to adopt its rules of procedure and to choose Clement Clay as Chief Justice. They then proceeded to issue nine published opinions, all of a civil nature, which became the genesis of Alabama's precedential case law. Perhaps the most significant decision confirmed that the Supreme Court was a tribunal limited primarily to appellate jurisdiction. Most of the other published decisions concerned technical matters such as venue and proof requirements in assumpsit actions (actions to enforce, or recover damages for the breach of, an oral contract or a written contract not made under seal), pleading requirements for actions to recover debts, set off and counterclaim requirements for suits on debts, and the requirements for an appeal bond. Less mundane was the review of a civil action brought against a person accused of killing a slave. In this case the court ruled that no action can be brought for a private injury sustained in a felony until after acquittal of the felony. Finally, in a case reflective of the region's colonial beginnings, the court held that former residents of the Territory of Louisiana subject to Spanish rule were not competent to serve as jurors in Alabama unless they could show they were naturalized U.S. citizens or citizens of Louisiana at the time of its admission into the Union.[47]

Not long after the Supreme Court completed its first session and while the Crocheron brothers were making every effort to get the State House ready for the accommodation of the Legislature, Alabama was stunned with the news of the death of Governor Bibb on August 10, 1820. Already in poor health, Bibb's condition steadily worsened due to injuries sustained when he was thrown from his horse while riding on his plantation near Coosada in Autauga County. The governor did not live to see the completion of the State House that he had pushed so hard for and his death left Cahaba without its principal supporter. The state was also bereft of the leadership

---

[46] Hobbs, "History of Early Cahaba," 166, 168; Owen, *History of Alabama*, 1: 186; *Alabama Watchman*, September 29, 1820.

[47] Brantley, *Three Capitals*, 70; *Minor's Reports*, 1–9; Meador, "Supreme Court of Alabama," 900–06.

of its politically astute founding father who was eulogized by Secretary of State Henry Hitchcock, who said of Bibb's political philosophy: "The sovereignty of the people, the accountability and responsibility of officers, and the supremacy of the laws, expressions common and much discussed, have been with him themes of deep and solemn reflection." In a separate obituary notice, Hitchcock further said of Bibb's personal life that "in the discharge of his domestic duties he was zealous, constant, and parental. . . ." As to Bibb's standing within the community, Hitchcock observed that "his enemies never contradicted the character given him by his friends," despite the presence of a myriad of fierce political factions.[48]

Governor Bibb's brother, Thomas Bibb, succeeded him in office as result of the constitutional provision calling for the President of the Senate to become acting governor in case of the governor's death. In addressing the General Assembly which met in Cahaba for the first time on November 6, 1820, Governor Thomas Bibb lamented that he had assumed the duties of governor "with the most peculiar sensations of pain . . . rising not only from the reflection of the loss of a more experienced officer than myself, but also from a recollection which is continually renewed, that of the loss of a friend and brother." Fittingly, one of the first matters addressed by Thomas Bibb as governor was the completion of the construction of the State House which had been commenced and supervised by his brother. In his message to the Assembly on November 20, 1819, Governor Bibb reported that the State House was almost complete, although not within in the time specified by the contract with the Crocherons. Since the delay was a result of unforeseen circumstances, and due to the immediate necessity of its occupation by the General Assembly, Bibb recommended that the Legislature go ahead and receive it with the stipulation of its completion shortly thereafter. The Crocherons, however, sought additional compensation due to extra work being performed and the difficulties under which the work was performed. After extensive debate the Assembly authorized an additional payment to them in the amount of $4,500, driving the total cost to $13,500, well above the $10,000 authorized previously.[49]

There were a myriad of other matters addressed in Governor Bibb's initial address to the General Assembly. As for an earlier act pertaining to the organization and disciplining of the Alabama militia, he reported that all actions required of the chief executive had been carried out with the exception of setting a time for the election of major generals. He delayed in carrying this provision out in hopes that the Assembly would amend the act to allow such elections to be held at the place of holding courts in each county, as opposed to just one location within each military division as originally enacted. He reported delays in the transmission of some civil and military commissions due to the difficulty of communicating with far-away

---

[48] Brantley, *Three Capitals*, 71–72 (quoting, in part, *Eulogium in Commemoration of His Excellency, William W. Bibb, late Governor of the State of Alabama*, 9–10).

[49] *Ala. Const. 1819*, Art. IV, Sec. 18; *Journal of the Senate at the Second Session of the General Assembly of the State of Alabama* (Cahawba, Ala.: Allen and Drichell, 1820), 10–11 (cited hereafter as *Ala. Senate Journal (1820)*); Brantley, *Three Capitals*, 82.

areas of the state. As to the reservation of lands for the use of a "Seminary of Learning," he reported that that the process had not been completed due to a few delays in surveying and asserted that the future disposition of these lands "imperiously demands your early attention." Other matters addressed by the governor included a report on the status of the building of a six hundred dollar brick structure to house public arms, the upcoming sale of an additional two hundred town lots in Cahaba, the employment of an engineer to examine certain rivers within the state, a delay in the settlement of accounts with the state of Mississippi, the status of a loan made to the state by the Planters and Merchants Bank of Huntsville, a forewarning that receipts into the treasury fell far short of covering the necessary government expenditures of the previous year, a report that census returns had been received from twenty-four counties reflecting an aggregate population of 129,227, and finally a suggestion that the Assembly appoint electors for the upcoming election of President and Vice-President. Upon completion of these various reports, Governor Bibb concluded by stating: "That your deliberations may result in the greatest possible good to the community at large is my anxious and only wish."[50]

Before the Assembly took on its legislative business in earnest, however, its members paid tribute to their fallen governor, to add to that already provided by Secretary of State Hitchcock. A joint legislative committee eulogized Bibb and "his revered memory," describing him as a "friend of liberty and of man," as well as "a pure republican . . . devoted to the service of his country." The joint committee also resolved that members of the Assembly would wear black crape on their left arm during the session then in progress, and that the Reverend Mr. Kennedy be requested to deliver a sermon at funeral services to be held in the State House on November 26, 1820. Finally, during this session, the Assembly passed an act changing the name of Cahawba County to that of Bibb County in honor of the deceased governor.[51]

As the second session of the General Assembly got down to the serious business before it, the overriding issue was reapportionment. This issue, however, would not be resolved during this session due to the fact that the Alabama River basin group favoring Cahaba as the permanent capital, formerly headed by William W. Bibb, did not trust their former leader's brother, who they ironically considered anti-Cahaba. Therefore, they wished to delay reapportionment at least until the 1821–1822 session when pending census returns would be available, and hopefully, in their minds, there would be a new governor. Their ultimate fear was that by 1825, without a favorable reapportionment, there would be a majority favoring a removal of the capital from Cahaba.[52]

Although reapportionment was not achieved during this session, the Assembly passed over one hundred laws and authored twelve resolutions.

---

[50] *Ala. Senate Journal (1820)*, 11–13.

[51] *Ala. Senate Journal (1820)*, 18–19; *Ala. Acts (1820)*, 63.

[52] Brantley, *Three Capitals*, 83–84.

Many of the laws enacted were simply amendments to acts passed in the first session of the Assembly. Others were designed to consolidate several enactments into one act. Routine legislation authorized St. Clair, Perry, Blount, Wilcox, Marengo, Montgomery, and Lauderdale counties to designate their "seats of Justice" and extended the boundaries of Baldwin and Autauga counties. The towns of Selma, Claiborne, Washington, Elyton, and the lower portion of the town of Tuscaloosa were also incorporated by acts of this session of the Assembly. The anticipated increase of traffic on the navigable rivers of the state as a result of the advent of steamboats was reflected in legislation which incorporated the Cahawba Navigation Company, the Steam-Boat Company of Alabama, the Flint River Navigation Company, and the Indian Creek Navigation Company. Another act granted John Fowler the right to operate a steam ferry boat between Mobile and Blakeley. Additional transportation projects were financed by lotteries, including one for the benefit of the navigation of the Buttahachee River, a tributary of the Tombigbee River rising in Winston County and flowing through Marion County to Mississippi, and one for the construction of a bridge over Clear Creek within the town of Cahaba. The use of lotteries were not limited to transportation projects as evidenced by an act authorizing lotteries for the benefit of three Masonic Halls to be built in Claiborne, Cahaba, and Tuscaloosa.[53]

Education was addressed in the 1820 legislative session by the passage of an act establishing the "Seminary of Learning," which had been mentioned in an act of the first legislative session authorizing commissioners to search for the most suitable site for a state university. The act passed in the second session designated the so-called seminary of learning as "The University of the State of Alabama," and appointed three commissioners for each county in which seminary lands were located who were tasked with leasing the lands at public auction at terms most advantageous to the state. Still, it would be another eleven years before Alabama's first university, denoted as the state's "capstone of education" by one of its future presidents, would open its doors to its first class consisting principally of the sons of wealthy planters.[54]

One of the more practical pieces of legislation passed during the Assembly's second session was an act granting the circuit courts of the new state jurisdiction to decree divorces, a power which had previously resided solely within the ambit of the General Assembly during territorial days. Now divorce actions could be filed for in the circuit courts. Decrees could be issued for the benefit of husbands whose wives committed adultery or left their bed and board voluntarily for two years with the intention of abandonment. Wives likewise could be granted divorce decrees for adultery and abandonment by their husbands, as well as for a husband's treatment of her that was "so cruel, barbarous, and inhuman, as actually to endanger her life." After a court issued its final decree, however, it was required to send a certified copy of its proceedings to the Speaker of the House of Representa-

---

[53] *Ala. Acts (1820)*, generally, and 13–14, 29–31, 34–35, 69–70, 82–83, 85–87, 93, and 97–99.

[54] Ibid., 4–6.

tives who was required to read the record in the presence of members of the
Assembly. The decree then would not take effect unless approved by a two-
thirds vote of both houses of the Assembly. Nothing suggests that this was
anything but a pro forma vote to rubber stamp the action of the circuit
courts who weighed the evidence in these cases.[55]

Governor Thomas Bibb was considered by many as a caretaker governor for his brother's unfulfilled term. He confirmed that belief by choosing
not to seek reelection. As the gubernatorial election to be held in August
1821 approached, north Alabamians pushed the candidacy of Dr. Henry
Chambers of Madison County who would run against Israel Pickens the
candidate favored in south Alabama. When it appeared that Pickens would
probably defeat Chambers, Bibb's protégés in Madison, Limestone, and
Tuscaloosa Counties who were in favor of moving the state capital from
Cahaba urged him to call a special session of the legislature. Their hope was
to enact a reapportionment bill prior to the election of Pickens who was
aligned with those sympathetic to keeping the capital in Cahaba. In view of
his belief that the constitution required a new apportionment law prior to
the 1821 annual session, Governor Bibb called the Assembly back into
session for the first special legislative session in the state's short history on
June 4, 1821.[56]

In a written address to the special session of the Assembly, Governor
Bibb chastised its members for failing to pass a reapportionment bill in the
previous session as required by the state's Constitution. Mincing no words,
and in dramatic fashion, Bibb asserted that their failure to do so "threat-
en[ed] the very existence of the legislative branch of the government." After
a rather complex recitation of constitutional principles which he argued
required the passage of a reapportionment bill, Governor Bibb asserted that
"the manifest imperfections in the existing laws for the collection of the
Revenue . . . would have been alone sufficient to have induced a called
session." Reporting that ostensibly high taxes were not enough to cover the
current charges upon the Treasury, Bibb also urged the Assembly to completely revamp the mode of tax assessments.[57]

The Senate objected to the governor's call for a reapportionment of its
body on the grounds that it could not be reapportioned until the expiration
of the first terms of the state's senators in August 1822. The House, however, amended the Senate bill to require the reapportionment of the Senate
also. The Senate brought on a stalemate when it outright rejected the House
amendment. The House finally capitulated and agreed to pass the Senate
bill, albeit by a very narrow margin of just one vote. Representative Samuel
Chapman of Madison County changed his vote in order for the Senate bill
to pass, citing a fear that if at least some form of reapportionment were not
passed, "the government would dissolve and society thrown into a state of

[55] Ibid., 79–80; *Ala. Const. of 1819*, Art. VI, Sec. 13.

[56] Brantley, *Three Capitals*, 84–85; *Journal of the Senate at the Called Session of the General Assembly of the State of Alabama, 1821* (Cahawba: Allen & Brickell, 1821) (cited hereafter as *Ala. Senate Journal (Called Sess., 1821)*).

[57] *Ala. Senate Journal (Called Sess., 1821)*, 4–9.

anarchy and confusion. . ." On June 18, 1821, however, Governor Bibb exercised the first gubernatorial veto in state history by refusing to the sign the compromise bill that only provided for a new reapportionment of the House. The Senate passed the bill over the governor's veto, but it failed to become law when the House did not have enough votes to overcome the veto.[58]

The Assembly did manage to pass, at Governor Bibb's urging, a bill that revised the methods for assessing and collecting taxes. In an effort to assure that taxable property would not be overlooked, this bill authorized the appointment of justices of the peace or other public officials as tax assessors in all militia mustering districts within each of the counties throughout the state. Other legislation of note passed during this short special session included that granting liens to those involved in the building trades until final payment was received pursuant to contracts relating to buildings under construction; imposing a tax on non-residents who imported, "goods, wares, merchandise, or other commodities" for sale within the state; authorizing "any licensed Minister of the Gospel of any denomination" to perform marriage ceremonies; and amending the insolvency law to allow debtors to be absolved of arrest or imprisonment upon posting a bond of sufficient security and surrendering property for the benefit of his or her creditors. Nevertheless, Alabama's first special session of its legislature adjourned on June 18, 1821, without achieving its primary goal of reapportionment.[59]

After the adjournment of the special session, two events occurred that would portend significant changes in the political landscape of the new state. First, in the summer and fall of 1821, Cahaba was hit hard by heavy rains and yellow fever, referred to as a "bilious remitting fever." Recurring floods and dangerous fevers for the next several years would eventually tilt the capital relocation vote in favor of those favoring to move the capital to Tuscaloosa. The second significant occurrence was Thomas Bibb's decision not to run for reelection. His decision opened the way for the election of Israel Pickens, who had rejected his prior allegiance to the Georgia faction. William Wyatt Bibb's death combined with the election of Pickens led to the ultimate demise of the influence of the Georgia faction in Alabama politics. Due to the wealthy Georgians' well-known influence in Washington, early Alabamians had trusted them to establish their state government. Once the foundation of the state's government had been laid, however, Alabama's electorate began to gravitate to so-called candidates of the "common man," such as Israel Pickens and, later, those supportive of the presidential candidacy of Andrew Jackson.[60]

---

[58] Brantley, *Three Capitals*, 84–87; *Ala. House Journal (Called Sess., 1821)*, 59–61.

[59] *Ala. Acts (Called Sess., 1821)*, 3–6, 18–19, and 26–29.

[60] Abernethy, *Formative Period*, 120–24; Brantley, *Three Capitals*, 89.

Andrew Jackson, 1824
Portrait by Philadelphia artist Thomas Sully

8

&

REJECTION OF THE GEORGIA FACTION AND REMOVAL OF THE CAPITAL FROM CAHABA

Israel Pickens became Alabama's third governor by taking advantage of public resentment that had been intensifying against the Planters and Merchants Bank of Huntsville whose capital was primarily under the control of wealthy former Georgians then dominating state government and federal patronage within the state. Ironically, Pickens had initially aligned himself politically with the Georgia faction when he had moved to Alabama from North Carolina in 1817 to become the register of the land office in St. Stephens. Equally as ironic, Pickens was himself a man of wealth and became the first president of the Tombeckbe Bank of St. Stephens, which had been created by the first session of the Alabama Territorial General Assembly.[1]

Perhaps the most adept politician in Alabama at that time, Pickens quickly distanced himself from the Georgia machine when he realized that it was out of favor with the common folks who regarded it as a party of the privileged few. Also, more and more voters were realizing the close association between the Georgia machine and the reviled Merchants and Planters Bank. The Huntsville bank, perceived as the advocate of the wealthy and the enemy of the common man, had earned a poor reputation by speculating with government specie, exchanging its own depreciated notes at par for government specie, over-extending loans, and suspending specie payments. In juxtaposition to the Planters and Merchants Bank was the Tombeckbe Bank of St. Stephens. As a result of Pickens' skillful management abilities, that bank was a success and avoided the unpopularity which had befallen the Huntsville bank. In an effort to maintain the bank's solvency and provide it specie during bad economic times, Pickens shrewdly arranged to have one of the Tombeckbe Bank's agents serve as the cotton factor for three-fourths of the cotton produced in the surrounding area. Because of this success, as well as Pickens' announced support for the chartering of a state bank that would transfer fiscal control away from private banks dominated by the wealthy planter class, Pickens became a "champion of the people."[2]

On the right side of the banking issue and with a more engaging personality, Pickens easily defeated the Georgia faction's candidate, Dr. Henry Chambers, an eminent physician who had emigrated from Virginia to

---

[1] Hugh C. Bailey, "Israel Pickens, People's Politician," *Alabama Review* 17 (April 1964): 83–84.

[2] Ibid., 84–85; Thornton, *Power and Politics*, 16.

Huntsville about 1815. Chambers' support was primarily limited to a small number of counties in north Alabama. The final tally was 9,616 in favor of Pickens and 7,129 for Dr. Chambers. John W. Walker, who certainly had more name recognition throughout the state than Dr. Chambers, had offered to leave the Senate to serve as the Georgia faction's candidate for governor, but by the time he made that offer, Dr. Chambers had already been chosen to take on Pickens. Henry Hitchcock, sensing the tide turning in Pickens' favor, expressed to Senator Walker that it was a blessing in disguise that he did not make the race due to its potential to bring Walker the "mortification of defeat." For this reason among others, Hitchcock further opined that "you may well congratulate yourself on being released from the trouble of the contest."[3]

Governor Israel Pickens

Courtesy of Alabama Department of Archives and History

[3] *Journal of the House of Representatives of the General Assembly of the State of Alabama, 1821* (Cahawba: William R. Allen & Co., 1821), 25 (hereafter *Ala. House Journal (1821)*); Bailey, *John Williams Walker*, 106–107; Willis Brewer, *Alabama: Her History, Resources, War Record, and Public Men, From 1540 to 1872* (1872; repr., Baltimore, Md: Genealogical Publishing Co., 2000), 350–51.

Upon taking the oath of office on November 9, 1821, Governor Pickens delivered his inaugural address to a joint session the General Assembly in which he remarked on the incredible rapidity of Alabama's emergence from the wilderness: "The fairest portion of our territory, and even the spot where we are assembled, was but yesterday unknown as the residence of civilized man. The prospects which nature alone presented have successfully invited a respectable order of emigration, and filled our forests with the improvements of good society." He then focused upon the need for further development of the state's navigable streams and overland transportation methods, "where the greatest practical benefits can be affected with the smallest means." Next he asserted that the constitution indisputably required the apportionment of one or both houses of the legislature, while at the same time diplomatically recognizing that the dispute over the apportionment issue was based upon unavoidable honest differences of opinion. The governor also asserted that speculation in public land sales had contributed to the state's "pecuniary difficulties" and the suppression of vigorous industry. He stated, however, that Alabama should be able overcome these problems as a result of more than two million dollars being pumped into the economy by the annual production of cotton within the state.[4]

Governor Pickens saved the specifics of his legislative proposals for a detailed written address presented to the Assembly four days after his inaugural address. In keeping with his assertion in his inaugural address that the state constitution required a new apportionment, he first pointed out that the latest census abstracts were available to enable the Assembly to proceed with the apportionment of representatives of both houses of the legislature. He next seized upon recommendations made by Governor Thomas Bibb on his way out of office concerning the University of Alabama. In this regard, he agreed with Bibb that University lands should be sold, but advocated that the lands be sold on an installment basis to yield more sales as opposed to cash sales as had been proposed by Bibb. He also agreed with Bibb's proposal that the yet to be built University be allowed to invest an amount not exceeding $100,000 in stock of a state bank. In order to ensure that the University would not need such funds for construction, Pickens managed to delay debate of the location of the University to future sessions of the legislature while pressing in the meantime for the incorporation of the university and allowing its trustees to sell land and invest the proceeds from these sales.[5]

Other items addressed by the governor included a recommendation that the state's Treasury refuse to accept any paper that was not the equivalent of specie; a call for the examination of ways to improve the navigation of the Alabama and Tombigbee Rivers and their tributaries, as well as establishing the best portages on the Tennessee River particularly in the Shoals area; a report to the Assembly from the Secretary of War "urging the propriety of preventing the sale of spirits to Indians;" a report that no court had yet convened in Henry County accompanied with a request that action

---

[4] *Ala. House Journal (1821)*, 58–64.

[5] Ibid., 40–43; Brantley, *Three Capitals*, 98.

be taken to ensure that court be "regularly holden" in that county; and a request that a committee be appointed to examine the records of Alabama's first two governors, asserting that proper books and records had not been maintained by those administrations. Pickens concluded his address with a platitude expressing the hope "that our joint labors . . . may result in promoting the best general interests and satisfying the just expectations of our constituents."[6]

Although Governor Pickens had not set forth the details for a state bank in his initial messages to the Assembly, the establishment of such a bank was the major concern of his administration. The newly elected governor had barely assumed office when the legislature—at the behest of those supporting the Planters and Merchants Bank of Huntsville—voted to amend a bill passed in the 1820 session that called for the incorporation of the Bank of the State of Alabama, with one half of the capital stock reserved to the state and the total amount of capital stock set not to exceed two million dollars. That bank had been a colossal failure due to an inability to attract the necessary subscribers for its stock. Private bank supporters thus proposed and passed what they termed as an amendment to the act that had set up the failed state bank. This amendment provided that the state would provide forty percent of the capital for a state bank and would correspondingly have forty percent control of the institution. Governor Pickens, however, vetoed this measure upon discovering that existing private banks could become branches of the state bank and would actually be in control of the state bank during its formative period well before the state would be authorized to exercise the control commensurate with its capital contribution. The governor was also concerned that by taking in the three private banks already chartered by the state—Planters and Merchants Bank of Huntsville, the Bank of Mobile, and the Tombeckbe Bank of St. Stephens—the state bank would be burdened by immense debt at its outset. The Assembly was unable to pass the bill over the governor's veto, the House's attempt to do so falling short by a vote of 26-20. Governor Pickens had won the day by stopping the private bank supporters in their tracks. He decided to let the dust settle a bit, however, before pushing for a banking bill more in line with what he and his common folk electorate had in mind.[7]

While the banking issue was put on the back burner, the Assembly was able to take up the previously controversial reapportionment question and quietly passed a new apportionment bill. Because the capital relocation issue was to be revisited in 1825, the opposing factions regarding this issue—the Tombigbee/Warrior basin group pushing Tuscaloosa and the Alabama/Cahaba River system group pushing Cahaba—cautiously kept an eye on each other during the creation of new senatorial districts. That they were able to come to an agreement is somewhat remarkable in light of the fact that the Alabama/Cahaba River system group who opposed reloca-

<hr />

[6] *Ala. House Journal (1821)*, 43–48.

[7] Abernethy, *Formative Period*, 114–15; Bailey, "Israel Pickens," 87; Brantley, *Three Capitals*, 102–04; Moore, *History of Alabama*, 117; *Ala. Acts (1820)*, 20–27; *Ala. House Journal (1821)*, 227–33.

tion—knowing that it would be impossible for them to take over the House—sought to create senatorial districts that would give them the best opportunity to gain control of the Senate by 1825. There were no guarantees for either side, however, as some newly created districts were composed of counties that benefited from both river systems, whereas some districts were not significantly benefited by either system.[8]

Although Governor Pickens was unable to get the bank bill he wanted during this session, the legislature did pass at his request a bill that provided for a Board of Trustees to govern the University of Alabama. The bill provided that two trustees were to be elected from each of the six judicial circuits in the state for a term of three years. More importantly, this Board was authorized to sell lands set aside for the University and to invest the proceeds. As outlined in his initial address to the General Assembly, Governor Pickens fully expected that the Board's investments would include a State bank, which would be established soon to take advantage of the fact that no funds were yet needed for the University whose location had still not been addressed.[9]

One of the more interesting bills in the 1821 session was one granting the first pension in the state's history to Samuel Dale, Indian scout and one of the heroes of the Canoe Fight during the Creek War. In response to Dale's lobbying on his own behalf, the Assembly bestowed the rank of brevet brigadier general upon him and awarded him a pension equivalent to half the pay of a colonel in the United States Army for life. Recognizing the services he rendered in protecting vulnerable frontier inhabitants "from Indian rapine and Indian barbarity" and recognizing that his services during the Creek War had subjected him "to privations, hardships and difficulties that have impaired his constitution and reduced him to indigence," the Assembly asserted that it had a duty "not only to remunerate him for losses actually sustained, but also to compensate him for his distinguished services." Keeping with this line of thought, the Assembly also discharged an indebtedness of $229.04¼ owed by Dale for the collection of taxes in Monroe County for the year 1817. The Assembly was not so generous with Jeremiah Austill, one of the other heroes of the Canoe Fight. While it passed a resolution of "unfeigned thanks" for Austill's "heroic exertions" during the Creek War, it did not provide him a pension as it had for Dale. Perhaps it was because Austill was a considerably younger man who appeared to have the ability to provide for himself as would later be demonstrated by several successful endeavors, including as a merchant, a member of the Alabama Legislature, and a plantation owner.[10]

---

[8] Brantley, *Three Capitals*, 104–05.

[9] Ibid., 105–06.

[10] Ibid., 101–02; *Ala. Acts (1821)*, 53, 60–61, 115–16. Concern for the unfairness of singling out just one person—albeit a deserving one—for a pension, and the belief that the public treasury was not intended for charitable purposes, prompted a group in the 1822 session of the General Assembly to attempt to take Dale's pension away. Although that attempt failed, the group was successful in taking away his designation as brigadier general. The 1823 session, however, succeeded in withdrawing his pension altogether. Dale went to court in an effort to retain his pension, but the Alabama Supreme Court ruled that the legislature was within its province to

Although there were no other major acts passed during this legislative session, several were enacted that reflected the raw character of the new state, as well as its need for further development. As a sign of the still violent times, the General Assembly found the need to extend a requirement that all public officials and attorneys take an oath affirming that they had not participated in a duel in the previous year nor would they do so during their term of office. In an effort to thwart vandalism inflicted upon the livestock, crops, and property of Alabama's frontier farmers, the Assembly passed a law authorizing a jury to impose a fine of up to four times the value of any property destroyed or damaged upon any person convicted of such acts of malicious mischief. With regard to internal improvements, the state's emerging river transportation continued to receive attention of the Assembly with its incorporation of the Mobile Steam Boat Company, the third such company to be incorporated since Alabama's entry into the Union. The General Assembly also continued to authorize lotteries to finance projects such as a bridge in Greene County, a turnpike road in Mobile County, and an academy in the town of Montgomery.[11]

Finally, the General Assembly of 1821 also dealt with individual acts pertaining to divorces and slave emancipations. The several divorces during this session were for the first time mere confirmations of the circuit courts who heard the cases in the first instance. With regard to slaves, a citizen in Dallas County was authorized to emancipate a female slave and her ten children provided that they leave the state with the warning that, "if any of the persons emancipated by this act shall return into this State and remain as residents of their own accord such person or persons shall be considered to be in the same state of slavery as if this act had never passed." For reasons not expressed, two slaves in other parts of the state were authorized to be emancipated without the requirement that they leave the state.[12]

The next session of the General Assembly in 1822 concentrated on political issues more so than legislation. During this session, the Assembly's election of two U.S. Senators effectively ended the political control of the Georgia faction whose influence had been rapidly declining since the election of Israel Pickens as governor. But before the political maneuvering began, Governor Pickens delivered a written address to the Assembly on November 18, 1822, in which he proudly proclaimed that they were "the first General Assembly chosen under the permanent system of representation provided by the constitution." He reported that the state's financial condition was improved because the Treasury's paper was circulating at par and the loan to the state from the Planters and Merchants Bank was almost paid off. He next outlined in great detail what he deemed vital requisites for "a State Bank established conformably to the Constitution—on correct principles—wisely and honestly conducted." In this regard, he stressed the need for the state to have significant influence in the governance of the

---

withdraw the pension. Brantley, *Three Capitals*, 116–17, 134; *Ala. Acts (1822)*, 138; *Acts (1823)*, 115; *Dale vs. The Governor*, 3 Stewart 387.

[11] *Ala. Acts (1821)*, 16–17, 24–25, 45–46, 54–56, 76–77, and 87–88.

[12] *Ala. Acts (1821)*, 99–100, 107–13.

corporation and to have an interest in the bank's capital in a degree proportionate to its control. His paramount concern however, was to ensure that
the state bank be organized before existing private banks were allowed to
be associated with it. At all costs, he wanted to prevent private interests in
gaining control of the state bank and burdening it with their debts, as he
had earlier indicated in his veto of the bank bill in the last session of the
Assembly.[13]

With respect to another banking issue, Pickens reported that the Planters and Merchants Bank of Huntsville had failed to resume payment of
specie within the time allotted by a bill enacted in the last session of the
Assembly. Accordingly, he had directed the prosecutor for the First Circuit,
in which Huntsville was located, to institute *quo warranto* proceedings (in
essence, a legal action to revoke the bank's charter) against the bank.
Finally, the governor shared with the Assembly the decrees and minutes of
the first meeting of the Board of Trustees of the University of Alabama. He
then expressed that it might become necessary to enact legislation concerning the lands of the University and the investment of its funds. There is no
doubt that this is what Pickens wanted in order to partially fund his desired
bank, but he stated that he would put off making any such recommendation
until the Board of Trustees convened again since the Board would have to
concur in any such proposed acts.[14]

Senator John W. Walker set the political maneuvering into motion
when he resigned his Senate seat due to declining health. In a letter to
Governor Pickens dated November 21, 1822, Walker announced his resignation: "Though improving, I improve but slowly; and though I may eventually be so fortunate as to regain my wonted strength, the period is uncertain and may be distant. Meantime the state ought not to suffer, nor lose a
portion of its representation on account of my infirmities." He also expressed the hope that in selecting his successor the Assembly would "fix on
an individual, who, to equal zeal and devotion for the interests of Alabama,
may unite happier talents and more vigorous health." The Georgia faction,
which had been aware of Walker's deteriorating condition for several
months, had serious doubts about their ability to retain his Senate seat in
view of their declining popularity. Their candidate, John McKinley of
Madison County, surprisingly lost by just one vote, 39-38, to William Kelly
of the so-called "People's Party."[15] However, a loss is a loss, and it was
compounded by the Assembly's reelection of Senator William Rufus King
over the Georgia faction's challenger, William Crawford. It took seven
ballots with a final vote of 38 to 35, but, as a result, the Georgians were

---

[13] Brantley, *Three Capitals*, 107–11; *Journal of the House of Representatives of the State of
Alabama, 1822* (Cahawba: William B. Allen & Co., 1823, 9–11 (hereafter *Ala. House Journal
(1822)*).

[14] Brantley, *Three Capitals*, 111; *Ala. House Journal (1822)*, 13.

[15] The "People's Party" of the 1820s representing the so-called common man is a distinct entity
from the People's, or Populist, Party that emerged in the 1890s in Alabama, as well as
nationally. In Alabama, this later party was made up primarily of small farmers and organized
labor. See Brantley, *Three Capitals*, 114, and Bailey, *John Williams Walker*, 177–81, for references to the earlier "People's Party."

virtually powerless for the first time since Alabama had achieved statehood as a result of their political influence in Washington.[16]

In addition to electing Alabama's two senators, the General Assembly of 1822 was otherwise primarily consumed with routine matters, such as delineating technical legal matters of jurisdiction, venue, and statutes of limitations; creating new counties; refining boundaries of existing counties; establishing county seats; incorporating new towns; authorizing public roads; emancipating slaves; and granting divorces. Of more significance, the Assembly followed Governor Pickens' recommendation in authorizing the University of Alabama's trustees to invest in any state bank to be established by it an amount not exceeding $100,000. It also provided for the suspension of *quo warranto* proceedings against the Planters and Merchants Bank of Huntsville in exchange for a pledge from the board of directors of the bank that they would resume specie payments during the course of the following year.[17]

The Assembly also again passed measures which reflected the need to bring order to its fledgling frontier society. For example, due to the unruliness of some of its citizens, the Assembly passed an act to prohibit "immoral and disorderly conduct at places of religious worship," providing for a fine of twenty dollars for any "wicked persons . . . found guilty of willfully raising a riot, getting drunk, swearing, or any other act by which the congregation shall be interrupted." In an effort to further ensure the sanctity of religious gatherings, the Assembly also provided for a fine of forty dollars for anyone retailing "spirituous liquors" within two miles of any camp meeting or other religious meeting, unless they actually resided within two miles of such a meeting and held a retailing license. In another measure addressing the sale of liquor, the Assembly made it illegal for "free Negroes and mulattoes" to retail, directly or indirectly, any kind of spirituous liquors. The fine for the first offense was only ten dollars, but the punishment for a second offense, in addition to a fine, included the receipt of up to twenty-five lashes on the bare back. However, the act exempted any "free negro or mulatto" or their descendants who had become citizens of the United States as a result of the treaty between Spain and the United States. In all probability such legislation was enacted out of fear that free persons of color would make sales to the enslaved population of African Americans. In any event, the Assembly kept a close eye on the sale of hard liquor to anyone due to their undoubted concern for alcohol induced violence on the frontier. According to A. J. Rorabaugh, hard drinking was common on the frontier "when the typical American annually drank more distilled liquor than at any time in our history." Indeed, as Alabama historian A.B. Moore put it with reference to the Alabama frontier, "Drinking was almost as common as eating." A fact not surprising to Moore in view of the fact that

---

[16] *Ala. House Journal* (1822), 47; Brantley, *Three Capitals*, 112–14; Bailey, *John Williams Walker*, 177–81. Unfortunately, Senator Walker continued to deteriorate and died just a few months later. He was only forty years old at the time of his death. The newly created Walker County was named in his honor in recognition of his many contributions to the young state.

[17] *Ala. Acts (1822)*, 3–139.

"every little village had its 'grog-shops,' 'dram-shops,' or 'tippling houses'" leading to frequent incidents of public drunkenness and rowdyism.[18]

The next session of the Assembly was preceded by a gubernatorial campaign in which Israel Pickens sought reelection. The Georgia faction again tapped Dr. Henry Chambers to run against Pickens. Tremendously weakened by the loss of their leaders William Bibb and John W. Walker, as well as by their loss of both Senate seats, the Georgia faction failed yet again with Pickens winning by a vote of 6,942 to 4,604. With this victory, Pickens took his second oath of office on November 25, 1823, and immediately began to push the legislature, with both houses now controlled by those loyal to the governor, to once and for all establish a state bank that would insure a sound currency. Also, the governor again sought to delay the location of the State's university so as to allow its board of trustees to invest in a bank rather than in the construction of buildings for the university. To this end, in his written address to the Assembly Pickens advanced the idea that the healthiness of any of the university's possible locations had not been sufficiently tested to warrant a selection at that time. Other matters urged by the governor in his initial address to the Assembly included a reformation of the judicial code designed to prohibit litigation from being disposed of by technicalities rather than on the merits; a regular reporting of decisions of the Alabama Supreme Court; adoption of a general law of incorporation to spare the Assembly of so many individual incorporations; an improvement of navigation on the Tombigbee, Black Warrior, and Coosa Rivers; and opposition to the introduction of slaves into the state for the purpose of trafficking, denoting the trade as a "public evil."[19]

Before enacting legislation establishing a state bank as requested by the governor, the 1823 session of the Assembly briefly turned its attention to national politics when both the Senate and House passed a resolution endorsing General Andrew Jackson as "a suitable candidate for the President of the United States." The resolutions passed with ease but neither was unanimous. Jackson's popularity in Alabama was such that those opposing the resolution were the subject of much criticism and felt the need to explain that their vote was not based upon any disrespect for the hero of Horseshoe Bend and New Orleans, but instead was based upon their beliefs that the resolution was not a constitutionally appropriate subject for the legislature, that the legislature should not support one candidate over another, and that their constituents had not communicated to them support for the resolution. Governor Pickens, despite Jackson's popularity, joined those opposing the resolution by vetoing it, agreeing that it was "not fairly within the legitimate sphere of legislation." Consummate politician that he was, Pickens still managed to please Jackson's supporters by praising Jackson's patriotism: "His signal gallantry has not merely given him a

---

[18] Ibid., 53–54, 61; A. J. Rorabaugh, *"The Alcoholic Republic: An American Tradition* (New York: Oxford University Press, 1979), 7; Moore, *History of Alabama,* 144.

[19] Brantley, *Three Capitals,* 122–24; Rogers, et al., *Alabama,* 78; *Journal of the House of Representatives of the State of Alabama, 1823* (Cahawba: William B. Allen & Co., 1823), 8–17 (hereafter *Ala. House Journal (1823)*), 8–17.

rank among the conquerors of modern times, but his uniform and eminent usefulness in the protection of our southern frontier has enlisted his name among the saviors of his country. . . ."[20]

Governor Pickens' popularity and his diplomatic handling of the Jackson resolution insulated him from the criticism that was bestowed upon some of those legislators who had voted against the resolution. The Georgia faction for the most part had originally opposed Jackson because of their support for Secretary of the Treasury William H. Crawford who was also running for President. The indignant reaction to their opposition to the Jackson resolution, however, caused many of those associated with them to reassess their positions. The most conspicuous case of realignment of allegiances occurred when Dr. Henry Chambers—twice previously supported by the Georgia faction in unsuccessful campaigns for governor against Israel Pickens—became an ardent Jackson supporter and served as a presidential elector on the Jackson ticket in the presidential election of 1824. Chambers' realignment served him well as he was elected to the U.S. Senate in 1824, beating William Kelly by a vote of 41-36. Dr. Chambers, however, however, died in Virginia on the way to Washington to assume his seat in the Senate.[21]

In the meanwhile, after putting national politics aside, the 1823 session of Alabama's General Assembly finally presented Governor Pickens with a bank he could accept. The act provided for an initial capitalization of a little more than $200,000. Approximately one-half of that amount was subscribed by the Trustees of the University of Alabama just as Governor Pickens had so carefully maneuvered to arrange. The rest of the capital came from the three percent fund that had been donated by Congress for internal improvements, state funds generated from the seat of government grant, monies due from the lease of the Salt Springs, funds generated as a result of escheats to the State, and the proceeds of state bonds sold on the New York market. The bank opened the next year in Cahaba and was directed by a president and a board of directors to be elected annually by both houses of the Assembly.[22]

The Bank of the State of Alabama was the state's first major institution that required the oversight of the legislature. Regrettably, as noted by historian Leah Rawls Atkins, members of the legislature "viewed the bank as an immense pork barrel waiting for their eager spoons." Indeed, the Senate rejected an amendment to the bank bill that would have prevented Assemblymen from doing business with the bank, but did make them ineligible for a bank office for at least five years. Politics, however, would dominate the election of bank officers and directors. This was evidenced

---

[20] Journal of the Senate of the State of Alabama, 1823 (Cahawba: William B. Allen, 1824), 83 (hereafter *Ala. Senate Journal (1823)*); *Ala. House Journal (1823)*, 77, 120–21, and 136–37; Brantley, *Three Capitals*, 127–30.

[21] Abernethy, *Formative Period*, 130; Moore, *History of Alabama, 119;* Brewer, *Alabama*, 351; *Journal of the Senate of the State of Alabama, 1824* (Cahawba: Wm B. Allen, 1825), 60–61 (hereafter *Ala. Senate Journal (1824)*).

[22] *Ala. Acts (1823)*, 3–11; Brantley, *Three Capitals*, 130; Rogers et al., *Alabama*, 79–80.

when a joint session of the Assembly chose the governor's brother, Andrew Pickens, to serve as the bank's first president, and such prominent attorneys and politicians as Henry Hitchcock, Jesse Beene, and Horatio G. Perry to serve on the bank's first board of directors. Soon after the state bank was created, it lost one of its major private bank competitors when the Planters and Merchants Bank of Huntsville—an institution which had been dominated by the Georgia faction—failed to resume specie payments within the time set by an act of the 1823 Assembly, thus requiring Governor Pickens to proclaim the institution "null and void."[23]

In addition to establishing a bank, the 1823 Assembly addressed a myriad of issues, including regulating the licensing of physicians and surgeons, allowing compensation for witnesses, increasing compensation for jurors to a total of a dollar per day and four cents a mile for travel, creating Walker County, providing for further internal improvements, compensating Ferdinand Sannoner $120 for making a map of the State, compensating Henry Hitchcock $1200 for superintending the printing of a digest of the laws of the state that had been compiled by the deceased Judge Harry Toulmin, confirming seven divorces, and emancipating eleven slaves. The 1823 Assembly also rejected a plan set forth by Governor Pickens providing that Alabama's presidential electors be chosen by districts instead of on a statewide basis. Pickens had so proposed because he was fearful that a statewide vote would result in Andrew Jackson receiving all of Alabama's allotted electors. Pickens, despite Andrew Jackson's popularity in the state, was a supporter of John Quincy Adams for President and apparently believed that voting by districts might result in Adams peeling off a couple of votes in south Alabama where the planter class was in control. Pickens' fears of a statewide election proved to be well founded when Jackson received all of the state's electors, with a majority in every county except for Montgomery, Butler, and Greene. Jacksonian Democracy was in now in full sway in Alabama.[24]

When Governor Pickens addressed the 1824 General Assembly on November 16, 1824, he prudently avoided mention of the presidential race and instead concentrated on local domestic issues. He first reported that the site of the University of Alabama had still not been selected, which, as we have seen, was in accord with his plan for the University trustees to be able to invest in the new state bank. As a matter of fact, the governor indicated that the bank had already received $39,667.31¼ of an expected total of $100,000 from the University's funds. The governor also announced that census returns would soon be available for the all-important apportionment of the 1825 Assembly that would decide the seat of government issue. The governor also made available for the Assembly's contemplation a plan adopted by the state of Ohio for the gradual emancipation and colonization of its slaves. In addition, Pickens spoke to a continuing pet peeve of his pertaining to the state's judicial practice. In this regard, he made another

---

[23] Rogers et al., *Alabama*, 80; Bailey, "Israel Pickens," 93; *Ala. Senate Journal (1823)*, 54; *Ala. Acts (1823)*, 28–29.

[24] *Ala. Acts (1823)*, 3–116; *Ala. Senate Journal (1823)*, 12; Brantley, *Three Capitals*, 135–36.

plea to the General Assembly to eliminate the technicalities in the legal system "which tend so materially to impede the administration of justice," asserting that "the course of proceeding in our courts should be regulated with no other view, than to the correct and speedy attainment of justice...." Again, he sought to ensure that cases were decided upon their merits rather than esoteric rules. The main culprit in the governor's view was the hyper-technical nature of the English pleading system that was confusing to Alabama's frontier lawyers, and instead "required a distinct class of legal professors" to decipher it.[25]

While generally steering clear of national issues, Governor Pickens did comment on the current visit to the United States by French General Marquis de Lafayette, a former allied aide to General George Washington and the last surviving general of the Revolutionary War. Lafayette, who had returned to France after the war, was on a tour of America in 1824–1825 honoring the nation's fiftieth anniversary. Pickens offered praise for the aging legendary hero from France, but expressed doubt that he would honor Alabama with his presence during his visit due to the state's "remote situation." Pickens and all Alabamians, however, were later pleased to learn that Lafayette had made a decision to visit all of the states in the Union. Accordingly, the Assembly passed a resolution requesting Governor Pickens to issue a formal invitation to Lafayette "in such manner as he shall deem most respectful" and if he accepted, that "he be received in such manner as shall best comport with the important services he has rendered the American people." The governor was also authorized to liberally draw upon the state treasury to properly entertain the state's most distinguished visitor in its short history. In response to the Assembly's request, on December 25, 1824, Pickens sent the formal invitation to Lafayette in which he referred to him as "the most distinguished benefactor of the republic now living."[26]

Before passing the resolutions concerning Lafayette's visit to the state, the Assembly had been busy enacting 135 pieces of legislation along with nine resolutions. First and foremost, the Assembly apportioned itself at a ratio of 2,086 white inhabitants to one representative and divided the state into twenty-one senatorial districts with each district being allotted one senator. As evidence that the state's civil court dockets were full, the Assembly passed an act to allow parties who agreed to submit their controversy to a mutually chosen referee so as to have their cases "rendered more speedy and less expensive than heretofore." In response to the governor's pleas, the Assembly also finally passed an act that prohibited the reversal of any case due to a defect in the pleadings to which an objection had not been previously asserted. Other legislation included that which regulated the sale of slaves by constables, established methods of compensation to owners of

---

[25] *Ala. Senate Journal (1824)*, 6–12; Brantley, *Three Capitals*, 137–38.

[26] *Ala. Senate Journal (1824)*, 6; Edwin C. Bridges, "The Nation's Guest": The Marquis de Lafayette's Tour of Alabama," *Alabama Heritage* (Fall 2011): 12; Tennant S. McWilliams, "The Marquis and the Myth: Lafayette's Visit to Alabama, 1825," *Alabama Review* 22 (April, 1969): 136; D. L. McCall, "Lafayette's Visit to Alabama, April 1825," *Alabama Historical Quarterly* 17 (Spring and Summer 1955): 34; *Ala. Acts (1824)*, 132.

slaves executed as a result of a criminal conviction, allowed illegitimates to inherit through their mother, created Dale County named for the hero of the Canoe Fight, incorporated a volunteer corps of infantry for the city of Mobile to be named the Mobile Republican Greens, incorporated the Montgomery Light Infantry, improved the navigation of the harbor and port of Mobile, and incorporated the Mobile Society for Literature that was authorized to establish a library or center of learning. Finally in addition to individual acts of emancipation, the 1824 Assembly enacted a manumission law that freed a group of a dozen slaves all at one time, describing them as "sundry persons of colour, descendants of the ancient creole population of that place [Mobile], whose owners have petitioned the Legislature that they be emancipated and freed from slavery, are honest, industrious and well-disposed people; and that their being emancipated would not tend to the injury of society, but would essentially contribute to the welfare of the individuals concerned, and be advantageous to the community at large."[27]

When the Assembly adjourned on Christmas Day 1824, its members fanned out all over the state to their homes, quickly spreading the exciting word of Lafayette's impending visit. The Assembly having given carte blanche to the governor to draw upon the treasury, Governor Pickens was determined to spare no expense in playing host to the state's most prominent visitor. After being informed of Lafayette's itinerary through the state, Pickens organized committees to plan extravagant festivities to be held for the most part in Montgomery, Cahaba, and Mobile. The plans were so meticulous that Pickens made arrangements for a New Orleans orchestra to make the difficult journey to Alabama to play for a ball to be held in Montgomery. Also, because of Alabama's remoteness, detailed plans were made for the storage of refreshments and supplies along the itinerary to ensure the comfort of Lafayette and his entourage.[28]

On March 31, 1825, accompanied by his son, George Washington Lafayette, his secretary, Auguste Levasseur, and his dog "Quiz," Lafayette arrived at the Fort Mitchell crossing on the Chattahoochee River where his Georgia escorts turned him over to an Alabama welcoming party. The party included Bolling Hall, a former member of Congress, John Dandridge Bibb, brother of Alabama's first two governors, and Samuel Dale. Led by William Taylor, the senior major general in the State militia, the Alabama military escort was composed of two troops of militia volunteers, one from Montgomery County under the command of Capt. James Abercrombie and one from Monroe County under the command of Gen. Samuel B. Moore. Because the first part of the Alabama itinerary was through Creek territory and, in light of Creek resentment over a recent treaty, Governor Pickens also arranged for General Thomas S. Woodward who was part Creek to form an Indian escort to accompany the entourage until out of Indian territory. Woodward included a detailed account of the visit in *Woodward's*

---

[27] *Ala. Acts (1824)*, 3–4, 10–12, 16–17, 41–42, 49–50, 79–82, 89–91, 103–04, 118–20, 122–24.

[28] Brantley, *Three Capitals*, 147–48; McCall, "Lafayette's Visit to Alabama," 33, 74.

Reminiscences, a collection of his personal observations of events in the history of early Alabama.[29]

Lafayette and his entourage were undoubtedly rather taken aback by the scene that greeted them on the shores of the Chattahoochee upon their arrival. According to Woodward's account, first to greet them was Chilly McIntosh, son of Creek leader Gen. William McIntosh, who was leading fifty Creek warriors "stripped naked and finely painted." Their duty was to ferry the distinguished entourage across the river. As the ferry boat reached the Alabama side of the river, the Indians took two ropes attached to the sulky in which Lafayette was seated and hoisted it eighty yards to the top of the river bank where the Alabama welcoming delegation was waiting. As Lafayette arrived atop the bluff, the Indians shouted war whoops, whereupon McIntosh introduced Lafayette to Bolling Hall who delivered a short statement of welcome. After a more formal welcoming address delivered by John Dandridge Bibb, Lafayette's entourage was treated to a game of ballplay—an intense competition similar to modern lacrosse—among the Indians.[30]

Gilbert du Motier, Marquis de Lafayette

---

[29] McWilliams, "The Marquis and the Myth," 138–39; Herbert J. Lewis, "Lafayette's Visit," *Encyclopedia of Alabama*, http://www.encyclopediaofalabama.org/face/Article.jsp?id=h-2152 (accessed January 31, 2013); Brantley, *Three Capitals*, 150; Thomas S. Woodward, *Woodward's Reminiscences of the Creek, or Muscogee Indians, Contained in Letters to Friends in Georgia and Alabama* (1859; repr., Mobile, Ala.: Southern University Press, 1969).

[30] Woodward, *Reminiscences*, 59; McWilliams, "The Marquis and the Myth," 137–39.

After attending the ball-play, Lafayette's entourage traveled a few miles
to the west on the Federal Road before spending the night at Haynes
Crabtree's Tavern at Uchee Creek. The next day Lafayette and his military
and Indian escorts began a one-hundred mile trek down the Federal Road
to Montgomery. This colorful convoy through Alabama's wilderness consisted of American cavalry troops bedecked in splendid blue uniforms
trimmed with gold, one hundred Creek warriors led by McIntosh—now
fully clothed in European attire—and three stylish carriages carrying the
distinguished guests. That night some of the party stayed at Kendall Lewis'
Tavern across from Fort Bainbridge while Lafayette traveled a few miles
further to Warrior Stand, the home of Big Warrior, an important Creek
chief who had died only three weeks earlier in Washington, D.C., where he
had been lobbying Congress.[31]

The next day the entourage's Indian escorts withdrew when they
reached the commencement of white settlements on the edge of the Creek
country at Line Creek. The final night before arriving in Montgomery was
spent at Walter B. Lucas' Tavern, which was later moved and now can be
seen at Old Town Alabama in Montgomery. The next day, April 3, 1825, the
convoy reached "Goat Hill"—at that time on the outskirts of Montgomery
and now the site of the current state capitol building—where a crowd of
three thousand had assembled to greet Lafayette. After being serenaded by
French horns and bugles and a band playing "Hail to the Chief," Lafayette
was formally introduced to Governor Pickens who was reportedly awed and
left speechless. General Woodward's account indicates that Pickens was so
overcome by emotion that he was unable to deliver a planned welcoming
speech. Other accounts, however, indicate that Pickens quickly recovered
and made an outstanding speech.[32]

After the official welcome, Governor Pickens reported that "all further
public honors and parades were discontinued" due to the fact that it was
Sunday. After enjoying "a private dinner" and attending a church service in
the evening Lafayette spent the night in the home of John Edmondson. One
of the finest homes in the city, Edmondson's residence was specially deco-
rated for the occasion with the finest furniture and draperies to be found in
the city and its pantry stocked with the finest French foods and wine. The
next evening Lafayette was feted with a public dinner and an elegant ball.
The ball was held on the second floor of Freeny's Tavern which was located
at the present-day corner of Commerce and Tallapoosa streets. Attendance
at the ball was limited to high-status state officials and the ranking officers
of the state militia, and their ladies. Also in attendance was Chilly McIntosh. Lafayette's secretary reported that McIntosh was no longer in his
Indian clothing and danced with several beautiful women who, the secretary presumed, "certainly had little idea that they were dancing with a

---

[31] Bridges, "The Nation's Guest," 14–15; McCall, "Lafayette's Visit to Alabama," 74–75.

[32] Bridges, "The Nation's Guest," 14–15; Lucile Cary Lowry, "Lafayette's Visit to Georgia and
Alabama," *Alabama Historical Quarterly* 8 (Spring 1946): 38; Lewis, "Lafayette's Visit,"
Encyclopedia of Alabama; "Lafayette," *Alabama Historical Quarterly* 18 (Spring 1956): 50–
51.

savage." The New Orleans band entertained the honored guests with both martial and ballroom music. As the band played on, Lafayette retired early due to his exhausting schedule, and his entourage boarded two steamboats, the *Balize* and the *Henderson*, to continue on their journey through the state.[33]

After leaving Montgomery, Lafayette stopped at Selma just long enough for some of its citizens to come aboard his boat for a brief visit. The next lavish ceremony took place shortly after, when Lafayette landed at Cahaba. As a band played "Lafayette's March," Governor Pickens escorted the General up the river bank that was lined by members of the Cahawba Guards, a company of local militia volunteers. When they reached the top of the bluff, Lafayette passed through a triumphal arch where a welcoming address was delivered by Henry Hitchcock, Alabama's Attorney General and grandson of Lafayette's wartime comrade, General Ethan Allen of Vermont. After a public barbeque and a private reception where Lafayette was visited by a number of his fellow countrymen who had settled in the Vine and Olive Colony near Demopolis, the party set out for Mobile, briefly stopping in Claiborne to attend a formal reception at the courthouse and the laying of the cornerstone for a Masonic Lodge.[34]

On April 7, 1825, Lafayette's party arrived in Mobile, the last stop on their journey through the state. Mobile's welcome was similar to the others, including church bells tolling, cannons roaring, and a walk through a triumphal arch to be formally welcomed. A ball held that evening—the grand finale of Lafayette's visit to Alabama—was perhaps the most extravagant event to date, with over six hundred in attendance. The next day Governor Pickens traveled with Lafayette down Mobile Bay to Mobile Point where an official party from Louisiana awaited to welcome him aboard the steamboat *Natchez* to take him to New Orleans on the next leg of his American tour.[35]

The afterglow left in the wake of Lafayette's triumphal procession through Alabama was dimmed by the strain it put on the state's treasury. The visit's total expenditures amounted to almost $17,000. Indeed, the 1825 General Assembly had to appropriate an additional $4,000 to cover the balance of unpaid expenses related to the visit. The cost would have been even more staggering had not the escorts, including two military cavalry units, paid their own expenses. Taking into account that the General Assembly had only allotted $10,000 for the construction of the state capitol building and that no funds had yet been expended for the construction of the University of Alabama, this was indeed a burden on the state's

---

[33] Bridges, "The Nation's Guest," 16–17; McWilliams, "The Marquis and the Myth," 142–43; Brantley, *Three Capitals*, 151.

[34] Lowry, "Lafayette's Visit," 38–39; Brantley, *Three Capitals*, 152; McWilliams, "The Marquis and the Myth," 143–45.

[35] McWilliams, "The Marquis and the Myth," 145–46; Lewis, "Lafayette's Visit," *Encyclopedia of Alabama*.

limited resources.[36]

Lafayette's visit to Alabama was generally considered a grand success as measured by the amount of excitement it generated among Alabama's citizens who, in some cases, traveled hundreds of miles from remote parts of the state to be able to say that they had seen the last living hero of the American Revolution and one of the world's most distinguished citizens. But the visit was not without negativity or mishaps. One amusing distraction in Montgomery briefly interrupted the dignity of that city's welcoming ceremony. Just as the welcoming speeches were concluding, an elderly Revolutionary War veteran by the name of Thomas Carr, who was apparently well in his cups in celebration of Lafayette's visit, fell down a well not far from where the ceremony was being conducted. The resulting hullabaloo sent ceremony spectators scrambling to his rescue. Unfortunately, a tragic incident also occurred in Montgomery when Joseph Toussint, a member of the New Orleans orchestra that performed at Montgomery's ball in honor of Lafayette, was stabbed to death as a result of an argument with a fellow band member. The town of Montgomery billed the state for medical services provided, a shroud for Toussint, and the cost of his burial. Finally, an accident that would have significant legal ramifications occurred on the Alabama River as Lafayette's steamboat traveled to Selma and Cahaba. A crewman on the boat was injured when a cannon was fired to announce the approach of Lafayette's party. Lafayette visited the wounded man who later sued the owner of the steamboat and obtained a verdict awarding $1,500 in "smart money," or punitive damages. This marked the first time in Alabama history that the state's high court reviewed a personal injury lawsuit; it was also of historical significance in that it was the first time the Alabama Supreme Court had confirmed the awarding of punitive damages.[37]

As Lafayette and his distinguished entourage exited the state, Alabama's citizens and leaders came back to earth and turned their attention to the long anticipated resolution of the permanent seat of government location issue scheduled to take place in the 1825 Assembly. As Governor Pickens readied for the convening of the Assembly, his days in the gubernatorial office were coming to an end. Yet his influence was not waning—as evidenced by the fact that he was able to handpick John Murphy of Monroe County as his successor who was elected without opposition. Before Murphy took over, Pickens convened the 1825 Assembly and delivered his final written address to its members on November 22, 1825, proudly proclaiming to them that they were assembled "at a period of peace and general prosperity."[38]

[36] Brantley, *Three Capitals*, 154–55; *Ala. Acts (1825)*, 88; Lewis, "Lafayette's Visit," *Encyclopedia of Alabama*.

[37] McWilliams, "The Marquis and the Myth," 142; Brantley, *Three Capitals*, 147; Mary Ann Neeley, ed., *The Works of Matthew Blue: Montgomery's First Historian* (Montgomery, Ala.: New South Books, 2010), 94; Woodward, *Reminiscences*, 72–73; *Rhodes v. Roberts*, 1 Stewart 145 (Ala. 1827).

[38] *Journal of the Senate of the State of Alabama, 1825* (Cahawba: William B. Allen, 1826), 5 (hereafter *Ala. Senate Journal (1825)*).

Following his call for a distinct Supreme Court limited to appellate jurisdiction, the outgoing governor next addressed the permanent location of government issue. Acknowledging that by law the governor could not veto the Assembly's choice of location, Pickens indicated that he "regarded the subject as one of peculiar delicacy, and shall leave it where the constitution has intended, to your own uncontrolled judgment." Since both he and the incoming governor were opposed to the capital's relocation to Tuscaloosa, Pickens proposed a plan that could allow the Alabama River system faction to hold on to the seat of government, albeit not in Cahaba. In this regard Governor Pickens proposed that if it were the decision of the Assembly to remove the capital from Cahaba, that it do as the federal government had in establishing its capital and acquire a tract of land "of sufficient extent, whereon to lay out and found an entire metropolis." This of course would, by design, disqualify the already existing town of Tuscaloosa, while at the same time allowing a new site to be selected in the Alabama River region that did not have the disadvantages encountered in Cahaba, particularly floods and health problems.[39]

In an effort to keep the legislature focused on the seat of government issue, Governor Pickens yet again urged the postponement of the location of the University of Alabama so as to be "disentangled" from that issue. While on the subject of higher education, Pickens again pushed for the establishment of a "department of female instruction" to provide for the "education of our daughters in the higher branches of literature and science." He next reported on the status of the State Bank of Alabama that had opened for business on March 9, 1825, commencing operations with a capital of $253,646.46—of which $56,613.91 was derived from the university fund—and having earned a net profit of $2,244.46 in the short time it had been in business. Commenting on the Lafayette visit, Pickens reported that "his route through this state was of unusual length . . . a distance by land and water estimated at 500 miles . . . receiving at all the prominent places, the gratifying salutations of our citizens."[40]

With his term of office coming to an end, Pickens completed his final address to the members of the Assembly with an acknowledgement "that the official relation between us is about to be dissolved." He then reflected upon his time in office during which the constitution was subjected to competing constructions, new institutions were founded, decisions were being made as to the expenditure of public funds, and revenues were being raised in support of the fledgling state government. The day after Pickens' final address, a joint session of the Assembly formally announced that John Murphy had been elected to succeed Pickens as governor. On November 28, 1825, Murphy delivered a short written inaugural address to the Assembly in which he expressed gratitude for the confidence placed in him by the members of the Assembly who cast no opposing votes. As the outgoing governor's handpicked successor, it was not surprising that Murphy de-

---

[39] Ibid., 6–8; Brantley, *Three Capitals*, 159–60.

[40] *Ala. Senate Journal (1825)*, 8–11.

scribed Pickens' farewell address as "a masterly union of particular and general views," rendering unnecessary a detailed address from him.[41]

John Murphy, Alabama's fourth governor, was born about 1785 in Robeson County, North Carolina. He moved as a child with his family to South Carolina. He later attended South Carolina College in Columbia (later to become the University of South Carolina), where he formed friendships with two fellow future Alabama politicians: John Gayle, who became Alabama's seventh governor, and James Dellet, who was the first Speaker of the Alabama House of Representatives and later a representative in the U.S. House. Upon his graduation from college in 1808, Murphy read law for a while, but never practiced. Instead, he served as the clerk of the South Carolina Senate for ten years.[42]

In 1818 Murphy moved to Monroe County in the Alabama Territory, where he had purchased land to establish a plantation. He quickly became engaged in Alabama politics by getting elected as a delegate to Alabama's constitutional convention of 1819, where he served on the prestigious Committee of Fifteen that had been assigned the task of drafting the state's constitution. In 1820, he was elected to the Alabama House of Representatives from Monroe County and, in 1822, was elected as that county's only member of Alabama Senate. By aligning himself with the "People's Party" headed by Israel Pickens and by supporting Pickens' attempts to create a state bank, Murphy was rewarded by receiving Pickens' endorsement to succeed him as governor. With this endorsement, Murphy was elected without opposition.[43]

Following the inauguration of Governor Murphy, the Assembly tackled the seat of government issue with a vengeance. Fiercely contested skirmishes over the issue broke out in both the House and the Senate. The most interesting and significant battle occurred in the Senate where the election of John "Red" Brown of Jefferson County, a known proponent of Tuscaloosa, was contested by his opponent John Wood. Wood, who had represented Jefferson County from its inception, became the target of the pro-Tuscaloosa faction because he was believed to be opposed to relocating the capital to Tuscaloosa. Further, Wood had not won friends among the common folks because he had opposed the popular "Jackson for President" resolution and had promoted the closure of Huntsville's Planters and Merchants Bank, which caused many of his constituents who held its notes to lose money. An all-out effort was thus made to unseat Wood, whom the Warrior River group would have to win over on the merits of the issue. Instead they favored Brown, who had clearly made known his support for Tuscaloosa. To this end, citizens of Tuscaloosa County just across the border from Jefferson County may have tipped the scales in favor of Brown by working hard to convince their neighbors—some of whom did most of their business in the Druid City—to vote for the pro-Tuscaloosa candidate.

[41] Ibid., 15, 25; *Journal of the House of Representatives of the State of Alabama*, 1825 (Cahawba: William B. Allen, 1826), 18 (hereafter *Ala. House Journal (1825)*).

[42] Hugh C. Bailey, "John Murphy," in *Alabama Governors*, 21–22.

[43] Ibid.

Suffering his first rejection by his constituents, Wood filed a contest of Brown's seat on November 25, 1825. The Committee of Privileges and Elections to whom the contest was referred for a decision ruled against Wood, rejecting affidavits submitted by him alleging fraud and illegality, because they were taken without notice to Brown and citing Brown's resulting inability to be present and cross-examine the affiants. Without these affidavits, there was no evidence in support of the charges of fraud and illegality. John "Red" Brown was therefore declared to be the legal Senator representing Jefferson County.[44]

The resolution of the contested Senate seat in favor of Brown was crucial as the proposed removal of the capital to Tuscaloosa passed by just one vote in the Senate—the Senator from Jefferson County made the difference. Before the House cast its vote in favor of Tuscaloosa, there was quite a bit of parliamentary maneuvering by the Alabama River system faction hoping to give such sites as Selma, Montgomery, and Wetumpka a chance to be considered. On December 12, 1825, however, the Senate bill providing for the removal of the capital to Tuscaloosa came before the House for consideration. The next day the House passed the Senate bill by a vote of 38 to 26, thereby establishing Tuscaloosa as the state's second capital city. Thus, Cahaba's reign as the first seat of government for Alabama would soon come to an end.[45]

The main focus of the 1825 Assembly, obviously, was resolving the seat of government issue. Very few major statewide issues were taken up, giving way to many bills of local interest, particularly those relating to education, such as those establishing Moulton Academy, Coosada Academy, Milton Academy in Montgomery, Concord Academy in Greene County, Tuscumbia Academy, Tuscumbia Female Academy, and Lafayette Academy in northwest Alabama. Florence was the most significant new town to be incorporated. In addition, there were six slaves emancipated and eight divorces confirmed.[46]

The seat of government issue having been resolved, it was incumbent upon the Assembly to provide for the mechanics of moving the state's offices to Tuscaloosa. Accordingly, legislation was enacted requiring the Comptroller, Treasurer, and Secretary of State "to adopt such measures for the removal of their respective offices . . . either by land or water conveyance, and also for the transportation of such furniture . . . as may be con-

---

[44] Brantley, *Three Capitals*, 162–67; *Ala.* Senate *Journal* (*1825*), 19, 31. The affidavits alleged that "several persons, non-residents of Jefferson County, voted at the general election; and also, that one was a minor; and some persons took ballots at the election for said Wood, but changed said ballots before they approached the ballot-box, and took tickets for Brown." Ironically, the citizens of Jefferson County sent John Wood back to the Senate as their representative when Brown's term expired.

[45] Brantley, *Three Capitals*, 177–85; *Ala. Senate Journal* (*1825*), 20. Although a petition was also filed on behalf of Centreville by developer Sara F. Chotard, Alabama's first female businesswoman, it received little consideration. Rhonda Coleman Ellison, *Bibb County Alabama: The First Hundred Years, 1818–1918* (Tuscaloosa: University of Alabama Press, 1999), 32–39; *Ala. Acts* (*1825*), 12.

[46] *Ala. Acts* (*1825*), 9, 59–64, 96–98, and 102–04.

venient." The Assembly also imposed upon the Senate door-keeper the duty of rounding up the furniture of each branch and storing it in the Senate chamber which was to be locked and the key given to the State Treasurer. In turn, the Treasurer was authorized to sell any of the property that was not taken to Tuscaloosa, as well as the State House itself so long as it sold for at least three thousand dollars.[47]

As a result of these legislative actions, Alabama's state government prepared to vacate Cahaba where its foundations had been forged. From October 1819 until January 1826, the General Assembly sitting in Cahaba had passed in excess of eight hundred legislative acts that helped to lay the foundation for the new state's government. Much of this legislation dealt with organizing the state government and its legal system; apportioning the legislature; organizing a state militia; creating towns and counties; raising revenue and imposing taxes; providing for internal improvements; providing funding for education by the sale of public lands; creating a state bank; and deciding upon a permanent seat of government. The biggest failure of the Assembly in its formative sessions was its postponement of establishing a "Seminary of Learning." The future state university unfortunately fell victim to political maneuvering involving both the creation of a state bank and the determination of a permanent seat of government. As a result, the University of Alabama would not open until five years after the capital itself moved to Tuscaloosa.

Like the General Assembly, the Supreme Court of Alabama's initial sessions took place in Cahaba. Pursuant to an act of the transitional territorial legislature, Alabama's five circuit judges were required to convene twice a year in Cahaba, the second Monday in May and the second Monday in November, sitting as the state's Supreme Court. Accordingly, Alabama's Supreme Court convened for the first time on May 8, 1820—well before the General Assembly's initial session the following November—to become the first official governmental proceeding in the state's history. The court met for eleven terms during the time it presided in Cahaba, deciding a total of 214 cases, most of which involved civil actions, particularly those related to commercial transactions engendered by a developing economy. A large majority of cases, regardless of the subject matter, involved questions concerning the technicalities of common law pleading. The court's jurisdiction to entertain appeals in criminal cases was limited to questions of law referred to it by one of their justices sitting as a circuit court judge.[48]

Not only was Cahaba the site of the laying of the foundation for the state's government and its judicial system, it also saw a sea change in the young state's politics. William Wyatt Bibb and his Georgia faction of wealthy planters had dominated politics in the territorial days and were responsible for attaining statehood for Alabama. Inevitably, however, Alabama's yeomen frontiersmen rejected the Georgia faction in favor of the so-called "People's Party" led by Israel Pickens from North Carolina. Those

[47] *Ala. Acts (1825)*, 46–47, 70–74.

[48] *Ala. Acts (1819)*, 10; Daniel J. Meador, "The Supreme Court of Alabama: Its Cahaba Beginning, 1820–1825," *Alabama Law Review* 61 (2010): 894–905.

who supported Pickens would adopt with fervor the presidential candidacy of Andrew Jackson. Ironically, Pickens was not a Jackson supporter, but he skillfully downplayed this to stay in power, and as we have seen, his popularity enabled him to handpick John Murphy as his successor as governor.[49] Pickens' quiet support of John Quincy Adams in 1824 notwithstanding, Andrew Jackson carried all but three counties in the presidential race of 1824. Alabamians continued to overwhelmingly cast their lot with Jacksonian Democracy and contributed to Andrew Jackson's ascension to the White House in 1828.

As state government packed up and began the 90-plus mile trek to its new home in Tuscaloosa, Cahaba lost its status as the center of Alabama politics. Although it retained its status as the county seat of Dallas County, many of its citizens who had been associated with state government left for Tuscaloosa. Other distinguished citizens tore down their houses and moved them down river to Mobile while many other houses were simply abandoned. For a time this once-bustling frontier capital was essentially deserted. It would recover again for one more stance as an important town on the Alabama River as it later became the shipping center for cotton by then being grown on the fertile lands surrounding it.[50]

While the sun was setting on Cahaba's reign as the state's first capital, a new era was set to begin in Tuscaloosa. The focus in Cahaba had been on organizing a state government and providing for the basic needs of its citizens, particularly with regard to safety and security. About the time that the state's government and its officers settled in Tuscaloosa, however, citizens began to focus upon national issues such as tariffs, internal improvements, slavery, Indian policy, and states' rights. Two of these issues— slavery and states' rights—would remain dominant as the state government left Tuscaloosa for Montgomery twenty years later. In the interim, the government in Tuscaloosa grappled with thorny issues of both national and local consequence.

---

[49] Governor Murphy rewarded his benefactor Pickens by appointing him to take the Senate seat that Dr. Henry Chambers did not live to fill. Some were disappointed as this went against the gentlemen's agreement in place that Alabama's senators would come from different sections of the state. Unfortunately, Pickens became seriously ill with tuberculosis and was bedridden for much of the term he served before resigning at the end of 1826. He then went to Cuba in the hopes of relief from his illness. Instead, he died there on April 24, 1827. Later the Alabama General Assembly appropriated funds to return Pickens' remains to his family cemetery near Greensboro for burial. Bailey, *Israel Pickens*, 95–100.

[50] Moore, *History of Alabama*, 121; Anna M. Gayle Fry, *Memories of Old Cahaba* (Nashville, Tenn.: Publishing House of the Methodist Episcopal Church, South, 1908), 14.

9
❧
STATE GOVERNMENT RESUMES IN TUSCALOOSA

Leaving Cahaba for the the falls of the Black Warrior River, Alabama's government convened for the the first time in Tuscaloosa on November 20, 1826. Because no permanent capitol building had yet been erected, the legislature met in the Bell Tavern, which was located at the intersection of present-day University Boulevard and Twenty-Second Avenue. The Bell Tavern—a local gathering spot since at least 1820—had been hurriedly enlarged and specially equipped to host the state's government temporarily in accordance with Tuscaloosa's pledge to provide rent free space for the first two sessions of the General Assembly. After one session, Alabama's General Assembly left the Bell Tavern to make do in a wooden framed building several blocks to the west until it selected a site for a permanent building.[1]

On November 1, 1826, Governor John Murphy delivered a written address to the Assembly in which he proclaimed that "neither famine, pestilence, or the sword, are permitted to ravage our land." To the contrary, he reported a statewide enjoyment of "the bounty of the seasons, the rich fruits of the earth, domestic comfort, and public harmony." Recognizing that "it is of the utmost consequence, that the laws for the preservation of peace and good order should be faithfully executed," he first urged the legislators give careful consideration as to whether the salary of the state's prosecutors was commensurate with the importance of their office. In this regard, he suggested their salary should be enough to attract persons of "ability, and zeal and high character." With further regard to "peace and good order," he also addressed the need for more discipline and training for the state militia, contending that discipline needed to be instilled during periods of peace rather than during a crisis demanding their attention. Education was another topic of major concern. Not only did he urge the Assembly to devote its attention to locating and commencing construction of the University of Alabama, he indicated that it was also their duty to encourage the development of "primary seminaries" to complement the state university.[2]

Like Alabama's three previous governors, Governor Murpy was a supporter of internal improvements, particularly those designed to improve navigation on the state's rivers. In his address to the Assembly he pushed for two "grand projects of improvement." One proposal was to make the

---

[1] Robert O. Mellown, "Alabama's Fourth Capital: The Construction of the State House in Tuscaloosa," *Alabama Review* 40 (October 1987): 260; "Historic Sites in Alabama," *Alabama Historical Quarterly* 15 (Summer 1953): 370.

[2] *Ala. House Journal (1826)*, 6–9.

Tennessee River navigable through the Muscle shoals so as to allow produce to be shipped by river from northern Alabama to New Orleans; the other was to cut a canal from the Hiwassee River in Tennessee to either the Coosa River or all the way to Fort Jackson at the confluence of the Coosa and Tallapoosa rivers to allow more areas of the state an outlet to Mobile Bay. Because the transportation of Alabama's agricultural products was the principal beneficiary of proposed improvements in river navigation, Murphy also recommended that the General Assembly establish agricultural societies, which were in essence a forerunner of today's county extension system, for the purpose of disseminating helpful information as to soil, climate, and diversification of crops, as well as for obtaining new seeds and plants for experimentation.[3]

Banking issues continued to dominate early Alabama politics as evidenced by Governor Murphy's report to the General Assembly outlining what he considered menaces to the recently established State Bank of Alabama. First, he warned of the assumption of banking privileges by the St. Stephens Steamboat Company, which had been incorporated earlier by the legislature to enhance transportation efforts upriver from Mobile. The governor's initial reaction to the company's attempt to enter the banking business was to consider filing *quo warranto* proceedings against it. But upon assurances from its president and directors that it would suspend banking operations until the legislature convened to consider amendments to its charter, Murphy agreed to wait for action by the General Assembly. Of considerably more consternation to Murphy than a local navigation company trying to tansfigure itself into the banking business, was the proposal of the Bank of the United States (BUS) to establish a branch in Mobile. The governor was fearful that competition generated by the entry of the BUS into Alabama would seriously infringe upon the operations of the state bank. Because of this, he urged the legislature to take whatever action necessary to oppose the BUS's proposed entry as "an invasion of our sovereignty."[4]

Other subjects addressed by Governor Murphy included the settlement of accounts left over from territorial days between Alabama and Mississippi; the improvement of the Salt Springs, which he touted as an important resource in times of both peace and war, so much so as to justify that its employees be exempted from military service; and a request of annexation by the citizens of West Florida, which, in his opinion, would be in the best interest of the United States in terms of defense of the southern frontier's sea coast. Before closing his remarks, Murphy acknowledged the "most singular coincidences" of the deaths of the second and third Presidents of the United States, Thomas Jefferson and John Adams, who died within hours of each other on July 4, 1826, the fiftieth anniversary of the signing of the Declaration of Independence. As a result of this historic irony, the governor indicated that plans would be made by state officials to honor the lives of these two venerated citizens who were "consecrated in

[3] Ibid., 9–10.

[4] Ibid., 10–11.

the affections of the American people."[5]

One of the first orders of business for the 1826 Assembly was for it to authorize the construction of a permanent capitol building in Tuscaloosa to house the state's government. Accordingly, on December 15, 1826, a joint resolution was adopted appointing a committee consisting of five members from the House and an equal number from the Senate, who were tasked with the duty of selecting two or more proposed sites for the capitol within the corporate limits of the town of Tuscaloosa. At the insistence of the Senate, the committee was also authorized to procure plans for any public buildings proposed to be built. Ultimately the committee chose five prospective sites from which the legislature could choose. On January 10, 1826, the Assembly selected a large lot known as "Childress' Hill," which had been cleared in 1816 by one of Tuscaloosa's earliest white settlers. This lot was deemed the perfect site because of its location at the end of Broad Street which put it near the center of town, as well as the river, which was a major means of transportation for many visitors to the capital. In an act authorizing the construction of the new capitol building, five commissioners were appointed to contract with a builder and to select a superintendent to oversee the work that began in 1827 with the laying of a stone foundation. During a cornerstone-laying ceremony, the assembled crowd was stunned when a cannon shot to commemorate the occasion burst into many pieces. The unexpected shrapnel was gathered up and the pieces were placed in the walls of the capitol as it was being built.[6]

As state government transitioned to a new capital in Tuscaloosa, its officials gradually began to gain distrust for the federal government, which would ultimately transform the state into a hotbed of states' rights advocates, particularly by the time the capital relocated again to Montgomery in 1846. Governor Murphy's characterization of the BUS's proposed entry into Mobile as "an invasion of our sovereignty" in his address to the 1826 Assembly appears to be the first instance of an Alabama politician invoking the doctrine of state's rights in opposition to an action of the federal government. While Alabama's state political leaders seemed to be unanimous in opposing the BUS, Mobile's *Commercial Register* reported that many in Mobile supported it because of the need for more specie to support commercial transactions in Alabama's only port city. Newspapers in north Alabama also pushed for the location of a branch of the BUS in their part of the state. It was the Mobilians that got their wish, however, as a branch of the BUS was in fact opened in Mobile despite the governor's objections and those of Alabama's congressional delegation. The

---

[5] Ibid., 11–13.

[6] *Journal of the House of Representatives of the State of Alabama, 1826* (Tuskaloosa, Ala.: Grantland & Robinson, 1827), 114 (hereafter *Ala. House Journal (1826)*); *Journal of the Senate of the State of Alabama, 1826* (Tuskaloosa: Grantland & Robinson, 1827), 69, 137–38 (hereafter *Ala. Senate Journal (1826)*); Mellown, "Alabama's Fourth Capital," 260–62; *Ala. Acts (1826)*, 3. The commissioners in charge of contracting were John B. Hogan, James H. Dearing, Henry Minor, and John L. Tindall. Matthew William Clinton, *Tuscaloosa, Alabama:* William Clinton, *Tuscaloosa, Alabama: Its Early Days, 1816–1865* (Tuscaloosa, Ala.: The Zonta Club, 1958), 62.

national bank's presence in Mobile remained a sore issue throughout the next decade as a result of the shrinking availability of paper currency for the state's debtors in need of credit. Political maneuverings concerning the branch bank in Alabama would continue until President Jackson vetoed the rechartering of the BUS in 1832.[7]

While Governor Murphy had struck a states' rights theme in his opposition to the BUS's entry into Mobile, he was certainly not a radical when it came to the state's relationship with the federal government. Indeed, during his administration the state was the recipient of the federal government's largesse in the form of a grant of land in north Alabama to be sold to finance the building of canals around obstructive shoals on the Tennessee River. Little Muscle Shoals, Big Muscle Shoals, and Elk River Shoals presented approximately thirty-seven miles of generally impassable obstacles for any meaningful river transportion. In need of a commercial outlet to the Mississippi Valley to the west, and effectively hemmed in by the Appalachian Mountains to the east, the area's settlers began to demand improved navigation on the Tennessee River. Significantly, improvement of navigation around these shoals had been recommended to President James Monroe in a report submitted by Secretary of War John C. Calhoun in December 1824. Secretary Calhoun's recommendation was based upon his assessment of the project's strategic military significance and the positive economic impact which would result from uniting the eastern population centers with the ever-expanding western frontier. In response to this report and following a survey of the shoals, Congress granted 400,000 acres of land to finance the project. Unfortunately, the hoped for result was not achieved because, although canals were completed around some of the shoals, other shoals were left unhindered. The failure to complete the Shoals project, however, was due to a lack of adequate funds from the sale of the donated land rather than a lack of cooperative effort between the state and federal governments.[8]

During his second administration, Governor Murphy once again demonstrated that he was a moderate with respect to states' rights issues. Like most other southern governors, Murphy was opposed to the passage of the Tariff of 1828, citing it to be an unconstitutional and an unjust measure against the South. Indeed, among southerners it was referred to as the "Tariff of Abominations" because of the negative impact it had on the economy of the southern states. In this regard, the tariff forced southern states to pay more for goods that their region did not produce. Also, the tariff's intended effect of reducing the importation of British goods had the concomitant effect of reducing the amount of cotton Britain imported from the South. South Carolina's John Calhoun led the charge in opposition to this tariff, which ultimately resulted in South Carolina's nullification of the tariff and a crisis involving its possible secession from the Union. Not desiring to go against the wishes of President Andrew Jackson, however,

---

[7] Rogers et al., *Alabama*, 84, 88.

[8] Hugh C. Bailey, "John Murphy," in *Alabama* Governors, 23; Adrian G. Daniel, "Navigational Development of Muscle Shoals, 1807–1890," *Alabama Review* 14 (October 1961): 251–55.

Governor Murphy did not join in South Carolina's clamoring for nullification and, instead, worked for a compromise of the issue. The governor stressed: "Let it ever be the boast of Alabama" that her people did not play a part in creating discord in the Union. Ironically, Murphy's moderate stance on this issue due to his loyalty to President Jackson cost him politically at home when he was defeated in 1831 in a race for a seat in the U.S. House of Representatives by Dixon Hall Lewis, the leader of Alabama's more radical states' rights faction. Lewis would later have a substantial influence on firebrand lawyer William Lowndes Yancey and others who eventually led Alabama out of the Union in 1861.[9]

The remainder of Governor Murphy's term as governor was rather uneventful, but did see the the completion of the capitol building in Tuscaloosa and, finally, the selection of a site to commence construction of class buildings for the University of Alabama. There were quite a number of sites under consideration besides Tuscaloosa, including among others, Greensboro in Greene County, LaGrange in Franklin County, Athens in Limestone County, Montevallo in Shelby County, Moulton in Lawrence County, Greenville in Butler County, and Elyton in Jefferson County. On December 29, 1827, it took a joint session of the Assembly nineteen ballots to finally achieve a majority vote in favor of Tuscaloosa at a site known as "Marr's Spring," described in the *National Intelligencer* as "high and healthy with several constant springs." The *Intelligencer* noted other advantages of the site including its inclusion of sufficient forests to provide fuel (wood) for years to come and a close proximity to the same quarry that had provided the attractive stone for the ground floor of the new state capitol. The Druid City thus became the state's capstone of education, as well as its seat of government.[10]

As progress was being made with respect to the capitol and the state university, the General Assembly passed a couple of interesting resolutions during its 1828 session. One authorized the appropriation of five hundred dollars to transport the remains of former Governor Israel Pickens from Cuba, where he had died on April 4, 1827, to his residence in Greene County. Pickens, who was suffering from tuberculosis, had traveled to Cuba seeking the refuge of its warmer climate to alleviate the effects of that debilitating disease. The other resolution called for an amendment to the U.S. Constitution providing that the President and Vice President of the United States be elected by a direct vote of the people rather than by the indirect system of the states voting for electors in the same numbers as its representatives in Congress. This amendment was urged out of fear that the

---

[9] *Ala. Acts (1828)*, 101–02; Hugh C. Bailey, "John Murphy," in *Alabama Governors*, 23. According to Alabama historian A. B. Moore, during the nullification crisis many Alabamians were even prepared to lend their service to Old Hickory if need be "to preserve inviolate our constitution and our Union." Almost thirty years later, similar sentiments would be hard to find. Moore, *History of Alabama*, 164.

[10] *Journal of the Senate of the State of Alabama, 1827* (Tuscaloosa: Dugald McFarlane, 1828), 101–10 (hereafter *Ala. Senate Journal (1827)*); Clinton, *Tuscaloosa*, 71; Suzanne Rau Wolfe, *The University of Alabama: A Pictorial History* (Tuscaloosa: University of Alabama Press, 1983), 7; *National Intelligencer*, Washington, D.C., April 19, 1828.

system in place might one day result in the election of a President opposed to the choice of the people. Despite widespread criticism of the electoral system throughout the country's history, that system remains in effect to this day.[11]

As the legislature continued to meet in its temporary quarters described by some as a "shabby old tenement" resembling a "gin-house," construction of the new statehouse had been proceeding at a slow pace. In February 1827, the five commissioners who had been appointed by the Assembly to select a building superintendent settled upon William Nichols, a former official state architect for the state of North Carolina who had recently remodeled the capitol building in Raliegh. In November 1827, Nichols, in view of only $40,000 having been appropriated for construction, presented a set of plans to the Alabama legislative committee for an attractive, but small, building. This plan was rejected and Nichols was asked to present plans for a larger building with an estimate for its cost. Accordingly, Nichols presented revised plans that provided for increasing the size of the building by one-fourth with a total adjusted cost of $55,000.[12]

These plans were finally approved by joint resolution of the General Assembly on December 20, 1827. The revised plans called for a neoclassical Greek style, cross-shaped structure consisting of two main bricked floors sitting atop a ground floor which was faced with locally quarried sandstone. The building was capped by a dome that allowed light into its rotunda. The main façade of the building looked east and featured a false gabled portico which was supported by imposing Ionic columns. The two branches of the General Assembly were housed on the main floor of the north and south wings of the building, the Supreme Court was located on the ground floor of the western wing, and the entrance vestibule occupied the ground floor of the eastern wing with two impressive curving flights of stairs to carry visitors to the main floor where the legislative branches were located. A striking rotunda occupied the center of the building, dividing the various wings. The ground floor of the north and south wings were occupied by the various offices of the executive branch including those of the governor, secretary of state, treasurer, and comptroller.[13]

As the capitol was nearing completion in June 1829, excited citizens of Tuscaloosa decided to hold a Fourth of July celebration on the town's new "Capitol Hill." It would not completely be finished for almost two more years at a final cost of about $150,000. Yet by November 1829 the structure was in sufficient state for the General Assembly to meet there for the 1829–

---

[11] *Ala. Acts (1827)*, 160–61; 165–66.

[12] Mellown, "Alabama's Fourth Capital," 263–65; *Ala. Senate Journal (1827)*, 46, 52, 66.

[13] Mellown," Alabama's Fourth Capital, 264–67; *Journal of the House of Representatives of the State of Alabama, 1827* (Tuscaloosa: Dugald McFarlane, 1828), 129 (hereafter *Ala. House Journal (1827)*).

Capitol Building — Tuscaloosa

Courtesy of Alabama Department of Archives and History

1830 session. In his November 17, 1829, address to the Assembly, while workmen were busy painting and plastering elsewhere in the building, Governor Murphy noted that the "taste, skill, and experience of the Architect, Captain Nichols, deserved the highest commendations." He also optimistically expressed his wishes that the capitol would "long remain a monument of the liberal ambition" as well as "long remain the council hall, and citadel of liberty."[14]

William Nichols' stay in Tuscaloosa did not end with the completion of the capitol. When the legislature fixed his salary—$1,749 annually—as architect for the capitol, it assigned him the additional task of super-intending the construction of buildings for the University of Alabama. Although he was not provided additional compensation from the state treasury for this task, he was allowed to receive supplementary payment from the University if appoved by its board of trustees. Accordingly, Nichols submitted his plans for the University's buildings to the board on March 24, 1828. As a result, the University of Alabama was finally ready to receive its first students a year and a half after the completion of the capitol building. On April 17, 1831, the first students were admitted to the elegant

---

[14] Clinton, *Tuscaloosa,* 63; Mellown, "Alabama's Fourth Capital," 274–75; *Ala. Senate Journal* (*1829*), 7.

new campus designed and constructed by Nichols. The focal point of the campus was the Rotunda, which was seventy feet in both diameter and height. Its ground floor accommodated an auditorium for chapel services and commencement exercises. The library and a natural history collection were located on the second floor under the dome. The remainder of the campus consisted of the Lyceum where classes were to be held, two dormitories, two faculty houses, and a dining hall. The dining hall, later to be known to Alabamians as the Gorgas House, would be the only structure designed by Nichols to survive the the burning of the University by Union troops some thirty-six years later. It still stands today nestled among trees near the Amelia Gayle Gorgas Library and the Quadrangle.[15]

Alva Woods, a Harvard graduate and an ordained Baptist minister from Vermont, became the first president of the University of Alabama. Woods had served as a professor at the new Columbian College (later to become Georgetown University) in Washington, D.C., where his first assignment sent him to Great Britain to raise funds and purchase books. He later served as a professor of mathematics and natural philosophy at Brown University in Providence, Rhode Island, before becoming the president of Transylvania University in Lexington, Kentucky in 1828. On April 12, 1831, Woods was installed as the University of Alabama's president in a ceremony held in Tuscaloosa's Christ Episcopal Church attended by a considerable audience of townspeople and dignataries. Prominent guests included Alabama's then governor, Samuel B. Moore, U.S. congressmen, members of the legislature, judges, and city officials. A Tuscaloosa news-paper reported that the "leading subject of the discourse was the importance of learning and knowledge to the safety, liberty, prosperity, and moral and religious improvement of man."[16]

Although Woods would serve as the University's president for the next six years, his tenure was beset with a boisterous student body consisiting primarily of wealthy planters' sons predominantly from the Black Belt counties of Greene, Dallas and Montgomery. Woods' austere New England background and training had not prepared him for the unruly habits of this frontier student body that was not susceptible to his penchant for rigid discipline and scholarship. Woods' attempt to have the sons of Alabama pioneers adhere to similar standards of conduct as had been imposed upon him and his somber classmates at Harvard resulted in a running battle between Woods and the student body during his entire term as president. There was one student rebellion after another in response to Woods' autocratic rule. The rebellious nature of the students was reflected in minor infractions such as talking in class, throwing paper balls, and carving benches with knives. Drinking and gambling were also problems that led to more serious offenses. One student was expelled for assaulting a professor with a deadly weapon and another was expelled for stabbing a fellow stu-dent. Woods himself literally had brickbats hurled at him on one occasion

---

[15] *Ala. Acts, (1827),* 8; Wolfe, *University of Alabama,* 10–13.

[16] Wolfe, *University of Alabama,* 14–15; James B. Sellers, *History of the University of Alabama* (Tuscaloosa, Ala.: University of Alabama Press, 1953), 3–5.

and on a few occasions had to run to escape groups of boisterous students bent upon causing harm.[17]

James Sellers, principal historian of the University of Alabama, described the student body Woods battled as "proud possessors of dirks, pistols, and bowie knives" who "could quickly and easily turn a roughhouse into an assault, or a student mass meeting into a mob." Woods did not back down from these students nor did he let the fear of retaliation from the politically influential parents of some of these students deter him from expelling disorderly students. The conflict between Woods and the students came to a head in 1836, strangely enough ignited by the circus coming to town. Students were not allowed to attend events such as circuses without the express permission of the faculty. Nevertheless, an estimated eighty to ninety University students slipped away to attend the circus in the spring of 1836. Six students were identified and were suspended for almost a year. This action resulted in the remainder of the students along with citizens from Tuscaloosa pleading for their reinstatement. When their pleas were denied by the faculty, forty of the students who had also attended the circus signed a confession to that effect, theorizing that the school could not possibly suspend them all when there was only a total of one hundred students on campus. They were wrong. They were all suspended until August.[18]

Woods had not backed down and, in fact, as a result of the continuing confrontation with the students he enacted even stricter rules to ensure a more firm system of discipline. These new rules were put in place in the spring of 1836, but met such resistance from the few students remaining on campus following the circus debacle that they were withdrawn until the next school year. In the spring of 1837, the new rules had engendered renewed resistance to such an extent that rioting and gunfire erupted when the faculty denied a petition by students to again withdraw the rules. When the students participating in the riots refused to surrender their firearms or sign an affimation of good conduct with a pledge to no longer harass the administration, the faculty voted to suspend them all. Most students left the campus and those that remained were completely uncooperative with the administration.[19]

---

[17] Sellers, *University of Alabama*, 55–62; James B. Sellers, "Student Life at the University of Alabama Before 1860," *Alabama Review* 4 (October 1949): 272–74, 289–91.

[18] Sellers, *University of Alabama*, 63–64; Clinton, *Tuscaloosa*, 72.

[19] Sellers, *University of Alabama*, 64. The root of the problem concerning rebellious students during Woods' tenure as president was best summarized by Willis G. Clark: "The students were largely influenced in their conduct and manners by the environment. The civilization of the State was at the time the civilization of a frontier people. The State had not yet been redeemed from the wilderness. A large part of the eastern and the northeastern regions was still in possession of the Creek and the Cherokee tribes of Indians. A large part of the white people had not yet learned to submit patiently to the wholesome restraints of the law. It is not strange that the sons of the pioneers were restless under the wise regulations of college government." Willis G. Clark, *History of Education in Alabama, 1702–1889* (Washington, 1889), 43.

President Woods resigned on December 6, 1837, and took his family back to Providence, Rhode Island. Woods had had enough with the South, its climate, and its rebellious youth. He desired to have his son educated in the North under more refined and disciplined circumstances. While student unrest did not completely dissipate after Woods' departure, the next president, Basil Manly, a southerner who was instrumental in the founding of what would become Furman University in South Carolina, had a better rapport with the students as evidenced by his reign of eighteen years. Although Woods had lost the battle with Alabama's pioneer sons, before leaving Tuscaloosa he was instrumental in the founding of the Tuscaloosa Female Athenaeum, a renowned seminary of higher learning for females that drew students from all over Alabama and Mississippi. In 1836, the Tuscaloosa Female Athenaeum was chartered by the Alabama General Assembly some fifty-seven years before female students would be admitted to the University of Alabama. Woods served as the president of the school's first Board of Trustees until he left for Providence.[20]

While Tuscaloosa was becoming the state's capstone of education by the hardest, state government continued to hold forth just a few blocks away. In addition to John Murphy, eight more governors would lead the state while Tuscaloosa remained its capital: Gabriel Moore of Madison County (1829–1831), Samuel B. Moore of Jackson County (1831), John Gayle of Greene County (1831–1835), Clement C. Clay of Madison County (1835–1837), Hugh McVay of Lauderdale County (1837), Arthur P. Bagby of Monroe County (1837–1841), Benjamin Fitzpatrick of Autauga County (1841–1845), and Joshua L. Martin of Tuscaloosa County (1845–1849).

Succeeding Governor Murhpy was Gabriel Moore, who, despite being embarrassed by his highly public divorce and a duel with his ex-wife's brother, had since then represented Madison County in the 1819 Constitutional Convention and in the U.S. Congress from 1821 until 1829. Moore had an ambitious agenda upon becoming governor, but for the most part was unsuccessful in obtaining legislative approval for his priorities. With respect to his number one priority, Moore was unable to get the Assembly to approve a project linking the Tennessee and Alabama Rivers. The Assembly did appoint so-called canal commissioners to study the improvement of the navigation of the Tennessee River. Moore's second major priority was to assist small farmers by establishing a more equitable system of disposing of the public lands relinquished to the federal government by various Indian treaties. In this regard, he argued for changes in federal statutes so that smaller parcels could be obtained at graduated prices commensurate with the quality of the soil. He was unsuccessful in getting the legislature to go along with this proposal to petition Congress. Likewise, the legislature rejected his avocation of a centralized state penitentiary system which emphasized rehabilitation of prisoners, as well as his pro-

---

[20] Sellers, *University of Alabama*, 65; Dubose, *Sketches of Alabama History*, 155; *Ala. Acts (1836)*, 101–02.

posal that branches of the State Bank of Alabama be established in the Tennessee Valley and south Alabama.[21]

Governor Moore was more successful with respect to judicial reform and the promotion of education. In order to streamline the judicial system, Moore had called for a separate three-judge supreme court rather than the existing system of calling upon the state's circuit judges to also sit as the state's supreme court on an ad hoc basis. Such a measure was enacted on January 14, 1832, which amended the constitution to authorize the legislature to elect three justices for a term limited to six years.[22]

The six-year term limit had been imposed by the first amendment to the state's constitution in 1830. Malcolm McMillan's study of Alabama's constitutional development concludes that the effort to end lifetime judicial tenure limited only by the "good behavior" of the justices was a contest between conservative and liberal interests that had not yet coalesced into clearly defined political parties. In opposing this amendment, the liberal element argued that it would weaken the independence of the judiciary. Those in favor of the amendment argued that it would make the judiciary more accountable to the people. Conservative forces had sought to limit the tenure of judges during the constitutional convention of 1819. When they failed to do so they were determined to remedy the situation by constitutional amendment and kept a limited tenure amendment proposal before the legislature from 1819 until the six-year tenure limit was presented to the people for a vote in 1828 and was later ratified by the legislature in 1830.[23]

Support for the passage of the limited tenure amendment had been strengthened by a popular revolt against the Alabama Supreme Court for a decision it rendered with regard to the usury laws of Alabama. A law passed by the territorial legislature in 1818 had removed all restrictions on interest rates. This law was quickly repealed by the new state legislature in 1819 when interest rates skyrocketed. Interest rates were then limited to eight per cent. William Kelly, Speaker of the House of Representatives and a member of the so-called "People's Party," then sought to make things even more favorable for debtors by seeking to repeal the statute of limitations pertaining to the recovery of excessive interest rates. His attempt was rejected by the legislature in 1825, and in 1827 the Supreme Court dealt Kelly and his party another blow when it confirmed that the statute of limitations prevented the recovery of excessive interest already paid under contracts negotiated under the 1818 law.[24]

---

[21] Although he supported Alabama's state bank, Moore, a Jacksonian Democrat, vehemently opposed the Bank of the United States (BUS). Accordingly, he recommended that the legislature urge Alabama's congressional delegation to vote against the recharter of the BUS, which he described as a "mammoth institution" that was "unfriendly to . . . our State sovereignty itself." Doss, "Rise and Fall of an Alabama Founding Father," 163–71; *Ala. Acts (1830)*, 3.

[22] Doss, "Rise and Fall of an Alabama Founding Father," 163–71.

[23] McMillan, *Constitutional Development in Alabama*, 47–51.

[24] Ibid.

This decision was extremely unpopular among the followers of the People's Party, and Kelly made it the focus of the election of 1828 within the Tennessee Valley, ranting against the court and the creditor class. Once reelected, Kelly brought charges against the three justices of the Supreme Court—Reuben Saffold, John White, and Anderson Crenshaw—under a provision of the constitution that allowed the removal of judges for "willful neglect of duty or other reasonable cause, which would not be sufficient ground for impeachment." Kelly served as the prosecutor in the "Trial of the Judges," which was conducted before the Alabama Senate. The prosecution was based upon alleged improper rulings and decisions by these judges particularly with regard to cases involving the usury laws. After four days of testimony elicited from the leading lawyers in the state, the judges were acquitted by a considerable vote. Although Kelly had not won the case, he had continued the anti-court sentiment that led to the six-year term limit amendment which was adopted in 1830.[25]

A measure of judicial reform having been achieved in the form of a separate supreme court, the Assembly responded moderately to Governor Moore's promotion of education by incorporating male academies in Florence, Cahaba, and Asheville, and by requesting a grant of lands by Congress for use as a female academy in each county of the state. Also during Moore's term, the Assembly authorized appropriations for the completion of the state capitol and petitioned Congress for indemnity for losses sustained by its citizens "from depredations of the Creek Indians." Perhaps the most interesting action of the legislature during Moore's time as governor was the adoption of a joint resolution to Congress opposing the suspension of the transportation of mail on Sundays, contending that it "would be a violation of the spirit of the Constitution, and be repugnant to the principles of a free government." The resolution further contended that "All religious sects, whether they observe the Christian sabbath or not, are equally entitled to the respect and protection of the government."[26]

Despite his limited success as the state's chief executive, Gabriel Moore managed to defeat incumbent John McKinley for a seat in the U.S. Senate prior to the expiration of his term as governor. Moore thus resigned on March 3, 1831. Pursuant to the state's constitution, the president of the state Senate (the equivalent of today's lieutenant governor), Samuel B. Moore, ascended to the governor's seat to finish out the remainder of Gabriel Moore's term. Samuel Moore, no kin to Gabriel Moore, was born in Franklin County, Tennessee, in 1789, and moved with his family to Jackson County, Alabama when it was still part of the Mississippi Territory. Moore read law there and was first elected to the state House of Representatives representing Jackson County in 1823. In 1828, he was elected to the state senate. Although he was not a dynamic individual, he got elected president of the state senate in 1830 by a margin of two votes, and therefore was in

---

[25] McMillan, *Constitutional Development in Alabama*, 47–48; Ala. Const. of 1819, Art. V, Sec. 13; Henderson Middleton Somerville, "Trial of the Alabama Supreme Court Judges in 1829....," *Alabama State Bar Association Proceedings,* June, 1899.

[26] *Ala. Acts (1830),* 88; *Ala. Acts (1831),* 42–47, 73.

line to become governor when Gabriel Moore resigned. Perhaps the most important occurrence during Samuel Moore's short term as governor came just a few weeks after his assumption of office when the University of Alabama opened its doors. As governor and chairman of the University's board of trustees, Moore had the privilege of presiding over the inauguration ceremonies for Alva Woods as the University's first president. Samuel Moore, like Gabriel Moore, supported penal reform and internal improvements involving connecting the Tennessee River with other river systems, but was no more successful in securing legislation in these areas. He also took strong states' rights positions in opposing the rechartering of the BUS and protective tariffs. In November 1831, Moore sought to become governor in his own right, but finished dead last in a three-man race that was won by John Gayle of Greene County.[27]

John Gayle, Alabama's seventh governor, was born in 1792 in the Sumter District of South Carolina. His father had served in the Revolutionary War under the legendary General Francis ("Swamp Fox") Marion. The Gayle family moved to Mount Vernon, Alabama, in 1812 while John remained in South Carolina to attend a private academy and then the South Carolina College. Upon his graduation in 1813, Gayle traveled through Creek territory to visit his parents who now lived near Fort Stoddert north of Mobile. Unfortunately he arrived just before the massacre at Fort Mims and the outbreak of the Creek War. Although Gayle had planned to return to South Carolina to pursue legal studies, he decided it best to stay in Alabama to organize militia units to help defend settlements near his family's home. After the war, Gayle was able to complete his legal studies reading law in St. Stephens in the office of Judge Abner Smith Lipscomb, who was the second chief justice of the Alabama Supreme Court. Gayle was admitted to the bar in 1818 and subsequently held numerous state offices, including solicitor for the First Judicial Circuit in 1818, Monroe County's representative in the House of Representatives in 1822, judge of the Third Judicial Circuit in 1823, Greene County's representative in the House of Representatives, and Speaker of the House in 1829.[28]

When John Gayle was elected governor in 1831, he was an ardent Jacksonian and he strongly supported the federal government's anti-nullification position. Within a year, however, Gayle would become em-

---

[27] Mary Jane McDaniel, "Samuel B. Moore," in *Alabama Governors*, 28–30. Due to his open alliance with John C. Calhoun in opposing confirmation of President Jackson's nomination of Martin Van Buren as ambassador to Great Britain, Gabriel Moore quickly lost favor with the electorate. He would only last one term in the Senate and could not get reelected to his old seat in the U.S. House of Representatives in 1836. Thereafter he encountered financial woes during the Panic of 1837, causing him to lose thousands of acres of land and slaves to creditors. By 1843, he had lost most of his property, but did manage to take eight of his slaves to Cincinnati where he executed deeds of emancipation for them. He then went briefly with his emancipated slaves to Mississippi before moving on to the Republic of Texas where he died on August 6, 1844. After his death, it was revealed that he had fathered a child by one of his slaves for whom he had executed a deed of manumission on September 27, 1842. Doss, "Rise and Fall of an Alabama Founding Father," 163–71.

[28] Sara Woolfolk Wiggins, "John Gayle," in *Alabama Governors*, 31–33; Brewer, *Alabama*, 402.

broiled in a conflict of his own with the federal government concerning Indian policy which precipitated a crisis that nearly led to a military confrontation. President Jackson eventually sent Frances Scott Key, author of the "Star-Spangled Banner," to Alabama in 1833 to negotiate a truce and to avert a military confrontation between the two governments.[29]

The crisis grew out of management of the lands that had been ceded to the United States by the Creeks in the Treaty of Cusseta of 1832. By this treaty the Creeks ceded all of their lands east of the Mississippi River to the United States, including their remaining lands in east central Alabama. Although the Creeks were granted lands west of the Mississippi to which the federal government urged them to move, the treaty did not compel them to go. Indeed, those deciding to stay were allowed to choose allotments of land for their families. The provision of the treaty that ultimately led to the confrontation between state and federal authorities was one that provided for the removal of white settlers from the territory until the lands were surveyed and the remaining Creeks received their allotments of lands. Hostilities ensued not only because white squatters refused to leave, but also because thousands more rushed in to lay a claim to the choicest lands. In the interim, however, Governor Gayle had obtained an assurance from Secretary of War Lewis Cass that no peaceable white settlers would be forcibly removed unless situated upon lands chosen by Creek chieftains for their families.[30]

The first military encounter came in response to an advance into Indian country by a group of white settlers who built the village of Irwinton (later to be renamed Eufaula) on the banks of the Chattahoochee River. On instructions from officials in Washington, the United States marshal for southern Alabama appealed to the settlers to leave peaceably. When they refused and threatened violence instead, a detachment of federal troops from Fort Mitchell burned the village. Authorities in Pike County, where these settlers had come from, responded by issuing an arrest warrant for the commanding officer. The deputy sheriff attempting to execute the warrant was bayoneted to death by a federal soldier. Within a few months of this violent incident, the Alabama General Assembly extended the jurisdiction of the state over the ceded Creek territory by creating eight counties: Coosa, Benton (now Calhoun), Talladega, Tallapoosa, Russell, Randolph, Chambers, Macon, and Barbour. The stage was then set for further confrontation as Governor Gayle insisted that the federal government could make no treaty in derogation of the rights of the state to exert its sovereignty within its own boundaries.[31]

---

[29] Wiggins, "John Gayle," 32.

[30] Treaty of Cusseta (1832), Art. 5; Thomas Chalmers McCorvey, "The Mission of Frances Scott Key to Alabama in 1833," *Transactions of the Alabama Historical Society* 4 (1899–1903): 141–46; Frank L. Owsley, Jr., "Francis Scott Key's Mission to Alabama in 1833," *Alabama Review* 23 (July 1970): 181–84; Theodore H. Jack, "Alabama and the Federal Government: The Creek Indian Controversy," *The Mississippi Valley Historical Review* 3 (December 1916): 301–17.

[31] McCorvey, "Mission," 146–48.

In July 1833, the issue came to a head when Hardeman Owens, commissioner of roads and revenue for newly created Russell County, was killed when resisting arrest by federal troops. Jeremiah Austill—one of the heroes of the "Canoe Fight" during the Creek War, then the marshal of the southern district of Alabama—had sent in federal forces in response to complaints from chiefs within the Indian territory of degradations committed by Owens, including the seizure of lands and severe beatings of some of their inhabitants. As a result of Owens' death, incensed white citizens throughout the state met in mass meetings and passed defiant resolutions. The *Niles Weekly Register* reported on one such meeting in Lowndes County on September 28, 1833, which declared that "the removal of our citizens from their settlements by force is unconstitutional, oppressive, and utterly subversive of the sovereignty of the State, and we cannot and will not submit to it." In face of these bellicose expressions, Governor Gayle urged calm, acceptance of any lawful process from the courts of the United States, and a refrain from violence. The governor nevertheless strongly protested federal military presence within the state and heightened the possibility of a military confrontation by ordering the organization of militia units within the newly created counties in the ceded territory. In the meanwhile, the Russell County grand jury indicted the federal soldiers responsible for the death of Owens and issued a formal demand to the commanding officer at Fort Mitchell to deliver the accused soldiers for trial by Alabama's civil authorities. The officer refused, thus leaving the state and federal governments at a dangerous impasse.[32]

Despite Governor Gayle's prior efforts in preparing the state for a confrontation with federal forces, when push came to shove he decided to avoid armed conflict by forwarding the court's legal process to the Secretary of War to pass along to the President for consideration, rather than to send in the recently organized militia to enforce it. In the interim, Alabama's congressional delegation worked behind the scenes to effectuate a compromise of the entire controversy. From this group, Senator William Rufus King and Representative John Murphy met privately with President Andrew Jackson and hammered out an agreement by which white settlers who had not interfered with the properties of Indian inhabitants would not be removed from their land. To further promote peace between the state and federal governments, President Jackson dispatched Frances Scott Key, then the district attorney for the District of Columbia, to Alabama as the federal government's on-the-scene representative in the ongoing conflict.[33]

Key first went to Fort Mitchell where he obtained a reluctant promise

[32] McCorvey, "Mission," 149–50; Jack, "Alabama and the Federal Government," 305–06; Owsley, "Key's Mission," 185–86. Frank Owsley labeled Owens "a complete scoundrel," in view of an article in the *Charleston Courier* on October 13, 1833, that reported that he "had come into the territory with the intention of tricking the Indians into signing their land over to him." The article further contended that Owens forcibly removed at least two Indians from their land and broke a young girl's arm in retaliation for her reporting his actions to the federal authorities. There were also accusations that he further enraged the native population by digging up Indian graves in search of valuables.

[33] McCorvey, "Mission," 152–53; Owsley, "Key's Mission," 187–88.

from the commander to surrender the soldiers involved in the death of Hardeman Owens as soon as a trial was scheduled. Key next went to work ensuring the completion of the survey of Creek lands and the final location of their chosen plots. He also met with Governor Gayle in order to ease tensions with regard to the Owens case. As luck would have it, the federal soldier accused of the murder had the good sense to abscond, thus obviating a trial and ending the crisis that had pitted the state's civil authorities against the federal military. As the *Niles Weekly Register* put it: "A Gordian knot has been cut!" With this conflict resolved, Key was able to work out a compromise with regard to the ceded territory that provided for the removal of only those white settlers occupying lands specifically reserved by Creek chiefs and heads of family. Titles to these lands could even be purchased from the occupying Indians, so long as they were given a fair price, which was deemed by the federal government to be no less than $1.25 an acre.[34]

Although violence had been avoided by Key's mission to Alabama, the confrontation left scars that would have far-reaching political effects in the state. Jacksonian Democrats hung on to their control of the state, but President Jackson's popularity within the state took a serious hit because of his role in the controversy. As a result, Governor Gayle backed away from his support of the President and even joined the Whig Party to oppose Martin Van Buren, whom Jackson had promoted to succeed him. All in all, this confrontation with the federal government paved the way for a vociferous states' right faction led by Dixon Hall Lewis to gain strength and to sway the state from its previous support of a strong central government.[35]

Gayle's attachment to the Whigs following the Creek controversy portended a day soon when Alabama would emerge into a true two-party state for the first time. Whiggery in Alabama began to coalesce at that time around a strong sentiment in favor of states' rights and a concomitant opposition to Jackson. Jackson's previous popularity in the state was mollified not only by his handling of the Creek crisis, but also by his veto of the BUS whose lending policies benefited quite a few Alabamians. States' rights advocates also were disappointed with Jackson's handling of the nullification crisis in South Carolina as they opposed high federal tariffs on imports and the resulting damage done to southern planters and merchants. The combination of these concerns led some to refer to the president as "King Andrew." Jackson's selection of Martin Van Buren to be his successor in 1836 was the last straw for many Alabamians, who then flocked to the Whig Party and voted for Hugh Lawson White because of their belief that Van Buren was opposed to slavery. Although Van Buren carried Alabama, the Whigs were able to garner forty-five percent of the popular vote, as well as

---

[34] Owsley, "Key's Mission," 189–92; Jack, "Alabama and the Federal Government," 306; Wiggins, "John Gayle," 32–33.

[35] Owsley, "Key's Mission," 189–92; McCorvey, "Mission," 153–57. Governor Gayle's withdrawal of support from President Jackson was not purely based upon politics. Gayle had taken personal umbrage at charges of corrupt land speculation aired by the Washington *Globe*, which Gayle believed had been with the approval of Jackson. Senator William Rufus King tried to convince Gayle that the allegations of the *Globe* did not reflect the views of the President, but to no avail.

to close in on the Democratic majority in the state legislature. They continued to strengthen during the late 1830s during a period of economic depression.[36]

Although the Whigs were ensconced as a viable party in Alabama by 1840, opposition to Jackson and Van Buren seemed to be the only matters that unified them. Members of the party took varying stances pertaining to the extent of power to be exercised by the national government, the extent of national expansion, or how to deal with slavery. They did come together in calling for the establishment of a new Bank of the United States to combat the effects of the economic depression generated by the Panic of 1837. They were also in basic agreement that economic development would benefit from a government banking system and supported aid for internal improvements such as roads, railroads, and canals.[37]

The party's nucleus in Alabama consisted primarily of wealthy planters in the southern part of the state who favored an active government necessary to promote King Cotton and its reliance upon international markets. On the other hand, self-sufficient yeomen farmers, isolated in the hill country of north Alabama, stuck with the "people's" wing of the Democratic Party, which had previously stripped the "royalist" Georgia faction of power some fifteen years earlier. Although the Whig Party would have an influence on Alabama politics for several years to come, the Whigs never won a statewide election nor delivered the state in a presidential election. This was in large part due to the efforts of Democrats to stifle Whig influence by requiring—albeit temporarily, as it turned out—that all congressional candidates be voted upon on a statewide basis rather than by districts. Also, a plan was instituted that made electoral representation based solely upon the white population rather than upon a mixture of the white and black populations where blacks counted as three-fifths of a person. Both of these measures, particularly the "white basis" for representation, limited the successes of the Whig Party whose strength was centered in the slave-laden counties of the Black Belt. The party was nevertheless able to obtain a majority in the state senate in 1849 and 1851, and held two congressional seats from 1829 to 1843. During the 1850s, the Whig Party in Alabama declined as its local members became more and more concerned with its national leaders' lack of support for slavery. By the end of the decade, the Whig Party no longer was a viable party in Alabama.[38]

Regardless of evolving party politics, Governor Gayle's states' rights stance during the Creek controversy did not have universal approval, as reflected by a few who had supported the federal government's policy of removal of white settlers. For example, historian Thomas Chalmers McCorvey noted that "the *Mobile Register*, especially, twitted the governor for what it considered his inconsistency in condemning nullification in

[36] Frederick M. Beatty, "Whig Party," *Encyclopedia of Alabama*, http://www.encyclopediaof alabama.org/ face/Article.jsp?id=h-1173 (accessed December 20, 2012).

[37] Ibid.

[38] Rogers et al., *Alabama*, 137–42; Beatty, "Whig Party"; Lewey Dorman, *Party Politics in Alabama from 1850 through 1860* (Tuscaloosa: University of Alabama Press, 1995).

South Carolina and virtually becoming the champion of the Alabama variety." Despite such limited criticism of Governor Gayle's handling of the Creek controversy, he was reelected without opposition in 1833.[39]

Although overshadowed by the Creek controversy, other significant events occurred while Gayle served as governor, including expansion of the state bank, chartering of Alabama's first railroad, and establishment of the state's first cotton mill. Branches of the State Bank of Alabama were established during his term in Montgomery, Mobile, Huntsville, and Decatur. On January 30, 1830, the General Assembly chartered the Tuscumbia Rail Company to build a short road of just two miles from the Tuscumbia River landing to the present city of Sheffield, becoming one of the first railroads in the country. Just two years later, the legislature chartered the Tuscumbia, Courtland and Decatur Railroad. This railroad was to run forty-four miles from Tuscumbia to Decatur, allowing a transportation route around the rapids on the Tennessee River at Muscle Shoals. The entire line was completed in June 1834. The state's first cotton mill, located about ten miles northeast of Huntsville on the Flint River, was incorporated in 1832 by the legislature. The mill, containing three thousand spindles and one hundred looms, was the first cotton manufacturing facility of any significance in the southeastern United States. The mill was known as the Bell Factory because it had a bell which daily summoned its slave labor force—consisting primarily of children between ten and fourteen years of age—to work.[40]

After John Gayle left office to practice law in Mobile, Clement Comer Clay was elected in 1835 as Alabama's eighth governor. Born in Halifax County, Virginia, on December 17, 1789, Clay moved with his family as a child to Grainger County, Tennessee. After attending Blount College (the predecessor of the University of Tennessee), and reading law in Knoxville, Clay moved to Huntsville in 1811. There he associated with the Broad River Group political machine and became a stockholder and director of the Planters and Merchants Bank. Because of his alliance with the influential Georgia faction, Clay was chosen to chair the Committee of Fifteen that prepared the draft of Alabama's first constitution. The state's inaugural legislature elected Clay as one of Alabama's first five circuit judges, who collectively sat as the state's Supreme Court. The other judges selected Clay as the state's first chief justice even though he was, at age thirty, their youngest member. Clay resigned from the court in 1823 and ran for Congress in 1825. When he was soundly defeated by Gabriel Moore because of his relationship with banking and creditor interests, Clay set about to take public positions more appealing to the common yeoman farmer. As a result, in 1828 he was elected to the state House of Representatives, where

[39] Wiggins, "John Gayle," 33; McCorvey, "Mission," 155.

[40] Randall Martin Miller, *The Cotton Movement in Antebellum Alabama* (New York: Arno Press, 1978), 18–19; Moore, *History of Alabama*, 309; J. Lawrence Lee, "Alabama Railroads," *Encyclopedia of Alabama*, http://www.encyclopediaofalabama.org/face/Article.jsp?id=h-2390 (accessed February 3, 2013). Alabama's original railroad was powered by horses, but it soon operated the first steam powered locomotive engine west of the Alleghenies.

he was chosen its speaker, and in 1829 he was elected to the U.S. Congress.[41]

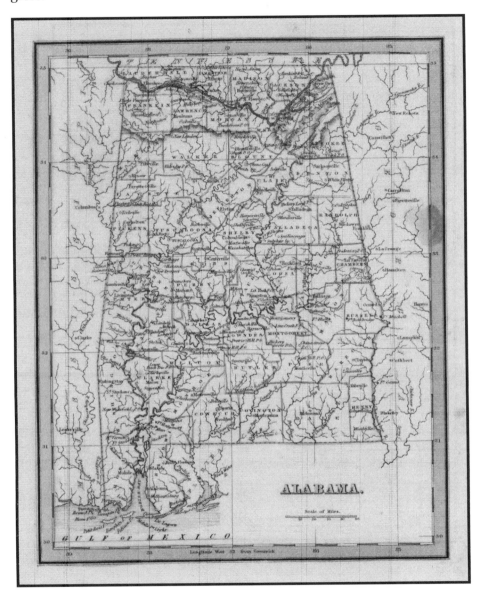

Map of the State of Alabama from Bradford's *Comprehensive Atlas*, 1835
By Boston mapmaker Thomas Gamaliel Bradford

Courtesy Barry Lawrence Ruderman Antique Maps, used by permission

---

[41] Mills Thornton III, "Clement Comer Clay," in *Alabama Governors*, 34–36; Frank L. Owsley, "The Clays in Early Alabama History," *Alabama Review* 2 (October 1949): 245–46; Brewer, *Alabama*, 356–57; Owen, *History of Alabama*, 4: 342.

By 1835, Clay was strongly ensconced as a Jacksonian Democrat and easily defeated the Whig candidate, Enoch Parson, for governor. In his first address to the legislature, Clay chose to focus upon the dangers of abolitionism spreading throughout the north. In order to prevent its spread to the south, he strongly advocated that northerners who had sent abolitionist propaganda to the south be punished. As a further precaution, he urged toughening of the state's laws against slave rebellions. Clay's administration, however, would be challenged by an Indian uprising and a severe economic downturn rather than slave insurrections. These challenges were presented by the Creek War of 1836 and the Panic of 1837.[42]

Although military confrontation with the federal government over the Creek controversy had been avoided during Gayle's administration, Governor Clay was faced with continuing violence committed by the Creeks remaining in Alabama. Skirmishes increased as pressure was exerted against the remaining Creeks to leave for their new lands west of the Mississippi, which had been provided for them in lieu of the lands in Alabama they had ceded as a result of the Treaty of Cusetta in 1832. Despite the previous efforts of Frances Scott Key, there was widespread fraud committed by land speculators against the Creeks to illegally obtain land from them before their relocation. Left in a desperate economic state after trading their allotments to speculators for pennies on the dollar, approximately three thousand Creeks joined in a final revolt against the white settlers.[43]

Several units of the Alabama militia were called up by Governor Clay after increasing hostilities occurred in the eastern section of Alabama in the spring of 1836. Communities attacked included Watson's near the Uchee Creek bridge in western Barbour County, as well as several communities in the Chattahoochee River valley as far south as Irwinton (present-day Eufaula). White settlers were also murdered along the Federal Road near Fort Bainbridge, seventeen miles southeast of present-day Tuskegee, Alabama, and near Midway in Bulloch County. Conditions had deteriorated to the point that stage contractors had difficulty in delivering the mail through this section of the state. On May 13, 1836, the *Columbus Enquirer* reported that "misguided Indians have at length commenced the work of death, which has so long been apprehended by our settlers in the new counties of Ala."[44]

Governor Clay took personal command of the state militia during this crisis. Renowned early Alabama historian Albert James Pickett was appointed as the governor's aide-de-camp. The "Montgomery Huzzars," or "Henry's Horsemen," were assigned directly to the governor. Other militia units helping to subdue the uprising included, among others, the Montgomery True Blues under the command of Captain George Chisholm, the Selma Guards under the command of John F. Connoley, a Montgomery

---

[42] Thornton, "Clement Comer Clay," 36.

[43] Ibid.

[44] Peter A. Brannon, "Creek Indian War, 1836–1837," *Alabama Historical Quarterly* 13 (1951): 156; *Columbus Enquirer*, May 13, 1836.

County unit under the command of Captain John Bonham, and an artillery unit under the command of Captain John Milton of Mobile. In June 1836, Secretary of War Lewis Cass finally sent in federal forces under the command of General Thomas Jessup to reinforce the state militia. These combined forces were joined by approximately 700 friendly Creeks, including David Moniac, grandnephew of Creek leader Alexander McGillivray and graduate of the United States Military Academy at West Point.[45]

With federal troops and Alabama militia in pursuit, many hostile Creeks took off for Florida to join the Seminoles. The last major battle of the war took place in March 1837 at Hobdy's Bridge on the Pea River, located near Louisville in Barbour County. There, Alabama volunteers under General William Wellborn attacked and defeated a party of Creeks finding refuge in nearby swamps as they moved toward Florida. During the so-called war, many thousands of Creeks had "voluntarily" begun the painful journey to their new unwanted lands in Oklahoma. At least two thousand others were rounded up as prisoners of war and taken under guard to Montgomery where they were put on steamboats and taken to Mobile. From there they were transported to New Orleans and on up the Mississippi River to the mouth of the Arkansas River, from where they trekked overland to Oklahoma.[46]

When the Creeks reached Mobile for transportation over to New Orleans for the long trip up the Mississippi River, they were placed in internment camps to wait for their kinsmen to return from the Second Seminole War. While they waited, they were subject to starvation and disease. On October 29, 1837, the Alabama Emigrating Company, contracted to transport the Creeks to "Indian Territory," crammed 1,500 Creeks and their slaves onto four steamboats. Of this number, approximately 500 people were dangerously crowded onto the steamboat *Monmouth* for their journey upstream. To the chagrin of most of these passengers, the journey began at night. To make matters worse it was not long before they ran into a rainstorm that significantly reduced visibility. As a result, the pilot apparently became confused and took the boat into a one-way channel that was for the use of downstream traffic only. As many of the passengers looked on in horror, the *Monmouth* took evasive measures, but nonetheless crashed into the *Trenton*, which was an empty vessel in tow of the *Warren*. As the *Monmouth* broke apart, many of its passengers were thrown overboard and fought desperately to cling to wooden debris in strong river currents. In all, it is estimated that 311 people, including two crew members and thirty-two slaves, lost their lives.[47] The Trail of Tears was tragically underway.

---

[45] Brannon, "Creek Indian War," 157; Owen, *History of Alabama*, 4: 1363.

[46] Brannon, "Creek Indian War," 158; Claudio Saunt, *Black, White, and Indian: Race and the Unmaking of the American Family* (New York: Oxford University Press, 2005), 50–52.

[47] This was the deadliest maritime accident in U.S. history until the *Sultana* exploded and sank in April 1865, as it was transporting approximately 2,300 freed Union soldiers back north. Approximately 1,700 soldiers, many recently released from the Cahaba Confederate prison camp in Alabama, lost their lives. Robert Gudmestad, *Steamboats and the Rise of the Cotton Kingdom* (Baton Rouge: Louisiana State Univ. Press, 2011).

With the end of hostilities, Governor Gayle was next confronted with the devastating effects of the Panic of 1837 that brought a crushing end to Alabama's "flush times." In the early 1830s Alabama was enjoying a period of economic prosperity described by Joseph G. Baldwin, well-known humorist of the times, as a "golden era, when shinplasters [paper money] were the sole currency; when bank—bills were 'thick as Autumn leaves in Vallambrosa,' and credit was a franchise." In Alabama, as throughout the nation, land speculation was running rampant. The bubble finally burst in 1837 as a result of a number of factors, including President Jackson's veto of the extension of the Bank of the United States which deprived the country of a stable currency. Further, in order to stem the tide of speculative fever, President Jackson had issued an executive order in July 1836, known as the Specie Circular, which required the payment for public lands be in gold and silver. This had the effect of eventually diminishing the value of much of the country's paper money. In Alabama, as all of its banks suspended specie payments, commerce and trade seriously declined and the price of land, cotton, and slaves were sent spiraling downward. Matthew P. Blue, early historian of Montgomery, described the effects of the depression on that city in this way: "The dockets of the Courts groaned under the civil suits, and the voice of the Sheriffs was a constant and most familiar sound, crying off the property of all classes involved in the universal ruin. All property and all kinds of business in Montgomery were paralyzed, which did not recover for several years."[48]

Governor Clay responded to the economic crisis by calling a special session of the legislature wherein he recommended legislation he believed favorable to Alabama's citizens burdened with debt. First and foremost, Clay desired to protect Alabama's banks from a provision of the state constitution that provided for a twelve per cent per annum penalty against banks that did not pay specie on demand unless the suspension was sanctioned by the General Assembly. If not sanctioned, the constitution also gave the legislature authority to forfeit the charter of a nonpaying bank. Realizing that it was unrealistic for the banks to resume specie payments before the state's cotton crop was harvested and sent to market, Governor Clay recommended that specie payments be suspended for at least another year. The Relief Act of 1837 enacted by the Assembly, in addition to sanctioning the suspension of specie payments by the banks, required the state bank and its branches to immediately suspend the collection of debts and to provide their debtors with another three years to pay off their loans. It further required the selling of five million dollars of bonds by the branch banks so that even more money could be lent to Alabama's already strapped borrowers. The unintended consequences of these actions left the bank with an unmanageable indebtedness that would continue to plague the

---

[48] Joseph G. Baldwin, *The Flush Times of Alabama and Mississippi*, American Century Series (New York: Sagamore Press, Inc., 1957 [1854]), 1; Rogers et al., *Alabama*, 138–39; William H. Brantley, *Banking in Alabama: 1816–1860*, 2 vols. (Birmingham, Ala.: Birmingham Printing, 1961), 2: 6; M. P. Blue, Beale and Phelan, *City Directory and History of Montgomery, Alabama* (Montgomery, Ala.: T. C. Bingham & Co. Printers and Binders, 1878), 28.

state and lead to the state bank's eventual closure.[49]

If the state banking system did not have enough problems, before the 1837 special session could finish its business, rumors were afloat in the state capital of misconduct on the part of officers of the state's main bank. The Assembly therefore appointed a committee to investigate possible acts of wrongdoing by the officers and directors of the bank in Tuscaloosa. The committee began its investigation by examining loans made by the main bank during February and March 1837, with particular focus on whether its directors were given preferences for accommodations. The investigation was soon expanded to see if any officer or director of the bank had at any time withdrawn specie for the bank's paper, and if so, in what amounts. As stated by William H. Brantley in his comprehensive history of banking in Alabama, "the misconduct alleged was preference in getting gold and silver in exchange for paper by insiders, while the ordinary citizen was being refused specie." Representatives were anxious to identify anyone who was "enjoying a preferential use of the bank's gold and silver during this painful time of specie famine." The investigation into these allegations, however, was cut short by the ending of the special session. Unfortunately, because of this, only the record to date was included in the journals of both houses with hardly any supporting evidence and with no findings, conclusions, nor even any recommendations.[50]

Amidst crises associated with a confrontation with the federal government, a second war with the Creeks, and an impending collapse of the economy, the legislature during Governor Clay's administration nevertheless managed to address a few other important matters. Foremost among these was the continued promotion of internal improvements. The number of acts pertaining to railroads seemed to increase dramatically during the 1836 annual session as a result of planters investing in this emerging alternative method of shipping their cotton to market. As examples, the Mobile and New Orleans Railroad Company was authorized to build a road from Mobile to Vincent's harbor in Grand Bay, near the Mississippi state line; the Mississippi and Alabama Railroad Company incorporated in Mississippi was authorized to construct a railroad from the Mississippi state line to the city of Mobile; the Wetumpka and Coosa Railroad Company was authorized to begin construction at the city of Wetumpka and to cross the Coosa River anywhere between Wetumpka and the Ten Islands and thence, within the discretion of its board of directors, proceeding either eastward to the Georgia state line or northeastward to the Tennessee River; and the Selma and Tennessee Railroad Company was authorized to commence construction in Selma and run northeastward to the Tennessee River near the Georgia state line.[51]

The 1836 session of the legislature also devoted significant attention to

---

[49] Brantley, *Banking in Alabama*, 2: 3–7; *Ala. Acts (1837, Called Sess.)*, 9ff; Ala. Const. of 1819, Art. VI (Establishment of Banks), Sec. 1; Thornton, *Alabama Governors*, "Clement Comer Clay," 37.

[50] Brantley, *Banking in Alabama*, 2: 12–16; *House Journal (1837, Called Sess.)*, 25.

[51] *Ala. Acts (1836)*, 46–44, 55–58, 61–64, and 87–90.

education and the making whole of those affected by the Creek War. Regarding education, the legislature expanded the number of female academies throughout the state by incorporating the Demopolis Female Academy in Marengo County, the Irwinton Female Academy in Barbour County, the Mesopotamia Male and Female Academy in Greene County, the Alabama Female Athenaeum in Tuscaloosa County, and the Tuscumbia Female Academy in Colbert County. With respect to expenses incurred as a result of the Creek War of 1836, the legislature appropriated $70,000 of the profits of the state bank for payment of the members of the militia who had been engaged in the defense of the state. Additionally, three other acts were passed to compensate various persons and businesses that had furnished troops with provisions and forage during the war. Finally, the governor was also authorized to appoint a commissioner to "receive, examine, audit and settle all claims against the State, growing out of the late Indian hostilities."[52]

In 1837, Arthur P. Bagby was elected to succeed Clay as governor by defeating Samuel W. Oliver, a former speaker of the house running as an anti-Van Buren independent. After the election, but before Bagby took office, Clay resigned as governor in July 1837 when the legislature unanimously elected him to succeed Senator John McKinley, who was appointed by President Martin Van Buren to the U.S. Supreme Court. Under the provisions of Alabama's constitution, Hugh McVay, then serving as the president of the Senate, became acting governor. Having no mandate from the people and because of his Jacksonian anti-bank attitude, pro-bank legislators deliberately withheld from McVay any of their legislative reports concerning the state bank and its branches. Because of this, McVay admitted in his message to the legislature that he could not update them as to the performance of the banks under the relief law passed in the special session of 1837. He did, however, manage to get in a jab at pro-bank legislators, stating: "As to the evils of the times, they have been brought upon this State and upon the whole Union, in a great measure, by a heedless creation of banks and wild and prodigal issues of bank paper." Not armed with sufficient information concerning the state's bank, McVay focused the remainder of his legislative message on the need for a revision of the criminal code as to punishments and the construction of a state penitentiary. Viewed as a mere caretaker, McVay's agenda was ignored as legislators bided their time awaiting the inauguration of Arthur Bagby.[53]

---

[52] Ibid., 7, 10, 66–67, 71–74, 84, 100–02, 132–33, and 137.

[53] Hugh McVay, born near Greenville, South Carolina in 1788, moved to Madison County, Alabama, in 1807. One of the first attorneys admitted to the Madison County Bar, McVay represented Madison County in the Territorial Legislature from 1811 to 1818. After moving to Lauderdale County, he represented that county in the Constitutional Convention of 1819, in the House of Representatives from 1820 to 1825 and in the Alabama Senate from 1825 to 1844—except for the few months that he served as governor. In 1836, McVay became the president of the Senate by a margin of just one vote and thus, under the provisions of Alabama's constitution, became interim governor when Clay resigned in July 1837. Owen, *History of Alabama* 4: 1141; Mary Jane McDaniel, "Hugh McVay," in *Alabama Governors*, 38–40; William Garret, *Reminiscences of Public Men in Alabama for Thirty Years* (Atlanta,

On November 22, 1837, Arthur P. Bagby was sworn in as Alabama's tenth governor. Born in Louisa County, Virginia, in 1794, Bagby moved in 1818 to Claiborne in Monroe County, Alabama, where he began to practice law a year later. He represented Monroe County in both houses of the legislature from 1821 until he was elected governor in 1837. In 1822, he became Alabama's youngest Speaker of the House and was again elected to that position in 1836, the year before he was elected governor. When Bagby took office as governor, Alabama was feeling the worst of the 1837 depression with real estate values at rock bottom and business basically at a standstill. Governor Bagby shared McVay's disapproval of the state banking system, albeit in a less hostile and confrontational manner. Despite his popularity as a recently elected governor, Bagby was still somewhat of an unknown quantity to a majority of the legislators. That, combined with his expressed negative attitude toward the banking system, prompted pro-bank legislators and the officers and directors of the banks to extend their withholding of information to the governor's office as they had done during McVay's interim term as governor.[54]

In his inaugural address, Bagby condemned "excessive issues of paper money" and complained that too many incurred excessive debt only to expect the state to rescue them from their self-inflicted predicaments. Bagby then adopted the stance of his predecessor in opposing the issuance of more state bonds to raise money for the banks. The new governor decided to say nothing further on this issue and did not even send the customary governor's annual message to the Assembly. Soon realizing that staying out of the fray in this manner was a mistake, Governor Bagby delivered a message to the Assembly in which he outlined what he saw as the state bank system's greatest flaws. In this regard, he called into question the method of appointing directors, the number of officers and directors needed, and their method of compensation. More specifically, Governor Bagby saw the potential for much abuse in a system that had a total of 73 officers and directors for just five banks that were each entitled to $35,000 in accommodations as a matter of right and who were elected annually by the legislature. The governor made recommendations to reduce the number of directors, to give the governor a role in the selection of the directors, and to pay fixed salaries to officers and directors rather than discount and accommodation privileges. He also questioned the wisdom of not requiring the banks to keep a sufficient amount of specie in their vaults in proportion to their circulation.[55]

As previously noted, Governor Bagby had indicated in his inaugural address that he was opposed to the issuance of more state bonds. He later asserted that unless the legislature called in the $5 million bond issue

Ga.: Plantation Publishing Company's Press, 1872), 39; Brantley, *Banking in Alabama*, 2: 20, 27–29; *Senate Journal (1837, Annual Sess.)*, 6–7.

[54] Mary Jane McDaniel, "Arthur P. Bagby," in *Alabama Governors*, 41; Garrett, *Reminiscences*, 205–06; Brantley, *Banking in Alabama*, 2: 50–51; Brewer, *Alabama*, 441–42.

[55] Brantley, *Banking in Alabama*, 2: 30–33; *Senate Journal (1837, Annual Sess.)*, 44ff; Garrett, *Reminiscences*, 65–66.

enacted in the Clay administration, specie payment would be delayed even further with a concomitant demand for more paper money. Not only did the legislature decline to cancel the previous bond issue, it authorized the issuance of additional bonds of $2.5 million. It also refused to reduce the number of bank directors as requested by the governor. Bagby did manage one victory when the legislature enacted a law ensuring more supervision of the state banks by requiring an audit of each bank twice a year by three commissioners to be appointed by the governor.[56]

The integrity of the state banking system—already damaged with allegations that its directors received undue privileges and preferences with respect to loan accommodations and payment of specie—was hit hard again as a result of excessive electioneering during the reelection of bank directors in December 1837. Samuel A. Hale, editor of Tuscaloosa's *Flag of the Union*, reported that during this election legislators could not leave their seats without being bombarded by dozens of hopeful candidates for these directorships. Although the tenure of bank directorships lasted only one year, incumbents were given the privilege of having up to $10,000 of their own paper discounted. Hale wished that everyone in the state could have witnessed what the *Montgomery Advertiser*'s capital correspondent described as a mad "scramble for office." Undoubtedly, had ordinary citizens been a witness to these elections, they would have been appalled by the cajoling of legislators for votes with good cigars, fine liquors, oysters suppers, and "other entertainments," as detailed by William Garrett, then Assistant Clerk of the House of Representatives and author of a comprehensive chronicle of the Alabama General Assembly and its members during the mid-nineteenth century. Garrett also reported on the cavalier fashion in which legislators sought votes for their favorite candidates for a bank directorship. In this regard, he told the tale of a conscientious legislator who sought support for a bill to improve the state's school system. He became disgusted when he was frequently told in response to his efforts, "I don't know anything about your bill, but will say that I have a friend I want elected a bank director, and if you will vote for him I will vote for your bill."[57]

During the regular session of the 1837 legislature, Governor Bagby finally managed to obtain legislative approval of his recommendation to reduce the number of directors for each bank. Indeed, the number was dramatically reduced from twelve to just six. More importantly, tougher restrictions were placed upon officers and directors prohibiting them from becoming liable or indebted in any manner to the state bank or its branches. They were further prohibited from obtaining any accommodation or discount in their own name or in the name of any other person or co-partnership. These reforms made bank directorships much less lucrative

---

[56] Brantley, *Banking in Alabama*, 2: 33–34; *Ala. Acts (1837, Annual Sess.)*, 46, 65–68; *Senate Journal (1837, Annual Sess.)*, 83–85.

[57] Brantley, *Banking in Alabama*, 2: 34–35; Garrett, *Reminiscences,* 42–43.

and thus less vigorously sought after as in the past with corruptive and excessive electioneering efforts.[58]

Arthur P. Bagby won a second term as governor in 1839 without much of an organized opposition, although there were a few votes cast for Arthur F. Hopkins, the leader of the Whig Party. Although he was almost universally supported for reelection, most legislators nevertheless consistently voted against Governor Bagby's recommendations concerning the state bank's ills, particularly those with regard to reforms aimed at the directorships and to requirements that banks keep a larger portion of specie in their vaults in proportion to their circulation. To further exacerbate matters, in 1840, the Merchants Bank of New York astounded Alabamians when it issued a report revealing that Alabama owed $11.5 million on state bonds without any visible means of satisfying them. The annual interest on these bonds alone was $600,000, a staggering amount that the state would struggle with for many years to come.[59]

Although the Whig candidate was soundly defeated by Arthur Bagby in the Alabama gubernatorial election of 1840, Democratic control of the Alabama legislature was seriously threatened by the election of many Whigs riding the coattails of William Henry Harrison, America's first Whig president. With only a narrow majority in the legislature, Governor Bagby sought to guard against further inroads by Whigs in Alabama by advocating a new manner of electing the state's representatives to the U.S. Congress. The Whigs already had majorities in the Tuscaloosa and Mobile districts and a win by Henry W. Hilliard over Dixon Hall Lewis in the Montgomery district would give the Whigs a three-to-two majority in Alabama's congressional delegation. Admittedly to stave off this possibility, Governor Bagby proposed the so-called *General Ticket* plan that required all of Alabama's congressional representatives to be elected from the state at large rather than from districts, so as to take advantage of the statewide majority held by the Democratic Party.[60]

The *General Ticket* bill was enacted in January 1841, and resulted in the election of Democrats in all five Congressional districts in a special election called by Governor Bagby in May 1841. State Whigs were outraged with this system, proclaiming in a Montgomery newspaper that "in order to punish the Whig portion of the State, the Loco Foco [a faction of the Demo-

---

[58] *Ala. Acts (1837, Annual Sess.)*, 13–14.

[59] Garrett, *Reminiscences*, 103; Brantley, *Banking in Alabama*, 2: 95; McDaniel, "Arthur P. Bagby," 42.

[60] Milo B. Howard, Jr., "The General Ticket," *Alabama Review* 19 (July 1966): 163–74; David I. Durham, *A Southern Moderate in Radical Times: Henry Washington Hilliard, 1808–1892* (Baton Rouge: Louisiana State University Press, 2008), 65–67. Had the general system not been used, the Whig candidates in the Tuscaloosa, Mobile, and Montgomery districts would have been elected. Although not winning the statewide race, Henry Hilliard's impressive outpolling of Alabama's leading states' rights activist in his own district set the stage for Hilliard to become leader of the Whig Party in Alabama. Hilliard, a moderate pro-Unionist, would later become the antagonist of William Lowndes Yancey, the leader of the Southern Radicals in Alabama, in the debate regarding secession. See Brantley, *Banking in Alabama*, 2: 124–25; Rogers et al., *Alabama*, 143.

cratic Party] majority in the Legislature, tyrannically proceeded to adopt a principle which in effect deprives South Alabama of representation in Congress, and transfers it entire to the Northern counties." The system, however, was short lived because a sufficient number of Democrats joined Whigs in repealing it in November 1841, resulting in the restoration of the district system of local representation to which most Alabamians had long been used to and preferred.[61]

Although the lion's share of Governor Bagby's attention while in office was directed toward economic issues, he nevertheless had to deal with two significant Indian issues. First, he oversaw the successful completion of the Indian removal that had commenced under Governor Clay. Secondly, he was required to raise militia in south Alabama as a result of a second Seminole War spilling into Alabama. Although Indians in north Alabama had removed peacefully following the brief Creek War of 1836, some Creeks in south Alabama fled to Florida where they joined Seminoles in violently resisting relocation. Warring bands of these Indians came out of the swamps of Florida to conduct guerilla-type raids on white communities in south Alabama, including several in Barbour, Dale, and Covington counties. As a result, a number of local militia companies were formed to protect these communities from further attacks.[62]

The legislature rarely supported Governor Bagby's recommendations with regard to the state's banking system, but significant legislative reforms in other areas were achieved during his administration. Foremost among these was the authorization to construct the state's first penitentiary, which was erected near the newly incorporated town of Wetumpka in 1841 at a cost of $84,899, and the prohibition of branding and whipping as forms of punishment within the penitentiary. In another reform measure, imprisonment for debt was abolished, except in cases where fraud was involved. Other noteworthy legislative acts included the establishment of separate courts of chancery (courts of equitable jurisdiction) and the appointment of commissioners to participate in the ascertainment of the boundary between Alabama and Georgia.[63]

---

[61] Brantley, *Banking in Alabama*, 2: 124–25; Rogers et al., *Alabama*, 142; McDaniel, "Arthur P. Bagby," 42–43. The special election was necessitated by President Harrison's call for a special session of Congress for May 1841. This presented a problem in that under existing state law the terms of Alabama's congressional representatives expired in March 1841, while the next regular election was not until August 1841. See also *Ala. Acts (1840)*, 41–42; *Ala. Acts (1841, Called Sess.)*, 3–4; Alabama *Acts, (1841, Regular Sess.)*, 3; *Alabama Journal*, April 14, 1841.

[62] McDaniel, "Arthur P. Bagby," 43; J. Leitch Wright, Jr., *Creeks and Seminoles: The Destruction and Regeneration of the Muscogulege People* (Lincoln: University of Nebraska Press, 1986), 270. At the request of Major General Winfield Scott who had been sent to Florida to command U.S. operations against the Seminoles, Governor Clement C. Clay had previously provided three volunteer companies of the Alabama militia to participate in the war in Florida. These companies were sent by steamboat from Mobile to Tampa Bay where they participated in a limited campaign against the Seminoles in central Florida. Phillip E. Koerper and David T. Childress, "The Alabama Volunteers in the Second Seminole War, 1836," *Alabama Review* 37 (January 1984): 3–12.

[63] *Ala. Acts (1838)*, 33–34, 44–51, 80–81, and 206; Garrett, *Reminiscences*, 204.

With regard to the criminal justice system, harsh punishments adopted from the English common law, including whipping, branding, and humiliation in the pillory, became the impetus for penal reform. Alabama's Constitution of 1819 urged the legislature to quickly pass a penal code "founded on principles of reformation, and not of vindictive justice." The penitentiary was seen by reformers as the perfect answer to cruel physical and public punishments. Milder punishments were also advocated so as to make the laws more enforceable and make it less likely that juries would convict of lesser penalties to spare a defendant from an unduly harsh result, such as the death penalty for committing forgery.[64]

Benjamin Faneuil Porter, a representative from Tuscaloosa County and former law partner of Alabama's first Speaker of the House James Dellet, led the fight in Alabama for the construction of a state penitentiary as well as for the reformation of the criminal code. The legislature rejected proposals for prison reform in 1831 and 1832, but in 1834, with support from Governor Gayle and newspaper editors, it decided to put the penitentiary issue directly before the electorate. While returns from cities such as Mobile, Tuscaloosa, Montgomery, and Huntsville were favorable, the proposal was overwhelmingly defeated statewide. Porter and likeminded legislators would not be deterred, however, and sought again to revise the penal code when Governor Bagby came out in support of criminal justice reform. As a result, on January 26, 1839, the legislature enacted a bill authorizing the construction of the state's first penitentiary. This bill authorized the legislature to elect three commissioners to reform the state's penal code so as to fit in with the penitentiary system. It also provided for three commissioners to supervise construction. Wetumpka was chosen as the site for the new facility, but due to political maneuvering by the commissioners and legislators, and slow-moving contractors, construction was not completed until of the fall of 1841.[65]

In his annual address to the legislature in November 1840, Governor Bagby made one of the first recorded speeches in Alabama history to defend slavery as a positive institution. An ardent supporter of slavery, Bagby asserted that since southern slaves had most of the necessities of life provided to them by their owners, they were better off than the free laborers of other regions. Despite their so-called advantages, Bagby nevertheless urged that the "peculiar character of a portion of our population" required the raising of local militia to address "emergencies" arising with respect to this population. Other politicians would soon follow suit in zealously defending slavery as Alabama began its journey toward secession. Meanwhile, Arthur Bagby finished his service as governor, which was succinctly described by

---

[64] Pruitt, *Taming Alabama*, 18–20; see also Mary Ann Neeley, "Painful Circumstances: Glimpses of the Alabama Penitentiary, 1846–1852," *Alabama Review* 44 (January 1991): 3–4.

[65] Pruitt, *Taming Alabama*, 19–24; Robert David Ward and William Warren Rogers, *Alabama's Response to the Penitentiary Movement, 1829–1865* (Gainesville: University Press of Florida, 2003), 35–46; Edward L. Ayers, *Vengeance and Justice: Crime and Punishment in the 19th-Century American South* (New York and Oxford: Oxford University Press, 1984), 43–49.

House Clerk (and later Secretary of State) William Garrett as follows, "He came into office as the storm was raging, and he left it after having been four years at the helm, while the winds yet howled in the deserted halls of commerce." Nevertheless in November 1841, Bagby was appointed to fill the vacancy in the U.S. Senate caused by the resignation of Clement Comer Clay. He was elected to a full term in 1842 and served until June 1848 when President James Knox Polk appointed him as foreign minister to the Court of St. Petersburg in Russia.[66]

In 1841, Benjamin Fitzpatrick of Elmore County became Alabama's eleventh governor by defeating James W. McClung of Madison County. Born on June 30, 1802, in Greene County, Georgia, Fitzpatrick was the first Alabama governor to be born in the nineteenth century. He was the son of William Fitzpatrick, who served in the Georgia legislature for nineteen years, and Anne Phillips Fitzpatrick. Orphaned by the age of seven and reared by his elder siblings, Fitzpatrick received very little in the way of a formal education. In 1816, when he was only fourteen, Fitzpatrick was sent by his bothers to manage property they had acquired on the east bank of the Alabama River about six miles north of Montgomery. Showing an ability to fend for himself on the Alabama frontier, young Fitzpatrick became a deputy for Autauga County's first sheriff. He was later employed as a clerk in a Wetumpka store before reading law in the office of Judge Nimrod E. Benson of Montgomery. By 1821, Fitzpatrick had been admitted to the local bar and had opened an office in Montgomery where he practiced law, first with Judge Benson and then with Henry Goldthwaite. He also served as the solicitor for Montgomery's judicial district for several years before health considerations forced him to retire to his plantation a few miles west of Wetumpka. In 1827, Fitzpatrick married Sarah Terry Elmore who came from a wealthy and influential family for whom Elmore County was later named. As result of this marriage, Fitzpatrick acquired a large plantation across the Alabama River from Montgomery and was thus able to leave the practice of law altogether to become a gentleman planter.[67]

For the next several years Fitzpatrick's life was devoted solely to agricultural and familial pursuits. Following the death of his wife, however, he increasingly turned his attention to politics, so much so that he was elected governor in 1841. During his campaign for governor, he made clear to voters his anti-banking Jacksonian position by assuring them, "I have never borrowed a dollar from a bank, neither was I ever president or director of one. I am a tiller of the earth and look to that as the only source of prosperity and wealth." In his inaugural address delivered on November 22, 1841, Governor Fitzpatrick emphasized a conservative view of the role of government and taxation, asserting "that in the practical administration of all

---

[66] Upon returning to Alabama, Bagby was appointed to a committee to codify the state's statutes. He then retired to private life, first living in Camden, then in Mobile, where he died from yellow fever in 1858. McDaniel, "Arthur P. Bagby," 43–44; Brewer, *Alabama*, 441–42; Garrett, *Reminiscences*, 205.

[67] Brewer, *Alabama*, 240; Owen, *History of Alabama*, 3: 582; J. Mills Thornton III, "Benjamin Fitzpatrick," in *Alabama Governors*, 45.

government, economy is one of the highest of public virtues. The essence of modern oppression is taxation. The measure of popular liberty may be found in the amount of money which is taken from the people to support the government; when the amount is increased beyond the requirement of a rigid economy, the government becomes profligate and oppressive."[68]

The banking issue remained dominant as Governor Fitzpatrick assumed office in November 1841. The 1841 session of the legislature, however, rejected any attempt at reform, with the minor exception of a bill requiring that any legislator nominating a candidate for president or director of any state bank to declare in writing any debts or liabilities of the candidate to the bank and to further state whether the candidate was solvent and competent to discharge his duties. Change was in the offing for the next session when the legislative elections of 1842 brought in a group of legislators who, for the most part, were not under the undue influence of the banks as so many had been in the past.[69]

In the months leading up to the 1842 election, which became a referendum on the banking issue, strong anti-bank sentiment was building such that the banks must be dealt with once and for all. Typical of sentiments as to how to do so was one expressed in the *Mobile Register* by an anonymous writer calling himself "A Citizen," who believed that the banks should either resume specie payments or be put out of business. The Mobile branch of the State Bank of Alabama in particular became the object of much scrutiny due to its mismanagement and its illegal purchase of one million dollars' worth of cotton in excess of what was needed to pay in specie all state bonds and the interest due on them in 1842. As to all banks in the state banking system, a proposal was gaining favor to adhere to the specie standard, also popularly known as the *True Measure of Value* standard. Another anonymous writer to the *Mobile Register*, referred to as the "Alabama Planter," proposed that this be achieved by closing the weakest of the branches, transferring any of their remaining assets to the other banks, and turning to direct taxation to pay down the state's bond indebtedness. The *Register* was joined by Tuscaloosa's *Flag of the Union* in keeping the pot stirring against the banks with their editorials. Reflective of their efforts, the *Register* noted on May 30, 1842: "The *Flag of the Union* . . . has taken grounds similar to ours, and is out strongly for the most searching reform . . . a resumption of specie payments, and the lopping off at once, of all the unsound banks."[70]

Shortly after the *Flag of the Union* urged the election of legislators not indebted to the banks, it was publicly announced on June 29, 1842, that John A. Campbell, an exceptional lawyer from Mobile and future Associate Justice of the United States Supreme Court, was seeking a seat in the legislature. Neither indebted to the banks nor in their pockets in any way, Campbell ran on a platform that called for the severance of the unhealthy

---

[68] Brewer, *Alabama*, 240; Thornton, *Politics and Power*, 49; Rogers et al., *Alabama*, 144.

[69] *Ala. Acts (1841, Annual Sess.)*, 14; Garrett, *Reminiscences*, 242.

[70] Brantley, *Banking in Alabama*, 2: 163–68, 174–79; Thornton, "Benjamin Fitzpatrick," 46.

relationship between the banks and the legislature. The idea of repudiation of notes of any bank being abhorrent to him, he first and foremost urged their redemption upon demand. His platform further asserted that banks should not be allowed to engage in any business that had the effect of increasing the number of their creditors. Campbell's entry into the race for the legislature was for the purpose of assisting Governor Fitzpatrick with the enactment of bank reform measures. Campbell and Henry Goldthwaite of Montgomery, two of Governor Fitzpatrick's most trusted friends, met with him during the summer of 1842 in Tuscaloosa to help prepare the proposals which would be presented by the governor to the legislature.[71]

After reflecting upon the advice received from Campbell and Goldthwaite, as well as from business and financial leaders throughout the state, Governor Fitzpatrick was determined to take dramatic action with respect to the Bank of the State of Alabama and its branches. To begin the process of reform, he had determined to seek the closure of the Mobile branch certainly, and possibly the Decatur branch. In his initial message to the 1842 legislature he went ahead and called for the immediate liquidation of the Mobile branch due to its gross mismanagement, which had resulted in excessive circulation and a colossal amount of suspended debt. The House of Representatives' Committee on the State Bank and Branches, chaired by John Campbell, reported out bills that not only provided for the liquidation of the Mobile branch but also for the closure of the Decatur branch. The Committee's report outlined an appalling condition of the state banks and Campbell warned that, "if the General Assembly does falter in the performance of its duty, that the character of the State will be degraded to the level of its currency; and that a condition will be attained, to which our gloomiest forebodings have not yet descended." In response, the legislature passed both of these liquidation measures while the Committee took a wait-and-see attitude toward the main bank in Tuscaloosa and the branches in Montgomery and Huntsville.[72]

Sentiment soon emerged, however, for total rather than partial liquidation of the state banks. Supporters of the doomed Mobile and Decatur branches, who did not enjoy being singled out for closure, began clamoring for the elimination of the state banking system in its entirety. In this venture, they were joined by those in the nine new counties of east Alabama, which had been carved out of the Creek cession. The new citizens of east

[71] Brantley, *Banking in Alabama*, 2: 179–86. Campbell, Goldthwaite, and Fitzpatrick were the nucleus of a faction to become known as the "Montgomery Regency" whose members were drawn together by strong family and personal ties rather than a particular political ideology. For example, both Fitzpatrick and Campbell had practiced law at different times with Goldthwaite in Montgomery, and Campbell married Goldthwaite's younger sister before moving to Mobile. Fitzpatrick had founded the Regency to support his brother-in-law Dixon Hall Lewis in his campaign against William Rufus King for a seat in the U.S. Senate. Other prominent members of this political machine other than those mentioned above included Crawford M. Jackson, Bolling Hall, John J. Seibels, and Albert Elmore. Thornton, *Politics and Power*, 373–74; Thornton, "Benjamin Fitzpatrick," 45; Robert Saunders, *John Archibald Campbell: Southern Moderate, 1811–1889* (Tuscaloosa: University of Alabama Press, 1997).

[72] *Ala. House Journal (1842)*, 14–30; *Ala. Acts (1842)*, 11–14, 53–56; Garrett, *Reminiscences*, 250–55; Brantley, *Banking in Alabama*, 2: 189–200.

Alabama had not been around when the banks had been created, but feared that they would be unduly taxed to pay for the banks' inadequacies. With growing opposition to the state banking system as a whole, bills were drawn up and enacted that put a death knell on the remaining branches at Montgomery and Huntsville. Governor Fitzpatrick reluctantly signed these measures as his plan for a gradual partial liquidation had been transformed by the legislature into an abrupt total liquidation. Other effective measures passed regarding the banks included a $200,000 revenue bill to take up the banks' slack in supporting state government, a requirement that all specie in state bank vaults be applied to the reduction of the state debt, the employment of an aggressive system of collection of debts due the state banks, and a provision that directors of the state banks be chosen from nominees submitted to the legislature by the governor.[73]

At the conclusion of the 1842 legislative session, all that was left of the state's banking system was the main branch at Tuscaloosa. Although it was not placed into liquidation as were its branches, it had no power to conduct any business other than to purchase bills of exchange for the purpose of effecting remittances to pay toward the reduction of the state's indebtedness. Fitzpatrick rode a wave of popularity for his handling of the bank question to be reelected as governor without opposition in the summer of 1843. In his message to the next session of the legislature, Governor Fitzpatrick candidly acknowledged that the previous legislature had been correct in choosing to liquidate all of the banks rather than employing a partial liquidation as Fitzpatrick had proposed. As the branch banks were steadily going about the business of terminating their affairs, very little further action regarding the banks was taken by the 1843 legislature. One other act regarding banking, however, was passed that reduced the number of directors at the main bank at Tuscaloosa from six to four and the number at the liquidating branches from six to two.[74]

As Governor Fitzpatrick's term as governor was winding down, he asked the 1844 legislature for a new revenue law to provide for payments on the state's debt as it matured. He further assured Alabamians that the liquidation of its banking system would not leave the populace without a circulating medium due to the fortuitous fact that a considerable amount of gold and silver had been pumped into Alabama to buy the last season's cotton crop. The governor then reminded the legislature that the State Bank of Alabama's charter was set to expire on January 1, 1845, with the recommendation that it not be renewed and that instead the State Bank and all its branches be finally liquidated. The legislature agreed with regard to the State Bank and enacted a law placing it in liquidation and requiring it to make a final settlement of its affairs. It did not follow his recommendation, however, with regard to enacting a revenue law, opting instead to use up all of the assets of the banks as they were collected from debtors before imposing taxes on ordinary citizens. In any event, after twenty years the State

---

[73] *Ala. Acts (1842)*, 37–40, 47–50; Garrett, *Reminiscences*, 250–55; Brantley, *Banking in Alabama*, 2: 189–200.

[74] Brantley, *Banking in Alabama*, 2: 200, 208, 211–12; *Ala. Acts (1843)*, 145.

Bank of Alabama's charter was terminated amidst allegations of fraud and corruption and because of gross mismanagement at the hands of the well to do and politically influential. Ironically, it had first been chartered in 1823 at the urging of Governor Israel Pickens to wrest fiscal control from the private banks dominated by the wealthy planter class.[75]

In addition to shutting down the State Bank, the 1844 legislature dealt with other issues that had far reaching implications for the state. First, it reapportioned the Assembly based upon the 1844 census that reflected a shift in the population southeastward, which had been brought about by the nine new counties carved out of the Creek treaty cession of 1832. While these southern and eastern counties were gaining representatives, western counties such as Tuscaloosa, Sumter, Bibb, and Pickens were losing them. This shift propelled a movement to move the capital from Tuscaloosa. Another action of the Assembly—a quiet harbinger of what was to come concerning the moving of the seat of government—involved legislation allowing the Montgomery & West Point Railroad and the Tennessee & Coosa Railroad to borrow from the two percent fund set aside for internal improvements. With the aid of this legislation, Charles T. Pollard, principal owner of the Montgomery & West Point Railroad, sought a joint venture with the Tennessee & Coosa Railroad to pursue the oft-dreamed connection of the Tennessee River and the Coosa–Alabama river system by which Tennessee Valley goods could be sent by water along the Tennessee River to Guntersville, then by rail to the Coosa River, and thence with the aid of the Montgomery & West Point Railroad down the Coosa and Alabama rivers to Mobile. Such a route threatened Tuscaloosa's continuing viability as the seat of government because it endangered the only established route between the Tennessee Valley and south Alabama that at that time ran through Tuscaloosa.[76]

Having already lost the main branch of the State Bank of Alabama for all practical purposes to closure and its location on the only major north–south trade route within the state now threatened by new river and rail routes, Tuscaloosa's likelihood of losing its status as Alabama's seat of government was all but assured when the legislature passed a joint resolution on January 24, 1845, proposing amendments to Alabama's constitution that would make it possible to move the seat of government. The same resolution called for an amendment to the constitution that would change the frequency of legislative sessions from annual to biennial.[77]

Sentiment had been growing for the removal of the capital from Tuscaloosa within just ten years of its replacement of Cahaba as the capital. As previously noted, the population of Alabama was shifting to the southeast as a result of Creek lands opening up in the early 1830s. Moreover, political power was shifting from north Alabama to the Black Belt as cotton was beginning to dominate the state's economy. The leading proponent for

---

[75] *Ala. Senate Journal (1844)*, 12–19; *Ala. Acts (1844)*, 27–28; Brantley, *Banking in Alabama*, 2: 232–38; see also *Ala. Acts (1823)*, 3–11.

[76] Brantley, *Banking in Alabama*, 2: 235, 239–40; *Ala. Acts (1844)*, 39.

[77] *Ala. Acts (1844)*, 208–09.

removal was Franklin W. Bowdon, an exceptional orator representing Talladega County in the legislature, who argued that Tuscaloosa was not readily accessible from all parts of Alabama due to its distance from the geographical center of the state. He also complained that the Black Warrior River was navigable for only a portion of the year, whereas the Alabama River was navigable at virtually all times of the year and had the further advantage of running through the most densely populated portion of the state. In August 1845, the Alabama electorate approved the amendment calling for biennial sessions of the legislature by a majority exceeding ten to one. The amendment removing the language permanently locating the seat of government in Tuscaloosa carried the day by a significantly more moderate margin of approximately 55 percent to 45 percent. Although approved by the electorate, the amendments still had to be approved by two thirds of the next legislature. Barely achieving the required majority, the legislature adopted both amendments. The way was thus opened for other Alabama cities and towns to make their pitch to take the seat of government away from Tuscaloosa.[78]

Just before the referendum on the removal of the seat of government and the frequency of legislative sessions, Alabamians had elected Joshua L. Martin to replace Benjamin Fitzpatrick as governor. His election, however, did not come about easily. Martin, like Fitzpatrick, was opposed to the State Bank, but surprisingly had to run as an independent to defeat Nathaniel Terry from Limestone County, who for many years had been a leading supporter of the so-called "Bank Junta" and who was indebted to three of the state banks for a total amount of $30,000. Terry's emergence as a candidate had occurred because of the difficulty encountered by many delegates in reaching Tuscaloosa to attend the 1845 Democratic gubernatorial convention as a result of the Black Warrior River becoming virtually impassable due to extremely low water levels. Taking advantage of this situation, pro-bank Democrats with hopes of reviving the state banking system rushed through the nomination of one of their own, Nat Terry. Rank and file Democrats were appalled at Terry's nomination because of his reputation as a gambler and fearful that he would go easy on bank debtors such as himself. These sentiments were best summarized in an editorial appearing in the Jacksonville *Republican* urging Democrats to seek out another candidate, disparaging Terry's candidacy succinctly: "A less acceptable candidate could not have been offered to the Democrats of Alabama. A professed Gambler and Horse Racer, glutted with Bank funds and opposed . . . to the policy of the late able Governor, in the collection of the Bank debts, in order to relieve the people from taxation.... Besides, it is well known, that the intellect of Mr. Terry is not suited to the office...."[79]

Concerned anti-banking Democrats thus prevailed upon Joshua Martin

---

[78] Brantley, *Banking in Alabama,* 2: 235, 239; Clinton, *Tuscaloosa,* 80; Rogers et al., *Alabama,* 148; Mellown, "Alabama's Fourth Capital," 278; Garrett, *Reminiscences,* 392; Malcolm Cook McMillan, "The Selection of Montgomery as Alabama's Capital," *Alabama Review* 1 (April 1948): 79–90.

[79] Rogers et al., *Alabama,* 145–48; Brantley, *Banking in Alabama,* 2: 246.

to run as an independent against Terry. Martin, the son of a farmer of modest means, was born near Maryville in Blount County, Tennessee, on December 5, 1799. At the age of twenty, he moved with his family to Alabama in 1819. Upon his arrival Martin read law with his brother-in-law in Russellville, was admitted to the bar, and opened a law office in Athens. In 1822, he was elected to represent Limestone County in the state legislature and did so, except for one year, until 1828. In 1829, he was elected Solicitor for the Fourth Judicial Circuit and then defeated incumbent Judge John White for a place on the Circuit Court in 1834. In 1835, Martin ran a successful campaign for one of Alabama's five seats in the U.S. Congress and was reelected in 1837. He resigned his congressional seat to return to private life for a short while before being elected in 1841 as chancellor for the Middle Chancery Division of the state. Martin held this position until he was approached to run for governor in 1845.[80]

By defeating Terry, Joshua Martin became Alabama's twelfth governor, and the last to preside in Tuscaloosa. Martin—with very little time to campaign—quickly made the State Bank the primary issue, emphasizing the money it had lost and the bad loans it had made. Garnering enough votes from Whigs, who had not put up a candidate, Martin won by a comfortable margin of approximately five thousand votes. Meanwhile, outgoing Governor Fitzpatrick warned the last legislature to sit in Tuscaloosa that, although the state bank was in liquidation, significant taxes would be necessary for years to come to pay off the bank's debts. He then summed up his accomplishments in reining in the banks: "The Banks are all in a state of final liquidation; the debts due them are in process of collection; and the faith of the State preserved and her credit maintained, as I trust it ever will be, with rigid punctuality." With that said, Governor Fitzpatrick turned over the reins of government to Martin when he took the oath of office on December 10, 1845.[81]

Not all had rejoiced in Martin's election as governor. For example, the Tuscaloosa *Monitor* credited Martin's win to the opposition Whigs and then doused his victory with a negative outlook: "The Governor elect will have no flowery path to tread. He has promised more than will come to pass. He has arrayed Bank debtors and Tax payers as antagonist parties." Weakened somewhat by the resentment of some Democrats over his run for governor as an independent, Martin nevertheless did not hesitate in going about the business of dismantling the banks, a process that had begun under Fitzpatrick. To this end, early in his administration Martin was successful in obtaining legislation that did away with the officers and director system and, instead, appointed a three-member commission to wind up the affairs of the bank with full power to collect as much of the debt owed to the banks as possible and to liquidate its assets and obligations. The commissioners named by the legislature were Francis S. Lyons, of Marengo County; former Governor Fitzpatrick, of Autauga County; and William Cooper, of Franklin County. Fitzpatrick declined the appointment,

[80] Hugh C. Bailey, "Joshua L. Martin," in *Alabama Governors*, 48–49.

[81] Brantley, *Banking in Alabama*, 2: 246–47, 251; *Ala. Senate Journal (1845)*, 12–13.

and Governor Martin appointed another former governor, Clement Comer Clay, in his stead. Lyons, who would become the sole commissioner in 1847, successfully finished the dismantlement of the State Bank of Alabama and paid most of its debts before he retired in 1853.[82]

One of the final items of business to be addressed by the last General Assembly to sit in Tuscaloosa dealt with the relocation of the seat of government. On January 21, 1846, the legislature enacted a law requiring that the seat of government remain in Tuscaloosa until a State House equivalent to the current one be constructed and completely furnished at a place to be selected by a joint vote of the two houses of the General Assembly. Accordingly, on January 28, 1846, the Senate and House of Representatives met in a joint session for the purpose of making the selection. Placed in formal nomination to be considered for the seat of government were Tuscaloosa, Wetumpka, Mobile, Montgomery, Statesville (a small community in Autauga County near the Dallas County line), Selma, Marion, and Huntsville. It took sixteen ballots for Montgomery to garner a majority of the votes cast, to be constitutionally declared the fifth seat of government for Alabama. Montgomery's acquisition of the capital assured that the already influential Black Belt would become the dominant political and economic section of the state.[83]

The loss of the state capital unavoidably had a devastating effect on Tuscaloosa. Its population in 1845, immediately prior to the capital's removal, was 4,250. Just five years later the 1850 census revealed that the population had been cut by more than half with a count of 1,950. Much of the decline in population was due to the loss of government officials, rank and file state employees, and lobbyists. As a result of this significant loss in population, business languished and real estate values plummeted. All was not lost, however, as the University of Alabama continued to flourish, and, despite varying river levels, Tuscaloosa continued to benefit economically from its position at the navigable headwaters of the Black Warrior River.[84]

During the capital's twenty-year presence in Tuscaloosa, the state government initially was consumed by its relationship with the federal government concerning the Indian removal policy. With the commencement of the Panic of 1837, state government became primarily concerned with how to deal with effects of an economic depression and a state bank system run amok. These issues, as significant as they were, would pale in comparison to the issue of secession that loomed on the horizon as the capital moved one last time to Montgomery.

---

[82] Brantley, *Banking in Alabama*, 2: 247, 255, 399 n.12; *Ala. Acts* (1845), 5–8; Garrett, *Reminiscences,* 580–81; Bailey, "Joshua L. Martin," 49–50.

[83] James B. Simpson, "The Alabama State Capital: An Historical Sketch," *Alabama Historical Quarterly,* 28 (Spring 1956): 87–90; McMillan, "The Selection of Montgomery," 90; *Ala. Acts (1845),* 28, 31.

[84] Clinton, *Tuscaloosa,* 81, 87.

Slave Market — Montgomery

Courtesy of Alabama Department of Archives and History

10

KING COTTON AND SLAVERY

While state government had been budding in Huntsville, Cahaba, and Tuscaloosa, cotton became increasingly more lucrative to grow and was emerging as a leader of Alabama's fledgling economy. By the time the state capital moved once again to Montgomery in 1846, "King Cotton" had become ensconced as the predominant economic and political force within the state.

The planting of cotton had commenced on a limited scale as early as 1772 in what was to become Alabama. By 1807, it had surpassed indigo as the predominant crop grown in the Tombigbee River region. Georgians, who were part of the Broad River faction immigrating to Madison County in 1809, came for the specific purpose of planting cotton. The rapid increase in cotton production was facilitated by Eli Whitney's invention of the cotton gin in 1793. Thereafter the crop was exceedingly profitable to cultivate with slave labor, particularly in view of the increasing demands from England's textile industry.[1]

As we have seen, the French own the distasteful distinction of importing the first slaves to what would become the state of Alabama. Some 120 slaves arrived in Mobile in 1721 on the French warship *Africane*. Twice that number had departed Guinea in West French Africa for Mobile, but extremely unsanitary conditions aboard the ship and a lack of sufficient water and food resulted in a fifty percent mortality rate before arrival. Two other ships soon arrived with more slaves—the *Marie* from Guinea with 338 aboard and the *Neride* from Angola with 238 aboard. The *Neride*'s human cargo was not without casualties as some 112 slaves lost their lives in transit. Because the first cotton plants had not yet been introduced to the Mobile area, these first slaves were used to clear the forests, work on Mobile's wharves, and cultivate crops other than cotton.[2]

Slaves continued to be imported to Mobile in such numbers that Governor Bienville had been ordered by King Louis XV to institute the *Code Noir*, the first formalized laws applied to slaves in the area to become Alabama. As previously discussed, the code placed severe restrictions upon

---

[1] Abernethy, *Formative Period*, 74; Pickett, *History of Alabama*, 326, 503; Moore, *History of Alabama*, 271–72. The Black Belt of Alabama did not become active in the cultivation of cotton until approximately 1830 because planters had not until then learned how to utilize its sticky soil.

[2] Rogers et al., *Alabama*, 30, 93–94. In 1730, the French introduced "Creole Black Seed" cotton and Phillip Miller, a West Indies botanist, introduced "Georgia Green Seed" cotton to the area. Charles C. Mitchell, "The Development of Cotton from the Old World to Alabama: Chronological Highlights in Alabama Cotton Production," *Agronomy and Soils Departmental Series No. 286* (Auburn University, Ala.: Agricultural Experiment Station, March 2008), 3.

slaves, such as prohibiting the gathering of slaves of different masters at any time of day or night, with recidivists of this offense subjected to a possible death penalty; forbidding them from carrying weapons, unless hunting with the permission of their master; and forbidding them from selling any commodities without the express permission of their masters. Any slave who struck his master or his family members in the face or drew blood was punished by death. More humane provisions were included to protect the well-being of the slave population, such as prohibitions against torture, separation of husbands and wives by sale, and separation of young children from their mothers.[3]

Like the first slaves in French Mobile, subsequent slaves in the Alabama section of the Mississippi Territory toiled to clear the woodlands, fence in the fields, and ready the soil for the cultivation of food producing crops. Whitney's invention of the cotton gin in 1793, which was a hand-cranked machine that separated seeds from the cotton, quickly engaged increasing numbers of slaves in the cultivation of cotton. This new gin could clean up to fifty pounds of cotton per day, thus making the production of cotton very profitable for those who owned slaves, as evidenced by the rise in the price of cotton in the years immediately following the War of 1812. By 1818 cotton's rise in price had reached its pinnacle at 34¢ per pound. This price rise along with the cession of Creek lands at the end of the war brought about Alabama's first great influx of settlers. After 1818, cotton's price fell steadily before bottoming out at 11¢ per pound in 1823. Nevertheless, the production of cotton continued to grow modestly on some large plantations during this period of falling prices. For example, production of cotton on one large plantation in Wilcox County grew from 117 bales in 1821 to 148 bales in 1825.[4]

The gins owned by most planters prior to 1822 still required that the cotton be hand-picked for trash and yellow flakes before being ginned. Also, after the ginning process, particles of seed had to be picked out by hand, or "moting." Then in 1822 a gin was introduced in Mississippi that did not tear the fiber while separating the seed, thus significantly improving the quality of the cotton. This new gin also added to the efficiency of cotton production by eliminating a large part of the moting process. General John Coffee brought one of these improved gins into the Tennessee Valley, and by 1824 a supply of these machines was taken delivery of in Mobile. Shortly after the introduction of the improved ginning process, a new "Mexican" variety of seed was introduced that produced larger pods, making the picking process easier. As a result, the amount of cotton that could be picked in one

---

[3] Everett, "Free Persons of Color," 22–23; *Édit du Roi*, 28–58.

[4] Rogers et al., *Alabama*, 95; Moore, *History of Alabama*, 271 n.2; James Benson Sellers, *Slavery in Alabama* (1950; repr., Tuscaloosa and London: University of Alabama Press, 1994), 32. The first cotton gin in Alabama was built by Abram Mordecai in 1804 on his plantation adjacent to the confluence of the Coosa and Tallapoosa rivers near present-day Wetumpka, Alabama. Mordecai was a Jewish trader transplanted to Alabama's "Indian Country" from Pennsylvania. Unfortunately, Mordecai's first gin was burned and Mordecai had his ears cropped by Indians in retaliation for an affair he had with a married woman of the attacking clan. Mitchell, "Development of Cotton," 4; Pickett, *History of Alabama*, 421, 469–70.

day doubled from 100 pounds to 200 pounds. Following on the heels of these improvements, planters in the 1830s began entering the Black Belt counties of Alabama after it was finally figured out that its rich black soil overlaying a chalky crust could be watered by artesian wells. As the planters moved into the Black Belt, the number of bales of cotton harvested in south Alabama jumped from 102,684 in 1830 to 445,725 in 1840.[5]

Increasing cotton production in south Alabama resulted in a proportionate increase in the export of cotton from Mobile. By 1840, Mobile became second only to New Orleans as an exporter of cotton, having overtaken Savannah and Charleston in the 1830s when the Black Belt opened up for widespread cotton cultivation. Most of the state's major rivers converged upon Mobile, making it easy for planters in south Alabama, particularly those whose plantations were on the river, to ship their cotton to Mobile by steamboat or barge. Planters on the river had their own private landings; planters in the interior utilized public landings or shared a neighbor's landing. Many landings were located at precipitous river banks necessitating that the bales of cotton be rolled from the warehouse on the landing to the top of the bluff where they were then pushed down a slide to the waiting steamboat or barge below. This created quite a spectacle particularly if a bale landed with such force to propel bales already on the deck into the river.[6]

Its status as a port city enhanced by increased cotton production within the fertile Black Belt, Mobile emerged as Alabama's largest city during the antebellum period. Mobile had been in continuous existence since 1702, but had grown very slowly until 1820. Then, from 1820 until 1860, it grew from a population of 1,500 to nearly 30,000. By the outbreak of the Civil War, Mobile was the only metropolitan area in the state in excess of 10,000 inhabitants. The 1860 population of the capital city of Montgomery was 8,843, that of Huntsville 3,634, that of Tuscaloosa 3,989, and that of Selma 3,177. With 29,259 inhabitants, Mobile dwarfed the other urban centers of the state. Mobile's population, its status as a port, its cotton trade, and its role in supplying the farmers and planters of the region made it the economic hub of the state. It had truly become Alabama's "metropolis by the sea," as dubbed by historian Weymouth T. Jordan.[7]

That Mobile's ascension to become Alabama's commercial center had been primarily due to the cotton trade is reflected in a traveler's description of the port city in the late 1850s as a "pleasant cotton city of some 30,000 inhabitants—where people live in cotton houses and ride in cotton carriages." This observer continued, "They marry cotton wives [and husbands],

[5] Abernethy, *Formative Period*, 81–82; Harriet E. Amos, *Cotton City: Urban Development in Antebellum Mobile* (Tuscaloosa, Ala.: University of Alabama Press, 1985), 20–21.

[6] Amos, *Cotton City*, 20–22. Planters in north Alabama had to ship their cotton by way of the Tennessee and Mississippi rivers some 1,500 miles to New Orleans. As we have seen, there had been several efforts to remedy this situation by constructing either a turnpike or a canal from the Tennessee River to the headwaters of the Alabama River. None of these succeeded and Mobile was denied the ability to market the totality of Alabama's cotton.

[7] Weymouth T. Jordan, *Ante-Bellum Alabama: Town and Country* (1957; repr., Tuscaloosa, Ala.: University of Alabama Press, 1987), 1.

and unto them are born cotton children.... It is the great staple, the sum and substance of Alabama. It has made Mobile and all its citizens." In all, south Alabama produced some 5,000,000 bales of cotton during the 1850s, most of which was shipped through Mobile, along with other goods, to such foreign ports as Liverpool, London, Havre, Amsterdam, Antwerp, Rotterdam, Hamburg, Bremen, St. Petersburg, Stockholm, Ghent, Gibraltar, Barcelona, Havana, Genoa, and Trieste. American ports receiving Mobile's exports included New York, Boston, Providence, Baltimore, and New Orleans. Even though cotton was the mainstay of Mobile's exports, by 1850 the port had begun exporting tallow, iron, shingles, laths, lime tar, hides, turpentine, rosin, rope, rice, bricks, leather, sugar, corn, timber, barrels, and staves, to name a few. In 1860 the value of exports from Mobile totaled $38,670,183. That same year steamboats from Mobile plying the Alabama, Tombigbee, and Warrior rivers were making 700 official stops at landings along these rivers to pick up passengers and cotton.[8]

With increasing numbers of cotton bales arriving in Mobile from the upcountry Black Belt, enterprising businessmen began to build facilities to receive, store, and compress the bales of cotton before their sale and shipment abroad. In the early 1820s there were a total of twelve private wharves; by the 1850s that number had grown to approximately fifty. In addition to the necessary facilities to store the cotton along the waterfront, planters needed the assistance of marketers for their cotton. While some sold their own, a majority employed the services of factors, or professional agents, to market their cotton. Factors generally charged a commission of 2 ½ percent of the sales price of the cotton. Factors also extended credit to cash-poor planters at a rate of anywhere from 8 to 12 percent. With their fees fairly standard, factors who had descended on Mobile wisely sought to develop close personal and professional ties to planters in the Black Belt counties to secure their business.[9]

Because the cotton trade demanded more credit and financial services than could be provided by factors, Mobile was fortunate to have the only local bank in the state to successfully endure all of the financial crises of the antebellum era. Chartered in 1819 as a privately owned bank, the Bank of Mobile was conservatively managed by William R. Hallett for approximately thirty years during which time the bank remarkably maintained its solvency. It was the only bank in Alabama that survived the Panic of 1837 and, by 1845, it was the only institution providing any banking services in the state. According to an investigator for the credit-reporting firm of R.G. Dun and Company, not only was the Bank of Mobile "the strongest Bank in Alabama," but it was "in fact as good as any in the United States," further praising it as "good as Gold." Other banks in Mobile during the antebellum era included a branch of the State Bank of Alabama chartered in 1832, which was closed by the legislature in 1844, and a branch of the Bank of the United States (BUS), which closed when the BUS's charter expired in 1836. The swell of cotton in Mobile also resulted in the opening of a number of

---

[8] Jordan, *Anti–Bellum Alabama*, 18–21; Amos, *Cotton City*, 23.

[9] Amos, *Cotton City*, 28–29.

insurance companies which offered protection against marine and river accidents and fires. In the late 1830s a few local companies such as the Mobile Marine Railway and Insurance Company and the Alabama Life Insurance and Trust Company began to issue such policies. By 1852, there were at least nine local insurance companies along with several national companies with much larger assets insuring against the risks of the cotton trade.[10]

Mobile's status as the commercial hub of the cotton trade resulted in upcountry planters pouring into the port city after the growing season in the fall to meet with their factors, to arrange their financing, and to insure their inventories of cotton. Often accompanied by their families seeking a respite from their rural plantations in exchange for the excitement of Alabama's largest city, Mobile became a winter resort for the planter class. After a day of conducting business, the visiting planters relaxed by attending soirées, balls, or the theater. Mobilians particularly promoted the building of theaters to keep their winter visitors amused and to prevent them from leaving early for home or moving on to New Orleans. To this end local newspapers extolled the virtues of the theater and local citizens repeatedly contributed to public subscription drives to build theaters. Providing suitable housing accommodations for their visitors was a continual problem.[11]

Accommodations in the 1820s consisted of sparse wooden structures with few amenities—structures that were frequently leveled by fires. Between 1835 and 1845 as the number of Mobile's winter visitors soared to three times the number of year-round residents, there was often a shortage of rooms. In the 1840s larger hotels such as the Waverly and the Mansion began providing more services to get the business of the planters wintering in Mobile. In 1850, however, these two hotels were destroyed by fire within a week of each other. In response to these losses, construction was begun on the Battle House Hotel, a five-story brick structure which would become the main meeting place of upcountry planters throughout the 1850s.[12]

Designed by a nationally renowned architect who had designed hotels in New York, Charleston, Richmond, Cincinnati, and New Orleans, the esteemed Battle House opened its doors for business on November 13, 1852. Located at the site of the old Waverly Hotel on the southeast corner of Royal and St. Francis streets, it was the largest hotel in Mobile at that time, with 240 guest rooms, dining rooms, and shops on the ground floor. During the winter season, weekly soirées were followed by suppers; frequent dances were also held where city residents mingled with the upcountry guests. The upcountry visitors also occasionally mingled with such famous guests as Millard Fillmore, former President of the United States; Sir Charles Lyell, the English naturalist; Henry Clay, Speaker of the House and candidate for president; and William Lowndes Yancey, Alabama's fire-

---

[10] Ibid., 34–37, 40–41.

[11] Ibid., 43–47.

[12] Ibid.

breathing secessionist. The Battle House was so popular with planters in south Alabama and Mississippi that it became the honeymoon location for many of their offspring.[13]

Elisha A. King and his son, Edwin W. King, of Perry County epitomized the increasing number of wealthy planters in Alabama's Black Belt whose collective success contributed greatly to Mobile's emergence as the state's commercial center. Elisha King was one of many Georgians coming into Alabama in 1819 to gobble up cheap land in the central part of the new state. In 1820 King purchased 1,028 acres of this land in Perry County. At that time cotton was not king; instead, the primary crop of Perry County was corn. By the 1830s, however, cotton had taken over as the chief crop because of improvements in the ginning process and the better quality of cotton seed that made the cultivation of cotton much more profitable. During this period Elisha King continued to buy more and more land and slaves, which he purchased on credit based on expected profits from cotton yet to be produced. While buying on credit devastated some planters due to the uncertain and fluctuating price of cotton, King was never caught significantly short as evidenced by the estate he had amassed at the time of his death in 1852: 8,000 acres of land, 186 slaves, and a large number of town lots in Marion.[14]

Elisha King, like most other large planters in the Black Belt, relied on cotton factors in Mobile to handle most of his financial transactions. In King's case factors advanced him money to purchase land and slaves, handled the sale of his cotton, and arranged for the purchase of plantation supplies and consumer goods. During his lifetime King utilized the services of a number of different factors. Correspondence from the factorage firm of Alexander and Pope indicates King and his son even experimented with shipping directly to dealers in Liverpool so as to increase their profits. The results of this experiment are not known, but the Kings usually went through factors in Mobile to sell their cotton. Elisha King also relied on Mobile factors to buy supplies for his plantation as well as such items as household furniture, books, and liquors. Like most of his fellow planters in the Black Belt, King made an annual trip to Mobile during the winter months to visit with his factors, purchase supplies, and often to relax with accompanying family members. Not all of his sales records are available, but those that are reveal he was very successful. Records for fifteen of the years between 1829 and 1852 reveal that King sold 1,438 bales of cotton that brought in gross receipts of $57,923. Expenses, including factorage fees, totaled $3,504, leaving a net of $54,418. Another 1,060 bales during

---

[13] Ibid., 45–46; James Frederick Sulzby, *Historic Alabama Hotels & Resorts*, (1960; repr., Tuscaloosa and London: University of Alabama Press, 1994), 42–45. Stephen Douglas was a guest in the historic Battle House the night he lost the presidential election to Abraham Lincoln. Jefferson Davis spent the night there on his way to Montgomery to be inaugurated President of the Confederate States of America. Ulysses S. Grant was a guest after the Civil War, but before he became president. "Battle House a Symbol of Hospitality," the Mobile *Press-Register*, May 4, 2007, http://blog.al.com/pr/2007/05/battle_house_a_symbol_of_hospi.html (accessed January 22, 2013).

[14] Jordan, *Ante-Bellum Alabama*, 41–44.

this time period bought a net profit of $45,869. At the time of his death in 1852, Elisha King left a considerable estate to his son, Edwin, who in turn became the second largest slaveholder in Perry County.[15]

James Asbury Tait and his father Charles Tait, Alabama's first federal judge, further personify successful Black Belt planters whose success enriched the cotton factors and made Mobile the "Cotton City." In 1817 James Tait preceded his father to the future state to claim choice lands along the Alabama River just a few years after he had been in Alabama fighting in the Creek War. As we have previously seen, his father, Charles, reluctantly remained in Georgia representing that state in the United States Senate while vigorously pushing for Alabama's entry into the Union.[16] James settled at Black's Bluff near Camden in Wilcox County. With the labor of twenty slaves he planted eighty acres in corn and 175 acres in cotton during his first year of farming. This was an extremely humble start to Tait's extensive planting efforts in Wilcox County. When Charles Tait died in 1835, his son inherited from him 100 slaves to add to those that James had accumulated since his arrival in Alabama. By 1848 James Tait owned in excess of 300 slaves that serviced six plantations, all equipped with their own gins, bailing presses, grist mills, saw mills, and blacksmith shops. With so many slaves, Tait's cotton production jumped from 148 bales in 1825 to 461 bales by 1851.[17]

The increasing number of slaves in the state paralleled the expanding production of cotton in the fertile Black Belt by planters such as the Kings and the Taits. In 1830 there were a total of 117,484 slaves in Alabama. That number more than doubled to 253,532 in 1840 as more and more planters entered the Black Belt. By 1850 the number increased to 342,844, reaching its pinnacle in 1860 when it topped out at 435,080. By 1860 tremendous wealth was concentrated in a relatively few large slaveholders who owned thirty per cent of the state's slaves, thirty per cent of its real estate and twenty-seven per cent of its personal property. Even though these planters owned 28.1 per cent of the total wealth of the state, they consisted of less than one-third of one per cent of Alabama's white population. This very small cadre of planters also possessed political clout far out of proportion to their numbers, as would be evidenced in the secession debate looming on the horizon.[18]

King Cotton's emergence in Alabama assured continued strict control of Alabama's slaves that had begun under the *Code Noir* implemented by the

---

[15] Ibid., 45–51.

[16] After successfully securing Alabama's statehood, Charles Tait moved to Alabama in 1819 to settle on lands recently acquired by his son approximately 30 miles from Claiborne on the Alabama River in Monroe and Wilcox counties. His plantations were known as "Weldon" and "Springfield." Herbert James Lewis, "Charles Tait," *Encyclopedia of Alabama*, http:// www. encyclopediaofalabama.org/face/Article.jsp?id=h-2338 (accessed February 4, 2013); Ulrich Bonnell Phillips, *Life and Labor in the Old South* (Boston: Little, Brown, 1929), 277.

[17] Peter A. Brannon, ed., "Journal of James A. Tait for the Year 1813," *Alabama Historical Quarterly* 2 (Winter 1940): 431–40; Sellers, *Slavery*, 31–33.

[18] Sellers, *Slavery*, 40–42.

French. Life for slaves became even harsher when the British took over from the French. As previously discussed, under British rule, slaves could be put to death or dismembered if found guilty of felonies such as burglary, robbery, burning of houses, or rebellious conspiracies. The punishment to be imposed—whether a death sentence, a lesser sentence consisting of a form of corporal punishment, or deportation from the colony—was within the discretion of at least two justices and a panel of freeholders. The death sentence, however, was mandatory, if a slave was found guilty of murdering a white person. The movement of slaves within the colony was again strictly regulated under the British with slaves restricted from traveling more than two miles from their plantation unless accompanying a white person or in possession of an official pass specifying the origin and destination of travel. Slaves were also forbidden from assembling in numbers of more than six after nine o'clock at night.[19]

Similar provisions for the stringent regulation of slaves were imposed by the Mississippi and Alabama territorial governments. Although Sargent's Code contained many of the same restrictions first imposed by the *Code Noir*, it did not adopt the French code's more humane provisions such as prohibitions against separation of husbands and wives by sale and separation of young children from their mothers, nor did it provide for emancipation under any circumstances. The territorial codes nevertheless did purport to adopt a humane prohibition against cruel and unusual punishments and empowered courts to impose fines of up to one hundred dollars on slave owners found guilty of authorizing or permitting such punishments.[20]

As previously discussed when Alabama became a state in 1819, its constitution addressed the status of slaves within the new state by guaranteeing its citizens the right to own slaves, while also guaranteeing certain basic rights to the slaves themselves. To keep state government from interfering with the right to own slaves, the General Assembly was prohibited from passing laws to emancipate slaves without the consent of their owners. The legislature was also denied the power to prohibit emigrants from bringing with them persons deemed slaves according to the laws of any of the other states. The legislature, however, was granted the power to prevent slaves from being brought into the state as commodities to be sold and was given the authority to pass laws to prevent the importation of slaves who had committed serious crimes in other states or territories. While the legislature could not free slaves without their owner's consent, it was given the power to establish the conditions under which their lawful owners could emancipate them, with an emphasis on protecting the rights of creditors and ensuring that any slaves freed did not become "a public charge."[21]

With respect to basic fundamental rights, the legislature was given the authority to require owners to treat their slaves "with humanity, to provide

---

[19] Robert R. Rea and Milo B. Howard, *Minutes, Journals, and Acts*, 342–46; Brown, "Colonial Mobile," 45.

[20] Ethridge, "Introduction to Sargent's Code," 192–96.

[21] McMillan, *Constitutional Development in Alabama*, 42–43; Ala. Const. of 1819, Art. VI.

for them necessary food and clothing, to abstain from all injuries to them extending to life or limb." Significantly, slaves were also accorded a constitutional right to a trial by jury for any crimes higher than that of petty larceny. However, they were obviously not allowed a jury of their peers. Finally, the constitution declared that any person who maliciously dismembered or killed a slave would be subjected to "suffer such punishment as would be inflicted in case the like offence had been committed on a free white person." The only exception was if such injury or death occurred during an insurrection.[22]

During the antebellum period, the Alabama General Assembly adopted laws pertaining to the regulation of slaves passed by the previous territorial governments and enacted a series of its own laws as evidenced in Toulmin's *Alabama Digest* of 1823 and Aiken's *Alabama Digest* of 1833. Many of the previous legislative enactments pertaining to slavery were finally incorporated into a comprehensive slave code in the 1852 Code of Alabama. This code, along with supplemental laws passed thereafter and judicial interpretations of the Alabama Supreme Court, defined the legal status of slaves and governed their everyday living. The law was clear in Alabama that slaves were the property of their owners and gave an owner "the right to the time, labor, and services of the slave, and to enforce obedience on the part of the slave, to all his lawful commands." Many of the laws as we have seen were designed to ensure that slaves were well controlled and confined to their plantations, unless they had a pass from their master to travel off the premises. The extent of control extended to prohibiting slaves from owning property, carrying weapons, keeping dogs, owning horses, and assembling in numbers more than five off their plantations without permission.[23]

Since territorial days an intricate patrol system had been in place to serve as a deterrent to slave insurrections. Slave patrols, referred to as "patterollers" by most slaves, consisted of no more than seven and no fewer than four patrollers who were to ride the countryside at night looking for runaways or slaves off their plantations without a pass. They were also to break up unlawful assemblies of slaves and to seize weapons from those who did not have the permission of their owner. All white males—both slaveholders and non-slaveholders—within each militia district were subject to serve in this paramilitary organization. It was the responsibility of the commanding officer of the militia in each district to make a list of all males within his territory subject to service. Those liable for service were subject to a forfeiture of five dollars for each patrol assembly which they failed to attend or to send a substitute in their stead. Similarly, leaders of patrol detachments were subject to a forfeiture of ten dollars for failure to give the required notice to persons liable for service or for failure to prose-

---

[22] McMillan, *Constitutional Development in Alabama*, 42–43; Ala. Const. of 1819, Art. VI.

[23] *Digest of the Laws of the State of Alabama...* Comp. Harry Toulmin (Cahawba, Ala., 1823), 627–46; *Digest of the Laws of the State of Alabama...* Comp. John G. Aikin (Philadelphia, 1833), 391–99; Code of Alabama (1852), 237–42, 390.

cute those who failed to attend duty noticed patrol meetings.[24]

Slave patrols were unfortunately the least of worries for slaves belonging to masters or working under overseers who had a penchant for delivering harsh punishments for violations of orders. As set forth above, by statute owners were given the right to "enforce obedience on the part of the slave, to all his lawful commands." The Alabama Supreme Court held that it was established law in the state that owners had the authority to impose "reasonable punishment" on their slaves to insure obedience. The court, however, failed to clearly define what was a reasonable punishment indicating that "what is reasonable punishment, and when it can be affirmed that correction has gone beyond this boundary, and become unreasonable and cruel, is a question which admits of no certain and uniform solution." Undoubtedly mindful of Alabama's statutory prohibition against the infliction of cruel and unusual punishment which had been in effect since 1805, the court further noted that "still there is a boundary, and the force must not be disproportionate to the offense." Such factors as the severity of the transgression and the attitude of the slave receiving the punishment were to be taken into account in determining the severity of the punishment, while keeping in mind that "the main purpose of correction is to reduce the offending and refractory slave to a proper state of submission, respect, and obedience to legitimate authority ... with as little risk of permanent injury or danger to the slave or his owner as is reasonably compatible with the surroundings." Such broad parameters, however, allowed individual owners and their overseers much discretion in determining the reasonableness of the punishments they imposed.[25]

All in all, slaves were at the mercy of their masters and their condition in life varied according to the temperament of their masters. Some masters were kind to their slaves and treated them as family, especially those who owned very few slaves and worked side by side with them on small farms. Others—generally those who owned large numbers of slaves on expansive plantations—entrusted the discipline of their slaves to overseers, many of whom were very cruel and often took extreme measures in enforcing discipline among the slaves under their supervision. The dichotomy in treatment is reflected in the narrative of former slave Charity Anderson, who was interviewed as part of the Federal Writers' Project administered by the Works Progress Administration (WPA) in 1937. Anderson was a house slave whose master ran a wood yard in Monroe County that supplied fuel to riverboats. She recalled that her master was kind to his slaves and took good care of them, but she also recounted that she saw slaves belonging to others "almos' tore up by dogs, and whipped unmercifully." Another of the

---

[24] Toulmin, *Digest of Laws*, 635–37. An encounter with a patrol on the way to church was related by Montgomery County slave Martha Bradley as if it were a routine occurrence: "When us'd pass by the patterollers, us jes hold up our pass and us'd go on." Horace Randall Williams, ed., *Weren't No Good Times: Personal Accounts of Slavery in Alabama* (Winston-Salem: John F. Blair, 2004), 112. For an extensive study of the slave patrol system as it was implemented in Virginia and the Carolinas, see Sally Hadden, *Slave Patrols: Law and Violence in Virginia and the Carolinas* (Cambridge, Mass.: Harvard University Press, 2001).

[25] *Tillman v. Chadwick, 37 Alabama*, 317 (1861).

WPA narratives reflects the cruelty often imposed by overseers even when the master himself was considered to be kind. Walter Calloway, a slave on a large plantation located a few miles south of Montgomery, indicated that his master "treated us purty good, but we hab to wuk hard." He continued, "Marse John good 'nough to us an' we get plenty to eat, but he had an overseer name Green Bush what sho' whup us iffen we don't do to suit him." The overseer did not administer the floggings himself; instead he gave this ignoble duty to a slave named Mose who was, according to Calloway, "mean as de devil an' strong as a ox" and "could sho' lay on dat rawhide lash." Mose's strength resulted in a thirteen-year-old girl being whipped so hard that she almost died. When the owner learned of this unmerciful beating, he fired his overseer, thus ending the whippings laid on by Mose.[26]

Unfortunately in some cases slaves were summarily executed by their masters, overseers, patrollers, or angry mobs. Historian Mills Thornton reports that on two occasions in the 1850s, accused slaves were burned alive in the presence of wealthy citizens of Mount Meigs, a planting community near Montgomery. According to Thornton, "The spectators listened to the screams of the tortured victims with all the impassivity of Aztec priests, observing sacrifices to gods equally as bloody and as terrible as the Furies who ruled the heart of the South." A slave by the name of Martha Bradley from Mount Meigs apparently was referring to one of these incidents when she reported in an interview that "they sho' burn that n____ alive for I seed him after he was burned up." A Sumter County slave charged with the murder of a young white girl was also the victim of vigilante justice when some seventy-five to one hundred white men stormed the jail where he was incarcerated awaiting trial and took him into their custody. As the lynch mob left the jail one of their leaders invited the sheriff and the citizens of Livingston to come witness the execution of their captive near the scene of the murder of the white girl. An estimated crowd of two thousand persons thereafter gathered and witnessed the slave being burned alive at the stake.[27]

These shameful incidents reveal that local law enforcement was often hard pressed to protect slaves from vigilante justice. Stunned by the gruesome incidents at Mount Meigs, Governor John Winston called upon the solicitor of the Montgomery circuit to seek indictments for those responsible. The solicitor, however, regrettably reported to the governor that he had previously sought an indictment after the first incident, but the grand jury took no action. Instead, the grand jury passed a resolution indicating that while in the normal course of events they would defer to local law enforcement's investigation and obey the decisions of the courts, there were "cases

[26] George P. Rawick, ed., *The American Slave: A Composite Autobiography* (Westport, Conn.: Greenwood Press, 1972–79), Supplement Series 1, 1: 13–16; see also Rawick, *The American Slave*, 6: 12–14, 51–54.

[27] Thornton, *Politics and Power*, 319; Williams, *Weren't No Good Times*, xxvi; Sellers, *Slavery*, 263.

in which a more summary and exemplary mode of vengeance should be resorted to."[28]

Slaves were not always the recipient of vigilante justice. As we have seen, Alabama's Constitution of 1819 had guaranteed slaves the right to a trial by jury for all offenses of a higher grade than petit larceny. In 1841, slaves were even given twelve peremptory challenges (allowing a prospective juror to be dismissed without explanation), while the state received only four. Lesser offenses were tried by a justice of the peace who was authorized to summarily impose a whipping of up to one hundred lashes. Physical punishments—ear cropping, branding, and whipping—were usually administered to slaves committing non-capital offenses because they did not have money to pay fines and their owners did not want them confined to jail instead of working their fields. Slaves were not always convicted whether tried by a justice of the peace or a jury. There were many instances where they were either acquitted or pardoned by the governor after being convicted.[29]

Slaves who were subjected to continued abuse by their owners or overseers decided to run away before they became the subject of a lethal punishment. Others ran away to avoid work or to seek freedom, while still others left to join family members who had been sold to another plantation. Runaways were subject to apprehension by any person in Alabama. Once apprehended, runaways were to be delivered to the nearest justice of the peace who were either to commit them to the county jail or, if their identity was known, to return them to their owner. For each slave returned, owners were required to pay the apprehending party six dollars plus reasonable costs and expenses. If a runaway was not claimed by an owner within ten days, the justice of the peace was required to publish a notice with a detailed description of the slave in a local newspaper for a period of thirty days. If still not claimed within that time, a notice was to be published for six months in the newspapers of the largest circulation in the state.[30]

While slaves fearing maltreatment often ran away, others were sold against their will if they were considered troublemakers. Advertisements for the sale of such slaves were usually sugar coated with exaggerated praise for the slave's qualities in an effort to hide the facts behind the sale. Not all slaves, however, were sold because they were perceived as troublemakers. Some were simply sold when the owner was experiencing economic hardships or a sale was forced in foreclosure proceedings. New slaves brought into the state by slave traders, as well as unclaimed runaways, were usually sold in large trading centers established in Mobile, Montgomery, and

---

[28] Thornton, *Politics and Power*, 319.

[29] Const. of 1819, Art. 6, Sec. 2; Sellers, *Slavery*, 216–18, 244. Slaves were sometimes even the beneficiary of legal technicalities. For example, in September 1821, attorney Henry W. Stevens secured the release of a slave accused of murder when a Shelby County court granted his motion to quash the venire summoning the jury on the ground that it was deficient by failing to specify the time that they were to appear in court. Lewis, "A Connecticut Yankee," 97.

[30] Toulmin, *Digest of Laws*, 630; John Hope Franklin and Loren Schweninger, *Runaway Slaves: Rebels on the Plantations* (Oxford: Oxford University Press, 1999), 151.

Huntsville. Initially, Mobile was the largest of these centers, but by 1840 Montgomery was home to the largest slave market in the state. A writer for the *New York Herald* reported on March 8, 1860, that sales were so brisk in Montgomery that he witnessed the sale of twenty lots of slaves during the course of just one day at Montgomery's fountain in plain view of the Capitol sitting atop Goat Hill at the other end of Dexter Avenue.[31]

For those slaves who did not run away or who were not sold, everyday life and living conditions varied, usually depending on the size of the plantation on which they toiled. Slave quarters were typically one-room log cabins furnished with cast-off furniture from the master's house. On larger plantations, slave families might occupy a wooden plank house of two or three rooms with an open hall. A garden and a poultry house were often located in the rear of each slave cabin. In addition to vegetables grown in their gardens, food provided to the slaves by their masters consisted primarily of meat and bread. Meat, usually pork, was typically rationed to them at a rate of about three pounds per slave per week. Corn meal was usually rationed at a rate of about a peck a week per person. Slaves sometimes supplemented the meat provided them by hunting and fishing near their quarters.[32]

The quality of slaves' daily lives, however, was more dependent upon the work they were required to perform rather than the quality of their living accommodations. Slaves on the plantation were classified as either field hands or household servants. Historian A. B. Moore concluded that household or domestic servants held the best positions within the slavery system, selected for their positions because of perceived superior qualities. Female domestic servants cleaned the house, cooked their owner's meals, ran nurseries for the owners' children, and often served as the plantation's seamstress. In addition to being household servants, male domestic workers held a variety of jobs as carpenters, millers, tanners, blacksmiths, and butchers. Life was worse for field hands who performed hard physical labor from sunup to sunset. The pace of their work on large plantations depended upon the ever-present overseer and head driver—a slave himself. If the slaves did not work at the pace prescribed by the overseer they were usually lashed on the spot with a leather whip by either the overseer or the head driver.[33]

Alabamians were hardened to its "peculiar institution" of slavery. Foreign visitors not familiar with everyday plantation life, however, were often taken aback with what they observed. Such was the case with Phillip Henry Gosse, an English naturalist who had traveled to Alabama in 1838. When Gosse first saw African American slaves working in cotton fields, his reaction was one of disgust: "It was revolting to me to observe women in this laborious occupation, whose clothing—if the sordid rags which fluttered by them deserve the name—was barely sufficient for the claims of decency.

---

[31] Sellers, *Slavery*, 143–44; 153–54.

[32] Moore, *History of Alabama*, 354–55.

[33] Ibid., 357–60.

Poor wretches! whose lot is harder than that of their brute companions in labour! For they have to perform an equal amount of toil, with the additional hardships of more whipping and less food." Indicating that he had perhaps not observed enough to be so judgmental, Gosse deferred to further observation. His opinion, however, did not change as time passed. Indeed, he later indicted Alabama's planters, stating that "his negroes he scarcely considers as human; they are but 'goods and chattels.'"[34]

Slaves were not always confined to the plantation. A significant number of slaves were hired out to work in city shops, factories, on construction gangs for emerging railroads, or on steamboats. Planters, however, were sometimes reluctant to lease their slaves for fear that they would be injured. This was particularly true with regard to leasing out slaves to work in the state's burgeoning coal mines, as evidenced by businessman William Phineas Browne's constant struggle to lease enough slaves to work his underground coal mines in Shelby County. Concerns for the safety of slaves—under hire or not—were for the most part based upon pure economics. When questioned why slaves loading bales of cotton worked on the riverbanks while Irishmen were on the boat receiving the bales, the boat mate gave a brutally honest answer: "The n____s are worth too much to be risked; if the Paddies are knocked overboard, or get their backs broke, nobody loses anything."[35]

Not only were slaves considered property, they generally were not allowed to own property of any significance. Alabama Supreme Court Justice Stone described their plight in this regard: "The status of a slave, under our law is one of entire abnegation of civil capacity. He can neither make nor receive a binding promise. He has no authority to own anything of value, nor can he convey a valuable title to another." Slaves were not even allowed to own horses or keep dogs. A slave could only enter into a contract with the consent of his owner and any property acquired by a slave became the property of his owner. To ensure that slaves did not acquire meaningful property, legislation was passed designed to prohibit owners from allowing their slaves to trade as a freeman. Despite legal obstacles to ownership of property by slaves, historian A. B. Moore reported that some slaves were allowed to make their own money in a variety of ways, including selling crops from a patch of land given them for that purpose, cutting wood for railroads and steamboats, or hiring out their services such as a carpenter or blacksmith on their free time.[36]

---

[34] Phillip Henry Gosse, *Letters from Alabama, Chiefly Relating to Natural History*, introduction by Harvey H. Jackson III (1859; rprt., Tuscaloosa: University of Alabama Press, 1993), 40. Gosse was in search of a teaching position on the Alabama frontier. He eventually landed a position to teach children of several planters in Dallas County. It was there that he was exposed to slavery for the first time.

[35] Sellers, *Slavery*, 195; Virginia Estella Knapp, "William Phineas Browne, A Yankee Business Man of the South" (M.A. Thesis, University of Texas, 1948), 61, 67; Moore, *History of Alabama*, 363.

[36] Toulmin, *Digest of Laws*, 629, 631; Aiken, *Digest of Laws*, 393–94; *Martin v.* Reed, 37 Ala. 198 (1861); *Trotter v. Blocker and Wife*, 6 Porter 269 (1838); Sellers, *Slavery*, 230–32; Moore, *History of Alabama*, 363.

When Alabama became a state, its constitution empowered the General Assembly to emancipate slaves so long as they had the consent of their owners. As we have seen in the years immediately following statehood, the legislature approved quite a few emancipations so long as the rights of creditors were protected and the owners pledged that their freed slaves would not become a charge against the state. As abolition fears increased, granting freedom to slaves was more frowned upon and occurred less frequently during the 1830s and thereafter. In 1834, the General Assembly relinquished its role in the process of manumission by transferring its power in that regard to county courts. The process then became a little more cumbersome due to new requirements that owners publish in county newspapers the time and court in which their application for emancipation would be sought. The judge upon good cause shown could then emancipate the slave, but only if he or she agreed to leave the state and never return. The legal status of freedom was not actually achieved until the slave left Alabama. Matters worsened such that by 1860 as the state headed toward secession, emancipation was prohibited altogether.[37]

Although possessing more rights than their enslaved counterparts, free blacks—referred to at the time as "free persons of color"—were certainly second-class citizens without the right to vote and with many constraints placed upon them. For example, they were prohibited from unlawful assemblies with slaves, retailing spirituous liquors, and visiting slaves or trading with slaves without the owner's permission. Free blacks were feared more and more as abolition efforts were on the rise. After 1832, no free persons of color coming into the state could settle in the state and they were required to leave the state within thirty days. If they did not leave within this time, upon conviction they would receive thirty-nine lashes. If they did not leave after this, they could be arrested again, tried, and sold into slavery for a period of one year. If they still did not leave after their period of servitude was up, they could have their freedom forfeited forever.[38]

The year 1831 was a seminal year with regard to how Alabamians felt about their "peculiar institution" of slavery. In that year a slave rebellion in Virginia lead by Nat Turner, and the advent of the abolition movement under the leadership of William Lloyd Garrison, had the effect of intensifying the defense of slavery within the state. Before 1831, there had at least been some lukewarm criticism of the evils of slavery and an open-mindedness with regard to eventual emancipation. For example, in 1824 the Tuscaloosa *Mirror* advertised subscriptions for the sale of an anti-slavery newspaper entitled *Genius of Universal Emancipation*, edited by abolitionist Benjamin Lundy. The next year the *Southern Advocate*, a Huntsville newspaper, ran an editorial critical of the domestic slave trade that it avowed was the main reason for the continuation of the evils of human bondage. Also, prior to 1831, there had been a limited movement

---

[37] Ala. Const. of 1819, Art. 4, Slaves, sec. 2; *Ala. Acts (1833)*, 29; *Ala. Acts (1859)*, 28; Sellers, *Slavery*, 236–37.

[38] Code of Ala. (1852), 241–42; *Ala. Acts (1831)*, 14.

toward the colonization of freed slaves led by Huntsville attorney James Birney from 1826 until he left for Kentucky in 1832.[39]

As a result of the commencement of the national abolition movement, white Alabamians became less tolerant of divergent views concerning slavery and did not welcome anti-slavery propaganda. So much so that in 1831 Governor Gayle sought the cooperation of other Southern governors to extradite abolitionists in the north for the publication and distribution of literature calling for slave insurrections. Practicing what he preached, on October 4, 1835, Governor Gayle persuaded a Tuscaloosa grand jury to indict an abolitionist editor in New York for circulating "within our state pamphlets and papers of a seditious and incendiary character," which made "illicit appeals to the passions, to incite to insurrection and murder our white population." To the extent that there were any suspected abolitionists in Alabama, several vigilante groups ran them out—whether real or imagined—of such places as Tuskegee, Wetumpka, Troy, and Auburn. Planters in Wilcox County joined the fray and resolved that "our right of property in slaves is fixed and guaranteed by the Federal Constitution and we regard the acts of the anti-slavery societies at the north as treason against the union."[40]

Just as abolitionism spurred aggressive opposition to the anti-slavery movement, Nat Turner's slave revolt in Virginia prompted a passage of laws further restricting the life of the slave. In this regard, the 1831 General Assembly made it illegal for anyone to teach blacks—slave or free—to read or write. Slaves in groups more than five were prohibited from congregating when not at work. The most draconian measure to evolve from this session of the legislature imposed the death penalty on anyone caught distributing anti-slavery literature.[41]

Despite criticism and legal maneuvers taken against abolitionists and the strengthening of the slave code, it was not until 1840 that the first major public official in Alabama spoke out in favor of the institution of slavery as a positive benefit for society. Addressing the legislature, Governor Arthur Bagby asserted that slaves in the South were better off than the poor laboring class in the northern states, or in any other country for that matter. Other defenses were more race-based, asserting that the Negro race was a separate species inferior to the white race, thus making slavery a blessing. Still others argued that slavery was ordained by God and was sanctioned in the Bible. Thus it was not surprising that the Methodist Conference of Montgomery in 1860 passed a resolution asserting that slavery was "wise, humane, and righteous." The primary legal argument in support of slavery was the assertion that slaves were property entitled to protection under the United State Constitution. Abolitionists countered

---

[39] Marshall Rachleff, "An Abolitionist Letter to Governor Henry W. Collier of Alabama: The Emergence of 'The Crisis of Fear' in Alabama," *Journal of Negro History* 66 (Autumn, 1981), 246–47.

[40] Rachleff, "An Abolitionist Letter," 247–48.

[41] *Ala. Acts (1831)*, 13–14, 16–18.

with the argument that slavery was contrary to the basic principles of equality as espoused in the Declaration of Independence.[42]

Most white laborers who did not own slaves defended slavery because of a fear that they would have to compete with freed slaves for jobs. Others, who saw the cruelty of slavery, were nevertheless opposed to abolition, worrying that the immediate freeing of some 400,000 slaves within the state's borders would pose a danger that those freed would take retribution against white citizens whether they had been slaveholders or not. Although there were some in the state who questioned the wisdom of the "peculiar institution," hardly any made their sentiments known publicly, particularly after 1831. One leading newspaper, however, did so. In January 1848, the *Tuscaloosa Monitor* voiced its concern: "We believe that the Southern States themselves would be better off without this institution than with it." It further asserted that if slavery had not already been in existence, a large majority within the South would be opposed to its introduction at that time.[43]

While slavery was generally defended to the hilt by most white Alabamians, there was nevertheless a concern that there were too many slaves in their midst. In some areas of the state—particularly the Black Belt—slaves were beginning to outnumber whites to such an extent that there were increasing fears of slave revolts. According to the 1840 census, slaves outnumbered whites by 23,500 in thirteen counties located in the central part of the state. At the urging of a group of Black Belt planter–politicians, a bill was introduced in the General Assembly to restrict the importation of slaves from outside the state. A special committee to which the bill was assigned for investigation reported that not only was the increasing slave importation becoming a threat to the security of the state, many of those imported came from the prisons of other states, which the committee asserted "could only create a spirit of unrest and insubordination among the slaves already here." Despite the committee's report predicting a slave rebellion unless the slave population was limited, the slave restriction bill failed to pass, prompting historian Marshall Rachleff to conclude that the action of the General Assembly was "an example of economic self-interest superseding racial anxieties."[44]

Alabama simply could not divorce itself from the economic benefits of slavery. As new territory was acquired as a result of the Mexican War, Alabamians became leading advocates of guaranteeing the rights of slaveholders to carry their slaves into the newly opened western territories. As the capital moved to Montgomery, increasing attention was devoted to the protection of slavery at home as well as in the territories.

---

[42] *Ala. House Journal* (1840), 17–20; Sellers, *Slavery*, 332–55; Moore, *Alabama*, 372.

[43] Sellers, *Slavery*, 351; Moore, *History of Alabama*, 372.

[44] Rachleff, "An Abolitionist Letter," 248.

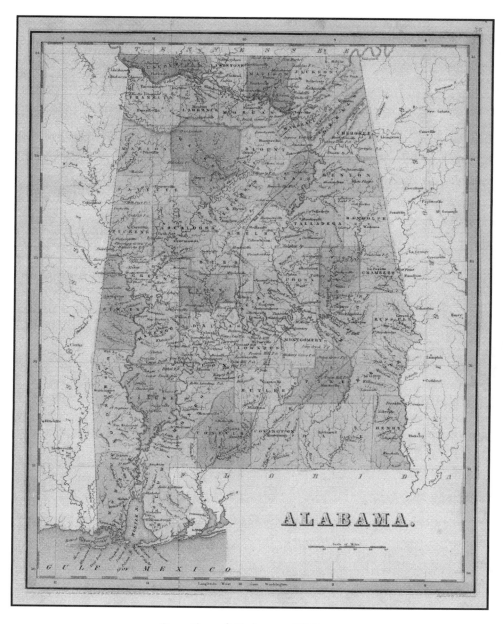

Counties of Alabama, 1841
By Boston mapmaker Thomas Gamaliel Bradford

Courtesy Barry Lawrence Ruderman Antique Maps, used by permission

11

❧

MONTGOMERY BECOMES CAPTIAL
AS SECESSION LOOMS

With the arrival of the evening stage from Selma on January 30, 1846, the citizens of Montgomery learned of their city's selection as the next state capital. According to Matthew P. Blue, Montgomery's earliest historian, the exciting news was greeted with great rejoicing such as had not been seen before in the town's history. Landowners were jubilant in anticipation of the increase in the value of their property. Investors quickly turned their attention to building hotels to cater to the flood of anticipated visitors during sessions of the General Assembly. Rapid construction thus began of the Exchange Hotel, the Madison House, and the Dexter House. One of the principals in the construction of the Exchange Hotel was Charles T. Pollard. Pollard was also the primary owner of the Montgomery & West Point Railroad. In that capacity he had formed a joint venture with the Tennessee & Coosa Railroad to provide a river–railroad route from the Tennessee Valley to Mobile. This route proposed to utilize the Alabama and Coosa rivers rather than the Black Warrior River, and, thus bypass Tuscaloosa in favor of Montgomery. The prospect of this route diverting traffic from the Black Warrior River had contributed to Tuscaloosa's inability to hold on to its status as the seat of Alabama's government.[1]

Andrew Dexter, the leading founder of Montgomery, had reportedly prophesied that the city would one day be home to the state's capital. More specifically, he foresaw a capitol building overlooking the city from a prominent hill looking down what would become Dexter Avenue toward the Alabama River. He therefore deeded the site to the city of Montgomery with the proviso that it could never be sold, but rather must be held in reserve for the location of the state capital if Montgomery was ever successful in securing the seat of government. This site was commonly referred to as "Goat Hill" because of the open pasturage it afforded to goats and other livestock in the area. This site had also been the scene of Montgomery's extravagant welcoming ceremonies for the Marquis de Lafayette during his triumphant tour through Alabama in 1825. Now that Montgomery had been successful in landing the seat of government, the removal act required its leaders to secure a site and to construct a capitol building at no expense to the state. Accordingly, the city issued construction bonds totaling $75,000 which were snatched up by Montgomery's leading real estate

---

[1] Blue, *History of Montgomery*, 30; Brantley, *Banking in Alabama*, 2: 235–40; Mary Ann Neeley, ed., *The Works of Matthew Blue: Montgomery's First Historian* (Montgomery, Ala.: New South Books, 2010), 63, 169.

dealers and capitalists at the urging of Charles Pollard.[2]

Pollard's influence in the new seat of government is further evidenced by his role as chairman of the capitol's building committee. Stephen D. Button was chosen to draw up the plans for the new capitol and the contract for construction was awarded to B. F. Robinson and R. N. R. Bardwell. After the city expended $5,000 in grading the Goat Hill site for construction, the Masonic Grand Lodge ceremoniously laid the corner stone of the building on July 4, 1846. Among the items placed inside the stone included a list of the current legislators, a Bible with a silver key, and a current local newspaper. Almost a year later on July 3, 1847, as construction continued, the ceiling in the House of Representatives chamber crashed to the floor killing two workers and seriously injuring another. Despite this tragic setback, in October 1847 the building was completed and ready for inspection by commissioners who had been appointed by the legislature to examine the building before its acceptance by the state. Upon the approval of the commissioners, the building and its keys, as well as the deed to the land, were turned over to the state in a formal ceremony held on November 2, 1847.[3]

After the state's formal acceptance of the capitol building, Secretary of State William Garrett readied the state's official records for transport from Tuscaloosa to Montgomery. The records were packed into 113 boxes and loaded onto 13 wagons for the trip. Under the direction of James H. Owen, the doorkeeper of the House of Representatives, the wagon train proceeded over the "Centreville Road," a route which in large measure parallels the present-day Tuscaloosa to Montgomery highway, U.S. Highway 82. The cost of transporting these records totaling 25,704 pounds was $1,325. Because of the legislative requirement that there be no expense to the state relative to the move, the transportation tab was picked up by Charles T. Pollard, the chairman of the building committee. The archival wagon train arrived in plenty of time for the legislators and executive officers to set up their offices before the convening of the General Assembly in the new capitol.[4]

The Montgomery that welcomed the new capital had been in existence for less than three decades. When initially chartered as a town in December 1819, it was a sleepy frontier village with a population of only 401 and a scattering of twenty-six frame houses and thirty-eight log cabins. Within just three years Montgomery's population nearly doubled and the town boasted a two-story framed courthouse with a distinctive cupola. Despite its frontier character, Montgomery was on the rise socially, religiously, and culturally. Montgomerians were soon enjoying theatrical performances,

---

[2] Williams, *Early History of Montgomery*, 38; Simpson, "The Alabama State Capitol," 91–93; Blue, *History of Montgomery*, 30.

[3] Blue, *History of Montgomery*, 30; Neeley, *The Works of Mathew Blue*, 173, 175; Peter Brannan, "Moving the Capital to Montgomery," *Montgomery Advertiser*, July 26, 1946; Simpson, "The Alabama State Capitol," 91–92.

[4] Garrett, *Reminiscences*, 460; Simpson, "The Alabama State Capitol," 95; Brannan, "Moving the Capital," *Montgomery Advertiser*.

such as *Julius Caesar*, starring future governor Benjamin Fitzpatrick. On December 3, 1837, it was chartered as a city with a mayor as its leader rather than a town intendant. Montgomery had also become host to meetings of the Alabama Conference of the Methodist Episcopal Church, the Agricultural Society of South Alabama, the Montgomery Lyceum Association, and numerous temperance organizations. In March 1844, Montgomery was considered significant enough to receive a visit from Henry Clay, the Whig candidate for president running against James K. Polk. Notably, Clay did not visit the capital in Tuscaloosa.[5]

Montgomery continued to grow such that by 1840 it had a population of 2,179 and by 1850 it had a population of 4,282. Despite this growth in population along with its cultural progression, Montgomery was still beleaguered with frontier violence in its streets during the 1840s and 1850s. In December 1841, the *Alabama Journal* lamented that Montgomery was "rife" with "murderous affrays." The criminal docket of the Montgomery Circuit Court for 1841–1843 documents eighty-nine cases of violent crimes, including eleven murders, twenty cases of assault with the intent to kill, thirty-two cases of assault or assault and battery, one case of mayhem, and eighteen cases of carrying concealed weapons. In 1848, a gunfight erupted in the streets of the new capital involving P. A. Wray, a prominent planter, and his former overseer. While no one was seriously hurt, this was just an example of the willingness of Montgomerians to rely on deadly weapons to quickly resolve disputes. That such a mindset continued to exist throughout the antebellum period was evidenced as late as 1859 when Justice George Stone of the Alabama Supreme Court denounced the "pernicious practice" of citizens carrying deadly weapons, complaining that "such deadly weapons are readily drawn, and fatally employed, in resentment of injuries and insults of the most trivial character."[6]

Against this background, Montgomery began its reign as Alabama's capital city. Secretary of State Garrett reported that the first session of the legislature "brought together an immense concourse of people" who crowded the city's hotels and boarding houses. Included within the numerous visitors were office seekers who "were thick as blackbirds in a fresh plowed field in the Spring." Most senators and representatives were in attendance

---

[5] Garrett, *Reminiscences*, 460–61; Clanton W. Williams, "Conservatism in Old Montgomery, 1817–1861," *Alabama Review* 10 (April 1957): 96–98; Neeley, *The Works of Mathew Blue*, 44, 89, 133–66. *Julius Caesar* was the Montgomery Thespian Society's first production. Debuting on December 17, 1822, the performance took place in the Montgomery Hotel, which was located at the corner of Commerce Street and Tallapoosa Street. Joining Fitzpatrick in the performance was a star-studded cast that included G. W. B Towns, a future governor of Georgia who played Octavius Caesar; Henry Goldthwaite, a future Chief Justice of the Alabama Supreme Court who played Marcus Antonius; and John Edmondson, a leading citizen of Montgomery who played M. Aemil Lepidus.

[6] Arthur F. Howington, "Violence in Alabama: A Study of Late Ante-bellum Montgomery," *Alabama Review* 27 (July 1974): 213–21. The actual number of crimes for 1841–1843 was undoubtedly significantly higher because these were just the number of violent crimes that reached the circuit court level. As Howington suggests in his study of violence in late antebellum Montgomery, not all crimes were prosecuted and many that were remain uncounted due to destroyed or unavailable records.

as Alabama's first biennial session of the General Assembly was gaveled to order on December 6, 1847. On the second day of the session, a message from outgoing Governor Joshua Martin was transmitted to both houses of the Assembly where it was read and ordered to be printed. The message referenced many topics, including those related to the dismantlement of the State Bank of Alabama, revenue and taxation, public education, and the condition of the state penitentiary in Wetumpka, which had undergone privatization in 1846 due to inefficient management by the state.[7]

Only in operation for five years at this point, with a maximum population of only 132 prisoners, the state penitentiary had been underfunded and mismanaged from the outset. Inefficiency was compounded by prison inspectors and a warden who were selected more for political reasons than for their expertise. It was thus not surprising that prisoners frequently escaped, prison manufactured goods did not compete successfully with private enterprise, and prisoners suffered high mortality rates. As a result, the legislature passed a bill which outsourced the operation of the penitentiary to a private concern for a period of six years.[8]

Martin spent a good portion of the remainder of his outgoing message defending his actions in expending monies out of the state's contingent fund to cover expenses for several volunteer companies that had been requisitioned by President Polk for service in the Mexican War. Martin acknowledged that he had questionable authority to make such expenditures, but did so since the Assembly was not in session and he felt that the payments were necessary "to preserve the honor and standing of the State." He further asserted his belief that Congress would refund most of the amount expended and urged the Assembly to petition for such. He concluded by stating, "I have acted in good faith, for the best interest of the State, in view of the emergency presented...."[9]

The next order of business for the Assembly was to convene in joint session to count the votes cast for governor in the last election between the Democrat candidate Reuben Chapman of Morgan County and the Whig candidate Nicholas Davis of Limestone County. After tabulating the official returns, the Assembly announced Chapman as the winner. Chapman had received 29,722 votes to Davis' 23,467. Born in 1799 in Caroline County, Virginia, Chapman moved to Huntsville in 1824 to study law in the office of

---

[7] Garrett, *Reminiscences of Public Men in Alabama*, 461.

[8] Ward and Rogers, *Alabama's Response*, 85; Mary Ellen Curtin, "Convict-Lease System," *Encyclopedia of Alabama*, http://encyclopediaofalabama.org/face/Article.jsp?id=h-1346 (accessed January 29, 2013); Neeley, "Painful Circumstances: Glimpses of the Alabama Penitentiary," 6–9. The leasing system continued through the end of the Civil War and was the forerunner of the infamous convict-lease system that developed after the war. Under that system prisoners were in essence "rented" by individuals and companies to perform labor at their farms, places of business, and coal mines. In many cases, the prisoners worked and lived in extremely harsh conditions, were poorly fed, and were subjected to cruel punishments.

[9] Garrett, *Reminiscences*, 460–63. Governor Martin, realizing that he was no longer popular within the Democratic Party because of his run for office as an independent, decided not to seek reelection. He instead returned to the practice of law in Tuscaloosa. In 1853, he was elected once again to the General Assembly. He died three years later in 1856, at the age of 56. Webb and Armbrester, *Alabama Governors*, Hugh C. Bailey, "Joshua L. Martin," 50.

his brother Samuel Chapman. He passed the bar in 1825 and practiced with his brother for a year before moving to Morgan County. In 1835 he was elected to the U.S. Congress where he served until 1847 when he received an unsolicited nomination of the Democratic Party to run for governor. During his career as a member of Congress, Chapman became a strong supporter of states' rights, aligning himself with such firebrands as Robert Barnwell Rhett of South Carolina, and fellow-Alabamians Dixon Hall Lewis and William Lowndes Yancey, in their unwavering defense of the rights of the southern states against what they saw as increasing encroachments by the northern states.[10]

Chapman's strong position on states' rights, particularly his opposition to the Wilmot Proviso which would have barred slavery from any of the western territories acquired as a result of the Mexican War, made him an attractive compromise candidate for governor. The Democratic Party had been divided ever since Joshua Martin left the party to run as an independent. Since Nathaniel Terry had been defeated in the last election by Martin, he was not favored. Neither was Henry W. Collier, who favored the Whig position on the use of privately chartered banks. Consequently, William Lowndes Yancey placed Chapman's name in nomination to give the party an alternative candidate. Because the party had changed its rules to require a two-thirds, rather than a simple, majority to obtain the nomination, it took ten hours and nineteen ballots for exhausted delegates to nominate Chapman to by acclamation. Defeating the Whig candidate, Nicholas Davis, by more than six thousand votes, Reuben Chapman was inaugurated as Alabama's thirteenth governor on December 16, 1847, and became the first governor to be sworn into office in the new capital city of Montgomery. The ceremonies were held in the chambers of the House of Representatives with Reverend Basil Manly—then serving as the second president of the University of Alabama—acting as chaplain for the occasion.[11]

Governor Chapman spent the overwhelming majority of his inaugural address ranting against the "General Government" rather than focusing upon the problems facing the state, such as debtor relief and an inadequate money supply. Of particular concern to Chapman was the danger presented by the possible passage of the Wilmot Proviso. In this vein he asserted that the proviso was not merely a measure to ban slavery from the territories acquired in the Mexican War, it was also a harbinger of "other still more direct measures in Congress to abolish slavery." He strongly urged Alabamians to guard against "outside interferences" and to never allow Congress to deprive slaveholders the right to take their slaves into any territory. What little attention Governor Chapman directed to local state issues was decidedly negative in tone and contained no proposals for legislative initiatives. He voiced strong opposition to the chartering of banks of any kind, whether

---

[10] John R. Mayfield, "Reuben Chapman," in Webb and Armbrester, *Alabama Governors*, 53–56; T. A. DeLand and A. Davis Smith, *Northern Alabama: Historical and Biographical Illustrated* (Birmingham: n.p., 1888), s.v. "Chapman, Reuben," 252–54.

[11] Mayfield, "Reuben Chapman," 53–56; Simpson, "The Alabama State Capitol," 96; Moore, *History of Alabama*, 184, 197.

privately or publicly owned. He also opposed expenditures for education or internal improvements because the state was too much in debt.[12]

No major legislative reforms or initiatives were sought by Governor Chapman during his one term in office. He basically ignored Alabama's many economic woes, taking a very laissez-faire attitude of letting things work out on their own. One of Chapman's few major achievements during his term was to reduce the commission responsible for the closure of the State Bank of Alabama from three members to just one—Francis S. Lyons. Chapman believed that negotiating issues involved with the closure of the bank would be more effective with all authority vested in just one person rather than three. Lyons proved himself up to the task and successfully finished the dismantlement of the bank and paid most of its debts before he retired in 1853. One other achievement of some note for Chapman was his success in securing the appointment of Michael Tuomey to teach geology, mineralogy, and agricultural chemistry at the University of Alabama. Tuomey was also to serve as the state's geologist and was tasked with completing a geological survey of the state. His Geological Survey of Alabama, completed in 1857, provided valuable information as to the state's mineral resources—particularly concerning coal and iron—that would lead to the founding of Birmingham after the Civil War.[13]

Governor Chapman became increasingly out of favor because of his opposition to any banks—whether private or public—and his unpopular proposal to tax recently acquired federal lands. He added to his disfavor by taking it upon himself to appoint successors to Alabama's two U.S. Senate seats, both of which had become open due to a resignation and death, rather than calling for a convention to elect the senators as urged by several north Alabama newspapers. What made matters worse, he appointed south Alabamians to fill both unexpired terms, violating the tacit understanding that the state's senate seats were to be divided between north and south Alabama. By the time the Democratic convention to nominate candidates for governor convened, Chapman had lost enough support that he failed to get his party's nomination for a second term as governor.[14]

Chapman's lackluster one term as governor was overshadowed by a pivotal U.S. senatorial election in December 1847, as well as by the pronouncement of a significant states' rights doctrine by Alabama Democrats in February 1848. With regard to the senatorial seat at issue, it initially became open when the incumbent senator, William Rufus King, was appointed by President John Tyler as America's minister to France. In April 1844, Governor Fitzpatrick appointed Dixon Hall Lewis to fill King's unex-

---

[12] Mayfield, "Reuben Chapman," 54–55.

[13] Ibid., 55; Deland and Davis, *Historical and Biographical Illustrated*, 253.

[14] Although he remained politically active, Chapman held only one other office during his lifetime after defeating Jeremiah Clemens, a candidate of the nativist Know-Nothing party, for a seat in the state legislature in 1855. During the Civil War, Chapman suffered greatly as his son was killed in battle, his home was burned down, and he was taken prisoner by northern troops. Chapman nevertheless recovered after the war and assembled a sizeable estate in Huntsville before dying on May 16, 1882. John R. Mayfield, "Reuben Chapman," 56.

pired term. Lewis, the brother-in-law of Fitzpatrick and a member of the so-called "Montgomery Regency," was Alabama's leading states' rights advocate at the time. When Lewis sought election for the seat in his own right, he was challenged by King, who had returned from his diplomatic post, and by Arthur F. Hopkins, the leader of the Whig Party. Despite the strong challenge from within his own party and a Whig party on the rise within the state, Lewis managed to win reelection.[15]

Historian Leah Rawls Atkins concludes that this was "probably the most significant senatorial election in the antebellum period" as "it pitted the Unionists—called 'Hunkers' by their south Alabama opponents who equated them with the blindly loyalist faction in New York state politics— against the states' rights group, called by their north Alabama opponents the 'Chivalry.'" To gain the support of enough Hunkers to win this frenetic contest, Lewis was compelled to support the national Democratic Party. This no doubt created some discomfort for Lewis in view of his states' rights views, particularly those pertaining to his support of the expansion of slavery into the territories.[16]

On February 14, 1848, state Democrats met in Montgomery to choose delegates to send to the national party convention being held in Baltimore to nominate a candidate for the presidential election of 1848. The Alabama Democrats were at first divided again between the Hunkers of north Alabama, who favored a Union candidate such as James Buchanan, and the Chivalry of south Alabama who favored a states' rights candidate. The south Alabama Democrats were successful in gaining control of the convention and were led by William Lowndes Yancey and other firebrands who stepped up their defense of southern rights, in particular demanding Congressional protection of slavery in the western territories acquired and created as a result of the Mexican War. Yancey had previously denounced the Wilmot Proviso as "antagonistic to every principle of the Constitution and of the democratic creed," and urged that it be resisted "at all hazards and to the last extremity." During the Montgomery convention, Yancey articulated with great passion resolutions in support of this sentiment. Soon to be known as the Alabama Platform, these resolutions in essence rejected the principle of "squatter sovereignty" for the territories—a principle endorsed by Lewis Cass of Michigan allowing the first settlers in a territory to decide whether or not to allow slavery—and instead declared that the federal government had a duty to protect slavery in the territories and slaveholders had the right to take their slave property into the territories without interference. Yancey also proposed that Alabama delegates to the national party convention in Baltimore refuse to vote for any candidate who would not pledge their support for these resolutions.[17]

In the excitement of the moment, the Montgomery convention adopted the Alabama Platform in total and instructed its delegates not to support

---

[15] Rogers et al., *Alabama*, 154–55.

[16] Ibid., 155.

[17] Rogers et al., *Alabama, 156*; Moore, *History of Alabama*, 199–200.

any presidential candidate who did not categorically reject the principles of squatter sovereignty and the Wilmot Proviso. Democratic conventions in Georgia, Florida, and Virginia endorsed the platform. Both Democratic and Whig newspapers supported it and Yancey was generally praised throughout the South. However, as the fervor of the Montgomery convention died down, opposition to Yancey and his platform began to surface among Alabama Democrats who were concerned that it would be rejected in the northern states and lead to a Whig victory in the presidential election. Historian A. B. Moore observed that "the people were not ready to break up the Union to overthrow 'squatter sovereignty,' especially as it was a doctrine close akin to the sort of democracy in which they believed."[18]

A group of Democrats under the leadership of future Governor John A. Winston ignored Yancey and his platform, as well as the instructions of the state party, by not leaving the national convention when former Secretary of War Lewis Cass, the principal advocate of the doctrine of squatter sovereignty, was nominated. Only Yancey and one other delegate complied with the instructions of the party by walking out of the convention and refusing to endorse Cass. Those who remained in Baltimore defended their actions and denounced Yancey. Yancey felt abandoned and contemplated forming a Southern Rights party to advance the cause of states' rights. Senator Lewis, however, who did not believe that Yancey's third party could carry a single county in the state, declined to join Yancey and instead encouraged him to seek control within in the Democratic Party. Yancey and his followers nevertheless worked against Cass and almost delivered the state for Whig candidate General Zachary Taylor, who won the election. With most Alabamians remaining loyal to the Union and Senator Lewis' rejection of Yancey's proposal for a third party, Yancey and his insurgents were kept in check for a while. In October 1848, however, Senator Lewis' death left Yancey as the leader of the states' rights advocates within the state. Under Yancey they would become more extreme in their views and less accommodating with Unionists. Indeed, they began to push wholeheartedly for an independent Southern nation. With Yancey ensconced as the leader of Southern secessionists, they would soon be known as "fire-eaters."[19]

Ironically, the South's leading revolutionary came from a household where abolitionism was advocated by his domineering stepfather. Yancey's radicalism was forged by a childhood and adolescence that was steeped in physical and mental abuse inflicted upon him by both his mother and stepfather. Yancey, who was born in Warren County, Georgia on August 10, 1814, was only three years old when his father, Benjamin Yancey, died. The elder Yancey—a veteran of the Quasi-War with France serving on the *USS Constellation*—was practicing law in Charleston at the time of his death. Four years later William's widowed mother married Nathan Beman, a Northern Presbyterian minister who was teaching school in Georgia. Beman took charge of his new wife's trust, sold her three slaves, and moved his family to Troy, New York. Beman, a strict disciplinarian, subjected his

---

[18] Moore, *History of Alabama*, 200–01.

[19] Rogers et al., *Alabama*, 156–58; Moore, *History of Alabama*, 201.

family to religious and abolitionist rants and engaged in violent fights with his wife. According to biographer Eric Walther, Yancey "devoted much of his life rebelling against his hated stepfather and that man's antislavery and unionist values."[20]

William Lowndes Yancey

Yancey rejoiced in escaping from his dysfunctional family in the fall of 1830 when he entered Williams College, a liberal arts college located in the small village of Williamston, Massachusetts. During his years at Williams College, Yancey engaged in rebellious activity in obvious reaction to being free of the constant oversight of a heavy-handed and stern stepfather. His foot-loose and fancy-free outlook resulted in his being fined by the college for such infractions as drunkenness, using profane language, playing cards, and breaking glass windows on campus. Despite his rebellious conduct, Yancey was a good student, studying rhetoric under the renowned Mark Hopkins. He also gained invaluable experience serving as the editor of the campus newspaper and sharpened his oratorical skills for which he would become famous by participating in the college's debate society. His skills were such that he was named the college's best orator in his senior year.[21]

---

[20] Eric H. Walther, *William Lowndes Yancey and the Coming of the Civil War* (Chapel Hill: University of North Carolina Press, 2006), 3–12; Rogers et al., *Alabama*, 152–53.

[21] Walther, *William Lowndes Yancey*, 17–22.

Although he finished his course work six weeks prior to commencement, for some reason—whether financial or otherwise—Yancey did not stay to officially graduate from Williams College. Not wishing to further endure the discord between Beman and his mother, Yancey did not return home, but instead, he headed south to read law under an acquaintance of his step-uncle in Sparta, Georgia. Quickly tiring of life in Sparta, Yancey moved to Greenville, South Carolina, where he continued his legal training under Unionist Benjamin Franklin Perry. He also helped to keep the books for his uncle's plantation, Rosemont, which was serviced by approximately 100 slaves. Having made known his fervent support of the federal union and his disdain of John C. Calhoun, in November 1834 Yancey was chosen to become editor of the Greenville *Mountaineer*, an anti-nullification Unionist newspaper. Not surprisingly, in his first editorial for the paper he lambasted Calhoun, nullification, and disunion.[22]

Before Yancey turned his attention to politics, he brought domestic order to his life by marrying Sarah Caroline Earle on August 13, 1835. Sarah was from a wealthy and politically influential family in Greenville. Her wedding dowry of thirty-five slaves instantly propelled Yancey into the planter slavocracy and exposed him to a totally different outlook on life from that which had been provided by his abolitionist stepfather. Not long after his marriage to Sarah and his acquisition of slaves, Yancey was struck with the urge to move once again to the frontier of the old Southwest where he could establish his own plantation.[23]

Yancey initially settled on a plantation near Cahaba, Alabama, in 1836, joining several relatives on his mother's side who had already settled there, including Jesse Beene who represented Cahaba in the state legislature. Upon his arrival, Yancey began practicing law and became the editor of the *Cahaba Democrat*. It was here that Yancey's transformation from a Unionist to a states' rights activist began. That transformation was temporarily interrupted, however, by a nasty turn of events that occurred on a return trip to South Carolina. During this visit, Yancey became engaged in a heated argument with his wife's uncle that ended with Yancey shooting him to death. Claiming self-defense at his trial for murder in October 1838, Yancey was convicted by the jury of the lesser offense of manslaughter. He was fined $1500 and sentenced to one year in prison. In January 1839, South Carolina's governor commuted the period of incarceration after Yancey had served only three months. Gaining his freedom, Yancey returned to Cahaba and resumed as editor of the Cahaba *Democrat*. It was not long after, however, that Yancey was devastated financially when most of his slaves died when they drank from a spring that had been poisoned by an overseer from another plantation who had hoped to kill Yancey's overseer. Yancey thus sold the *Democrat* and moved to Wetumpka to start over. There he began practicing law and, with his brother, began editing the Wetumpka *Argus and Commercial Advertiser*.[24]

---

[22] Ibid., 24–32.

[23] Ibid., 32–35.

[24] Ibid., 47–55; Rogers et al., *Alabama*, 153.

It was in Wetumpka that Yancey would complete his transformation from a Unionist and enter into politics on his road to becoming the South's leading secessionist. His political career began in 1841 with his election as Elmore County's representative in the state House of Representatives; in 1843 he was elected to the state Senate. At first Yancey devoted his attention to reform measures such as bank reform, public education, revisions in the penal code, and prison reform. Although by then a staunch supporter of slavery, he favored apportioning congressional districts on a white population basis which gave the advantage to the non-slaveholding counties in north Alabama. His stance in this regard was based upon his opposition to wealthy Whigs and his support of yeoman farmers. In 1844 Yancey was elected to Congress on a platform of strict construction of the U.S. Constitution and, at long last, a rejection of Unionism. Yancey was reelected in July 1846, but subsequently resigned. Officially citing financial reasons for his resignation, Yancey nevertheless also made public a letter in which he criticized the Democratic Party as lacking in principles. Thereafter Yancey would lead the fight for Southern independence free from party constraints or elective office.[25]

As Yancey had begun to emerge as the leader of the Southern radicals upon the death of Senator Dixon Hall Lewis, Alabamians elected a more moderate Henry W. Collier as the state's fourteenth governor. Reuben Chapman's falling out of favor with the party faithful had put Collier in a position to become a compromise candidate for the Democrats. Opposition to Chapman had been particularly strong in north Alabama, which was predominantly Unionist and upset with Chapman's filling both vacant senate seats with south Alabamians. Oddly, completely diverse factions came together to support Collier for governor—a north Alabama states' rights group led by Clement Comer Clay, Jr., and south Alabama Unionists led by William Rufus King. Collier also benefitted from a decision by the Whig Party not to field a candidate because of their belief that he shared their view that one of the principal functions of government was to stimulate economic growth. With only token opposition from several rogue candidates, Collier received 37,221 votes to just 704 for his nominal opponents to win the governorship.[26]

Governor Henry Collier, born in Lunenburg County, Virginia, on January 17, 1801, followed his family to South Carolina and then on to Huntsville in the Alabama Territory in 1818. Collier, having read law under Judge John Haywood of the Tennessee Supreme Court, practiced in Huntsville for a while before relocating in Tuscaloosa where he practiced with Sion L. Perry. In 1827 Collier was elected to the Alabama legislature on a platform of calling for the construction of a new capitol building in Tuscaloosa. After he served just one term in the legislature, his fellow legislators elected him as the judge of the Third Circuit Court, a position which at the time also made him an ad hoc member of the Alabama Supreme Court. When the Supreme Court was finally made a distinct entity in 1836, Collier became its

[25] Rogers et al., *Alabama*, 153–54; Walther, *William Lowndes Yancey*, 56–73.

[26] Leah Rawls Atkins, "Henry W. Collier," in *Alabama Governors*, 57–58.

chief justice. Collier's service in that capacity over the next twelve years earned him the respect that helped propel him into the governor's office as a compromise candidate.[27]

On December 14, 1849, just three days before governor-elect Collier took the oath of office, the capitol building in Montgomery, then only two years old, burned to the ground. The roof of the capitol was discovered to be on fire with both houses in session. In obvious haste, members of the House did not bother to record a formal adjournment, noting in their journal that "the roof of the Capitol was discovered to be in flames, and in three hours from the first alarm the broken walls alone remained." Remarkably, due to the valiant efforts of members of the legislature, workers in the executive departments, members of the Supreme Court's staff, and quite a few citizens, many public documents were saved. After salvaging the records of his office, Secretary of State William Garrett led a group to the third floor to save what they could in the Supreme Court's library. They managed to throw many of its books out the window before the extreme heat forced them to leave. Unfortunately many valuable documents, records, and law books could not be saved.[28]

Despite the fire, the work of the legislature went interrupted while alternate plans were made for the inauguration of governor-elect Collier. The day after of the fire, both houses of the legislature temporarily met in Montgomery Hall, one of Montgomery's finest hotels. It was determined that on the day of the inauguration, the legislature would initially convene in Montgomery Hall and then escort the governor-elect to the Court Street Methodist Church for the swearing-in ceremonies. Addressing a large crowd that had assembled at the church, Governor Collier barely mentioned the destruction of the capitol, indicating his confidence that the legislature would take appropriate steps to make the inconvenience as minimal as possible. In the meantime, arrangements were made for the House of Representatives to meet in the ballroom of the Exchange Hotel, and for the Senate to meet in the Tilley building, a brick building adjoining the Exchange Hotel. The Governor's office, various other executive offices, and the Supreme Court were relegated to temporary quarters in the Madison House Hotel.[29]

Immediately, there were legislative proposals to fund the rebuilding of the capital in Montgomery at state expense. However, some who had opposed Montgomery being the site of the capital saw this as an opportunity to have the capital moved out of Montgomery, with many favoring a move back to Tuscaloosa. Over nearly a two-month period, some fifty proposals were made in an effort to remove the capital from Montgomery temporarily or permanently. On February 11, 1850, however, the House finally passed a Senate bill that called for the appropriation of $60,000 for the rebuilding of the capitol in Montgomery on the foundations of the first

---

[27] Ibid., 58.

[28] Simpson, "The Alabama State Capitol," 96–97; "The Capitol Fire of 1849," *Alabama Bench and Bar Historical Society Newsletter* (November/December 2010): 11.

[29] Simpson, "The Alabama State Capitol," 98–101.

structure. In 1852 the General Assembly appropriated an additional $2,527 for the completed capitol building. With the capital now secure in Montgomery, on February 9, 1852, by joint resolution, the General Assembly authorized the city of Montgomery to place its town clock on the capitol building. Prominently perched just beneath the building's imposing dome, that historic clock has been a familiar sight for more than 160 years to Montgomerians and visitors traveling up Dexter Avenue.[30]

Ironically, a free black engineer by the name of Horace King was engaged to construct the framework of the new capitol, which within a few years would briefly serve as the home of the Confederate States of America. King also reportedly designed and built the capitol's double spiral entry staircases, which were cantilevered and thus appearing to be without support. King had already achieved a reputation as the South's most respected bridge builder, constructing dozens of bridges in Alabama, Georgia, and Mississippi. Many of these were built by King with his former owner, John Godwin, who—aided by Tuscaloosa entrepreneur Robert Jemison—not only secured King's freedom, but wrestled a waiver from the Alabama General Assembly of the usual requirement that an emancipated black must leave the state within a year.[31]

After resolution of the issue concerning the rebuilding of the capitol, Governor Collier's administration focused on reform issues. Supporting an organized state public education system, in 1850 Collier unsuccessfully pushed the legislature to create a state superintendent's office to provide direction for the county school systems. Lamenting the state's failure to adequately fund its schools, he called it a "blighting apathy that pervades the community." Collier more successfully promoted reforms in other areas, including a constitutional amendment allowing the people to elect their circuit and probate judges. During his administration the number of Supreme Court justices was increased from three to five and the legislature apportioned the state into seven Congressional districts. A visit to Alabama by social reformer Dorothea L. Dix, in 1850, inspired Collier to support the establishment of a state hospital for the mentally ill, which the legislature authorized in 1851. The facility in Tuscaloosa, originally named the Alabama State Hospital for the Insane, would not open until 1861; it was later named for its first superintendent, Dr. Peter Bryce.[32]

Collier, a moderate who supported the Compromise of 1850, nevertheless believed it prudent for Alabama to send delegates to a convention being held in Nashville in June 1850 to discuss how the slave states would react

[30] Brannan, "Moving the Capital," *Montgomery Advertiser*, July 26, 1946; Simpson, "The Alabama State Capitol," 103–05; *Ala. Acts (1849)*, 140–41; see also Donna C. Hole, "Daniel Pratt and Barachias Holt: Architects of the State Capitol?," *Alabama Review* 37 (April 1984): 83–97.

[31] John S. Lupold and Thomas L. French, *Bridging Deep South Rivers: The Life and Legend of Horace King* (Athens, Georgia: University of Georgia Press, 2004), 134–45; Rev. F. L. Cherry, "Horace King," in "The History of Opelika and Her Agricultural Tributary Territory," *Alabama Historical Quarterly* 15, no. 2 (1953): 178–339, and nos. 3, 4 (1953): 383–537; *Ala. Acts (1845)*, 207.

[32] Atkins, "Henry W. Collier," 59; *Ala. Acts (1849)*, 37–40; *Ala. Acts (1851)*, 8, 28, 10–19.

to any Congressional ban of slavery in the territories acquired as a result of the Mexican War. For the most part, Alabamians selected moderate delegates to attend the convention who were in favor of saving the Union if at all possible. Believing that becoming an independent nation was the only solution for a beleaguered South, Alabama's leading secessionist, William Lowndes Yancey, opposed the convention since it appeared to be committed to a policy to preserve the Union. Strangely enough, Alabama Whig leader Henry Hilliard also opposed the convention because of the contradictory fear that it could possibly offend the North and interfere with the Union's salvation.[33]

It turned out that Yancey's fears were more well-founded as moderates in the Nashville Convention rejected secession as an appropriate response to the restriction of slavery in the territories while at the same time reaffirming the constitutionality of its so-called "peculiar institution." Although moderates controlled the convention, the delegates declined to support the Omnibus Bill proposed by Henry Clay, which would eventually be enacted and known as the Compromise of 1850. The delegates nevertheless did manage to offer an apparent concession by proposing an extension of the geographical dividing line between slave and free territory—first established by the Missouri Compromise of 1820—to the Pacific Ocean.[34]

After the legislation encompassing the Compromise of 1850 passed in September 1850, it became the central issue in the 1851 elections in Alabama, as a result of which Unionists won five out of seven congressional seats, losing only those representing Mobile and Wetumpka. The secessionists were soundly defeated as moderation continued to prevail. Support for the preservation of the Union and compromise had grown stronger within the state when the national Democratic Party backed the Compromise of 1850 and nominated Franklin Pierce as President and Alabama's William Rufus King as Vice President. In 1852, the state was bestowed another honor when President Pierce appointed Alabama's John A. Campbell to the United States Supreme Court. For now, participation in the national government, restraint, and compromise ruled the day.[35]

---

[33] Moore, *History of Alabama*, 241.

[34] The Compromise of 1850 consisted of five bills that collectively were intended to ease tensions between the North and the South. These bills contained the following proposals: California was to be admitted into the Union as a free state; New Mexico and Utah would be allowed to utilize the doctrine of popular sovereignty to decide the issue as to whether they would be admitted as slave or free states; Texas would relinquish claims to lands in New Mexico and was to be given $10 million to pay its indebtedness to Mexico; the slave trade was to be abolished in the District of Columbia; and the Fugitive Slave Act was to provide for strengthened measures to assure the return of runaway slaves, including fines of $1,000 to be imposed on federal officials who failed to arrest runaways.

[35] Rogers et al., *Alabama*, 162–63; Moore, *History of Alabama*, 251–53. King, who had been ill with tuberculosis throughout the presidential campaign, went to the warmer climate of Cuba at the advice of his doctors. With his condition worsening and it becoming obvious that King could not travel to Washington for the inauguration, Congress passed a special act allowing him to take the oath of office in Cuba. King thus owns the distinction of being the only American elected official to assume office on foreign soil. When King realized that he was not going to improve, he returned to his Alabama plantation in Dallas County where he died the day after his arrival on April 18, 1853. Daniel Fate Brooks, "William Rufus King,"

During the 1851 congressional elections, fiery secessionist William Lowndes Yancey participated in a series of debates with Henry Hilliard, a Unionist and the leader of Alabama's Whig Party. Oddly, Yancey and Hilliard were not themselves candidates for Congress, but were speaking on behalf of candidates seeking to represent the Montgomery district in the House of Representatives—James Abercrombie of the Whig Party and John Cochran of the Southern Rights faction of the Democratic Party. Both Yancey and Hilliard had previously served in Congress but were now leading their respective interests without the burdens of office. While Hilliard had become disillusioned with Congress and did not wish to seek reelection, he was resolute in his desire to prevent his former seat from falling into the hands of the Democrats and agreed to stump for Abercrombie. Similarly, Yancey, who had resigned his seat in Congress because he did not believe that he could wield enough power in that body, was eager to help elect another Southern Rights advocate.[36]

Although having willingly agreed to speak on Abercrombie's behalf throughout the district, when Yancey's supporters urged a series of debates between Hilliard and Yancey instead of the candidates, Hilliard announced his intention not to participate in any heated exchanges, but rather would "confer quietly with my old constituents without interruption." This announcement resulted in acrimonious criticism from the secessionist press which proclaimed that Hilliard was afraid to take on Yancey face to face. Hilliard eventually gave in when Yancey and his supporters showed up for an announced engagement in Union Springs and demanded to be heard on the issues important to the voters of the district. With his hand thus forced, Hilliard agreed to proceed, but only under an organized structure of debate with Hilliard having the right to make the closing remarks.[37]

During the ensuing debates, Hilliard and Yancey repeated the positions that they had formulated over the last few years. Hilliard emphasized his

---

Encyclopedia of Alabama, http://www.encyclopediaofalabama.org/face/Article.jsp?id=h-1886 (accessed February 5, 2013).

[36] Durham, *A Southern Moderate in Radical Times*, 120–21. Henry Hilliard, like Yancey, was a fascinating figure with talents as a lawyer, scholar, preacher, editor, politician, and orator. A native of North Carolina, Hilliard graduated from South Carolina College (now the University of South Carolina) in 1826, was admitted to the bar in Athens, Georgia, in 1829, served as a Methodist minister, and was appointed to chair the English Department at the newly opened University of Alabama in 1831. Thereafter, he practiced law in Montgomery and served in the state House of Representatives from 1836 until 1838. He later was a member of the Whig National Convention of 1839 in Harrisburg, Pennsylvania. En route to the convention, he developed a relationship with future president John Tyler of Virginia. That relationship would ultimately secure him appointment as Chargé d'Affaires to Belgium in May 1842. After his diplomatic stint in Belgium, Hilliard served three terms in the U.S. Congress from March 4, 1845 until March 3, 1851, where he preached Unionism and became a supporter of the Compromise of 1850. Despite his strong pro-Union stance, Hilliard served as a brigadier general in the Confederate Army once the issue of secession had been decided. After the war, he served as the U.S. Minister to Brazil from 1877 until 1881 and during that service became a supporter of the emancipation of Brazil's slaves. Hilliard died in Atlanta, Georgia, on December 17, 1892, and was buried in Montgomery's Oakwood Cemetery.

[37] Durham, *A Southern Moderate in Radical Times*, 120–21; George F. Mellen, "Henry W. Hilliard and William L. Yancey," *The Sewanee Review* 17 (January 1909): 41–43.

support of the Compromise of 1850 and his firm belief that no state could legally secede from the Union. Yancey, on the other hand, condemned the Whig administration of President Fillmore as anti-slavery, repeated his opposition to the Compromise of 1850, and promoted secession as the answer to the South's problems. On a more personal level, Yancey condemned Hilliard for currying favor and friendships with northern abolitionists, while Hilliard warned that if the South yielded to Yancey's call for secession, a bloody war would follow resulting in the destruction of the world's greatest government. Hilliard also attacked Yancey's previous vote in Congress for a bill to organize a territorial government for Oregon. That bill also contained the Wilmot Proviso which would prohibit slavery in the new territory. Yancey tried to explain that his intent was to vote for a bill to *organize* the Oregon territory. Unfortunately, he had inadvertently used the word *admit* instead of *organize*, and thus Hilliard took advantage of the misstatement. A Whig newspaper, the *Eufaula Southern Shield*, reported that Yancey was so angered by Hilliard's hypercritical tactics that he used "rough and uncouth language" and was "anything but courteous" due to the perceived "unfairness and disingenuousness" of Hilliard's attack.[38]

Hilliard and Yancey concluded their canvassing in Montgomery with a lavish barbecue and a five-hour debate that the *Alabama Journal* described as a "struggle of giants—both were worthy champions." The *Journal* further noted that although "[n]o one could have defended a bad cause better than did Mr. Yancey, . . . his heart did not seem to be in it." Yancey was undoubtedly disheartened because he sensed the victory that was soon to envelop the Whig Party. In the Montgomery district in which Yancey and Hilliard had pushed so hard for their respective candidates, James Abercrombie of the Union Whig ticket easily out-polled John Cochran, the secessionist candidate, 56.2 percent to 43.8 percent. Even more disturbing to Yancey and the secessionists was the fact, as seen previously, that Unionists won five out of seven congressional seats, losing only those representing Mobile and Wetumpka. At least for now the secessionist movement in Alabama was thwarted.[39]

---

[38] Walther, *William Lowndes Yancey,* 139–40; Durham, *A Southern Moderate in Radical Times,* 122–23; Mellen, "Henry W. Hilliard and William L. Yancey," 44–46. Unionists and anti-Unionists had been going after each other since the 1840s and on at least one occasion went further than "rough and uncouth language" in their ongoing contest. In this regard, in April 1841 a Montgomery newspaper reported, "Serious riots, in which life has been lost, have occurred at the recent elections in Cahaba between the Unionists and anti-Unionists...." *Alabama Journal,* April 14, 1841.

[39] Despite these victories, the Whig Party soon began to fall apart nationally over the slavery issue. This left Hilliard and other southern Whigs scrambling for political cover as many northern Whigs aligned with the anti-slavery Free Soil Movement. Hilliard's call for party leaders to reorganize the party was too late causing Hilliard and others to temporarily align with the nativist Know-Nothing Party. Although Hilliard was uncomfortable with the anti-Catholic and anti-foreigner sentiments of the Know-Nothings, he was attracted to the party due to his support for Millard Fillmore and the fact that there was really nowhere else to turn. During Hilliard's tenure with the Know-Nothings he was criticized for his inconsistency as he began to espouse positions that were more attuned with that of the radical Southern Rights faction than those moderate positions he previously advocated during his years in the Whig Party. With Fillmore's defeat and the demise of the Know-Nothings, Hilliard wound up in the

Alabama's Unionist propensity continued for a while with the election of John A. Winston as governor in 1853. Winston had defied fire-eater William Lowndes Yancey at the 1848 Democratic convention by persuading Alabama's delegates not to walk out in protest over the convention's failure to give credence to Yancey's Alabama Platform. With the enactment of the bills encompassing the Compromise of 1850, Winston again rejected the radicalism of Yancey and his fellow fire-eaters. In reaction to the formation of the Unionist Whig Party—a coalition of north Alabama Democrats and south Alabama Whigs—in 1850-51, Winston reorganized the Democratic Party along its established partisan lines. He brought north Alabama Democrats back into the fold by disparaging the arrogance of the Whigs and extolling the virtue of the Democratic spoils system. For his efforts, he was awarded the Democratic nomination for governor in 1853. The Whig candidate, Richard Wilde Walker, became ill and had to withdraw, leaving Winston with only token opposition. As a result, Winston was easily elected as Alabama's fifteenth governor.[40]

John Winston, who was born on September 4, 1812, in Madison County, Alabama, became the first Alabama governor to be born within the state. After attending LaGrange College in Florence, Alabama, and Cumberland College in Nashville, Tennessee, he married Mary Agnes Walker in 1832. In 1835 Winston and his wife moved to Sumter County where they settled on a large plantation. Winston soon entered politics as a states' rights Democrat and was elected to the Alabama House of Representatives in 1840 and reelected in 1842. Thereafter, he served in the state senate from 1843 to 1853, and became a leader of the states' rights faction of the Democratic Party when he served as president of the senate from 1845 to 1849.[41]

In addition to being a successful political leader, Winston was a thriving businessman as well. He operated a cotton commission firm in Mobile and owned large plantations in Alabama, Mississippi, Arkansas, and Texas. Despite his political influence and business success, Winston demonstrated that he was the product of the frontier society that still prevailed in Alabama. After his first wife died in 1842, Winston married Mary W. Longwood. His new wife soon thereafter commenced an affair with Dr. Sidney S. Perry, who was their family physician as well as Winston's friend and fellow legislator. When Winston found out about the affair in 1847, he took matters into his own hands and shot Perry to death. Winston, however, escaped facing a jury of his peers when the county magistrate ruled that the shoot-

---

Democratic Party since Alabama was then a one-party state. Unable to secure public office in the party of his former opponents, Hilliard returned to his roots as a Whig and continued his promotion of sectional tolerance and support of the Union. He also locked horns with Yancey once again by lobbying against his forces and the Alabama Platform at the 1860 Democratic convention in Charleston. Hilliard continued to resist secession and only agreed to support the Confederate government after Lincoln called for troops to resist the secessionist states. Durham, *A Southern Moderate in Radical Times*, 126–41; Mellen, "Henry W. Hilliard and William L. Yancey," 47; Walther, *William Lowndes Yancey*, 140.

[40] William L. Barney, "John A. Winston," in *Alabama Governors*, 61–62; Rogers et al., *Alabama*, 163.

[41] Barney, "John A. Winston," 61.

ing constituted "justifiable homicide." Undoubtedly, Winston's political influence and an informal code of frontier justice protected him from even a charge of manslaughter. Winston's conduct was further legitimated when the legislature granted him a divorce in 1850 and when the people of Alabama elected him governor in 1853.[42]

During his inaugural address on December 20, 1853, Winston reiterated his Jacksonian campaign stances in opposition to the use of state funds to aid private corporations engaged in transportation and banking. He indicated a willingness to use state funds for internal improvements only if the state's debt resulting from the failure of the State Bank of Alabama was completely eradicated. He would then, and only then, favor the use of a treasury surplus to fund adequately secured loans for such purposes. With the State still in debt, however, Winston steadfastly resisted the efforts of those pushing state aid for railroads by vetoing the bills, often with acrimonious messages that further acerbated those seeking to keep pace with the surrounding states' expansion of their railroads. The legislature did manage to enact a few state-aid bills over Winston's veto during his first term, including one providing for a loan of $400,000 to the Mobile and Ohio Railroad, to which the city of Mobile had already provided $1.1 million.[43]

Although often at odds, the legislature and Governor Winston managed to come together a few times to pass legislation beneficial to the state, particularly that which created Alabama's free public education system on February 15, 1854. The most significant legislation passed during Governor Winston's first term created a state superintendent of education, appropriated $100,000 to be divided among the counties, and authorized the counties to collect real estate and personal property taxes for educational purposes. In a circular outlining the provisions of the Public Education Act, William F. Perry, who was elected by the legislature as the state's first superintendent of education, urged Alabama's citizens to "not be deaf to the mute persuasions of her one hundred thousand ignorant and neglected children, or insensible to the claims which posterity holds upon them for an inheritance of intelligence, virtue and freedom."[44]

Despite his willingness to fund free public education in the state, Governor Winston's frugalness prompted him to veto another worthy bill appropriating $150,000 for the completion of the State Hospital for the Insane, which had been authorized by the legislature in 1851. While Governor Winston frustrated his fellow Democratic politicians with his vetoes, particularly those involving aid to the railroads, most voters approved of his efforts in protecting the public's money and he was thus nominated with ease by the Democratic Party in 1855 for a second term. His opposition in the general election came from George D. Shortridge, who received the

[42] Ibid.

[43] Barney, "John A. Winston," 62; Moore, *History of Alabama*, 254; Rogers et al., *Alabama*, 166.

[44] *Ala. Acts (1853)*, 8–18; J. L. M. Curry pamphlet collection, LPR 100, Alabama Department of Archives and History (ADAH), Montgomery, Alabama. See also Perry, "The Genesis of Public Education in Alabama," 14–27.

nomination of the new Know-Nothing Party. Also known as the American Party, the Know-Nothing Party was composed of a fusion of former Whigs and Union Democrats. Starting out as a secret organization with grips and passwords, the Know-Nothings were openly prejudiced against foreigners and Roman Catholics, while also supporting Congressional protection of slavery in the territories. Shortridge aimed his message to those favoring state aid to the railroads and reformers who were upset with Governor Winston's vetoes. Although Winston won the election with almost sixty percent of the vote, Shortridge managed to poll the largest vote to date against a Democratic candidate for governor, in part due to the railroad aid issue.[45]

While at first ecstatic over his overwhelming victory—as evidenced by his November 1855 biennial message to the legislature in which he praised the "sober common sense of the people" in rejecting the "mania" of the railroad lobby—Governor Winston soon discovered that the new legislature was even more sympathetic to giving state aid to the railroads than the previous one. This came about as a result of north Alabama Democrats nominating railroad men for the legislature in an effort to stop defections to the Know-Nothing Party. These Democrats, along with the Know-Nothings who were elected to the legislature, forced Governor Winston to a position of further defiance from which he would not back down. In his second term Winston stood his ground by vetoing thirty-three bills which primarily dealt with the lending of state funds or concessions to private corporations. Twenty-seven of these vetoes, however, were overturned by the legislature.[46]

During Winston's tenure as governor, the nation continued to wrestle with how to deal with slavery in the territories. In 1854 the Kansas–Nebraska Act was passed which created the territories of Kansas and Nebraska, repealed the Missouri Compromise of 1820, and left it to the settlers of those territories to determine whether or not their states would be admitted as slave or free. The turmoil created by this act resulted in the creation of the Republican Party, which would become the predominant party of the North. It also resulted in violence as pro-slavery and anti-slavery forces vied to gain control in Kansas. The fear that the violence in Kansas evoked prompted Governor Winston to recommend in his last message to the legislature that the state undergo military preparation.[47]

---

[45] Barney, "John A. Winston," 63; Moore, *History of Alabama*, 255–56. According to A. B. Moore, the campaign between Winston and Shortridge was tense, and the Know-Nothing mania resulted in ministers attacking the Catholic Church and a priest and a few foreigners being flogged in Mobile.

[46] Garrett, *Reminiscences*, 620; Barney, "John A. Winston," 63.

[47] Moore, *History of Alabama*, 261. Although the voting public had approved of Winston's austere fiscal policies while governor, party leaders who favored state aid for railroads were opposed to his advancement in politics. Because of this, and as a result of incumbent Clement Comer Clay's stronger states' rights credentials, Winston failed in his bid to become a U.S. Senator in 1857. Winston's next involvement in Alabama politics came on the eve of the Civil War when he attended the 1860 Democratic convention in Charleston, South Carolina, where he supported the candidacy of Stephen A. Douglas—whom he believed could keep the Union intact—before the Alabama delegation walked out of the convention. During the Civil War,

Andrew B. Moore succeeded Winston as Alabama's sixteenth governor in 1857. Although a moderate on the issue of secession when elected, Moore was governor when Alabama finally seceded from the Union in January 1861. Moore was born in the Spartanburg district of South Carolina on March 7, 1801. His father, Charles Moore, was a veteran of the Revolutionary War and the War of 1812. Charles joined an elder son in Perry County, Alabama, in 1820, where they established a plantation a few miles west of Marion. Andrew Moore did not join his family until 1826, at which time he began to teach school in Marion. Two years later he read law with two local lawyers and was admitted to the bar in 1833. He served as justice of the peace for several years before winning election to the state House of Representatives in 1839 on the Democratic ticket.[48]

Defeated by a Whig in the next election, Moore was nonetheless able to regain his seat in 1842. In the next legislative session, Moore oddly went against the sentiments of his electorate by supporting the white basis for determining representation in the legislature. Because of this, he again received strong opposition from the Whigs. This time, however, he managed to get reelected despite his unpopular stance on the representation issue. His strength in the Whig stronghold of Perry County was demonstrated by his successful elections in 1843, 1844, and 1845, and his election as Speaker of the House for these three terms.[49]

As Speaker of the House, Moore supported Governor Fitzpatrick's efforts to liquidate the State Bank of Alabama, the move of the state capital from Tuscaloosa to Montgomery, and the constitutional amendment providing for biennial sessions of the legislature instead of annual sessions. Upon retiring from public office in 1846, Moore resumed the practice of law in Marion and remained active in Democratic Party politics. In 1848 he served as a presidential elector for the Democratic ticket of Lewis Cass and William Butler and was a delegate to the 1850 Nashville Convention, which debated the issue of secession. He returned to public service in 1851 when he was appointed by Governor Winston to fill a vacancy of the First Circuit Court. He remained on that court until 1857 when he was nominated by the Democratic Party as its candidate for governor.[50]

Moore's gubernatorial nomination did not come easily, as he faced stiff opposition from several opponents, three of whom were extreme states' rightists. Moore nevertheless took a moderate stance on secession arguing that there was not yet sufficient justification for secession and that the national Democratic Party would adequately defend Southern rights within

Winston raised troops and served with the Eighth Alabama Infantry during the Virginia peninsula campaign of 1862. After the war, he was finally elected to the U.S. Senate in 1867, but was denied his seat by the Republican Congress for refusing to take an oath of allegiance to the United States. Winston died on December 1, 1871. Barney, "John A. Winston," 64–65; Garrett, *Reminiscences*, 726–27.

[48] Owen, *History of Alabama*, 4: 1222; Brewer, *Alabama*, 490; Leah Rawls Atkins, "Andrew B. Moore," in *Alabama Governors*, 65–66.

[49] Garrett, *Reminiscences*, 720.

[50] Owen, *History of Alabama*, 4: 1222; Atkins, "Andrew B. Moore," 66–67; Garrett, *Reminiscences*, 721.

the Union. It was only after twenty-six ballots that he was able to secure the nomination. Moore easily won the general election, however, since no formal opposition was forthcoming from the Whigs or Know-Nothings. The Democratic Party was now the only viable political party within Alabama, but it would soon be splintered when its extreme states' rights wing attempted to break ties with the national Democratic Party to form a Southern Rights party.[51]

Despite the unease that prevailed over the nation as the slavery issue continued to fester, Moore's first term as governor was relatively uneventful. The legislature, however, did authorize the governor to call a state convention in the event that Congress refused to admit Kansas under the pro-slavery Lecompton constitution. On the domestic front, construction was begun on the state hospital for the insane in Tuscaloosa, and the school for the deaf and blind opened in Talladega. Unlike Governor Winston, Moore supported railroad construction and urged the completion of the Alabama and Tennessee Rivers Railroad. He also called for increased appropriations for the new Alabama public school system.[52]

In the meantime, William Lowndes Yancey continued to push for immediate secession in concert with Edmund Ruffin of Virginia and Robert Barnwell Rhett of South Carolina. To this end, in 1858 Yancey began to form the Leagues of United Southerners and urged the creation of Committees of Safety, which he hoped would spawn a revolution among the cotton states. Within this fiery climate, Moore's previous moderate stance on the issue of secession drew him opposition in his bid for reelection. Although Moore was renominated by the Democratic Party, William F. Samford, an avid secessionist and member of the Yancey faction, ran against him as an "independent Southern Rights candidate." Samford campaigned against Moore asserting a lack of "earnest, active, outspoken sympathy" in Moore's support of the Southern cause. Moore nevertheless won decisively and continued his cautious approach toward secession in light of his belief that there still was not sufficient cause to force Alabama out of the Union.[53]

Moore soon changed his mind and became more open to secession after the raid led by abolitionist John Brown at Harpers Ferry, Virginia, in October 1859. White Alabamians, like most white Southerners, were terrified by Brown's attempt to instigate an armed slave revolt by seizing the United States Arsenal at Harpers Ferry. While the attack was repelled by a unit of U.S. Marines led by Col. Robert E. Lee and Brown was hung for treason, the psychological impact of the raid was tremendous.[54]

As evidence of the concern Brown's raid generated in Alabama, during the 1859–1860 legislative session of the Alabama General Assembly, Governor Moore secured the passage of several acts to ready the state to

---

[51] Moore, *History of Alabama*, 258; Atkins, "Andrew B. Moore," 67.

[52] Moore, *History of Alabama*, 261; Atkins, "Andrew B. Moore," 67.

[53] Malcolm C. McMillan, ed., *The Alabama Confederate Leader* (1963; repr., Tuscaloosa: University of Alabama Press, 1991), 1–2; Moore, *History of Alabama*, 258–59.

[54] Atkins, "Andrew B. Moore," 67.

defend itself from attacks such as that carried out at Harpers Ferry. The most sweeping bill provided for a militia of no more than 8,000 men to be composed of volunteers from each county in the state. The bill also appropriated $200,000 to equip these volunteer units. Another bill provided for funding to send two young men from each county to a military school who agreed to return to their counties and utilize their learning to help train their county's volunteers. Other bills provided for the establishment of a military department at the University of Alabama and the furnishing of arms to cadets at LaGrange College and Military Academy.[55]

As the push for leaving the Union continued, Governor Moore—despite becoming more open to the idea of secession—opposed South Carolina Governor William H. Gist's call for a convention of the slaveholding states to consult on secession prior to the election of 1860. Instead, Moore supported a joint resolution of the Alabama Legislature passed on February 24, 1860, that required him to call for an election of delegates to a secession convention in the event of the election of a "black Republican" as president. A convention was required to be called within forty days of such an election for delegates "to consider, determine and do whatever in the opinion of the said convention, the rights, interests and honor of the State of Alabama requires to be done for their protection." Moore's stance was dictated by his belief that the Democratic candidate would win in 1860, thus forestalling secession once again.[56]

The chance that a Democratic candidate would win the 1860 presidential election, however, was made impossible by the split in the national party fueled by Yancey and the other so-called "fire-eaters." Alabama Democrats met in January 1860 to elect delegates to the national Democratic convention to be held in April in Charleston, South Carolina. Yancey's supporters beat out conservatives who supported Stephen A. Douglas' nomination, to gain control of the meeting. Yancey's delegates were therefore validated by the credentials committee chairman John Tyler Morgan. These delegates included such personages as Francis S. Lyons, John A. Winston, Reuben Chapman, Leroy Pope Walker, and Alexander Beaufort Meek. Alabama's delegation was instructed to follow the mandate of the Alabama Platform and walk out of the national convention if a guarantee was not included in the Democratic platform for the protection of slavery in the territories.[57]

Yancey and his supporters succeeded in having the Alabama Platform included within the majority report of the platform committee at the national Democratic convention. Amidst thunderous applause and flowers thrown by women in the gallery, Yancey eloquently argued for adoption of the majority report but was unable to win over enough northern delegates to secure its adoption by the full convention. As a result, the Alabama delegates walked out of the convention after Leroy Pope Walker read a formal

---

[55] *Ala. Acts (1859)*, 25–26, 36, and 90–92.

[56] *Ala. Acts (1859)*, 685–87; Atkins, "Andrew B. Moore," 68.

[57] Rogers et al., *Alabama*, 181–82.

protest. Other slave states followed and the shocked remaining delegates voted to adjourn and meet later in the summer to nominate a candidate.[58]

The northern Democrats reconvened in Baltimore in June 1860 and nominated Stephen A. Douglas, who continued to champion the popular sovereignty doctrine. The southern Democrats, meeting separately in Richmond, Virginia, also in June 1860, nominated Kentuckian John C. Breckinridge, who was the outgoing vice president serving with President James Buchanan. Breckinridge was nominated to run on a pro-slavery platform that held the rights of slave owners in the territories as sacrosanct. John Bell of Tennessee was nominated by the Constitutional Union Party composed of former southern Whigs and Know-Nothings, advocating a compromise between the North and South in hopes of preserving the Union. The Republican Party, which had been gaining strength among anti-slavery advocates in the North since its founding in 1854, nominated Abraham Lincoln.[59]

The split in the Democratic Party virtually assured a Republican victory. Yancey, in yet another futile effort, nevertheless campaigned in the North for Breckinridge. Almost as futile, Douglas campaigned in Alabama where he only carried five counties—Mobile, Lauderdale, Lawrence, Madison, and Marshall. Douglas' prospects in Alabama were not good to begin with, but obviously were not improved by a quote attributed to him in which he injudiciously proclaimed that he "would hang as high as Virginia hung John Brown, any man who would not submit to Lincoln rule." Ironically, Douglas was a guest in Mobile's Battle House Hotel the night that he and the other candidates lost the election to Lincoln. Lincoln, who was not even on the ballot in the South, won the election with only 39 percent of the popular vote. With the Democratic Party severely fragmented, Lincoln was able to carry all but one of the more populous northern states, thus gaining the necessary majority of the electoral votes. Breckinridge, who carried most of Alabama's counties, finished second in the Electoral College ahead of Bell and Douglas. Surprisingly, Douglas who finished second to Lincoln in terms of the popular vote, finished last in the Electoral College.[60]

Lincoln's election forced Governor Moore's hand to call for a special election to choose delegates for a convention to consider secession. With some thought of waiting for the formality of the vote of the Electoral College, on December 6, 1860, Moore nevertheless issued the summons for the election to be held on December 24, 1860. Obviously anticipating secession and a likely war, the governor also sent agents up north to obtain arma-

---

[58] Ibid.

[59] Moore, *History of Alabama*, 266–67.

[60] Rogers et al., *Alabama*, 182–83; *Mobile Register*, May 4, 2007, http://blog.al.com/pr/2007/05/battle_house_a_symbol_of_hospi.html; Melvin Durward Long, "Political Parties and Propaganda in Alabama in the Presidential Election of 1860," *Alabama Historical Quarterly* 25 (Spring and Summer 1963): 131; Carter Smith, *Presidents: Every Question Answered* (New York: Metro Books, 2008), 102.

ments for the state's militia as well as commissioners to compatriot southern states to seek their views on secession.[61]

On January 3, 1861, just four days before Alabama's secession convention was scheduled to convene, Governor Moore suddenly ordered the seizure of federal military installations within the state. Moore had taken this extraordinary step after receiving a telegram from Georgia's governor suggesting that federal military assets should be taken over as a precautionary measure. Moore was also possibly motivated by rumors that the federal government was about to reinforce its installations in the South and the unexpected appearance in Mobile Bay of the *USS Crusader*, a small naval vessel that was incorrectly believed to be carrying federal troops. In any event, Governor Moore telegraphed the state militia colonel at Mobile to immediately seize the federal arsenal at Mount Vernon, which was located approximately thirty miles north of Mobile. The seizure of the arsenal—probably the most valuable military asset in the state—resulted in a treasure trove for the state militia consisting of 20,000 rifles, 150,000 pounds of gunpowder, a number of canons and various other munitions. The seizure was accomplished in the middle of the night without a fight while its inhabitants slept. Bloodless seizures also occurred at minimally defended Forts Morgan and Gaines, which were located on opposite shores at the entrance to Mobile Bay.[62]

Governor Moore informed President Buchanan of the seizures and assured him that they were undertaken "simply as a precautionary movement to protect the State and not an act of hostility towards the Federal Government, of which we continue an integral part." Alabama's status, however, was about to change with the convening of the secession convention in Montgomery on January 7, 1861. The main contest for delegates to that convention had been between "straight-out secessionists," who favored immediate secession and "cooperationists," who favored secession in concert with other Southern states. There were also factions that opposed secession including "Unionists," who favored giving the North one more chance to redress their grievances, and the "ultra-Unionists," who opposed secession under any circumstances. The "straight-out secessionists" led by Yancey managed to get control of the convention by electing a slight majority of the delegates—electing 54 delegates while all the other factions combined elected 46 delegates.[63]

When the delegates convened there was an attempt by north Alabama cooperationists to have the secession ordinance submitted directly to the people for ratification. With the "straight-out secessionists" in control of the

---

[61] Rogers et al., *Alabama*, 183; Atkins, "Andrew B. Moore," 68; William L. Barney, *The Secessionist Impulse: Alabama and Mississippi in 1860* (Princeton, N.J.: Princeton University Press, 1974), 203.

[62] Adam Goodheart, "Caught Sleeping," Disunion Series, Opinion Section, *New York Times*, January 3, 2011: http://opinionator.blogs.nytimes.com/2011/01/03/caught-sleeping/ (accessed January 31, 2013); Moore, *History of Alabama*, 418.

[63] Rogers et al., *Alabama*, 183; Moore, *History of Alabama*, 412–16.

THE CITY OF MONTGOMERY, ALABAMA, SHOWING THE STATE HOUSE WHERE THE CONGRESS OF THE SOUTHERN CONFEDERACY MEETS ON FEBRUARY 4, 1861.

Secession Ordinance Approved February 4, 1861

Courtesy of Alabama Department of Archives and History

convention, however, this proposal failed, and an ordinance for immediate secession was passed by a vote of 61 to 39 on January 11, 1861, proclaiming: "Be it declared and ordained by the people of the State of Alabama in Convention assembled, That the State of Alabama now withdraws, and is hereby withdrawn from the Union known as 'the United States of America', and henceforth ceases to be one of said United States, and is, and of right ought to be, a Sovereign and Independent State." The resolution also contained an invitation to the other slaveholding states to meet in Montgomery on February 4, 1861, "in order to frame a provisional as well as a permanent Government upon the principles of the Constitution of the United States."[64]

Alabama had only been a state for forty-one years when it withdrew from the Union. Not appreciating the terrible consequences that this drastic step would bring on Alabama and the rest of the South, Montgomerians wildly celebrated when they learned that the secession ordinance had passed. Canons were fired, bells were ringing, bonfires blazed, bombastic speeches were made, music blared, and citizens joyfully demonstrated throughout the night. Montgomerians had not seen such a celebration since the visit of a Revolutionary War hero, the Marquis de Lafayette, in 1825. While most citizens rejoiced in Montgomery and south Alabama, quite a

---

[64] *Alabama Ordinance of Secession* (1861); Moore, *History of Alabama*, 420; "The Secession Convention" and "Delegates to the Alabama Secession Convention," *Alabama Historical Quarterly* 3 (Fall and Winter 1941): 287–356, 368–71.

272 • CLEARING THE THICKETS

few staunch Unionists in north Alabama considered seceding from Alabama and forming the new state of "Nickajack" that would include north Alabama and parts of east Tennessee and north Georgia that opposed secession. Likewise, Unionists in Winston County also threatened to secede from Alabama to form "the Free State of Winston."[65]

In response to the invitation in Alabama's ordinance of secession, delegates from the states that had seceded to date—Alabama, Florida, Georgia, Louisiana, Mississippi, and South Carolina—met in Montgomery on February 4, 1861, to form a provisional government to be known as the Confederate States of America. These delegates also elected Jefferson Davis as president and Alexander H. Stephens as vice president of this new government. During the few months that Montgomery served as the seat of the new national Confederate government, Governor Moore kept a low profile. He did quietly go about the business of appointing an adjutant general and a quartermaster general for the state and taking measures to protect the state's supplies and food from unscrupulous speculators.[66]

Moore was the last governor to serve before Alabama's secession. He continued to serve after secession, until December 2, 1861, when he was succeeded by John Gill Shorter. Governor Shorter then appointed Moore as a special aide de camp to coordinate the procurement and transportation of supplies to Confederate forces in north Alabama led by General Albert Sydney Johnston. At the conclusion of the war, Moore was arrested by federal troops and imprisoned at Fort Pulaski near Savannah, Georgia, along with other Confederate officials. He was released in August 1865 due to health concerns, and returned to Marion where he resumed the practice of law until his death in 1873.[67]

When Montgomery became Alabama's fifth capital in 1846, the nation was divided over the slavery issue. This division intensified even more after the Mexican War when the debate began as to how slavery was to be dealt with in the territories acquired as a result of that war. As Montgomerians rejoiced upon learning of the movement of the state's capital from Tuscaloosa to Montgomery, few believed that the dispute would lead to Alabama actually seceding from the Union and Montgomery serving briefly as the capital of a rogue nation. In the short span of fifteen years, however, that exact unlikely scenario came to reality. As a result, Alabama's frontier stage ended with a war rather than a period during which its cotton based economy would be diversified by the development of the state's plentiful natural resources. Alabamians' decision in favor of secession and war would set them back socially, politically, economically, and psychologically for generations to come.

---

[65] Rogers et al., *Alabama*, 183–84; Moore, *History of Alabama*, 421.

[66] Moore, *History of Alabama*, 423–24; Atkins, "Andrew B. Moore," 68–69.

[67] Atkins, "Andrew B. Moore," 68–69.

Montgomery County Court House, 1854

Courtesy of Robert Fouts, from his collection www.HistoricMontgomery.com, used by permission

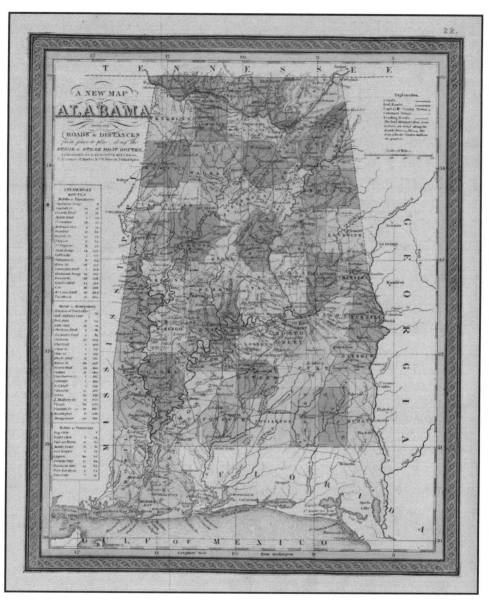

"A New Map Of Alabama with its Canals, Roads, Distances from Place to Place, along the Stage & Steam Boat Routes"

1849, published by Philadelphia mapmaker Samuel Augustus Mitchell

Courtesy Barry Lawrence Ruderman Antique Maps, used by permission

12

.𝕩.

SOCIAL AND ECONOMIC ADVANCES
OF FRONTIER ERA END WITH WAR

Alabama was emerging from its frontier stage in the 1850s, ironically, just as the disastrous course of secession loomed on the horizon. Secession ensured that Alabama's emergence from its frontier phase would carry it into a devastating war rather than into a period of industrialization and a diversification of its slave-based agricultural economy. The previous chapters have chronicled the efforts of colonial powers to bring pockets of civilization to Alabama before it came under American control. They further related how territorial Alabama emerged from a raw frontier into a fully functioning state providing much needed order to its citizens. Specifically, we saw how government was shaped to provide protection for its new citizens who had suffered from the violence associated with an untamed frontier. This violence emanated from both a rough and rowdy element that flourished in the absence of lawful authority and from that imposed upon them by Native Americans whose lands they had invaded upon their arrival in the territory that was to become Alabama.

In relating Alabama's transformation from a frontier society, this book has concentrated on political and governmental issues such as the development of the government in its formative stages, the politics involved in the efforts to decide upon a permanent seat of government, how banking issues dominated early politics, and how the state's reliance on its "peculiar institution" of slavery led to its fateful decision to secede from the Union. In this final chapter, we take a closer look at the social and economic transformations that were occurring during this time frame and how they were also interrupted by the tragedy of secession and war.

Alabama's frontier psyche was persistent even in the face of the social development of the state prior to the Civil War. In the 1850s after Alabama began emerging from its frontier status, vestiges of a frontier code of justice remained. As we have seen, as late as 1859 Associate Justice George Stone of the Alabama Supreme Court lamented that too many Montgomery citizens carried deadly weapons that "were readily drawn, and fatally employed, in resentment of injuries and insults of the most trivial character." This is an indication that that at least remnants of the violent nature of frontier life remained in Alabama up until secession when it was replaced by the collective sanctioned violence afforded by the advent of the Civil War.[1]

---

[1] Howington, "Violence in Alabama," 215. Matthew Blue recorded several violent incidents involving the use of deadly weapons on the streets of Montgomery during the 1850s, including

The violence of Alabama's frontier was no better evidenced than by *Code Duello*'s presence within Alabama from its territorial days up until the time of secession, despite stringent laws against it. Dueling had been first outlawed by the Mississippi Territorial Assembly by laws enacted in 1803 and 1804, which were incorporated into the Territorial Digest of 1807. These laws made it a felony punishable by a fine of $1,000, imprisonment for twelve months, and a five-year prohibition against holding a government office for any person even participating in an arrangement for a duel. If a duel was actually held and either party was killed, the survivor and all those who had aided and assisted in the duel were to be deemed guilty of "willful murder" and were subject to a death penalty if convicted. Similar laws were enacted by Alabama's first legislature in 1819. An additional measure was then enacted that required all public officials and attorneys to take an oath affirming that they had not participated in a duel since January 1, 1820, nor would they do so during their term of office. Furthermore, anyone guilty of proclaiming in a newspaper or hand bill "any other person or persons, as a coward, or use any opprobrious and abusive language," for not accepting a challenge or fighting a duel, would be subject to a fine of up to five hundred dollars.[2]

Hot-headedness and false chivalry nevertheless often ruled the day. As we have seen, this was certainly true among some of Alabama's early leaders. If tempers flared too quickly, some disputants were unfortunately shot on sight without the benefit of a gentlemanly challenge to a duel. Such was the case with John A. Winston, Alabama's fifteenth governor. In 1847 Winston shot his physician in cold blood upon learning that the doctor was having an affair with his wife. Winston, however, never faced a jury of his peers because the county magistrate ruled that the shooting constituted "justifiable homicide." Choosing the more gentlemanly approach, Gabriel Moore, another early Alabama governor, was involved in a duel with his ex-wife's brother. Although neither party was killed, Moore's opponent did sustain a bullet wound in his arm. A third major figure in Alabama politics, secessionist William Lowndes Yancey, was convicted of manslaughter for shooting his wife's uncle during a heated argument while visiting family in South Carolina in 1838. Yancey, who had pled self-defense, was fined $1,000 and sentenced to one year in prison. Yancey only served three months of his imprisonment before South Carolina's governor commuted his sentence, freeing Yancey to return to Alabama to resume his political career.[3]

Alabama was also the site of duels between antagonists from out of state. One such duel involved General Sowell Woolfolk and Major John T.

---

murders in front of the Exchange Hotel and in a popular restaurant. Neeley, *The Works of Matthew Blue*, 217, 222, 226, and 234.

[2] Peter A. Brannon, "Dueling in Alabama," *Alabama Historical Quarterly* 17 (Fall 1955): 97–98; Toulmin, *Digest of Laws, 1823*, 261–66; Toulmin, *Digest of Laws, 1807*; Ala. Acts (1819), 64–67.

[3] Barney, "John A. Winston," 61; Doss, "An Alabama Founding Father," 163–71; Walther, *William Lowndes Yancey*, 47–55.

Camp, two Georgia legislators who had become embroiled in a dispute during the 1832 session of the Georgia legislature. Their dispute continued via anonymous correspondence in a Columbus, Georgia, newspaper and finally resulted in Major Camp challenging Woolfolk for "personal satisfaction." Arrangements were then made for a duel to be held at Fort Mitchell, a military reservation in Alabama, which was on the Federal Road that ran between Milledgeville, Georgia, and St. Stephens, Alabama. This site was chosen because the Georgia antagonists claimed exemption from their own state laws there and argued that Alabama laws did not apply either because Fort Mitchell was a U.S. military reservation within the Creek Nation. In any event, the first shots of the duel resulted in the death of General Woolfolk.[4]

In its early days, Alabama's vast remote areas attracted reckless and violent criminals. Although border towns near the Indian country such as Phenix City were "a favorite location for fugitives from justice, traffickers in whiskey, and rascals of every description," more populous areas including Mobile, Montgomery, and Huntsville were not devoid of desperadoes. Anne Royall reported during her journey through the South that "Mobile has always, is now and will long be the rendezvous of *Renagadoes, Outlaws, Pirates,* and obnoxious characters." As for Montgomery, the *Montgomery Republican* ended its report of an 1822 murder with this telling observation: "Recent transactions in the village are such as would disgrace even Algerine." In 1825, when Huntsville was a town of only 2,000, it was the scene of five murders. Additionally, during that same year the Huntsville *Democrat* reported two dozen horses rustled, seven slaves kidnapped, one house robbed, two instances of embezzlement, one act of counterfeit, one act of forgery, and numerous items stolen including pocketbooks, saddles, bridles, coats, blankets, and watches.[5]

Historian Jack Williams, who surveyed crime in Alabama between 1819 and 1840, attributed the frequency of homicides to the raw character of the frontier where hair-trigger temperaments, often fueled by alcohol, prevailed. In such an environment, insults were not tolerated and minor disagreements often escalated into lethal combat. Such escalations were facilitated by the fact that Alabamians were allowed "to go about armed to the teeth." After much criticism of this practice by newspaper editors and concerned members of the public, in 1839 the Alabama General Assembly made it unlawful for anyone to "carry concealed about his person any species of firearms, or any Bowie knife, Arkansaw toothpick, or any other ... deadly weapon."[6]

Williams also noted that the number of homicides and other serious crimes in frontier Alabama were difficult to keep in check in large part due to the failure of juries to convict if any modicum of evidence supported a

---

[4] Brannon, "Dueling," 99–100. Ironically, two years later Major Camp was shot to death on the streets of Columbus.

[5] Jack K. Williams, "Crime and Punishment in Alabama, 1819–1840," *Alabama Review* 6 (January 1953): 14–16.

[6] Ibid., 16 and 25.

plea of self-defense. Even where a jury could not sustain a self-defense plea, it often would bring in a verdict of manslaughter rather than murder. Another contributing factor was the abysmal shape of most jails, which made it exceedingly easy for prisoners to escape. The sentiment of Alabama juries, however, gradually became more hardened as more and more citizens became victims of nefarious crimes. Travelers were waylaid by highway robbers who often murdered their victims; thievery was widespread, particularly horse thievery; slaves were kidnapped in increasing numbers; citizens were being fleeced in land frauds and other confidence games; and arsons of small businesses and homes were occurring more frequently. As a result juries were less tolerant and the number of criminals apprehended and punished—sometimes with the assistance of citizen posses or militiamen—increased as secession approached and the state's frontier stage came to an end.[7]

Even in its earliest days, Alabama was not devoid of religious instruction to attempt to counterbalance its violent frontier temperament. In 1703 the Catholic Church established itself as the first Christian denomination in what was to become Alabama when the French bishop at Quebec designated Mobile as the area's first Catholic parish. The religion flourished among the French settlers of Mobile as the *Code Noir* in 1724 forbade the practice of any religion within the colony other than Roman Catholicism. Furthermore, among other restrictions, the *Code* ordered the expulsion of Jews from the colony and invalidated the marriage of non-Catholics. Even when the British took over from the French in 1763, Catholicism was tolerated, albeit with the understanding that the Anglican Church was the official church of the colony. The Catholic Church regained preeminence when Spain became the next colonial power to rule Mobile from 1780 to 1813.[8]

It was not until 1829 when Mobile was a city within the new state of Alabama that the Catholic Church created the Diocese of Mobile and named Michael Portier, a Frenchman, as its first bishop. Portier soon sent missionaries to take the faith to isolated Catholics in Montgomery, Tuscaloosa, Huntsville, Moulton, Courtland, Tuscumbia, Florence, Carthage, Greensboro, and Demopolis. More importantly, within his first year at the helm, in 1830 he founded Spring Hill College in Mobile, claimed by some to be the first institution of higher learning to open its doors within the state.[9]

Although the Catholic Church had been established as Alabama's first Christian denomination by European colonists, it would not assimilate in

---

[7] Ibid., 17–27.

[8] Andrew S. Moore, "Archdiocese of Mobile," *Encyclopedia of Alabama*, http://www.encyclopediaofalabama.org/face/Article.jsp?id=h-1070 (accessed January 31, 2013); *Édit du Roi*, 28–58; Rogers et al., *Alabama*, 33.

[9] Oscar Hugh Lipscomb, "Catholic Missionaries in Early Alabama," *Alabama Review* 18 (April 1965): 124–31. It appears that LaGrange College actually became Alabama's first institution of higher learning when it opened its doors on January 11, 1830, and was chartered by the Alabama General Assembly on January 19, 1830. Harry V. Barnard, "LaGrange College, A Historical Sketch," *North Alabama Historical Association* Bulletin, II (1957): 10; Charles W. Watts, "Student Days at Old LaGrange College, 1844–45," *Alabama Review* 24 (January 1971): 65.

any significant numbers the new settlers coming to the region. It would prove to be a hard and rocky road, however, for any denomination to assimilate these early settlers. Protestantism did not make its first significant appearance in what was to become Alabama until 1803 when Lorenzo Dow, an eccentric Methodist preacher, began riding the circuit to spread the gospel to the isolated communities of the Tombigbee District. His hell-fire and damnation sermons condemned drinking, gambling, dancing, and womanizing, activities which were prevalent among rowdy pioneers. Conditions were such that Dow described St. Stephens—the future capital of the Alabama Territory—as "a godless place."[10]

Soon after Dow's appearance, Methodists and Baptists began to send other ministers into the area to ride the circuit. These circuit riders typically wore heavy coats and wide brimmed hats to protect them from the elements and carried a Bible and a hymnal in their saddlebags. They were not always met with open arms by the settlers in the remote communities. Historian A. B. Moore says that they were often "scoffed at and scolded" and sometimes were forbidden from praying in certain homes. Legend has it that one minister—believed by some to be Lorenzo Dow—was rowed across the river from St. Stephens and let out with a warning that he would be tarred and feathered if he returned.[11]

Protestant circuit riders withstood the lack of hospitality exhibited by some of the more rowdy settlers and began to preach to larger groups at camp meetings held under brush arbors, which were makeshift shelters built out of logs, sticks, and brush to protect the worshippers from the elements. These highly emotional meetings sometimes lasted for several weeks. After fiery sermons sinners were called forth to confess, often resulting in "groaning, shouting, shrieking, singing, exhorting, laughing, dancing, jerking, and swooning." Camp meetings were not always devoted to purely evangelical activities as some attendees resorted to drinking, horse racing, and rowdyism to pass the time. Such conduct usually drew censure from the preacher. Quite a few preachers, however, joined their flock in imbibing during services to get "at least some of their inspiration from the god of wine."[12]

Considerably more prim and proper Protestant congregations emerged from the days of brush arbors and camp meetings to build permanent structures within the growing number of towns and villages in antebellum Alabama. In 1860, the Baptists, with some 800 churches, were the largest

---

[10] As early as 1764, during the British rule of Mobile, Reverend Samuel Hart, who had been sent by the Missionary Society of the Episcopal Church of Charleston, left after only one year because he found Mobile to be "spiritually sterile" and "the atmosphere so uncongenial." Moore, *History of Alabama*, 129–32; Anson West, *A History of Methodism in Alabama* (Nashville: Publishing House, Methodist Episcopal Church, South: 1893), 27–34; Rogers et al., *Alabama*, 63; Richard J. Stockham, "The Misunderstood Larenzo Dow," *Alabama Review* 26 (January 1963): 20–34.

[11] Moore, *History of Alabama*, 132; G. Ward Hubbs, "Methodism in Alabama," *Encyclopedia of Alabama*, http://www.encyclopediaofalabama.org/face/Article.jsp?id=h-1857 (accessed February 5, 2013).

[12] Moore, *History of Alabama*, 144, 151–52.

denomination within the state. During the 1850s the number of Baptist churches had grown from 576 to 805 at an average cost of $600. Close behind were the Methodists with 777 churches, costing an average of $780. Presbyterians and Episcopalians had far fewer churches but spent considerably more on their structures. The Presbyterians had 135 churches at an average cost of $2,400, while the Episcopalians had thirty-four churches built at an average cost of $5,766. Although the Catholics only had nine churches in the state by 1860, the Catholic Cathedral in Mobile was reportedly the most impressive church in the state, built at a cost in excess of $80,000.[13]

While the physical structures of Alabama's churches were becoming more permanent and impressive as compared to the rough brush arbors from which they emerged, by the 1840s Alabama's denominations were beginning to separate from their northern brethren over the issue of slavery. In 1844 Alabama Methodists became the first to do so when the Methodist general conference ordered Georgia Bishop James O. Andrew to sell his slaves. Refusing to do so, Andrew and his parishioners joined other southern Methodists to create the Methodist Episcopal Church, South. The very next year Alabama Baptists broke away from their national church organization when it refused to appoint a Georgia man as a missionary because he was a slaveowner. It took until the outbreak of the Civil War, but Alabama Presbyterians and Episcopalians also split from their national churches. Some of these Protestant divisions did not end after the war and some of those that did would rekindle in the next century during the Civil Rights movement.[14]

One of the enduring legacies provided by Alabama's pioneer churches was the number of schools founded by them. In January 1830 LaGrange College was established by the Tennessee Conference of the Methodist Church in northeast Franklin County to become the first college chartered by the Alabama General Assembly on January 19, 1830, and Alabama's oldest institution of higher learning. Although founded by the Methodists, LaGrange College was not to become a religious or theological school. Instead, the Conference provided that its instruction should be "purely literary and scientific." In 1855 the school moved to Florence and was chartered under the name of Florence Wesleyan University. After the Civil War it became the State Normal College, then Florence State Teachers College, and finally the University of North Alabama. Also, as noted above,

---

[13] Minnie Clare Boyd, *Alabama in the Fifties: A Social Study* (New York: Columbia University Press, 1931), 156–61.

[14] Rogers et al., *Alabama*, 125; Wayne Flynt, "Southern Baptists in Alabama," *Encyclopedia of Alabama*, http://www.encyclopediaofalabama.org/face/Article.jsp?id=h-1836 (accessed February 5, 2013); W. Jason Wallace, "Presbyterian Church in America (PCA)," *Encyclopedia of Alabama*, http://www.encyclopediaofalabama.org/face/Article.jsp?id=h-1626 (accessed February 5, 2013). Ironically, while Alabama's Christian denominations were breaking away from their northern counterparts, they were also bringing masters and slaves together to worship under the same roof where they worshipped at the same altar, served bread by the same hands, and drank out of the same cup. Slaves often sat in the balconies or in separate sections cordoned off on the main floor. Some churches, however, held separate services for their slave membership. Sellers, *Slavery*, 296–97.

in 1830 the Catholics established Spring Hill College in Mobile. While not the oldest institution of higher learning within the state as some claim, Spring Hill College is certainly the second oldest and, like LaGrange College, it was operational before the University of Alabama opened its doors in 1831. In its early years Spring Hill was more of a boarding school attended by boys from wealthy non-Catholic families in Mobile, New Orleans, and Pensacola. It was not until 1836 that Spring Hill College was chartered by the Alabama General Assembly and given full power to award degrees in the arts and sciences.[15]

Quite a few other schools were established by Alabama's churches during the state's formative period. Included among these were Judson Female Institute (later renamed Judson College) and Howard College, both of which were founded by Baptists and were located in Perry County at Marion. Judson, named for America's first female foreign missionary, was established in 1838 as a Baptist institution to provide higher education for women and was Alabama's only college specifically for women at that time. The initial curriculum was geared to honing the skills of women in the arts of needlework, dancing, drawing, and penmanship, while also providing them with a solid foundation in theology, literature, and the fine arts. Judson was chartered by the Alabama General Assembly in 1841, and by 1855 it had 239 students. Also by 1855 the curriculum had broadened to stress English, mathematics, history, and foreign languages in addition to the fine arts. Most of the same group who had been involved in the founding of Judson opened a new school for men in Marion in 1841. The school, named Howard College, opened its doors in January 1842 to only nine students. The next year the school's attendance grew to 77 students and by the school-year 1853–1854 it had 152 students. After the Civil War, the college moved to the East Lake area in Birmingham. In 1957 the school moved again to its present site in Homewood where it achieved university status in 1965 and became known as Samford University.[16]

Significant schools founded by Alabama Methodists include Athens Female College (1840), Tuskegee Female College (1856), Southern University (1856), and East Alabama Male College (1856). A meeting of the Methodist Conference in 1855 in Eutaw, Alabama, resulted in the decision to establish the Southern University in Greensboro, Hale County. Col. John Erwin, an influential lawyer and former senator and representative for Greene County, was appointed to obtain a charter from the legislature. He did so in 1856, but only over the veto of Governor Winston. After a sum in

---

[15] Barnard, "LaGrange College," 10; Watts, "Student Days," 65; Charles Stephen Padgett, "Spring Hill College," *Encyclopedia of Alabama*, http://www.encyclopediaofalabama.org/face/Article.jsp?id=h-1029 (accessed February 5, 2013).

[16] Elizabeth Crabtree Wells, "Judson College," *Encyclopedia of Alabama*, http://www.encyclopediaofalabama.org/face/Article.jsp?id=h-2492 (accessed February 5, 2013); Francis Dew Hamilton and Elizabeth Crabtree Wells, *Daughters of the Dream: Judson College, 1838–1988* (Marion, Ala.: Judson College, 1989); Sean Flynt, "Samford University," *Encyclopedia of Alabama*, http://www.encyclopediaofalabama.org/face/Article.jsp?id=h-1590 (accessed February 5, 2013); Mitchell Bennett Garrett, *Sixty Years of Howard College, 1842–1902* (Birmingham, Ala.: Howard College, 1927).

excess of $200,000 was raised, Southern University opened its doors for its first session on October 3, 1859. The school remained open during the Civil War, but at one point there were only fourteen students in attendance. After many lean years following the war, Southern University was merged with Birmingham College, another Methodist institution, to become Birmingham-Southern College.[17]

The supporters of Southern University in Greensboro had beat out a bid by a group in east Alabama who wanted the Methodists to establish an institution of higher learning for men in Auburn. The group nevertheless succeeded in obtaining a charter in February 1856 for the East Alabama Male College to be established in Auburn. It too had to overcome a veto by Governor Winston. The school finally opened on October 1, 1859, but would soon suspend operations during the Civil War and convert into a hospital for wounded soldiers. After the war the school reopened, but struggled as many others did. In 1872, because of serious financial difficulties, the Methodist Church transferred its control of the school to the state, which in turn made it the state's first-land grant institution under the Morrill Act and renamed it the Agricultural and Mechanical College of Alabama—the forerunner of today's Auburn University.[18]

The schools founded by Alabama's early churches were in direct competition with Alabama's only state university in Tuscaloosa. As we have previously seen, the University of Alabama finally opened in 1831 after having been put on the back burner as a result of political maneuvering in relation to the funding of the state bank and the location of the state capital. Once established it attracted the sons of Alabama's wealthy planters who were not amenable to the discipline imposed by the University's first president, an austere New England graduate of Harvard University. Before Alva Woods resigned as president in 1837, he had faced one student rebellion after another. The next president, Basil Manly, was a southerner who had a better rapport with his students as evidenced by his eighteen-year tenure as president during which rebellious and rowdy conduct declined, but did not totally disappear.[19]

Baptists in Alabama rejoiced when Dr. Manly—dubbed by them as a "mighty magnet"—left the University in 1855 because they were concerned with the number of Baptist sons that he had enticed away from Howard College. Manly's successor, Dr. Landon C. Garland, in turn complained of the competition emanating from the church schools, asserting that "the church steps out of her legitimate and proper sphere when she attempts to

---

[17] William Edward Wadsworth Yerby, *History of Greensboro Alabama, From Its Earliest Settlement* (Montgomery, Ala.: Paragon Press, 1908), 85–90; G. Ward Hubbs, "Birmingham-Southern College," *Encyclopedia of Alabama*, http://www.encyclopediaofalabama.org/face/Article.jsp?id=h-1844 (accessed February 5, 2013).

[18] William Warren Rogers, "The Founding of Alabama's Land Grant College at Auburn," *Alabama Review* 40 (January 1987): 14–37; Dwayne Cox and Rodney J. Steward, "The Old South, Civil War, and Reconstruction," *The Auburn University Digital Library: Auburn History*, http://diglib.auburn.edu/auburnhistory/oldsouth.htm (accessed February 1, 2013).

[19] Wolfe, "University of Alabama," 14–15; Sellers, *University of Alabama*, 65; Dubose, *Sketches*, 155; Sellers, "Student Life," 277, 289–90.

control public education." Church leaders then came forth with a rejoinder extolling the virtues of providing a Christian education to the youth of Alabama, which was undoubtedly offered as a slap at the unruliness still prevalent to some extent at the University of Alabama.[20]

With the establishment of Judson Female Institute, Athens Female College, and Tuskegee Female College (later Huntingdon College), the churches partially filled the gap in female education left by a failure of the Alabama legislature to make good on establishing a female branch of the University of Alabama. In December 1821 the legislature had supplemented the act creating the state university by giving university trustees the power and the specific duty "to select a city for a female institution" which would be considered as a "branch of the University of the State of Alabama." Although no action was ever taken to establish this female branch, the legislature did seek a grant from Congress for as much as two sections of land in each county for the use of a female academy. Congress did not support this request and thus female higher education in the state was left to private academies charted by the legislature, or academies and colleges founded by churches, towns, or benevolent organizations.[21]

As detailed above, the first institutions of higher learning in Alabama did not open until 1830. Primary education, however, got off to a much earlier start in 1799 when Connecticut native John Pierce established the first American school in Alabama at Boat Yard Lake in the Tensaw community, approximately thirty-five miles north of Mobile. Pierce taught children of the descendants of such notable area families as the McGillivray's, Taits, Weatherfords, Durants, Linders, and Mims. The first legislation in Alabama pertaining to education did not inure until the Mississippi territorial legislature chartered the Washington Academy at St. Stephens in 1811 and the Green Academy in Huntsville in 1812.[22]

The need for primary education in Alabama had been emphasized from the state's very inception. In addition to requiring that two townships be set aside for "the use of a seminary of learning," the state's Enabling Act required that the sixteenth section of each township be reserved for the use of schools. Although not providing for centralized state control of education, in 1822 the legislature did authorize the creation of school districts to act in concert with the governing board of commissioners of each township in providing for schools at the local level. It was the duty of the commissioners for each township to manage the sale or lease of school lands and distribute the resulting monies to the schools in proportion to the number of students enrolled in each. The commissioners were further entrusted with the responsibility to examine and certify teachers for the schools in their township. Working together with the commissioners were trustees elected by the people of each school district whose responsibilities included the

---

[20] Moore, *History of Alabama*, 347.

[21] *Ala. Acts (1821)*, 3–8; Moore, *History of Alabama*, 338.

[22] Forrest David Matthews, *Why Public Schools? Whose Public Schools?: What Early Communities Have to Tell Us* (Montgomery, Ala.: NewSouth Books, 2002), 50–53; Pickett, *History of Alabama*, 469.

construction of a school in their district, the employment of teachers, the purchase of supplies, and the regulation of the admission of students.[23]

Unfortunately, this localized system was fraught with problems based in large part on the mismanagement of much of the lands designated for school use. The sale of public lands, particularly in north Alabama, often failed to provide adequate funding for local schools. In what should have been a boon to education in the state, in 1836 Alabama received $669,086.78 from the federal government, which comprised its share of the surplus from national land sales. These monies were deposited into the State Bank of Alabama in a fund for public schools, but were lost when that bank collapsed in 1843. By 1840 there were only 753 students enrolled in public schools and the emerging number of private academies. The public schools that existed were primitive at best, usually occupying a one-room building unsuited for other purposes and devoid of sanitary conditions. The state of education was such that in 1848 the legislature asserted that the sixteenth sections had "utterly failed to accomplish the noble object" for which they had been set aside. Another six years would pass before the legislature would improve the situation by providing for public education to be managed on a statewide basis.[24]

Until the 1850s most of the schools in Alabama were not financed by the sale of school lands, but rather were chartered by the legislature to private corporations, many of which were allowed to raise funds by conducting public lotteries. During the antebellum period some 250 private academies were chartered by the General Assembly. In 1860 there were 206 of these academies in service with 10,778 students being taught by 400 teachers. Significant academies included the Greene Springs School for Boys founded in 1847 by Henry Tutwiler, former professor at the University of Alabama; the Valley Creek Academy established at Summerfield in Dallas County in 1829; and the Barton Academy established in Mobile in 1836.[25]

The Greene Springs School for Boys, in spite of its name, later admitted girls as did the Valley Creek Academy, which became a part of the Centenary Institute established by the Methodists in 1841. Since there were not many such coeducational institutions, girls from wealthy families were sent to female seminaries, which were basically finishing schools, while middleclass families sent their daughters, along with their sons, to small one-teacher community schools to learn the basics of mathematics, reading, grammar, spelling, and geography. Although girls who were able to receive an advanced education studied literature, poetry, and music, for the most part their studies were directed at preparing them for household chores such as sewing, needlework, and knitting, and at polishing their manners,

---

[23] Enabling Act for Alabama (1819), Fifteenth Congress, Second Session, Sec. 6; *Ala. Acts (1822)*, 73–78.

[24] Moore, *History of Alabama*, 321–24; Gordon Harvey, "Public Education in Antebellum Alabama," *Encyclopedia of Alabama*, http://www.encyclopediaofalabama.org/face/Article.jsp?id=h-2599 (accessed February 5, 2013).

[25] Rogers et al., *Alabama*, 118–19; Moore, *History of Alabama*, 336.

comportment and etiquette. As we have seen, more progressive subjects, including English, math, foreign languages, and history, in addition to the fine arts, began to be offered to women attending Judson College in Marion.[26]

Paving the way for public education in Alabama in its formative period was the founding of the Barton Academy in Mobile. The school was named for Willoughby Barton, a legislator from Mobile who in January 1826 secured passage of an act that created the Board of School Commissioners of Mobile County. The construction of the Barton Academy, the system's largest school, began in 1836 under the direction of Henry Hitchcock—Alabama's first attorney general and Mobile's first millionaire—and Silas Dinsmore, a former U.S. lands surveyor. It was completed in 1839 at an estimated cost of $100,000. Financing came not only from sixteenth section land revenue, but also from revenues generated from certain city fines and taxes. An additional $50,000 was raised in a lottery that had been authorized by the legislature. Despite these various sources of revenue, the Mobile system experienced hard times resulting in the emergence of a vocal segment that advocated the sale of the Barton Academy to reduce mounting indebtedness. The Mobile commissioners secured the passage of an act allowing the Academy to be sold if the electorate approved. As a result, on August 2, 1852, a referendum was held that pitted those who wanted to sell and continue the operation of public and private schools (with their prohibitive high tuition fees) and parochial free schools, or those who favored keeping Barton Academy as a public school supported by direct taxation. The "no sale" and public school proponents won overwhelmingly by a vote 2,225 to 244.[27]

Mobile's experience inspired a push for statewide free public education. As a result, under the leadership of Mobile's Alexander Beaufort Meek—lawyer, poet, historian, associate newspaper editor, and chairman of the Alabama House committee on education—the Public School Act of 1854 was enacted on February 15, 1854. The act created a state superintendent of education, appropriated $100,000 to be divided among the counties, and authorized the counties to collect real estate and personal property taxes for educational purposes. William F. Perry, chosen by the legislature to serve as the first superintendent of education, immediately introduced into the curriculum of the state's public schools previously neglected subjects such as U.S. history and geography. He also introduced standard textbooks such as McGuffey *Readers* and Webster's *Blue-Backed Spelling Book*.[28]

Even with the advent of a statewide public school system, for the most part Alabama's schools continued to be fiscally mismanaged and struggled to stay open for most of the year. In 1858 the average school term was six and one half months, although several counties were able to stay open for nine months. School enrollment at that time stood at 98,274, or 54.5 per

---

[26] Rogers et al., *Alabama*, 117–18; Wells, "Judson College."

[27] *Ala. Acts (1825)*, 35–36; Nita Katherine Pyburn, "Mobile Public Schools Before 1860," *Alabama Review* 11 (July 1958): 177–88.

[28] *Ala. Acts (1853)*, 8–18; Rogers et al., *Alabama*, 119; Harvey, "Public Education."

cent. Many schools still met in primitive log structures and were fortunate if their students were provided with textbooks. The promise for the future envisioned with the passage of the Public School Act not only was slow to take hold but was totally obliterated by the advent of secession and war.[29]

The only specialized school for children with disabilities during the antebellum period was a school for the deaf, established by Dr. Joseph Henry Johnson in 1858. Johnson had previously served as a teacher at the Georgia Asylum for the Deaf. Internal friction at that school caused Johnson to look for opportunities to found his own school and he was encouraged to establish such a school in Alabama by Governor Andrew B. Moore and Alabama's new Superintendent of Education William Perry. On October 4, 1858, Johnson opened the Alabama School for the Deaf in Talladega. In 1860 the state of Alabama purchased the Talladega campus and retained Johnson as its president. Even with the intrusion of the Civil War, Johnson was able to add the Alabama School for the Blind in 1867. The combined schools were the forerunner of the current Alabama Institute for the Deaf and Blind.[30]

There was little in the way of education for the professions during Alabama's antebellum period. However, in the 1840s the legislature did authorize the building of medical colleges at Wetumpka and Montgomery, though neither project ever got off the ground. With no medical school in the state, concern over the laxity of licensing standards for physicians and the level of skills possessed by Alabama physicians led to the formation in 1847 of the Medical Association of the State of Alabama (MASA). That organization's goal was to establish a code of ethics and provide for medical education within the state.[31]

In 1859 the state's first medical school—the Medical College of Alabama—was finally opened in Mobile, largely due to the efforts of Dr. Josiah C. Nott, a Mobile physician who was the author of controversial books and articles concerning differences between the races. He also wrote many articles on yellow fever and has been credited as being the first to suggest that insects could transmit the disease. Dr. Nott served as the president of the Medical Association of the State of Alabama in 1857 and 1859 and served as the Medical College of Alabama's Professor of Surgery in 1860. Unfortunately, the school held only two sessions before having to shut down as a result of the commencement of the Civil War. The school would reopen in 1868, be made part of the University of Alabama system in 1907, and be relocated to Tuscaloosa in 1920 and finally to Birmingham in 1944.[32]

---

[29] Moore, *History of Alabama*, 334.

[30] Jack Hawkins, Jr., "Alabama Institute for the Deaf and Blind," *Encyclopedia of Alabama*, http://www.encyclopediaofalabama.org/face/Article.jsp?id=h-1855 (accessed January 8, 2013).

[31] Moore, *History of Alabama*, 345; A. J. Wright, "Medical Association of the State of Alabama (MASA)," *Encyclopedia of Alabama*, http://www.encyclopediaofalabama.org/face/Article.jsp?id=h-1156 (accessed January 8, 2013).

[32] Strangely enough, Dr. Nott was the physician who delivered William Crawford Gorgas. Gorgas later utilized the theory that yellow fever was transmitted by mosquitoes to eradicate that disease in Panama. Perhaps Alabama's most prominent physician, Gorgas also served as U.S. Army Surgeon General and received numerous awards and honorary degrees for his work

Legal education in antebellum Alabama was primarily limited to "reading law," which amounted to an apprenticeship involving a period of study under the supervision of an experienced attorney. This system was necessitated by the fact that there were very few law schools in the United States prior to the Civil War. Of the sixteen Alabama governors who served during the antebellum period, thirteen were lawyers. Of these, twelve had read law in the office of an experienced practitioner, with only one having attended a formal law school. After reading law, prospective lawyers were required by an 1819 statute to produce evidence of a good moral character and to stand for an examination before the Alabama Supreme Court as a prerequisite to receiving a license to practice law. A statute passed two years later allowed any two circuit court judges to license candidates to practice at the trial court level in circuit and county courts. That statute implied examinations were to be given but did not so specifically provide. The rigorousness of the tests imposed on prospective candidates varied from judge to judge, allowing the admission to practice of a good number of ill-trained lawyers to deal with complex issues involving "land titles, Indian rights, and contract law."[33]

Because there were no local law schools, the few Alabama lawyers that had the benefit of a formal legal education attended out-of-state schools such as the Litchfield Law School in Connecticut, the University of Virginia, Harvard Law School, and the Cumberland School of Law—then located in Lebanon Tennessee, but which would move to Birmingham in 1961. With a growing sense that law office apprenticeships were not adequately preparing the state's young lawyers, in 1845 Benjamin F. Porter, a prominent lawyer and University of Alabama trustee, pushed to establish a law school at the University. To this end Porter, who was appointed as Professor of Law during the winter of 1845–1846, intended to operate a law school which would provide a two-year course of study, involving a reading of the basic legal treatises, attendance at lectures, and frequent moot courts. The school never really got off the ground due to onerous regulations imposed by the university's board of trustees, such as not allowing undergraduates to take law courses, not allowing law students to use the school's dormitories or dining halls, and not allowing Porter to teach his students on the University's campus. Paul Pruitt, a University of Alabama law librarian and historian, surmises that the trustees' discouraging regulations were the result of their opposition to "grafting a professional school onto a liberal arts curriculum" or, perhaps, simply an indication of Porter's ability to make enemies. Whatever the reason, Porter's attempt was an utter failure.[34]

---

in improving sanitary conditions throughout South America and Africa. William B. Bean, M.D., "Josiah Clark Nott, A Southern Physician," *Bulletin of the New York Academy of Medicine* (April 1974): 529–35.

[33] Paul M. Pruitt, Jr.,"The Life and Times of Legal Education in Alabama, 1819–1897: Bar Admissions, Law Schools, and the Profession," *Alabama Law Review* 49 (Fall 1997): 283–84; *Ala. Acts (1819)*, 68–69. In 1847, there were only fifteen university affiliated law schools in the United States. David J. Langum and Howard P. Walthall, *From Maverick to Mainstream, Cumberland School of Law, 1847–1997* (University of Georgia Press, 1997), 1.

[34] Pruitt, "The Life and Times of Legal Education in Alabama," 287–88.

The only law school to open during the antebellum period was the Montgomery Law School founded by Wade Keyes, who had been chancellor of Alabama's southern district equity courts. In 1859 former Alabama Supreme Court chief justice Samuel F. Rice shepherded a bill through the legislature authorizing Keyes' Montgomery Law School to award degrees to its students who were also given a "diploma privilege," which allowed them to practice law without submitting to an examination. The bill further put the school under the dual supervision of the justices of the Alabama Supreme Court and the University's board of trustees. Unfortunately the school was able to award diplomas to just one class before the Civil War forced its students into military service. The present University of Alabama School of Law in Tuscaloosa would not be founded until 1872.[35]

Although education, at all levels, was slow to develop for the benefit of Alabama's free white population during the antebellum period, it was practically nonexistent among African Americans, whether free or slaves. Although some plantation owners provided a rudimentary education for their slaves, after 1832 it became illegal to "attempt to teach any free person of color, or slave, to spell, read or write." Thereafter, any person caught teaching a black person was subject to fines from $250 to $500. On the other hand, technical training of blacks was not prohibited and slaves and free persons alike were trained to be blacksmiths, carpenters, brick masons, wheelwrights, seamstresses, and cooks. In any event, with the exception of a few schools in Mobile that taught "Creole" children as a result of their being guaranteed rights as American citizens by the Louisiana Purchase Treaty, there were no known formal schools in Alabama prior to the Civil War that allowed blacks, free or slave, to attend.[36]

Despite the slowness with which formal education developed in the state's early days, Alabamians were not completely devoid of literary interests. The first books to be published, however, were practical in nature rather than literary works of art. In 1822, Henry Hitchcock, Alabama's first attorney general and a future chief justice of the Alabama Supreme Court, published the first book in the state which was a manual for justices of the peace—"a combination digest of the laws and a comprehensive guide to legal and judicial procedure." Following on its heels in 1825 was a medical treatise published by Dr. Jabez Heustis on the subject of fevers in Cahaba during 1822–1823. In 1833 a work entitled *The Lost Virgin of the South: A Tale of Truth Connected with the History of the Indian War of the South, 1812 to '15*, became the first novel to be published in Alabama. The book was written under the pseudonym of Don Pedro Casender, whom some literary historians have identified as Wiley Conner, an editor of the Courtland *Herald* from 1826 to 1841. The book recounted the "saga of a virginal heroine, shipwrecked, captured, cast in the tumults of the great wars of the Southwest, eventually united with a faithful lover and, after a sojourn in

---

[35] Ibid., 291–92.

[36] Sellers, *Slavery*, 117–20.

Europe returned to happy domesticity in New York."[37]

Much of what early Alabamians read—practical or literary in nature—was contained in the state's newspapers. Even before Alabama became a state, two experienced newspapermen hauled a printing press from Chattanooga to Fort Stoddert to begin publishing the first newspaper in the Alabama portion of the Mississippi Territory in May 1811. Despite its locale at Fort Stoddert, the paper was called the *Mobile Centinel* [sic]. Explaining this geographical anomaly in the first issue, the editors indicated that although it had been their intention to set up shop in Mobile, they had been thwarted to date by a failure of Americans to wrest control of that city from the Spanish. While this statement explained the reason for the paper's name, it did not address—nor correct—its embarrassing misspelling. Not surprisingly the paper went out of business after just two years.[38]

More newspapers followed the *Centinel*, beginning in the spring of 1812 with the founding of the *Madison Gazette* (which became the *Huntsville Republican* in 1816); the *Alabama Republican* in 1818; and the *Southern Advocate and Huntsville Advertiser* in 1825. Serving as the organ of the Georgia faction, the *Madison Gazette* and its progeny played a prominent role in the political machinations of early Alabama. Other newspapers during Alabama's territorial period included the *Mobile Gazette* (1813), which was absorbed into the *Mobile Commercial Register* in 1822; St. Stephens' *The Halcyon* (1815); Blakeley's *Sun and Alabama Advertiser* (1818); Claiborne's *Alabama Courier* (1819); the *Tuscaloosa Republican* (1819); and Cahaba's *Press and Alabama Intelligencer* (1819). By the time Alabama became a state there were six weekly or semi-weekly newspapers in publication—the *Alabama Republican*, the *Mobile Gazette, The Halcyon*, the *Alabama Courier*, the *Tuscaloosa Republican,* and the *Press and Alabama Intelligencer*. After Alabama became a state, the capital in Cahaba was home to a second transitory paper by the name of the *Alabama Watchman*, founded in 1820.[39]

These early Alabama newspapers and others that followed usually consisted of just four pages and contained very little in the way of current news. Two pages were typically devoted to advertisements of goods, notices of runaway slaves and lands sales, and announcements of public meetings. The other two pages contained dated reprints of news stories from national papers and editorials concerning local issues, usually of a political nature. Any unfilled spaces were taken up by poems and short stories, sometimes

---

[37] According to Philip Beidler, the subject of the state's first known book spoke volumes as to the needs of its frontier population: "To put things simply, in its desperate need to implement the rule of law and order in arguably some of the most lawless precincts of the English-speaking world, Alabama had a justice system that needed a jump start as far as some guide to basic operations were concerned." Beidler, *First Books*, 8, 25 (quote), 32–46. See Benjamin Buford Williams, *A Literary History of Alabama: the Nineteenth Century* (Cranbury, NJ: Fairleigh Dickinson Press, 1979), 167–78.

[38] Daniel Savage Gray, "Frontier Journalism: Newspapers in Antebellum Alabama," *Alabama Historical Quarterly* 37 (Fall 1975): 183–84; see also F. Wilbur Helmbold, "Early Alabama Newspapermen, 1810–1820," *Alabama Review* (January 1959): 53.

[39] Gray, "Frontier Journalism," 185–87.

supplied by local authors, but more often reprinted from European sources. Local and national politics prompted the founding of quite a few newspapers after Alabama's statehood in the 1820s. In 1823 Henry B. Long of Kentucky founded the *Huntsville Democrat,* which became an organ of the so-called "People's Party" and ended the Georgia faction's media monopoly in Madison County. The presidential election of 1824 spawned many more newspapers that became supporters for either John Adams or Andrew Jackson in their bids for the presidency. Fifty additional newspapers were founded in the 1830s, and by the 1850s larger cities in the state published daily papers. As the Civil War approached, however, the number of papers dwindled, partly as a result of papers having a Unionist sentiment leaving the field to firebrand states' rights and secessionist papers. Journalism historian Daniel Savage Gray summarized the plight of newspapers at this time, stating, "The final irony is that the establishment of the Confederacy which these papers so heartily endorsed and which they so loudly cheered in 1861, gave rise to the war that would cause them as well as the remaining Unionist papers and more moderate newspapers to pass into oblivion."[40]

During the antebellum period a small cadre of literary personages gave Alabamians something to read in addition to newspapers. First among these chronologically, but not in prominence, was Lewis Sewall, an official in the Land Office of the Mississippi Territory, who authored *The Last Campaign of Sir John Falstaff The II; or, The Hero of the Burnt-Corn Battle, A Serio-Comic Poem.* This work—published in 1815 and believed to be the first work of literature published in the Mississippi Territory—took satirical aim at Col. James Caller who commanded a militia unit that was routed at Burnt Corn Creek by a much smaller Indian party. Caller's men had gained the early advantage with a surprise attack, but soon lost it by foolishly ransacking the Indian's packhorses giving the Indians time to regroup and launch a counterattack resulting in an embarrassing rout. In true boisterous frontier fashion, Sewall penned this satirical prose—comparing Caller to the bumbling Shakespearean character John Falstaff—in retaliation for Caller publicly accusing him of embezzling funds from the Land Office.[41]

More prominent and talented Alabama poets included William Russell Smith and Alexander Beaufort Meek, two lawyer-politicians who had acquired an interest in poetry while under the tutelage of Professor Henry W. Hilliard—himself a lawyer and politician—at the University of Alabama. While still a student in 1833, Smith published a collection of poems entitled *College Musings: or Twigs from Parnassus,* which was the first book of poetry published in the state by an Alabamian. In 1835 Smith also had the distinction of publishing the first literary periodical in the state, entitled *The Bachelor's Button.* Smith achieved yet another literary first with his play *Aaron Burr, or the Emperor of Mexico,* which was the first play written by an Alabamian to be performed by a professional acting company—

---

[40] Ibid., 188–91.

[41] Beidler, *First Books,* 14–22; Ben P. Robertson, "Lewis Sewall," *Encyclopedia of Alabama,* http://www.encyclopediaofalabama.org/face/Article.jsp?id=h-3004 (accessed January 8, 2013).

the Ludlow-Smith company of Mobile. After these literary achievements, Smith edited Tuscaloosa's *The Independent Monitor,* served in the state legislature as well as the U.S. Congress, was a Unionist delegate to the Alabama Secession Convention, and served briefly as the president of the University of Alabama after the Civil War.[42]

Despite the number of firsts achieved by Smith, Alexander Beaufort Meek is generally considered to be the foremost literary figure in Alabama's antebellum period. Meek graduated from the University of Alabama in 1833, edited Tuscaloosa's *Flag of the Union* at the age of 21, was admitted to the bar in 1835, and received one of the University's first Master's degrees in 1836. After his education, Meek served as an ensign in the Seminole War. Political and legal experience included an appointment as Alabama's Attorney General, service as a law clerk to solicitor of the U.S. Treasury in Washington, D.C., and an appointment as the U.S. Attorney for the Southern District of Alabama in Mobile. Meek developed an early reputation as an orator, frequently lecturing at colleges and before learned societies. In 1839 he started a monthly literary magazine entitled *The Southron.* This publication survived only six months due to a lack of subscriptions which was typical of similar publications of the era. Meek's most well-known literary work, *The Red Eagle: A Poem of the South,* published in 1855, weaves a love story into the historical events of the Creek War of 1813–1814, with William Weatherford—dubbed for the first time as Red Eagle—as its protagonist. According to Benjamin Buford Williams, it is considered one of the best epic poems to be written in the South during the antebellum period. Other important works of Meeks include *Romantic Passages in Southern History,* a collection of previously delivered or published orations and historical sketches, and *Songs and Poems of the South,* a collection of his best poems and compositions that had previously appeared in failed periodicals.[43]

Literary fame in early Alabama was not limited to male politicians. Two women, Caroline Lee Hentz and Augusta Jane Evans, gained national notoriety for novels they published in the 1850s. Neither of them were natives of Alabama but both of them lived in the state for an extended period. Hentz moved from Massachusetts to Florence in 1835 with her husband who was a school teacher, and they lived for a while in Tuscaloosa and Tuskegee before moving out of state. Hentz wrote several novels that focused on plantation life and usually were filled with fast action, violence, and romantic twists and turns. Perhaps her most significant work was *The Planter's Northern Bride,* published in 1854. This was not the first novel that brought her national attention, but it was particularly noteworthy since it was considered to be a Southern literary retort to Harriet Beecher Stowe's *Uncle Tom's Cabin* with its depiction of allegedly happy slaves in the South

---

[42] Benjamin Buford Williams, "William Russell Smith," *Encyclopedia of Alabama,* http://www.encyclopediaofalabama.org/face/Article.jsp?id=h-2340 (accessed January 8, 2013).

[43] Benjamin Buford Williams, "Alexander B. Meek," *Encyclopedia of Alabama,* http://www.encyclopediaofalabama.org/face/Article.jsp?id=h-1127 (accessed January 8, 2013); Beidler, *First Books,* 47–50.

by comparison to the miserable white working poor of the North. Even more widely read was Augusta Jane Evans who moved with her family to Mobile from Texas, where in 1854 at the age of sixteen, she wrote *Inez: A Tale of the Alamo,* an anti-Catholic romantic novel set during the Texas Revolution. Although *Inez* did not sell well, in 1859 Evans published *Beulah,* which became a bestseller. *Beulah,* which chronicled the struggles of an orphaned teenage girl seeking independence as she transcended into young adulthood, attained critical acclaim, selling 22,000 copies in the first nine months. Even more popular was her novel *St. Elmo,* whose female heroine struggled to establish a writing career but gave it up to marry a man whom she had converted to Christianity. It was published in 1866 and is considered by some as the most popular American novel in the era immediately following the Civil War.[44]

Another prominent female of letters during the antebellum period was Octavia Walton Le Vert. Born near Augusta, Georgia, she moved with her family to Pensacola when her father became the first territorial secretary of Florida. Octavia was tutored at home by her highly educated mother and grandmother. She had a special aptitude for foreign languages and by the age of twelve was proficient in Spanish and French and beginning to master Italian. Octavia traveled extensively with her mother in the early 1830s and also spent a good deal of time in Washington, D.C. During her travels she met the author Washington Irving with whom she remained friends until his death in 1859. While in Washington, Octavia frequently visited the Capitol to attend Congressional debates where she gained the acquaintance of the most prominent political lions of the era—Daniel Webster, John C. Calhoun, and Henry Clay. She formed a special relationship with Clay whom she would later accompany through Alabama during his quest for the presidency in 1844.[45]

George Walton moved his family to Mobile in 1834 when his term as Florida territorial secretary expired. Two years later Octavia married a prominent physician of French descent. From her new luxurious home on Government Street, Le Vert soon established a "salon" in which she hosted gatherings of prominent politicians and professionals, writers, actors, artists, foreign visitors, and other celebrities to discuss a wide range of topics including literature, music, politics, history, and philosophy. Known by many of the socially elite simply as Madame, Le Vert hosted these gatherings on a weekly basis and reigned as the leader of Mobile's privileged society for almost four decades. She became somewhat of a literary figure in her own right in 1857 when she published *Souvenirs of Travel,* a small two-volume work chronicling her travels to Europe in the mid-1850s, which related a meeting with the Pope in Italy, being escorted to the opera

[44] Rogers et al., *Alabama,* 130; Beidler, *First Books,* 102–03; Sarah Frear, "Augusta Jane Evans Wilson," *Encyclopedia of Alabama,* http://www.encyclopediaofalabama.org/face/Article.jsp?id=h-1072 (accessed January 24, 2013).

[45] Harriet E. Amos Doss and Sara Frear, "Octavia Walton Le Vert," *Encyclopedia of Alabama,* http://www.encyclopediaofalabama.org/face/Article.jsp?id=h-2355 (accessed January 24, 2013); Neeley, *The Works of Mathew Blue,* 166–67.

in Paris by former President Millard Fillmore on a night when Queen Victoria and the Emperor of France were in attendance, and a meeting with the poets Robert and Elizabeth Browning in Florence, Italy. Although Le Vert lost favor in Mobile after the Civil War due to her strong Unionist leanings and her entertainment of Union soldiers, two years before her death an Alabama newspaper praised her as "beyond question . . . the most famous woman the South has yet produced."[46]

In contrast to the sophisticated European travel accounts of an erudite socialite was the widespread popularity of a genre of humorous accounts of the disorderly frontier society of the old Southwest. First in Alabama to author such a work was Johnson Jones "Jonce" Hooper, who moved from North Carolina in 1835 to Lafayette in Chambers County where he practiced law and edited the *East Alabamian*. In 1844, the *East Alabamian* introduced Hooper's best-known character, Captain Simon Suggs, a conniving confidence man whose credo was reflected by his most quotable line, "It is good to be shifty in a new country." In 1845, *Some Adventures of Captain Simon Suggs* gained a national following when it was published in Philadelphia. In it Hooper told tales of unsurpassed trickery as evidenced by Captain Suggs' ability to con fellow con-men as well as his own father. Utilizing an exaggerated dialect, Hooper poked fun at the gullibility of the masses on the unsettled frontier. Perhaps Suggs' most notable adventure was his attendance at a camp meeting where—despite being dubbed by one of the preachers as a sinner and "a missubble old critter"—Suggs proceeded to con the flock by staging a humorous religious conversion and collecting money from them on the pretense of building a church in his own neighborhood. In addition to the confidence man theme, however, Hooper, who was a staunch Whig, wrote Suggs' episodic adventures in the form of a campaign biography that was intended as spoof of Whig rival Andrew Jackson. In this regard, Captain Suggs was a candidate for sheriff and the premise was that his adventures constituted a hoodwinking campaign biography similar to that of Jackson.[47]

Another Alabamian contributing to the genre of Southwest humor was Joseph Glover Baldwin, who, like Hooper, was a lawyer and a journalist. Baldwin, originally from Virginia, lived in Mississippi before settling in

---

[46] Rogers, et al., *Alabama*, 132–33; Doss and Frear, "Octavia Walton Le Vert"; Beidler, *First Books*, 58; Williams, *A Literary History*, 64–66.

[47] Cynthia Quinn White, "Johnson Jones Hooper," *Encyclopedia of* Alabama, http://www.encyclopediaofalabama.org/face/Article.jsp?id=h-2514 (accessed January 7, 2013); Rogers et al., *Alabama*, 130–31; Notes, "Simon Suggs: A Burlesque Campaign Biography," *American Quarterly* 15 (Autumn 1963): 459–63. See also Johnson Jones Hooper, *Some Adventures of Captain Simon Suggs, Late of the Tallapoosa Volunteers; Together with "Taking the Census," and Other Alabama Sketches. By a Country Editor with a Portrait from Life, and Other Illustrations, by Darley* (Philadelphia: Carey and Hart, 1845), 118–33. Suggs' camp meeting episode is credited with inspiring Mark Twain's Pokeville camp meeting in the *Adventures of Huckleberry Finn*. Twain's cousin, Jeremiah Clemens, was another Alabama lawyer studying under Professor Henry Hilliard who supplemented his legal career with writing. Clemens wrote three novels prior to the Civil War—*Bernard Lile: An Historical-Romance Embracing the Period of the Texas Revolution and the Mexican War* (1856), *Mustang Gray* (1858), and *The Rivals* (1860), a novel examining the animosity between Alexander Hamilton and Aaron Burr.

Alabama in 1837. He first practiced law in Gainesville and later in Livingston, both located in Sumter County. In 1843 he was elected to the Alabama
legislature as a Whig, serving just one term. After running unsuccessfully
for the U.S. Congress in 1849, Baldwin began to concentrate on his writing
career. Baldwin's sketches were more sophisticated than Hooper's and,
with the exception of Simon Suggs, Jr., the fictional son of Hooper's Captain Suggs, his characters did not speak with an exaggerated dialect. By
1852 Baldwin's sketches began appearing in the *Southern Literary Mes-
senger*, the South's leading literary journal, at one time edited by Edgar
Allen Poe. In 1853 these sketches were collected and published in book
form in a work entitled *The Flush Times of Alabama and Mississippi*.[48]

In *Flush Times*, Baldwin recounted his experiences as a lawyer during
the boom times of the expanding frontier of the old Southwest, which
included Mississippi and Alabama. Interwoven with humorous tales of
fictional lawyers of questionable repute and confidence men in this unsettled frontier, Baldwin wrote serious biographies of those he had actually
come across in his career that for the most part were depicted as irrespon-
sible and unethical. Since Baldwin—a Whig and respected lawyer—was dis-
mayed with the legal, moral, and financial chaos prevalent on the frontier,
it is not surprising that the hero of his book was Francis Strother Lyons, the
commissioner of Alabama's troubled state banks who was deemed by
Baldwin as scrupulously honest and responsible for bringing order to the
state's financial chaos by successfully recovering the banks' bad debts.[49]

In 1854 Baldwin followed up *Flush Times* with a book of sketches of
prominent politicians entitled *Party Leaders*, which was not nearly as
widely read. That same year Baldwin left Alabama for California, which was
in the final throes of the Gold Rush. There he became a prominent attorney
and was appointed as an associate justice of the California Supreme Court.
During the Civil War, Baldwin traveled to Washington, D.C., where he
secured a meeting with President Abraham Lincoln. During that meeting
the president purportedly flattered Baldwin by telling him that he slept
with a copy of *Flush Times* under his pillow. Attracting new readers in each
generation, *Flush Times* has been continuously in print since its original
publication in 1853.[50]

Not as well-known as Hooper and Baldwin, John Gorman Barr was another Alabama contributor to the satire genre of the Old Southwest. Barr
lived a remarkable but short life, dying at the age of thirty-four. In 1835 he
moved from North Carolina to Tuscaloosa with his widowed mother. His
mother died shortly after, leaving Barr and his sister orphans. Adopted by a

---

[48] Adam L. Tate, "Joseph Glover Baldwin and *The Flush Times of Alabama and Mississippi*,"
Encyclopedia of Alabama, http://www.encyclopediaofalabama.org/face/Article.jsp?id=h-
1566 (accessed February 2, 2013).

[49] Charles S. Watson, "Order Out of Chaos: Joseph Glover Baldwin's *The Flush Times of
Alabama and Mississippi*," *Alabama Review* 45 (October 1992): 257–72; Eugene Current-
Garcia, "Joseph Glover Baldwin: Humorist or Moralist?," *Alabama Review* 5 (April 1952):
122–41.

[50] Michael H. Hoffheimer, "Race and Terror in Joseph Baldwin's *Flush Times of Alabama and
Mississippi* (1953)," *Seton Hall Law Review* 39 (2009): 725.

Tuscaloosa merchant, Barr entered the University of Alabama at the age of fifteen. He graduated tied with another student for the highest scholastic average and served as his class's valedictorian. His scholastic achievements continued with receipt of a Master's degree in 1842. By 1846, after reading law in the office of Harvey W. Ellis, he was practicing his profession. A few months later he was appointed the United States Attorney for the Middle District of Alabama. After running unsuccessfully for the Alabama House of Representatives in 1847, Barr recruited a group of volunteers to fight in the Mexican War. Although his unit never saw action, Baldwin rose to the rank of lieutenant colonel.[51]

Barr resumed the practice of law when he returned to Tuscaloosa in 1848 and became managing editor of the *Tuscaloosa Observer*. About this time he also began to publish his works of fiction and was welcomed to an illustrious literary group, which included Alexander Beaufort Meek, William Russell Smith, and G. P. Blevins. Led by Professor Frederick A. P. Barnard, one of the University's most distinguished professors who later became president of Columbia University, this acclaimed group was known as Tuscaloosa's "Brilliant Galaxy of young men." Barr gained national attention between 1855 and 1857 when he published some of his humorous stories under the pseudonym *Omega* in two New York weeklies, Porter's *Spirit* and the *Spirit of the Times*. Shortly after, Barr tragically died at sea of sunstroke en route to Melbourne, Australia, in May 1858. He had been appointed as the U.S. Consul to Australia by President Buchanan as a reward for his support of Buchanan and for giving up his race for a seat in Congress for party unity.[52]

Unlike Hooper and Baldwin, who were Whigs and who focused on the lives of landed gentry, Barr, a Democrat, concentrated more on common people, such as ordinary laborers, small businessmen, immigrants, and yeomen farmers. Inspired by his Democratic leanings, Barr more often poked fun at aristocratic planters and lawyers rather than at the working class. His tales carried such intriguing titles as "Old Charley and His Impromptu Ride," "A Steamboat Captain's Love Adventure," "New York Drummer's Ride to Greensboro," and "John Bealle's Accident—or, How the Widow Dudu Treated Insanity." These stories and other rowdy tales provide a comprehensive view of everyday antebellum life in Tuscaloosa and west Alabama.[53]

The backwardness of Alabama's frontier as often depicted in the works of Baldwin, Hooper, and Barr was a product of the region's physical, economic, and psychological isolation from the older eastern states. Due to poor methods of communication and transportation, as well as a fledgling

---

[51] W. Stanley Hoole, ""John Gorman Barr: Forgotten Alabama Humorist," *Alabama Review* 4 (April 1951): 83–116; James L. Jolly, Jr., *Encyclopedia of Alabama*, "John Gorman Barr," http://www.encyclopediaofalabama.org/face/Article.jsp?id=h-2455 (accessed February 2, 2013).

[52] Hoole, "John Gorman Barr," 95; Jolly, "John Gorman Barr."

[53] G. Ward Hubbs, ed., *Rowdy Tales from Early Alabama: The Humor of John Gorman Barr* (Tuscaloosa: University of Alabama, 1995), 1–10.

agricultural-based economy increasingly dependent upon slave labor, Alabama settlers struggled in their efforts to fully develop their state. In Alabama's territorial days travel was primarily by foot and horseback over primitive Indian trails and former colonial trade routes. Settlers coming into the state from the north utilized a wagon road, referred to as the Natchez Trace, provided for in treaties in 1801 with the Chickasaw and Choctaw nations. The roadway crossed the Tennessee River at Muscle Shoals and proceeded south through Colbert County into Mississippi on the way to Natchez. There were many other Indian trails or footpaths that were utilized in various parts of the territory, but the most significant roadway into the new territory was the Old Federal Road, which at the outset ran from the Ocmulgee River in Georgia to Fort Stoddert in Alabama. Initially it was a horse path through Creek country authorized by the Treaty of Washington in November 1805; in 1811 the U.S. Army rerouted and widened the path so as to allow rolling vehicles—rolling hogsheads, carts, and wagons—to bring settlers and their household goods into the territory. This redirected route now connected Fort Stoddert with Fort Wilkinson in Georgia near Milledgeville.[54]

A few years after the widening of the Federal Road, another significant roadway was blazed through a portion of north Alabama. After the Battle of New Orleans in 1815, General Andrew Jackson proposed this road as a shorter and improved route for military movements between Nashville and New Orleans. When completed on May 17, 1820, the new road was 483 miles long. The road crossed the Tennessee River near Florence, Alabama, intersected the Gaines Trace at Russellville, Alabama, proceeded southward and crossed the Tombigbee River in Columbus, Mississippi, to continue southward toward Madisonville, Louisiana, on the north shore of Lake Pontchartrain just above New Orleans.

Alabama's first legislature also ambitiously authorized the construction of a series of public roads throughout the state. One road was to run from the Military Road in Lauderdale County to Tuscaloosa. Other major projects included a road to run from the falls of the Black Warrior at Tuscaloosa by way of Cahaba and Claiborne to Blakeley located across Mobile Bay from Mobile, as well as one from Cahaba via Coffeeville to the Washington County courthouse, thence to the post road leading from St. Ste-

---

[54] Peter Joseph Hamilton, "Early Roads of Alabama," Transactions of the Alabama Historical Society 2 (1897–98): 47–55; Peter Brannon, *Peter Brannon's Alabama Travel Logs: A Series of Historic Stories of Trips Through Alabama* (Montgomery, Ala.: Paragon Press, 1928), 46–56. The following colorfully sums up the extensive use of the Federal Road:

> Over this route passed post riders for remote New Orleans, militiamen to reinforce forts, stagecoaches bearing European travelers and touring theatrical companies, Aaron Burr under arrest, freight wagons, the maverick evangelist Lorenzo Dow and Peggy (his sensible wife), the horses of highwaymen, the Marquis de Lafayette in a grand entourage, Creeks taking a last look at what had been their lands, and, of course, thousands of pioneers seeking a fresh start.

Henry deLeon Southerland, Jr. and Jerry Elijah Brown, *The Federal Road* (Tuscaloosa: University of Alabama Press, 1989), 2.

phens to Natchez. Each county through which these roads passed was to appoint three commissioners to direct the construction efforts within their respective counties. The legislature also appointed commissioners to study the feasibility of a road from Cahaba to connect with the Federal Road.[55]

As the number of roadways within the young state increased, stage-coach lines began operating which in turn increased the number of taverns in the state. Some coach lines carried the mail in addition to passengers. Principal among the mail stagecoach contractors were Charles Pollard of Montgomery, who later became a pioneering railroad executive, and Robert Jemison of Tuscaloosa, who also owned toll roads, turnpikes, and plank roads. All principal towns in Alabama were serviced by stagecoach lines, which maintained regular schedules, and all parts of the state were con-nected by long-distance lines. Later, as river and rail travel increased, many stagecoaches were routed to river landings and rail heads. Drivers and horses were replaced at relay stations that were spaced twelve to fifteen miles apart. Prior to 1840 there were three separate stage lines that ran between Columbus, Georgia, and Montgomery along the Old Federal Road—the "Mail Line," the "Telegraph Line," and the "People's Line." There was even an "Express Mail" line operating between New York and New Orleans that rapidly carried important news and market reports at a speed nearly three times that of a regular stagecoach.[56]

According to a project of the Works Progress Administration, there were some seventy taverns and stage stops in the state prior to 1840, some dating back to territorial days. Several were located along the Federal Road in Russell, Montgomery, and Lowndes counties and along the old Natchez Trace in Colbert County. At least two of these taverns—Big Warrior's Stand in Russell County and Freeny's Tavern in Montgomery—hosted General Lafayette in 1825 during his celebrated visit to the state. The stops identi-fied by the WPA included several hotels in Tuscaloosa and Montgomery, as well as crude accommodations in the wilderness, such as Bear Meat Cabin in Blount County and Buzzard Roost Tavern along the old Natchez Trace in Colbert County. Of note also was the Green Bottom Inn in Madison County, frequented by General Andrew Jackson when attending horse races in the area, and Milly's Tavern in Montgomery County near present-day Mount Meigs, run by a widow of a purported deserter from the British Army who also operated a toll bridge where the Federal Road crossed a nearby creek.[57]

Abundant contemporary accounts of travel in early Alabama give us a glimpse of the generally primitive conditions along the state's highways and byways. In 1820 Adam Hodgson, a traveling Christian philanthropist from Liverpool, England, reported that a previously excellent roadway for horse-back became "wretchedly bad" when it descended into swampy territory.

[55] William A. Love, "General Jackson's Military Road," *Publications of the Mississippi His-torical Society* 11 (1910): 409; Hamilton, "Early Roads," 50; *Ala. Acts (1819)*, 76–78, 80–81, and 92–93.

[56] Moore, *History of Alabama*, 295–98; Brannon, *Alabama Travel Logs*, 59.

[57] Peter A. Brannon, "Principal Stage Stops and Taverns In What Is Now Alabama Prior to 1840," *Alabama Historical Quarterly* 17 (Spring and Summer 1955): 80–87.

Hodgson related that the going was so rough that their horses became exhausted making their way through the sticky muck of the swamp and that the travelers had to dismount their horses to cut their way through heavily entangled vegetation. Another foreign visitor to Alabama in January 1826, Bernard, Duke of Saxe-Weimar-Eisenach, who was a veteran of the Netherland Army's campaigns against Napoleon, reported that a stretch of road in Russell County was so rough that his carriage overturned on eight separate occasions, fortunately not seriously injuring any of the passengers. Anne Royall, a female journalist from Virginia, writing of the road between Fort Mitchell and Montgomery in 1830, stated that "the whole country is a waste, scarcely a house is seen, and the road badly cut up." Famed showman P. T. Barnum who visited Alabama in February 1837 indicated that the "Indian Nation" between Columbus and Montgomery was fraught with danger posed by hostile Creeks who refused to join the forced migration of their people to the Arkansas territory. Barnum reported that these hostiles "almost daily murdered passengers" who traveled through the Nation. He further indicated that just the day before his journey began the mail stage had been stopped, all the passengers killed, and the stage burned. Violence had been a problem off and on for many years. In 1818 so many people were murdered—entire families being wiped out—that a military contingent led by Sam Dale and Maj. White Yungs of the Eighth U.S. Infantry was sent in to sweep the area of hostiles.[58]

By the 1830s the steamboat had become the main mode of travel in antebellum Alabama as the most important towns sprung up along the state's navigable rivers. As indicated previously, steamboat travel was complemented by stagecoach passenger service to river landings. The arrival of steam-powered river craft was celebrated by Alabama's planters, many of whom abutted or had convenient access to the Alabama and Tombigbee rivers. Previously, they slowly floated their cotton to market in Mobile on primitive flat-bottomed boats. In 1818 the steamboat *Alabama,* constructed by the St. Stephens Steamboat Company, is believed to have been the first steamboat to ply Alabama's waters. Unfortunately, after steaming down river from St. Stephens to Mobile, it was unable to generate enough power to return back upstream. The disappointment of its performance was ameliorated somewhat in May 1820 when the steamboat *Tensas* made it upstream as far as Cahaba. On October 22, 1821, the *Harriet* became the first steamboat to make it as far north as Montgomery, having made the trip in just ten days from Mobile, including three days spent in stops at Claiborne, Cahaba, and Selma. On the return trip, in addition to passengers, the *Harriet* carried 265 bales of cotton on board and another 210 bales in tow on a separate barge. From then on, the steamboat would be the transportation work horse of the cotton trade.[59]

---

[58] Jeffrey C. Benton, *The Very Worst Road: Travelers' Accounts of Crossing Alabama's Old Creek Indian Territory, 1820–1847* (Historic Chattahoochee Commission of Alabama and Georgia, 1998), 14–15, 27–29, 64, and 125; Southerland and Brown, *Federal Road,* 57.

[59] Jack N. Nelms, "Early Days with the Alabama River Steamboats," *Alabama Review* 36 (January 1984): 13–14.

Often impassable conditions of the roads during rainy weather, uncomfortable rides over rough dry roads, and risk of violent attack led many Alabamians and those visiting the state increasingly to opt for steamboat travel instead of overland routes. Steamboat travel, however, was not without risk and inconvenience. Boats were often grounded on sandbars that led to frustrating delays. Sunken logs or snags stranded boats or, worse, caused boats to sink and, occasionally, passengers to drown. Also, boats were sometimes stricken by exploding boilers and consuming fires that resulted in tragic deaths. One of the worst accidents during Alabama's steamboat era occurred on March 5, 1850, when the *Orline St. John* caught fire on the Alabama River near Camden's Bridgeport Landing. The fire spread so rapidly that most passengers were trapped aboard, with forty of the approximately sixty passengers—many of whom were women and children—dying either on board or drowning after escaping from the fire onboard. The news of this disaster spread quickly up and down the river and generated many tales of tragic loss, heroism, and mystery. Heroism was achieved by a slave by the name of Abram, who, at great risk to his own personal safety, rescued nine people found floating in the river several miles downstream from the wreck. Mystery surrounded a lost cargo of substantial quantities of gold that were being brought back from California by a number of prospectors as well as by an official of the U.S. Navy. Unsubstantiated rumors abounded that someone—possibly the captain of the *Orline St. John* himself—brought in divers from the Caribbean who searched for the downed ship during the summer when the waters had receded, and removed the lost gold from the wreckage.[60]

The breadth of steamboat travel is reflected by the number of boats operating on Alabama's rivers. An unofficial inventory conducted by Judge A. H. Benners reveals that at least 337 steamboats plied Alabama's rivers between 1819 and 1869. Landings along the Alabama River alone numbered 314. The boats often carried names reflective of the era, including *Alabama, Andrew Jackson, Alamo, Cahawba, Chickasaw, Choctaw, Cotton Plant, Governor Israel Pickens, John C. Calhoun, Lewis Cass, Mobile, Sam Dale, Tombeckbe,* and *William R. King.* By the 1850s the larger steamboats had become very comfortable and elegant floating palaces, equipped with well-stocked bars, gaming tables, ballrooms for dancing, and, in some cases, a calliope. Gunfire announced their approach, generating great excitement at the towns and landings along the route. This was especially so at night when the waiting crowds were in awe of the approaching vessels all aglow from a bellowing furnace and bright lights from the ballroom. An orchestra

---

[60] Jackson, *Rivers of History*, 87–97; Nelms, "Alabama River Steamboats," 16–17; James T. Lloyd, *Lloyd's Steamboat Directory and Disasters on the Western Waters* (Cincinnati, Ohio: James T. Lloyd & Co., 1856), 207–09. See also Robert O. Mellown, "Steamboats in Alabama," *Encyclopedia of Alabama,* http://www.encyclopediaofalabama.org/face/Article.jsp?id=h-1803 (accessed February 4, 2013). In 1826, the General Assembly imposed the state's first transportation regulations by requiring steamboats to be inspected annually and be certified as "staunch and well found, both in hull and machinery." Those without the certification were assigned the burden of proof in lawsuits for damages. *Ala. Acts (1826)*, 5.

playing in the ballroom or a calliope steaming a tune contributed to the exhilaration of the locals who rushed to the scene.[61]

Although Alabama's first railroad began operating in 1832, the steamboat would remain the main mode of transportation prior to the Civil War. A major impediment to river traffic on the Tennessee River at Muscle Shoals, however, triggered the development of railroads in the Tennessee Valley. On January 30, 1830, the General Assembly chartered the Tuscumbia Rail Company to build a short road of just two miles from the Tuscumbia River landing to the present city of Sheffield, becoming one of the first railroads in the country. Powered at first by horses, the line soon boasted the first steam locomotive west of the Alleghenies. Just two years later, the legislature chartered the Tuscumbia, Courtland and Decatur Railroad. This railroad was to run forty-four miles from Tuscumbia to Decatur, allowing a transportation route around the rapids on the Tennessee River at Muscle Shoals. In 1847 these two railroads were purchased and merged into the Tennessee Valley Railroad, which was later taken over by the Memphis & Charleston Railroad Company.[62]

Between 1830 and 1840, some twenty-five railroad companies were chartered in Alabama, but few got off the ground due to the Panic of 1837. One of those that did eventually succeed was the Montgomery Railroad Company, which was chartered by the legislature in 1834 with an authorized capital of one million dollars. Two wealthy planters, Abner McGhee and Charles T. Pollard, pushed for this railroad, envisioning a way to capture the trade of northwest Georgia and parts of the Tennessee Valley with a railway between Montgomery and Columbus, Georgia. Such a railway would also provide rail traffic between the Atlantic and the Alabama River. After opening its first twelve miles of track in 1840, just two years later the company, staggering from the effects of the economic downturn, failed and its property was sold under foreclosure. The company was reorganized by McGehee and Charles Pollard as the Montgomery & West Point Railroad. This road, completed in 1851, was a success in part because of its receipt of federally backed loans, but also because of its use of slave labor for construction.[63]

With the assistance of the Montgomery & West Point Railroad, the Alabama & Florida Railroad Company was the first to take rail traffic to the Gulf of Mexico from Montgomery. With the further assistance of federal land grants, the Alabama & Florida reached Pensacola in 1861. In furtherance of making Montgomery the state's first rail hub, Charles Pollard obtained three charters to connect Montgomery with Selma. The first charter involved the Western Railroad of Alabama, which purchased the Montgomery & West Point Railroad. Pollard's plan was to connect this railroad with the Alabama & Mississippi Rivers Railroad and the Alabama & Tennessee Rivers Railroad at Selma. The Civil War would hinder Pollard's plan for a

[61] J. H. Scruggs, Jr., *Alabama Steamboats, 1819–1869* (Birmingham, Ala. 1953); Nelms, "Alabama River Steamboats," 16.

[62] Moore, *History of Alabama*, 309; Lee, "Alabama Railroads."

[63] Moore, *History of Alabama*, 310–12; Lee, "Alabama Railroads."

highly integrated rail system within the state to compete with river transportation. During the 1850s, as the Civil War approached, in excess of seventy railroads were chartered by the state legislature, but few were actually built, due in large part to Governor Winston's vetoes of any state financial aid to proposed railroad companies. In 1856, however, with increasing pressure of the railway lobby, the legislature enacted legislation over Winston's vetoes and granted a loan of $200,000 to the Alabama & Tennessee Rivers Railroad and $300,000 to the Memphis & Charleston Railroad. During the war, a number of Alabama's railroads were utilized to move Confederate troops, while at least one was dismantled so that its rails and equipment could be used by other railroads closer to the theater of war.[64]

Despite the emergence of railroads, the steamboat was still the primary conveyance for delivering cotton to market and thus remained the predominant mode of travel before the Civil War. We have previously seen that the highly profitable production of cotton was the mainstay of Alabama's agriculturally based economy. However, there was increasing concern that cotton was overproduced to the detriment of other needed farm staples. Agricultural literature and a growing number of county agricultural societies began to advocate a reduction of cotton acreage to free up land and capital for a diversification of crops. Despite the advocacy of more progressive methods, cotton acreage was not significantly reduced. In fact, during the 1850s even more slaves were bought by planters to plant even more acres of cotton to such an extent that by 1860 cotton production was more than seventy-five per cent above that of 1850. This profitable continual cycle would not be broken until the advent of war.[65]

While there was relatively little industrial development in Alabama during the antebellum period, the state's first major manufacturers not surprisingly took advantage of Alabama's plentiful cotton production. The first cotton mill in the state, The Bell Factory of Madison County, was incorporated by the Alabama legislature in 1832. Despite the abundance of cotton grown locally, the 1850 census documented only twelve cotton mills within the state with a total capitalization of $651,900 and employing a total of 736 workers. In 1860, with the addition of two more mills, Alabama was producing cotton goods valued at $1,040,147.[66]

Alabama's production of cotton also prompted the founding of cotton gin factories, most notably that founded by Daniel Pratt in Autauga County. Originally from New England, Pratt ventured south in 1819 to Georgia, where he used his skills as a woodworker to build fine plantation homes in the cotton-rich vicinity of Milledgeville and Macon. Several years later Pratt became the factory manager for Samuel Griswold, a fellow transplanted New Englander who manufactured cotton gins. Eager to follow the westward expansion of cotton, Pratt took his family to central Alabama where, with

---

[64] Moore, *History of Alabama*, 311–17; Lee, "Alabama Railroads."

[65] Jordan, *Ante-Bellum Alabama*, 106–39; Moore, *History of Alabama*, 271, 279–83.

[66] Moore, *History of Alabama*, 284–86; Jordan, *Ante-Bellum Alabama*, 140.

the help of two slaves and enough materials to construct fifty gins, he founded the Daniel Pratt Gin Company about 1833. Initially he leased a site on Autauga Creek known as McNeil's Creek where he began manufacturing his gins. Around 1838 he purchased 1,822 acres of land further up this creek where he constructed a permanent factory and founded the town of Prattville.[67]

Daniel Pratt's Gin Company
One of the few businesses that survived the Civil War

Library of Congress

Pratt, generally recognized as Alabama's first major industrialist, was a passionate member of the Whig Party who advocated Southern self-sufficiency by pushing for a balanced economy, the development of more industries, state aid to railroads, and other types of internal improvements. He practiced what he preached when he made Prattville a self-sufficient community by diversifying its industries, building homes and churches for his workers, and establishing one of Alabama's first free public schools. In

---

[67] Herbert James Lewis, "Daniel Pratt," *Encyclopedia of Alabama*, http://www.encyclo-pediaofalabama.org/face/Article.jsp?id=h-1184 (accessed February 4, 2013); see also Merrill E. Pratt, *Daniel Pratt: Alabama's First Industrialist* (New York: The Newcomen Society of England, American Branch, 1949); Ethel Armes, *The Story of Coal and Iron in Alabama* (Birmingham, Ala., 1910), 174–76, 280–82.

addition to cotton gins, Pratt's facilities produced various kinds of cloth, tin, carriages, wagons, windows, and door sashes. Pratt's most successful enterprise at Prattville, however, was the manufacture of cotton gins for planters all over the world in such faraway places as Russia, Great Britain, France, Cuba, Mexico, and countries in Central and South America. By 1860, Alabama was producing more cotton gins than any other state in the Union, with Pratt's factory producing about one fourth of the state's total at the rate of 1,500 gins per year. Unlike most, Pratt's success would continue after the Civil War when he invested the fortune he had made from manufacturing cotton gins into developing north Alabama's mostly untapped mineral sources. Along with his ward and eventual son-in-law, Henry F. DeBardeleben, Pratt invested in a new railroad venture, the South and North Railroad, the Red Mountain Iron and Coal Company, and the rebuilding of the Oxmoor furnaces in Jefferson County destroyed by Wilson's Raiders at the end of the Civil War.[68]

Although most of Alabama's early industries were in some fashion related to cotton, in the early 1830s crude iron manufacturing began in Bibb and Shelby counties. This signaled a meager start to the development of Alabama's plentiful mineral resources. In the 1840s it was becoming increasingly evident that Alabama was sitting on top of a rich bed of natural resources which could be developed with plenty of available water power. In 1847 Michael Toumey, Alabama's newly appointed state geologist, indicated that Alabama's coal and iron deposits were quite remarkable. In 1853 *DeBow's Review* complained that "[t]oo much time is given to the growing of cotton," and asked, "How long, with all the advantages which God has given her, shall Alabama remain in the background, with her countless millions of wealth buried beneath her soil?"[69]

One of the first entrepreneurs to take advantage of Alabama's mineral resources on a significant scale was Massachusetts native Horace Ware. In 1835, at the age of sixteen, he partnered with his father, Jonathan, to construct and operate several rudimentary forges in Shelby and Bibb counties. Just four years later Horace had taken over his father's share of the business and went on to build Alabama's first permanent ironworks and the state's first rolling mill. Ware's Shelby County Iron Manufacturing Company, locally known as the Shelby County Ironworks, progressed from its modest beginnings in the 1840s into a significant industrial complex, similar to that developed by Daniel Pratt at Prattville. By 1860 his community, located a few miles south of Columbiana, contained a blast furnace, forge, foundry, school, church, and homes housing several hundred people.

---

[68] Lewis, "Daniel Pratt"; Jordan, *Ante-Bellum Alabama*, 152. The Pratt's cotton gin company was acquired by the Continental Gin Company in 1899. The company later became the Continental Eagle Corporation and manufactured cotton gins in several of the original brick structures that Pratt built until 2009, when the company outsourced most of its operations to India. These surviving buildings are believed to be the longest continuously occupied industrial buildings in Alabama. In March 2012 an Atlanta-based commercial real estate developer announced the signing of a contract to keep the structures intact and to redevelop the historic property.

[69] Jordan, *Ante-Bellum Alabama*, 142–44; *DeBow's Review*, XIV (1853), 67–68.

Ware's company, like many others of the era, utilized slave labor, preferring if at all possible to hire them from their owners rather than purchase them. Hired slaves were fed, clothed, and housed at company expense. Hard-to-find skilled white workers were also hired as laborers, most often filling supervisory positions.[70]

In its early years the Shelby Iron Works sold much of its iron to local plantation blacksmiths or made it into hollow ware such as bowls, pitchers, teapots, and trays, as well as several castings used for making kitchen ware or farm implements. Ware's business began to expand when he hauled his product by wagon to the Coosa River where he transported it by river to Montgomery, Prattville, Selma, and Mobile. As a result he was able to ship his iron to more affluent customers, such as Daniel Pratt. During the Civil War, Ware sold most of his interest in the company but retained a minor role sitting on the company's board of directors. During the war, the company added a larger furnace and became Alabama's primary supplier of iron to the Confederate Naval Arsenal in Selma. The Shelby Iron Works continued its role as a major supplier of the Confederate arsenal until its furnace's blast engine and boilers were destroyed by a detachment of Wilson's Raiders on March 31, 1865, near the end of the war.[71]

About the same time that Horace Ware and his father were starting up his rudimentary iron forges in Shelby and Bibb counties in the 1830s, gold was discovered in a large section of east Alabama, which included Chilton, Lee, Elmore, Coosa, Tallapoosa, Chambers, Talladega, Randolph, Clay, and Cleburne counties. While this discovery generated a flurry of excitement and so-called "gold fever" for adventurous prospectors, it was relatively short-lived and pretty much died out in 1849 when the majority of prospectors followed the "Gold Rush" to California. Nonetheless miners rushed into east Alabama in the 1830s and 1840s to create such mining communities as Goldville, Goldberg, Silver Hill, and Abracoochie. Perhaps the most prominent of these communities was Abracoochie, located in Celburne County. It was a town of some 5,000 inhabitants in 1845 and possessed twenty general stores, five saloons, two mining equipment companies, two hotels, a fire department, a race track, a school, two churches, over a hundred permanent homes, and numerous tents and temporary shacks. Not far behind was Goldville—located in northern Tallapoosa County— with approximately 3,000 residents, twelve stores, three saloons, a hotel, a mining supply house, a race track, a school, and several churches. Signifi-

---

[70] Robert H. McKenzie, "Horace Ware: Alabama Iron Pioneer," *Alabama Review* 26 (July 1973): 157–72; Herbert J. Lewis, "Horace Ware," *Encyclopedia of Alabama*, http://www.encyclopediaofalabama.org/face/Article.jsp?id=h-1174 (accessed February 4, 2013).

[71] McKenzie, "Alabama Iron Pioneer," 167–72; Lewis, "Horace Ware." Ware was able to resurrect the Shelby Iron Works after the Civil War when he and John W. Lapsley succeeded in attracting northern capital to rebuild it and convert it into a nationally renowned railroad-car wheel manufacturer. Although Ware sold his interest in the company in 1881, it continued in operation until August 1923.

cant mines in the Goldville District, in addition to Goldville, included Birdsong, Log Pits, Hog Mountain and Dutch Bend.[72]

For the most part armed with just picks, shovels, and buckets, and facing a rough terrain over which they had to haul their meager equipment and supplies, Alabama's prospectors by 1840 had succeeded in mining a considerable quantity of gold—some individual nuggets valued as much as $1200. Ironically, however, more money was probably made by those benefiting from the land booms in the various mining districts than was realized from the actual mining of gold. Indeed, by 1860, according to the records of the United States mint, only $367,000 worth of gold had been sent to them between 1830 and 1860. But, as conjectured by a researcher of Alabama's gold mining, most of the ore mined within this time frame probably never made it directly to the mints and was instead used for money locally to defray expenses, to purchase supplies out of state, or to pay many miners' way to the more alluring fields of California.[73]

Alabama's mini gold rush, while creating quite a hullabaloo for a while, did not have the long lasting or widespread economic significance as did the commencement of Alabama's coal and iron production. William Phineas Browne, yet another native New Englander promoting industrial development in antebellum Alabama, is credited with operating the state's first regular systematic underground coal mines near Montevallo in Shelby County. A native of Vermont, Browne moved to Alabama in the early 1830s where he became involved in many enterprises as a lawyer, engineer, and real estate investor. Notably, after investing in canal projects in Muscle Shoals and New Orleans and running a steamship company that carried mail and freight daily between New Orleans and Mobile, in the mid-1830s he partnered with Henry Hitchcock—a fellow former Vermonter and a future Alabama Supreme Court chief justice—in the acquisition of prime real estate in Mobile. Struggling to recover after the Panic of 1837, Browne purchased land near his wife's family in Shelby County, portions of which were located within the rich Cahaba coal field.[74]

As soon as Browne discovered the coal seams on his land, he began to lobby the legislature and the railroads to build a rail line to Montevallo so that he could more easily market the coal on his property. In support of his proposal, he reported to the Alabama and Tennessee Rivers Railroad company that his land contained 1.6 million tons of coal. Utilizing slave labor, in 1851 Browne began hauling his coal by wagon to the Cahaba River where it was taken by barge to Selma to be sold. Browne transported his coal to market in this manner for two years before the Alabama and Ten-

---

[72] Robert A. Russell, "Gold Mining in Alabama Before 1860," *Alabama Review* 10 (January 1957): 5–14; Moore, *History of Alabama*, 289.

[73] Ibid.

[74] Virginia E. Knapp, "William Phineas Browne, Business Man and Pioneer Mine Operator of Alabama," Part 1, *Alabama Review* 3 (April 1950): 111; James Sanders Day, "'Diamonds in the Rough': A History of Alabama's Cahaba Coal Field," Ph.D. diss., Auburn University, 2002; Herbert J. Lewis, "William Phineas Browne," *Encyclopedia of Alabama*, http://www.encyclopediaofalabama.org/ face/Article.jsp?id=h-1119 (accessed February 4, 2013); Armes, *Story of Coal and Iron*, 70, 75, 154–55, and 169.

nessee River Railroad extended to Montevallo, from where Browne was able to lay a short branch line to the coal mines on his property. Although his transportation problems eased with the arrival of the railroad to his property, Browne was frequently beset with labor problems. Free labor was unreliable and planters were hesitant to allow their slaves to be hired out to work underground. Nevertheless, by 1856 Browne's labor force was such that he was able to remove five tons of coal per day from his mines. Browne's business continued to grow as the Civil War approached. In 1858 he contracted to supply 1,000 tons of coal to the Montgomery Gas and Light Company, in the summer of 1861 in excess of 1,500 tram-loads of coal was extracted from his mines, and in 1862 was he was under contract with the Confederate government to furnish it 4,000 tons of coal. Although Browne made a fortune selling his coal, he lost it at the end of the war since most of his assets were tied up in Confederate bonds and slaves.[75]

The triumvirate of native New Englanders—Daniel Pratt, Horace Ware, and William Phineas Browne—had a different vision of Alabama's future and represented an alternative to Alabama's cotton-dominated frontier economy. While they all utilized slave labor to some extent, Pratt—the more publicly visible of the three—favored a more diverse economy that would make the South self-sufficient and suggested that slavery would become less profitable and thus unsustainable. In a public statement made in 1859, Pratt demonstrated that he was a moderate in the midst of fiery secessionists. Although professing to be a strong defender of Southern rights, Pratt indicated that he would take "somewhat a different course from that of the politicians." In this regard, he stated that he "would not make any flaming fiery speeches and threats," but instead "would go quietly and peaceably to work, and make ourselves less dependent on those who abuse and would gladly ruin us." He then urged the local production of a laundry list of goods from firearms and farm implements to cotton gins with the state's own natural resources. As for slavery, he was opposed to "fencing it in or penning it up" for it would "eventually go where it can be made profitable, and nowhere else is it wanted."[76]

Although Pratt, Ware, and Browne were all ahead of their time, their pioneering efforts paved the way for future industrialists, such as Truman H. Aldrich, James W. Sloss, Henry F. DeBardeleben, and Enoch Ensley, who would not be strapped by a slave-based cotton economy. As early as 1849, Pratt's significance was recognized by *DeBow's Review*, which asserted that "no man in Alabama has contributed more than Daniel Pratt to its prosperity; none had done more to bring the loom, the plough, and the anvil into closer proximity." As for Browne, his biographer summed up his importance by simply stating that he "was a Yankee who foresaw the industrial possibilities of the South and went to work to develop those possibilities."[77]

---

[75] Lewis, "William Phineas Browne."

[76] Jordan, *Ante-Bellum Alabama*, 159.

[77] Lewis, "Daniel Pratt"; Virginia E. Knapp, "William Phineas Browne, A Yankee Business Man of the South," Master's Thesis, University of Texas, 1948, 81.

The initial stages of industrial development in Alabama, primarily at the hands of Pratt, Ware, and Browne, in essence marked the beginning of the end of Alabama's frontier. Like most everything else, however, Alabama's industrial development was seriously interrupted by the Civil War. All of the state's attainments and developments during its formative antebellum period were in utter ruins. Alabama historian Leah Rawls Atkins precisely summarized the devastating effects of the war: "Alabama society had collapsed under the strain of wartime conditions. Specie had vanished, spent for military supplies and food or secretly buried for its safety. Barter replaced inflated paper currency. Many schools and churches were closed, and probably one-fourth of the newspapers ceased publication. Cotton was piled on plantations or stored and would be burned by invading armies or confiscated as matériel of war."[78]

Of course, the one redeeming effect of the war was the freedom accorded to hundreds of thousands of African American Alabamians who had been held in bondage all of their lives. Their emancipation, however, was just the beginning of a long struggle to obtain full justice and equality, which would frame many of the issues and events of the twentieth century. The freed slaves crossed over into a new frontier on a journey seeking the full rewards of freedom—having just witnessed the end of the frontier society that they, while enslaved, had toiled to help develop.

꧁

[78] Rogers et al., *Alabama*, 222.

Acknowledgments

My acknowledgments must begin with those who came before me and who instilled in me a keen interest in history, and eventually a desire to write a book concerning Alabama's early history. In the introduction, I mentioned how my father initiated me to Alabama's fascinating past by taking the family on weekend excursions to places such as the site of the Battle of the Holy Ground in Lowndes County, Horseshoe Bend National Park, Moundville, and the ruins of old Cahaba. If it had not been for my father introducing to these venues and others, I may never have had any real interest in my past nor the lives of my ancestors. Although I majored in history in college, my legal career did not leave much time for me to do much in the way of research and writing with regard to my interest in history.

When I headed off to law school in 1971, my father informed me that I would be a fifth generation lawyer if I successfully completed my studies and passed the bar exam. This intrigued me and I hoped one day to learn more about my ancestors. In 2003, as I neared retirement from the U.S. Department of Justice, I finally began to research my ancestors and discovered that I was a seventh generation lawyer, instead of a fifth generation lawyer as my father had believed. During my research, I discovered two more generations of lawyers on my mother's side of the family of which my father was apparently unaware.

I wish to acknowledge these six generations of lawyers because learning about them further had inspired me to write this book. James Brooks, my fourth great grandfather, immigrated from Ireland, fought in the American Revolution, and practiced law in Albemarle County, Virginia. Henry Wilbourne Stevens, my third great grandfather, graduated from the Litchfield Law School in Connecticut before emigrating to Mobile in 1814, where he joined the Mississippi Territorial militia for a short while before eventually becoming Montgomery County's first justice of the peace and the register of its orphans' court and later serving on the county court in Bibb County (then Cahawba County). William Phineas Browne, my second great grandfather, was admitted to the Vermont bar in 1811 and subsequently moved to Alabama, where he became involved in many business ventures including operating the state's first regular systematic underground coal mines near Montevallo in Shelby County. William Bradford Browne, my great grandfather, practiced law in Columbiana, where he also served as Columbiana's mayor for many years. Frederick G. Koenig, my grandfather, practiced law in Columbiana before moving to Birmingham in 1924 where he practiced law until he died in 1949. Herbert J. Lewis, Jr., my father, graduated from Birmingham-Southern College and the University of Alabama School of Law, served in the Army Air Corps during World War II, and became Chief Counsel of the Veterans Administration in Alabama.

In 2003, I decided to attempt to write an article concerning my third great grandfather, Henry Wilbourne Stevens. Not sure where to turn, I decided to call Dr. Jeff Jakeman, who was then the Editor of the *Alabama Review*. I asked Jeff what I needed to do to have my article submitted for possible publication by the *Review*, thinking at that time that publication of the article would indeed be a long shot. Jeff took his time to explain that the best course of action was for me to submit a paper to the Alabama Historical Association (AHA) for presentation to its upcoming annual meeting. I expressed my reluctance, but Jeff thought I had a reasonable chance to have my paper accepted for presentation. He explained, however, that even if it were accepted, that did not guarantee that the paper would be published by the *Review*. In any event, I pressed forward.

As I was preparing for my AHA presentation, I was introduced to Steve Murray, then the Managing Editor of the *Alabama Review* and currently the Director of the Alabama Department of Archives and History. Steve ably shepherded me through my presentation and encouraged me to submit an expanded version of my paper for consideration for publication by the *Alabama Review*. I did, and after submission for peer review, my proposal was thankfully accepted for publication. I then went through a detailed editorial process with Steve, who showed great patience for a novice such as myself to the publication business. After the publication of my article in the *Review* in 2006, Steve contacted me to inquire of my interest in writing a couple of entries for the online *Encyclopedia of Alabama* (EOA). I readily agreed and began submitting a few articles to the EOA. Shortly thereafter I was approached by Jeff Jakeman to work under contract as a free-lance writer and editor for the EOA. While all of this was transpiring, I was kicking around the idea of writing a book about Alabama's formative period.

I obviously owe everyone associated with the EOA for giving me the opportunity to improve my research and writing skills and giving me the confidence to take on a project such as this one. My confidence was significantly boosted by the complimentary remarks made to me and the encouragement given to me by EOA's Editor-in-Chief, Dr. Wayne Flynt. In addition to Wayne Flynt, Jeff Jakeman, and Steve Murray, I need to acknowledge the help and support offered by James P. Kaetz, managing editor; Claire Wilson, senior content editor; Christopher Maloney, content editor; Laura Newland Hill, communications director; Benjamin Berntson, production editor; and Donna Siebenthaler, graduate research assistant.

Of vital assistance to me during the period in which I was seeking a publisher for this book were James L. Noles, Jr. and Dr. Paul Pruitt, Jr. Jim Noles, a lawyer, author, and chairman of the board of directors of the Alabama Humanities Foundation, read portions of my manuscript and gave me prudent advice throughout this process. Paul Pruitt, legal historian and librarian at the University of Alabama School of Law, read the entire manuscript and offered detailed constructive criticism that made the end product considerably better. Others to whom I owe a debt of gratitude, for reasons not necessarily known to them, include Virginia Estella Knapp (deceased), biographer of William Phineas Browne; Dr. Leah Rawls Atkins; Martin Everse, former director of Tannehill Ironworks Historical State Park and Brierfield Ironworks Historical State Park; Dr. James S. Day, Assistant Vice

President of Academic Affairs and Associate Professor of History at the University of Montevallo; Carey Cauthen, former Associate Editor of the *Alabama Review* and currently web designer at the University of Alabama at Birmingham; Judge Melford O. Cleveland of Wilton, Alabama; Robert Stewart, former Executive Director of Alabama Humanities Foundation; Garland Cook Smith, Wilcox County Historical Society, Camden, Alabama; Bobby Joe Seales, President of the Shelby County Historical Society; Elizabeth C. Wells, coordinator of the Special Collections Department, Samford University Library, Birmingham, Alabama; the research staff at the Alabama Department of Archives and History; the staff of the North Shelby County Library; and the staff of the Birmingham Linn-Henley Library.

I also express my thanks, in the publication process, to Dr. Steven Alan Childress, Publisher of Quid Pro Books, for his helpful editorial and presentation suggestions, as well as to Barbara Merchant, for her insightful contributions as an experienced academic editor and aficionado of Alabama's rich history.

Finally, I want to thank my wife Becky, my daughter Emily L. Rich, and my sister, Myra L. Daniel, who researched family genealogical issues that proved helpful to me in the writing of certain parts of this book. The danger in acknowledgments is the fear that you leave someone out that deserves mention. This I hope I have not done.

— H. J. L.

Selected Bibliography

Books

Abernethy, Thomas Perkins. *From Frontier to Plantation in Tennessee—A Study in Frontier Democracy*. Chapel Hill: University of North Carolina Press, 1932.

———. *The Formative Period in Alabama, 1815–1828*. Tuscaloosa: University of Alabama Press, 1995. Reprinted from Montgomery, Ala.: Alabama State Dept. of Archives and History (Historical and Patriotic Series no. 6), 1922.

Amos [Doss], Harriet E. *Cotton City: Urban Development in Antebellum Mobile*. Tuscaloosa: University of Alabama Press, 1985.

Armes, Ethel. *The Story of Coal and Iron in Alabama*. Birmingham, Ala., 1910.

Ayers, Edward L. *Vengeance and Justice: Crime and Punishment in the 19th-Century American South*. New York: Oxford University Press, 1984.

Bailey, Hugh C. *John Williams Walker: A Study in the Political, Social, and Cultural Life of the Old Southwest*. Tuscaloosa: University of Alabama Press, 1964.

Baldwin, Joseph G. *The Flush Times of Alabama and Mississippi*. American Century Series. New York: Sagamore Press, Inc., 1957. Reprinted from original edition, New York: D. Appleton & Co., 1854.

Barnes, Celia. *Native American Power in the United States, 1783–1795*. Madison, NJ: Farleigh Dickinson University Press, 2003.

Barney, William L. *The Secessionist Impulse: Alabama and Mississippi in 1860*. Princeton, New Jersey: Princeton University Press, 1974.

Bassett, John Spencer, ed. *Correspondence of Andrew Jackson*. Washington, DC: Carnegie Institution, 1926–1935.

Beidler, Philip D. *First Books: The Printed Word and Cultural Formation in Early Alabama*. Tuscaloosa: University of Alabama Press, 1999.

Betts, Edward Chambers. *Early History of Huntsville, Alabama, 1804–1870*. rev. ed. Montgomery, Ala.: The Brown Printing Co., 1916.

Beirne, Francis. *The War of 1812*. New York: E. P. Dutton, 1949.

Benton, Jeffrey C. *The Very Worst Road: Traveller's Accounts of Crossing Alabama's Old Creek Indian Territory, 1820–1847*. Historic Chattahoochee Commission of Alabama and Georgia, 1998.

Blaufarb, Rafe. *Bonapartists in the Borderlands: French Exiles and Refugees on the Gulf Coast, 1815–1835*. Tuscaloosa: University of Alabama Press, 2005.

Blue, M. P., Beale and Phelan, *City Directory and History of Montgomery, Alabama*. Montgomery, Ala.: T. C. Bingham & Co. Printers and Binders, 1878.

Borneman, Walter R. *1812: The War that Forged a Nation*. New York: Harper Collins Publishers, 2004.

Bosmajian, Haig A. *Metaphor and Reason in Judicial Opinions*. Carbondale: Southern Illinois University Press, 1992.

Boyd, Minnie Clare. *Alabama in the Fifties: A Social Study*. New York: Columbia University Press, 1931.

Brands, H. W. *Andrew Jackson: His Life and Times*. New York: Doubleday, 2005.

Brannon, Peter. *Peter Brannon's Alabama Travel Logs: A Series of Historic Stories of Trips Through Alabama*. Montgomery, Ala.: Paragon Press, 1928.

Brantley, William H. *Banking in Alabama: 1816–1860*. 2 vols. Birmingham: Birmingham Printing Co., 1961.

———. *Three Capitals, A Book About the First Three Capitals of Alabama: St. Stephens, Huntsville & Cahawba, 1818–1826.*, 1947. Reprint. Tuscaloosa: University of Alabama Press, 1976.

Braund, Kathryn E. *Deerskins & Duffels: The Creek Indian Trade with Anglo-America, 1685– 1815*. Lincoln: University of Nebraska Press, 1993.

Brewer, Willis. *Alabama: Her History, Resources, War Record, and Public Men, From 1540 to 1872*. 1872. Reprint. Baltimore, Md.: Genealogical Publishing Co., 2000.

Buchanan, John. *Jackson's Way: Andrew Jackson and the People of the Western Waters*. New York: Wiley, 2001.

Burke, Ulick Ralph. *A History of Spain from the Earliest Times to the Death of Ferdinand the Catholic*. 2nd ed. London: Longman's, Green, and Co., 1900.

Carter, Clarence E. ed., *Territorial Papers of the United States*, vols. 5 and 6, *Mississippi*. Washington, D.C.: Government Printing Office, 1937.

Caruso, John Anthony. *The Great Lakes Frontier: An Epic of the Old Northwest*. Indianapolis: Bobbs-Merrill, 1961.

Caughey, John Walton. *McGillivray of the Creeks*. Norman: University of Oklahoma Press, 1938.

Cashin, Edward J. *Lachlan McGillivray, Indian Trader: The Shaping of the Southern Colonial Frontier*. Athens: University of Georgia Press, 1992.

Channing, Edward. *A History of the United States*, vol. 1. *The Planting of a Nation in the New World, 1000–1600*. New York: Macmillan, 1905.

Clark, Willis G. *History of Education in Alabama, 1702–1889*. Washington, 1889.

Clayton, Lawrence A., Vernon J. Knight, and Edward C. Moore. *The De Soto Chronicles: The Expedition of Hernando de Soto to North America in 1539–1543*. Tuscaloosa: University of Alabama Press, 1993.

Clinton, Matthew William. *Tuscaloosa, Alabama: Its Early Days, 1816–1865*. Tuscaloosa, Ala.: The Zonta Club, 1958.

Cox, Isaac J. *The West Florida Controversy, 1798–1813: A Study in American Diplomacy*. Baltimore: John Hopkins Press, 1918.

Crockett, Davy. *A Narrative of the Life of David Crockett of the State of Tennessee*. 1834. Reprint. Lincoln: University of Nebraska Press, 1987.

Davis, William C. *The Rogue Republic: How Would-Be Patriots Waged the Shortest Revolution in American History*. Boston: Houghton Mifflin Harcourt, 2011.

DeLand, T. A. and A. Davis Smith. *Northern Alabama: Historical and Biographical Illustrated*. Birmingham: n.p., 1888. s.v. "Chapman, Reuben."

Dorman, Lewey. *Party Politics in Alabama from 1850 through 1860*. Tuscaloosa: University of Alabama Press, 1995.

Dubose, Joel C. ed. *Notable Men of Alabama: Personal and Genealogical with Portraits*. vol. 1. Atlanta, Ga.: Southern Historical Association, 1904.

————. *Sketches of Alabama History*. Philadelphia: Eldredge & Bro., 1901.

Dupre, Daniel S. *Transforming the Cotton Frontier: Madison County, Alabama, 1800–1840*. Baton Rouge: Louisiana State University Press, 1997.

Durham, David I. *A Southern Moderate in Radical Times: Henry Washington Hilliard, 1808–1892*. Baton Rouge: Louisiana State University Press, 2008.

Eggleston, George Cary. *Red Eagle and the Wars with the Creek Indians of Alabama*. New York: Dodd, Mead & Co., 1878.

Ellis, Joseph J. *American Creation: Triumphs and Tragedies at the Founding of the Republic*. New York: A. A. Knopf, 2007.

Ethridge, Robbie. *Creek Country: The Creek Indians and Their World*. Chapel Hill: University of North Carolina Press, 2003.

Fabel, Robin F. A. *Bombast and Broadsides: The Lives of George Johnstone*. Tuscaloosa: University of Alabama Press, 1987.

Field, Vena Bernadette. *Constantia: A Study of the Life and Works of Judith Sargent Murray, 1751–1820*. Orono, Me.: University Press, 1931.

Foster, Thomas, ed., *The Collected Works of Benjamin Hawkins, 1796–1810*. Tuscaloosa: University of Alabama Press, 2003.

Frank, Andrew K. *Creeks and Southerners: Biculturalism on the Early American Frontier*. Lincoln: University of Nebraska Press, 2005.

Franklin, John Hope and Loren Schweninger. *Runaway Slaves: Rebels on the Plantations*. Oxford: Oxford University Press, 1999.

Fry, Anna M. Gayle. *Memories of Old Cahaba*. Nashville, Tenn.: Publishing House of the Methodist Episcopal Church, South, 1908.

Garrett, Mitchell Bennett. *Sixty Years of Howard College, 1842–1902*. Birmingham, Ala.: Howard College, 1927.

Garret, William. *Reminiscences of Public Men in Alabama for Thirty Years*. Atlanta, Ga.: Plantation Publishing Company's Press, 1872.

Gayarré, Charles. *Louisiana; Its Colonial History and Romance*. New York: Harper & Brothers, 1851.

Gosse, Phillip Henry. *Letters from Alabama, Chiefly Relating to Natural History*. Introduction by Harvey H. Jackson III. 1859. Reprint. Tuscaloosa: University of Alabama Press, 1993.

Griffith Jr., Benjamin W. *McIntosh and Weatherford: Creek Indian Leaders*. Tuscaloosa: University of Alabama Press, 1988.

Griffith, Lucille. *Alabama: A Documentary History to 1900*. rev. ed. Tuscaloosa: University of Alabama Press, 1972.

Gudmestad, Robert. *Steamboats and the Rise of the Cotton Kingdom*. Baton Rouge, La.: Louisiana State University Press, 2011.

Hadden, Sally. *Slave Patrols: Law and Violence in Virginia and the Carolinas*. Cambridge, Mass.: Harvard University Press, 2001.

Halbert, Henry S. and T. H. Ball. *The Creek War of 1813 and 1814*. 1895. Reprint. Tuscaloosa, Ala.: University of Alabama Press, 1995.

Hamilton, Francis Dew and Elizabeth Crabtree Wells. *Daughters of the Dream: Judson College, 1838–1988*. Marion, Ala.: Judson College, 1989.

Hamilton, Peter J. *Colonial Mobile*. 1910. Reprint. Tuscaloosa: University of Alabama Press, 1976.

————. *The Founding of Mobile: 1702–1718: Studies in the History of the First Capital of the Province of Louisiana, with Map Showing Its Relation to the Present City*. Mobile, Ala.: Commercial Print Co., 1911.

————. *Colonial Mobile: An Historical Study Largely from Original Sources, of the Alabama-Tombigbee Basin and the Old South West . . .* Rev. ed. Boston: Houghton Mifflin Co., 1910.

Hamilton, William Baskerville. *Anglo-American Law on the Frontier: Thomas Rodney and his Territorial Cases*. Durham, N.C.: Duke University Press, 1953.

Hamilton, Virginia Van der Veer. *Alabama a Bicentennial History*. New York, 1977.

Hanger, S. "'The Most Vile Atrocities': Accusations of Slander against Maria Cofignie, Para Libre (Louisiana 1795)," in *Colonial Lives: Documents in Latin American History, 1550–1850*, eds. Richard Boyer and Geoffrey Spurling. New York: Oxford University Press, 2000.

Haynes, Robert V. "The Formation of the Territory," in *A History of Mississippi*. ed. Richard Aubrey McLemore. Jackson: University & College Press of Mississippi, 1973.

Higginbotham, Jay. *Mobile: City by the Bay*. Mobile, Ala.: Azalea City Printers, 1968.

Hill, Mabel. *Liberty Documents, with Contemporary Exposition and Critical Comments, Drawn from Various Writers*. London: Longmans, Green, and Co., 1901.

Hitchcock, Henry. *The Alabama Justice of the Peace: Containing all the Duties, Powers and Authorities of that Office as Regulated by the Laws Now in Effect in this State*. Cahawba: William B. Allen Press, 1822.

Hooper, Johnson Jones. *Some Adventures of Captain Simon Suggs, Late of the Tallapoosa Volunteers; Together with "Taking the Census," and Other Alabama Sketches. By a Country Editor with a Portrait from Life, and Other Illustrations, by Darley*. Philadelphia: Carey and Hart, 1845.

Hubbs, G. Ward. ed. *Rowdy Tales from Early Alabama: The Humor of John Gorman Barr*. Tuscaloosa: University of Alabama, 1995.

————. *Guarding Greensboro: A Confederate Company in the Making of a Southern Community*. Athens: University of Georgia Press, 2003.

Jackson III, Harvey H. *Rivers of History: Life on the Coosa, Tallapoosa, Cahaba, and Alabama*. Tuscaloosa: University of Alabama Press, 1995.

Jackson, Walter M. *The Story of Selma*. Birmingham, Ala.: The Birmingham Printing Company, 1954.

James, Marquis. *The Life of Andrew Jackson*. New York: Bobbs Merrill Company, 1938.

Jenkins, Ned J. and Richard A. Krause. *The Tombigbee Watershed in Southeastern Prehistory*. Tuscaloosa: University of Alabama Press, 1986.

Jordan, Weymouth T. *Ante-Bellum Alabama: Town and Country*. 1957. Reprint. Tuscaloosa: University of Alabama Press, 1987.

Kappler, Charles J. ed. *Indian Affairs: Laws and Treaties*, II, Treaties. Washington: Government Printing Office, 1904.

Kennedy, Roger G. *Burr, Hamilton, and Jefferson: A Study in Character*. Oxford and New York: Oxford University Press, 2000.

Kent, James. *Commentaries on American Law*. New York: O. Halsted, 1826.

Kieth, Todd. *Old Cahawba*. Brierfield, Ala.: Cahaba Trace Commission, 2003.

King, Grace Elizabeth. *Jean Baptiste Le Moyne Sieur de Bienville*. New York: Dodd, Mead, and Company, 1892.

Kirschke, James J. *Gouverneur Morris: Author, Statesman and Man of the World*. New York: Thomas Dunne Books, 2005.

Knight, Vernon J. ed. *The Search for Mabila: The Decisive Battle between Hernando de Soto and Chief Tascalusa*. Tuscaloosa: University of Alabama Press, 2009.

Langum, David J. and Howard P. Walthall. *From Maverick to Mainstream, Cumberland School of Law, 1847–1997*. University of Georgia Press, 1997.

Laver, Harry S., *Citizens More Than Soldiers: The Kentucky Militia and Society in the Early Republic*. Lincoln: University of Nebraska Press, 2007.

Linklater, Andro. *An Artist in Treason: The Extraordinary Double Life of General James Wilkinson*. New York: Walker, 2009.

Lloyd, James T. *Lloyd's Steamboat Directory and Disasters on the Western Waters*. Cincinnati, Ohio: James T. Lloyd & Co., 1856.

Lovette, Leland P. *Navy Customs, Traditions and Usage*. Annapolis, Md.: United States Naval Institute, 1939.

Lowery, Woodbury. *The Spanish Settlements Within the Present Limits of the United States, 1513–1561*. New York: G.P. Putnam's Sons, 1901.

Lupold, John S. and Thomas L. French. *Bridging Deep South Rivers: The Life and Legend of Horace King*. Athens, Georgia: University of Georgia Press, 2004.

Luttrell III, Frank Alex. ed. *Historical Markers of Madison County, Alabama*. Huntsville–Madison County Historical Society, 50th Anniversary, 1951–2001.

McCaleb, Walter Flavius. *The Aaron Burr Conspiracy*. New York: Wilson-Erickson, 1936.

McDonald, William Lindsey. *A Walk Through the Past: People and Places of Florence and Lauderdale County, Alabama*. Florence, Ala.: Bluewater Publications, 2003.

McLoughlin, William Gerald, Walter H. Conser and Virginia Duffy McLoughlin. *The Cherokee Ghost Dance: Essays on the Southeastern Indians, 1789–1861*. Macon, Ga.: Mercer, 1984.

McMillan, Malcom Cook. *Constitutional Development in Alabama, 1798–1901: A Study in Politics, the Negro, and Sectionalism*. Chapel Hill: University of North Carolina Press, 1955.

McNeeley, Mary Ann. ed. *The Works of Matthew Blue: Montgomery's First Historian*. Montgomery, Ala.: New South Books, 2010.

Martin, Joel. *Sacred Revolt: The Muscogees' Struggle for a New World*. Boston: Beacon Press, 1991.

Matthews, Forrest David. *Why Public Schools? Whose Public Schools?: What Early Communities Have to Tell Us*. Montgomery, Ala.: NewSouth Books, 2002.

Matte, Jacqueline A., Doris Brown, and Barbara Waddell. Eds. *Old St. Stephens: Historical Records Survey*. St. Stephens Historical Commission, 1997.

Matte, Jacqueline Anderson. *The History of Washington County, First County in Alabama*. Chatom, Ala.: Washington County Historical Society, 1982.

Merriman, Roger Bigelow. *The Rise of the Spanish Empire in the Old Word and in the New*. vol. 1, *"The Middle Ages."* New York: Macmillan, 1918.

Miller, Randall Martin. *The Cotton Movement in Antebellum Alabama*. New York: Arno Pr., 1978.

Moore, Albert Burton. *History of Alabama*. 1934. Reprint. Tuscaloosa: Alabama Book Store, 1951.

Neville, Bert. *A Glance at Old Cahawba, Alabama's Early Capital*. Selma, Ala.: Coffee Printing Co., 1961.

Newmyer, R. Kent. *The Treason Trial of Aaron Burr: Law, Politics and the Character Wars of the New Nation*. Cambridge, UK: Cambridge University Press, 2012.

O'Brien, Sean Michael. *In Bitterness and in Tears: Andrew Jackson's Destruction of the Creeks and Seminoles*. Westport, Conn.: Praeger, 2003.

Owen, Thomas McAdory. *History of Alabama and Dictionary of Alabama Biography*. Chicago: S. J. Clarke Publishing Company, 1921.

Owsley Jr., Frank Lawrence. *Struggle for the Gulf Borderlands: The Creek War and the Battle of New Orleans, 1812–1815*. Gainesville: University Presses of Florida, 1981.

Perdue, Theda and Michael D. Green. *The Columbia Guide to American Indians of the Southeast*. New York: Columbia University Press, 2005.

Peterson, Merrill D. *Thomas Jefferson and the New Nation: A Biography*. Oxford University Press: London, 1975.

Phillips, Ulrich Bonnell. *Life and Labor in the Old South*. Boston: Little, Brown, 1929.

Pickett, Albert James, *History of Alabama, and Incidentally of Georgia and Mississippi, from the Earliest Period*. 1851. Reprint. Birmingham, Ala.: Birmingham Book and Magazine Co., 1962.

Pratt, Merrill E. *Daniel Pratt: Alabama's First Industrialist*. New York: The Newcomen Society of England, American Branch, 1949.

Priestley, Herbert I. *Tristán de Luna: Conquistador of the Old South, A Study of Spanish Imperial Strategy*. Glendale, Calif.: Arthur H. Clark Co., 1936.

Pruitt Jr., Paul M. *Taming Alabama: Lawyers and Reformers, 1804–1929*. Tuscaloosa: University of Alabama Press, 2010.

Purcell, Richard J. *Connecticut in Transition: 1775–1818*. Middletown, Conn.: Wesleyan University Press, 1963.

Rawick, George P. ed. *The American Slave: A Composite Autobiography*. Westport, Conn.: Greenwood Press, 1972–79. Supplement Series 1.

Rea, Robert R. *Major Robert Farmar of Mobile*. Tuscaloosa: University of Alabama Press, 1990.

Rea, Robert R. and Milo B. Howard, comps. *The Minutes, Journals, and Acts of the General Assembly of British West Florida*. Tuscaloosa: University of Alabama Press, 1979.

Rorabaugh, A. J. *The Alcoholic Republic: An American Tradition*. New York: Oxford University Press, 1979.

Rogers, William Warren et al. *Alabama: The History of a Deep South State*. Tuscaloosa: University of Alabama Press, 1994.

Rothbard, Murray N. *Panic of 1819*. New York: Columbia University Press, 1962.

Rowland, Dunbar, ed., *The Mississippi Territorial Archives, 1798–18. . .* (Nashville: Brandon Print. Co., 1905.

————. *Courts, Judges, and Lawyers of Mississippi, 1798–1935*. Jackson: State Department of Archives and History and the Mississippi Historical Society, 1935.

Rowland, Eron. *Mississippi Territory in the War of 1812*. 1921. Reprint. Baltimore: Genealogical Publishing Company, 1968.

Royal, Anne Newport. *Letters from Alabama on Various Subjects*. ed. Lucille Griffith. Tuscaloosa: University of Alabama Press, 1969.

Saunders, Robert. *John Archibald Campbell: Southern Moderate, 1811–1889*. Tuscaloosa: University of Alabama Press, 1997.

Saunt, Claudio. *A New Order of Things: Property, Power, and the Transformation of the Creek Indians, 1733–1816*. New York: Cambridge University Press, 1999.

————. *Black, White, and Indian: Race and the Unmaking of the American Family*. New York: Oxford University Press, 2005.

Schachner, Nathan. *Aaron Burr: A Biography*. 1937. Reprint. New York: A. S. Barnes, 1961.

Scruggs Jr., J. H. *Alabama Steamboats, 1819–1869*. Birmingham, Ala., 1953.

Saugera, Eric. *Reborn In America: French Exiles and Refugees in the United States and the Vine and Olive Colony Adventure, 1815–1865*. Tuscaloosa: University of Alabama Press, 2011.

Sellers, James B. *History of the University of Alabama*. University, Ala.: University of Alabama Press, 1953.

————. *Slavery in Alabama*. 1950. Reprint. Tuscaloosa and London: University of Alabama Press, 1994.

Sicking, Louis. *Neptune and the Netherlands: State, Economy, and War at Sea in the Renaissance*. Leiden, Netherlands: Brill, 2004.

Smith, Carter. *Presidents: Every Question Answered*. New York: Metro Books, 2008.

Sonne, Niels H. *Liberal Kentucky, 1780–1828*. New York: Columbia University Press, 1939.

Southerland Jr., Henry deLeon and Jerry Elijah Brown. *The Federal Road through Georgia, the Creek Nation, and Alabama, 1806–1836*. Tuscaloosa: University of Alabama Press, 1989.

Stiggins, George. *Creek Indian History: A Historical Narrative of the Genealogy, Traditions and Downfall of the Ispocoga or Creek Indian Tribe of Indians*. Birmingham, Ala.: Birmingham Public Library Press, 1989.

Sulzby, James Frederick. *Historic Alabama Hotels & Resorts*. 1960. Reprint. Tuscaloosa and London: University of Alabama Press, 1994.

Summersell, Charles Grayson. *Mobile: History of a Seaport Town*. University, Ala.: University of Alabama Press, 1949.

Thomas, Daniel H. *Fort Toulouse: The French Outpost at the Alabamas on the Coosa*. 1960. Reprint. Tuscaloosa: University of Alabama Press, 1989.

Michael V. R. Thomason. ed. *Mobile: The New History of Alabama's First City*. Tuscaloosa: University of Alabama Press, 2001.

Thornton III, J. Mills. *Politics and Power in a Slave Society: Alabama, 1800–1860*. Baton Rouge: Louisiana State University Press, 1978.

Tucker, Glenn. *Poltroons and Patriots: A Popular Account of the War of 1812.* Indianapolis: Bobbs-Merrill, 1954.

Walthall, John A. *Prehistoric Indians of the Southeast: Archeology of Alabama and the Middle South.* Tuscaloosa: University of Alabama Press, 1990.

Walther, Eric H. *William Lowndes Yancey and the Coming of the Civil War.* Chapel Hill: University of North Carolina Press, 2006.

Ward, Robert David and William Warren Rogers. *Alabama's Response to the Penitentiary Movement, 1829–1865.* Gainesville: University Press of Florida, 2003.

Waselkov, Gregory A. *A Conquering Spirit: Fort Mims and the Redstick War of 1813–1814.* Tuscaloosa: University of Alabama Press, 2006.

————. *Old Mobile Archeology.* Tuscaloosa: University of Alabama Press, 2005.

Webb, Samuel L. and Margaret E. Armbrester, eds. *Alabama Governors: A Political History of the State.* Tuscaloosa: University of Alabama Press, 2001.

West, Anson. *A History of Methodism in Alabama.* Nashville: Publishing House, Methodist Episcopal Church, South: 1893.

Wheelan, Joseph. *Jefferson's Vendetta: The Pursuit of Aaron Burr and the Judiciary.* New York: Carroll & Graf Publishers, 2005.

Williams, Benjamin Buford. *A Literary History of Alabama: the Nineteenth Century.* Cranbury, NJ: Fairleigh Dickinson Press, 1979.

Williams, Clanton W. *The Early History of Montgomery and Incidentally of the State of Alabama.* University, Ala.: Confederate Publishing Company, 1979.

Williams, Horace Randall. ed. *Weren't No Good Times: Personal Accounts of Slavery in Alabama.* Winston-Salem: John F. Blair, 2004.

Wolfe, Suzanne Rau. *The University of Alabama: A Pictorial History.* Tuscaloosa: University of Alabama Press, 1983.

Wood, Gordon S. *Empire of Liberty: A History of the Early Republic, 1789–1815.* New York: Oxford University Press, 2009.

Woodward, Grace Steele. *The Cherokees.* Norman: University of Oklahoma Press, 1982.

Woodward, Thomas S. *Reminiscences of the Creek, or Muscogee Indians, Contained in Letters to Friends in Georgia and Alabama.* 1859. Reprint. Mobile, Ala: Southern University Press, 1969.

Wright Jr., J. Leitch. *Creeks and Seminoles: The Destruction and Regeneration of the Muscogulge People.* Lincoln: University of Nebraska Press, 1986.

Yerby, William Edward Wadsworth. *History of Greensboro, Alabama, From Its Earliest Settlement.* Montgomery, Ala.: Paragon Press, 1908.

Articles

Abernethy, Thomas Perkins. "Aaron Burr in Mississippi." *Journal of Southern History* 15 (February 1949): 9–21.

Atkins, Leah. "The First Legislative Session: The General Assembly of Alabama, Huntsville, 1819." *Alabama Review* 23 (January 1970): 30–44.

Austill, Henriosco. "Jeremiah Austill." *Alabama Historical Quarterly* 6 (Spring 1944): 81–91.

Bailey, Hugh C. "Israel Pickens, People's Politician." *Alabama Review* 17 (April 1964): 83–101.

———. "John W. Walker and the 'Georgia Machine' in Early Alabama Politics."
Alabama Review 8 (July 1955): 179–95.

Barnard, Harry V. "La Grange College, A Historical Sketch." *North Alabama Historical Association* Bulletin, II (1957), 10.

Bean, William B. "Josiah Clark Nott, A Southern Physician." *Bulletin of the New York Academy of Medicine.* (April 1974): 529–35.

Beidler, Philip. "Toulmin & Hitchcock: Pioneering Jurists of the Alabama Frontier."
Alabama Heritage, no. 81 (Summer 2006): 18–25.

Bigham, Darrell E. "From the Green Mountains to the Tombigbee: Henry Hitchcock in Territorial Alabama, 1817–1819." *Alabama Review* 26 (July 1973): 209–28.

Blaufarb, Rafe. "Alabama's Vine and Olive Colony." *Alabama Heritage*, no. 81 (Summer 2006): 26–35.

Brannon, Peter A. "Creek Indian War, 1836–1837." *Alabama Historical Quarterly* 13 (1951): 156–58.

———. "Principal Stage Stops and Taverns In What Is Now Alabama Prior to 1840."
Alabama Historical Quarterly 17 (Spring and Summer 1955): 80–87.

———. "Dueling in Alabama." *Alabama Historical Quarterly* 17 (Fall 1955): 97–109.

———. "Interesting Characters of the Constitutional Convention of Alabama of 1819."
Alabama Lawyer 8 (October 1947): 388–89.

———. "Spruce McCall Osborne: A Mississippi Territorial Volunteer at Fort Mims."
Alabama Historical Quarterly 5 (Spring 1943): 68–70.

Brannon, Peter A. ed. "Journal of James A. Tait for the Year 1813." *Alabama Historical* Quarterly 2 (Winter 1940): 431–40.

Brantley, Jr., William H. "Henry Hitchcock of Mobile: 1816–1839." *Alabama Review* 5 (January 1952): 3–39.

Braund, Kathryn E. Holland. "Reflections on 'Shee Coocys' and the Motherless Child: Creek Women in a Time of War." *Alabama Review* 64 (October 2011), 255–84.

Briceland, Alan V. "Ephraim Kirby: Mr. Jefferson's Emissary on the Tombigbee–Mobile Frontier in 1804." *Alabama Review* 24 (April, 1971): 83–113.

———. "Land, Law, and Politics on the Tombigbee Frontier, 1804." *Alabama Review* 33 (April 1980): 92–124.

Bridges Edwin C., "'The Nation's Guest': The Marquis de Lafayette's Tour of Alabama."
Alabama Heritage (Fall 2011): 12.

Burton, Gary. "Pintlala's Cold Murder Case: The Death of Thomas Meredith in 1812."
Alabama Review 63 (July 2010): 163–91.

Cherry, Rev. F. L. "Horace King," in "The History of Opelika and Her Agricultural Tributary Territory." *Alabama Historical Quarterly* 15, no. 2 (1953): 176–339, and nos. 3, 4 (1953): 383–537.

Childress, David T. "The Alabama Volunteers in the Second Seminole War, 1836." *Alabama Review* 37 (January 1984): 3–12.

Clinton, Thomas P. "Early History of Tuscaloosa." *Alabama Historical Quarterly* 1 (Summer 1930): 169–78.

Coker, William S. "The Last Battle of the War of 1812: New Orleans. No. Fort Bowyer!."
Alabama Historical Quarterly 43 (Spring 1981): 42–63.

Cruzat, Héloise H. trans. "Records of the Superior Council of Louisiana." *Louisiana Historical Quarterly 5* (April 1922): 239–76.

———. "Records of the Superior Council of Louisiana." *Louisiana Historical Quarterly 7* (October 1924): 676–705.

Current-Garcia, Eugene. "Joseph Glover Baldwin: Humorist or Moralist?." *Alabama Review* 5 (April 1952): 122–41.

Daniel, Adrian G. "Navigational Development of Muscle Shoals, 1807–1890." *Alabama Review* 14 (October 1961): 251–58.

Dart, Henry Plauchè. "The Legal Institutions of Louisiana." *Louisiana Historical Quarterly* 2 (January 1919): 76–79.

Doss, Harriet Amos. "Rise and Fall of an Alabama Founding Father." *Alabama Review* 52 (July 2000): 163–176.

Doster, James F. "Early Settlements on the Tombigbee and Tensaw Rivers." *Alabama Review* 12 (April 1959): 83–94.

Elkins, Stanley and Eric McKitrick. "A Meaning of Turner's Frontier: Part II: The Southwest Frontier and New England." *Political Science Quarterly* 69 (December 1954): 570.

Emerson, O. B. "The Bonapartist Exiles In Alabama." *Alabama Review* 11 (April 1958): 135–43.

Ethridge Jr., William N. "An Introduction to Sargent's Code of the Mississippi Territory (1798–1800)." *American Journal of Legal History* 11 (April 1967): 148–51.

Everett, Donald E. "Free Persons of Color in Colonial Louisiana." *Louisiana History* 7 (Winter 1966): 21–50.

Gray, Daniel Savage. "Frontier Journalism: Newspapers in Antebellum Alabama." *Alabama Historical Quarterly* 37 (Fall 1975): 183–91.

Guice, John D. W. "The Cement of Society: Law in the Mississippi Territory." *Gulf Coast Historical Review* 1 (Spring 1986): 76–99.

Guyton, Pearl V. "Sam Dale, from J. F. H. Claiborne." *Alabama Historical Quarterly* 7 (Spring 1945): 7–25.

Halbert, Henry Sale. "Creek War Incidents." *Transactions of the Alabama Historical Society* 2 (1897–98): 99–100.

Hall, John C. "Prince Madoc and the Stubborn Persistence of a Legend." *Alabama Heritage*, no. 96 (Spring 2010): 30–37.

Hamilton, Peter Joseph. "Early Roads of Alabama." *Transactions of the Alabama Historical Society* 2 (1897–98): 47–55.

Haynes Jr., Robert V. "Early Washington County, Alabama." *Alabama Review* 18 (July 1965): 183–200.

———. "Law Enforcement in Frontier Mississippi." *Journal of Mississippi History* 22 (January 1960): 27–28.

———. "The Revolution of 1800 in Mississippi." *Journal of Mississippi History* 19 (October 1957): 234–51.

Helmbold, F. Wilbur. "Early Alabama Newspapermen, 1810–1820." *Alabama Review* (January 1959): 53–68.

Higginbotham, Jay. "The Battle of Mauvila, Causes and Consequences." *Gulf South Historical Review* 6 (Spring 1991): 19–33.

"Historic Sites in Alabama." *Alabama Historical Quarterly* 15 (Spring 1953): 25–55.

Hobbs, Sam Earle. "History of Early Cahaba, Alabama's First State Capital." *Alabama Historical Quarterly* 31 (Fall and Winter 1969): 155–182.

Hoffheimer, Michael H. "Race and Terror in Joseph Baldwin's *Flush Times of Alabama and Mississippi* (1853)." *Seton Hall Law Review* 39 (2009): 725.

Hole, Donna C. "Daniel Pratt and Barachias Holt: Architects of the State Capitol?" *Alabama Review* 37 (April 1984): 83–97.

Holmes, Jack D. L. "Alabama's Forgotten Settler: Notes on the Spanish Mobile District, 1780–1813." *Alabama Historical Quarterly* 33 (Summer 1971): 87–97.

———. "Law and Order in Spanish Natchez, 1781–1798." *Journal of Mississippi History* 25 (July 1963): 186–201.

———. "The Abortive Slave Revolt at Point Coupée, Louisiana, 1795." *Louisiana History* 11 (Fall 1970): 341–62.

———. "The Role of Blacks in Spanish Alabama: The Mobile District, 1780–1813." *Alabama Historical Quarterly* 37 (Spring 1975): 5–18.

Hoole, W. Stanley. "John Gorman Barr: Forgotten Alabama Humorist." *Alabama Review* 4 (April 1951): 83–116.

Howard, Jr. Milo B. "The General Ticket." *Alabama Review* 19 (July 1966): 163–74.

Howington, Arthur F. "Violence in Alabama: A Study of Late Ante-bellum Montgomery." *Alabama* Review 27 (July 1974):213–31.

Jack, Theodore H. "Alabama and the Federal Government: The Creek Indian Controversy." *The Mississippi Valley Historical Review* 3 (December 1916): 301–17.

Jenkins, William H. "Alabama Forts, 1700–1838." *Alabama Review* 12 (July 1959): 163–80.

Johnson, Jerah. "La Coutume de Paris: Louisiana's First Law." *Louisiana History* 30 (Spring 1989): 145–55.

Jones, Charles Edgeworth. "Governor William Wyatt Bibb." *Transactions of the Alabama Historical Society* 3 (*1898–99*): 128–32.

Jones, Pam. "William Weatherford and the Road to the Holy Ground." *Alabama Heritage*, no. 74 (Fall 2004): 24–32.

Knapp, Virginia. "William Phineas Browne, Business Man and Pioneer Mine Operator of Alabama." Part 1, *Alabama Review* 3 (April 1950): 108–70.

"Lafayette." *Alabama Historical Quarterly* 18 (Spring 1956): 44–52.

Lengel, Leland L. "The Road to Fort Mims: Judge Harry Toulmin's Observations on the Creek War, 1811–1813." *Alabama Review* 29 (January 1976): 16–36.

Lewis, Herbert J. "A Connecticut Yankee in Early Alabama: Henry Wilbourne Stevens and the Founding of Ordered Society, 1814–1823." *Alabama Review* 59 (April 2006): 83–106.

Lipscomb, Oscar Hugh. "Catholic Missionaries in Early Alabama." *Alabama Review* 18 (April 1965): 124–31.

Long, Melvin Durward. "Political Parties and Propaganda in Alabama in the Presidential Election of 1860." *Alabama Historical Quarterly* 25 (Spring and Summer 1963): 120–35.

Love, William A. "General Jackson's Military Road." *Publications of the Mississippi Historical Society* 11 (1910): 409.

Lowery, Charles D. "The Great Migration to the Mississippi Territory, 1798–1819." *Journal of Mississippi History* 30 (August 1968): 173–92.

Lowry, Lucile Cary. "Lafayette's Visit to Georgia and Alabama." *Alabama Historical Quarterly* 8 (Spring 1946): 35–40.

Lyon, Anne Bozeman. "The Bonapartists in Alabama." *Alabama Historical Quarterly* 25 (Fall and Winter 1963): 227–41.

McCall, D. L. ed. "Lafayette's Visit to Alabama, April 1825." *Alabama Historical Quarterly* 17 (Spring and Summer 1955): 33–77.

McCorvey, Thomas Chalmers. "The Mission of Frances Scott Key to Alabama in 1833." *Transactions of the Alabama Historical Society* 4 (1899–1903): 141–65.

McDaniel, Mary Jane. "Tecumseh's Visits to the Creeks." *Alabama Review* 33 (January 1980): 3–14.

McKenzie, Robert H. "Horace Ware: Alabama Iron Pioneer." *Alabama Review* 26 (July 1973): 157–72.

McLemore, Richard A. "Division of Mississippi Territory." *Journal of Mississippi History* 5 (1943): 79–82.

McMillan, Malcolm Cook. "The Alabama Constitution of 1819: A Study of Constitution-Making on the Frontier." *Alabama Lawyer* 12 (January 1951): 74–98.

———. "The Selection of Montgomery as Alabama's Capital." *Alabama Review* 1 (April 1948): 79–90.

McWilliams, Tennant S. "The Marquis and the Myth: Lafayette's Visit to Alabama, 1825." *Alabama Review* 22 (April, 1969): 135–46.

Meador, Dean Daniel J. "The Supreme Court of Alabama: Its Cahaba Beginning, 1820–1825." *Alabama Law* Review 61 (2010): 891.

Mellen, George F. "Henry W. Hilliard and William L. Yancey." *The Sewanee Review* 17 (January 1909): 32–50.

Mellown, Robert O. "Alabama's Fourth Capital: The Construction of the State House in Tuscaloosa." *Alabama Review* 40 (October 1987): 259–83.

Mitchell, Charles C. "The Development of Cotton from the Old World to Alabama: Chronological Highlights in Alabama Cotton Production." *Agronomy and Soils Departmental Series No. 286* (Auburn University, Alabama: Agricultural Experiment Station, March 2008), 3–8.

Moffat, Charles H. "Charles Tait: Planter, Politician, and Scientist of the Old South." *Journal of Southern History* 14 (May 1948): 206–33.

Napier, John. "Martial Montgomery: Ante Bellum Military Activity." *Alabama Historical Quarterly* 29 (Fall and Winter 1967): 107–31.

Neeley, Mary Ann Oglesby. "Lachlan McGillivray: A Scot on the Alabama Frontier." *Alabama Historical Quarterly* 36 (Spring 1974): 5–14.

———. "Painful Circumstances: Glimpses of the Alabama Penitentiary, 1846–1852." *Alabama Review* 44 (January 1991): 3–16.

Nelms, Jack N. "Early Days with the Alabama River Steamboats." *Alabama Review* 36 (January 1984): 13–23.

Notes. "Simon Suggs: A Burlesque Campaign Biography." *American Quarterly* 15 (Autumn 1963): 459–63.

Nuermberger, Ruth Ketring. "The 'Royal Party' in Early Alabama Politics." *Alabama Review* 6 (April and July 1953): 81–98, 198–212.

Nunez Jr., Theron A. "Creek Nativism and the Creek War of 1813–14 (George Stiggins Manuscript)." *Ethnohistory* 5 (Winter, Spring, Summer 1958): 1–47, 131–75, 292–301.

Owen, Thomas McAdory. ed., "Burr's Conspiracy." *Transactions of the Alabama Historical Society* 3 (1898–99): 167–77.

———. "The Visit of President James Monroe to Alabama Territory, June 1, 1819." *Transactions of the Alabama Historical Society* 3 (1898–99): 128–130.

Owsley Jr. Frank L. "Francis Scott Key's Mission to Alabama in 1833." *Alabama Review* 23 (July 1970): 181–92.

Owsley, Frank L. "The Clays in Early Alabama History." *Alabama Review* 2 (October 1949): 243–68.

Parker, James C. "Blakely: A Frontier Seaport." *Alabama Review* 27 (January 1974): 39–51.

Parker, James W. "Fort Jackson after the War of 1812." *Alabama Review* 38 (April 1985): 119–30.

Parkhurst, Helen H. "Don Pedro Favrot, a Creole Pepys." *Louisiana Historical Quarterly* 28 (July 1945): 679–734.

Pearson, Theodore Bowling. "Early Settlement around Historic McIntosh Bluff: Alabama's First County Seat." *Alabama Review* 23 (October 1970): 243–55.

Perry, William F. "The Genesis of Public Education in Alabama." *Transactions of the Alabama Historical Society* 2 (1898–99): 14–27.

"Portrait of Judge Toulmin Presented." *Alabama Lawyer* 1 (April 1940): 157.

Pruitt Jr., Paul M. "The Life and Times of Legal Education in Alabama, 1819–1897: Bar Admissions, Law Schools, and the Profession." *Alabama Law Review* 49 (Fall 1997): 283–84.

Pyburn, Nita Katherine. "Mobile Public Schools Before 1860." *Alabama Review* 11 (July 1958): 177–88.

Rachleff, Marshall. "An Abolitionist Letter to Governor Henry W. Collier of Alabama: The Emergence of 'The Crisis of Fear' in Alabama." *Journal of Negro History* 66 (Autumn, 1981), 246–53.

Reynolds, Susan E. "William Augustus Bowles: Adventurous Rogue of the Old Southwest." *Alabama Heritage*, no. 103 (Winter 2012): 18–27.

Rodgers, Thomas G. "Night Attack at Calabee Creek." *Journal of the Historical Society of the Georgia National Guard* 4 (Spring 1995): 12.

Rogers, William Warren. "The Founding of Alabama's Land Grant College at Auburn." *Alabama Review* 40 (January 1987): 14–37.

Russell, Robert A. "Gold Mining in Alabama Before 1860." *Alabama Review* 10 (January 1957): 5–14.

Sellers, James B. "Student Life at the University of Alabama Before 1860." *Alabama Review* 4 (October 1949): 269–93.

Simpson, James B. "The Alabama State Capital: An Historical Sketch." *Alabama Historical Quarterly*, 28 (Spring 1956): 81–125.

Somerville, Henderson Middleton. "Trial of the Alabama Supreme Court Judges in 1829....." *Alabama State Bar Association Proceedings* (June, 1899).

Stockham, Richard J. "The Misunderstood Larenzo Dow." *Alabama Review* 26 (January 1963): 20–34.

Strong, Russell W. "Governor Bienville and the Fate of French Louisiana." *Gulf Coast Historical Review* 8 (Spring 1993): 7–17.

Stumpf, Stuart O. ed. "The Arrest of Aaron Burr: A Documentary Record." *Alabama Historical Quarterly* 42 (Fall and Winter, 1980): 113–23.

Taylor, Thomas Jones. "Early History of Madison County And, Incidentally of North Alabama." *Alabama Historical Quarterly* 1 (Spring 1930): 101–11.

———. Early History of Madison County And, Incidentally of North Alabama" (second installment). *Alabama Historical Quarterly* 2 (summer 1930): 149–68.

Tetley, William. "Maritime Law as a Mixed Legal System, With Particular Reference to the Distinctive Nature of American Maritime Law . . ." *Tulane Maritime Law Journal* 23 (Spring 1999): 317–50.

"The Capitol Fire of 1849." *Alabama Bench and Bar Historical Society Newsletter* (November/December 2010): 11.

"The Secession Convention" and "Delegates to the Alabama Secession Convention." *Alabama Historical Quarterly* 3 (Fall and Winter 1941): 287–356, 368–426.

"The Visit of President James Monroe to Alabama Territory, June 1, 1819." *Transactions of the Alabama Historical Society* 3 (1898–99): 154–58.

Thomas, Daniel H. "Fort Toulouse—In Tradition and Fact." *Alabama Review* 13 (October 1960): 243–57.

"Towns in the Alabama Territory." *Alabama Historical Quarterly* 3 (Spring 1941): 74–82.

Ward, David. "Albert James Pickett and the Case of the Secret Articles: Historians and the Treaty of New York of 1790." *Alabama Review* 51 (January 1998): 3–36.

Waselkov, Gregory A. "Return to Holy Ground: The Legendary Battle Site Discovered." *Alabama Heritage,* no. 101 (Summer 2011): 28–37.

Watson, Charles S. "Order Out of Chaos: Joseph Glover Baldwin's *The Flush Times of Alabama and Mississippi*." *Alabama Review* 45 (October 1992): 257–72.

Watts, Charles W. "Student Days at Old La Grange College, 1844–45." *Alabama Review* 24 (January 1971): 63–76.

Welborn, Aaron. "A Traitor in the Wilderness: The Arrest of Aaron Burr." *Alabama Heritage,* no. 83 (Winter 2007): 10–19.

Whitfield, Jr., Gaius. "The French Grant in Alabama." *Transactions of the Alabama Historical Society* 4 (1899–1903): 321–55.

Williams, Clanton W. "Early Antebellum Montgomery: A Black Belt Constituency." *The Journal of Southern History* (November 1941): 495–525.

Williams, Jack K. "Crime and Punishment in Alabama, 1819–1840." *Alabama Review* 6 (January 1953): 14–30.

Wright Jr., J. L. "Creek American Treaty of 1790: Alexander McGillivray and the Diplomacy of the Old Southwest." *Georgia Historical Quarterly* 51 (December 1967): 379–400.

Wunder, John. "American Law and Order Comes to the Mississippi Territory: The Making of Sargent's Code, 1798–1800." *Journal of Mississippi History* 38 (May 1976): 131–155.

Wyman, Justus. "A Geographical Sketch of the Alabama Territory." *Transactions of the Alabama Historical Society* 3 (1898–99): 109–27.

Legal References

Acts Passed at the First Session of the First General Assembly of the Alabama Territory in the Forty-Second Year of American Independence. St. Stephens: Thomas Easton, 1818.

Acts Passed at the Second Session of the First General Assembly of the Alabama Territory in the Forty-Third Year of American Independence. St. Stephens: Thomas Easton, 1818.

Acts of the General Assembly of the State of Alabama, 1819–1860.

Alabama Ordinance of Secession (1861).

Code of Alabama (1852).

Digest of the Laws of the State of Alabama ... Comp. Harry Toulmin (Cahawba, Ala., 1823).

Digest of the Laws of the State of Alabama ... Comp. John G. Aikin (Philadelphia, 1833).

Enabling Act for Alabama (1819), Fifteenth Congress, Second Session, Sec. 6.

Martin v. Reed, 37 *Alabama,* 198 (1861).

Mississippi Territorial Statutes. Birmingham, Ala.: Historical Records Survey, 1939.

Rhodes v. Roberts, 1 *Stewart,* 145 (1827).

Sargent's Code: A Collection of the Original Laws of the Mississippi Territory Enacted 1799–1800 by Governor Winthrop Sargent and the Territorial Judges. Jackson, Miss.: Historical Records Survey, 1939.

The Constitution of the State of Alabama, adopted August 2, 1819.

Tillman v. Chadwick, 37 *Alabama,* 317 (1861).

Treaty of Cusseta (1832), Art. 5.

Treaty with the Chickasaw. July 23, 1805. 7 Stat. 89

Treaty with the Cherokee. Jan. 7, 1806, 7 Stat. 101.

Trotter v. Blocker and Wife, 6 *Porter,* 269 (1838).

U. S. Statutes at Large, III, 371–373.

Archival Material

"Address to Inhabitants of Mississippi Territory," in Rowland, Dunbar. ed. *The Mississippi Territorial Archives, 1798–18.* . . . Nashville: Brandon Print. Co., 1905.

"Address to Militia Officers." Rowland, *Mississippi Territorial Archives.*

Brightwell to Robert Williams, July 20, 1805. "General Correspondence, 1795–1815." *Mississippi Territorial Transcripts.*

"Divorce Petition to Governor and Legislature," September 16, 1799. Governor's Records, Administration of Winthrop Sargent, May 1798–April 1801. series A , vol. 1, Mississippi Department of Archives and History, Jackson, Mississippi (MDAH).

Evans to Andrew Ellicott, August 7, 1798. Andrew Ellicott Papers, MSS Division, Library of Congress.

"Information to the Inhabitants of the Mississippi Territory." Rowland, *Mississippi Territorial Archives.*

J. L. M. Curry pamphlet collection, LPR 10., Alabama Department of Archives and History (ADAH), Montgomery, Alabama.

J.S.W. Parkin to Jno. R. Parker, May 15, 1815. J.S.W. Parker Letters. SPR 101. Alabama Department of Archives and History (ADAH), Montgomery, Alabama.

"Order for the Regulation of Militia." Rowland, *Mississippi Territorial Archives.*

Ross to Sargent, July 15, 1798. Winthrop Sargent Papers. Massachusetts Historical Society, Boston, MA.

Sargent to Pickering. June 16, 1798, August 20, 1798, September 18, 1798, December 11, 1798, and December 20, 1798. Rowland, *Mississippi Territorial Archives.*

Thomas C. Hunter to Gov. William Wyatt Bibb, March 29, 1818 and William Johnston to Gov. William Wyatt Bibb, April 16, 1818. Records of Gov. William Wyatt Bibb concerning Appointments, Commissions, and Resignations, 1817–1819, SG24709, reel 22, Alabama Department of Archives and History (ADAH), Montgomery, Alabama.

Toulmin to D. Holmes, June 10, 1811, Mississippi (Territory). Judge of the Superior Court, Correspondence, 1805–1816. SG3111, Alabama Department of Archives and History, Montgomery, Alabama (ADAH).

Toulmin to Holmes, May 27, 1810, 3–5, Mississippi (Territory). Judge of the Superior Court, Correspondence, 1805–1816. SG3111, Alabama Department of Archives and History, Montgomery, Alabama (ADAH).

Toulmin to Holmes, July 7, 1810, 8–9 and Toulmin to Holmes, July 21, 1810. Mississippi (Territory), Judge of the Superior Court, Correspondence, 1805–1816, SG3111, Alabama Department of Archives and History, Montgomery, Alabama (ADAH).

Toulmin to His Excellency D. Holmes, Governor of the Mississippi Territory, September 16, 1810. Mississippi (Territory). Judge of the Superior Court, Correspondence, SG3111, Alabama Department of Archives and History, Montgomery, Alabama (ADAH).

Toulmin to Governor, January 19, 1807, Mississippi (Territory). General Correspondence (1795–1815). SG3105–SG3106, Alabama Department of Archives and History, Montgomery, Alabama (ADAH).

Toulmin to Mingo Pooshmatahaw, May 18, 1810. Mississippi (Territory), Judge of the Superior Court, Correspondence, 1805–1816, SG3111, Alabama Department of Archives and History, Montgomery, Alabama (ADAH).

Toulmin to Secretary of State James Madison, July 6, 1805. "General Correspondence, 1795–1815." *Mississippi Territorial Transcripts.*

Dissertations and Theses

Elliott, Mary Joan. "Winthrop Sargent and the Administration of the Mississippi Territory, 1798–1801." PhD diss., University of Southern California, 1970.

Day, James Sanders. "'Diamonds in the Rough': A History of Alabama's Cahaba Coal Field." Ph.D. diss., Auburn University, 2002.

Knapp, Virginia. "William Phineas Browne, A Yankee Business Man of the South," Master's Thesis, University of Texas, 1948.

Newspapers and Magazines

Alabama Watchman, September 29, 1820.

Brannan, Peter "Moving the Capital to Montgomery." *Montgomery Advertiser*, July 26, 1946.

Columbus Enquirer, May 13, 1836.

Goodheart, Adam "Caught Sleeping." Disunion Series, Opinion Section, *New York Times*, January 3, 2011: http://opinionator.blogs.nytimes.com/ 2011/01/03/caught-sleeping/ (accessed January 11, 2011).

Mobile *Press-Register*, May 4, 2007, http://blog.al.com/pr/2007/05/battle_house_a_symbol_of_hospi.html (accessed August 26, 2010).

National Intelligencer, Washington, D.C., April 19, 1828.

Internet References

Beatty, Frederick M. "Whig Party," *Encyclopedia of Alabama*, http://www.encyclopediaofalabama.org/face/Article.jsp?id=h-1173

Blaufarb, Rafe. "Vine and Olive Colony," *Encyclopedia of Alabama*, http://www.encyclopediaofalabama.org/face/Article.jsp?id=h-1539

Brooks, Daniel Fate. "William Rufus King," *Encyclopedia of Alabama,http://www.encyclopediaofalabama.org/face/Article.jsp?id=h-1886*

Cox, Dwayne and Rodney J. Steward. "The Old South, Civil War, and Reconstruction." *The Auburn University Digital Library: Auburn History*, http://diglib.auburn.edu/auburnhistory/oldsouth.htm

Doss, Harriet E. Amos and Sara Frear. "Octavia Walton Le Vert," *Encyclopedia of Alabama*, http://www.encyclopediaofalabama.org/face/Article.jsp?id=h-2355

Flynt, Sean. "Samford University," *Encyclopedia of Alabama*, http://www.encyclopediaofalabama.org/face/Article.jsp?id=h-1590

Flynt, Wayne. "Southern Baptists in Alabama," *Encyclopedia of Alabama*, http://www.encyclopediaofalabama.org/face/Article.jsp?id=h-1836

Frear, Sarah. "Augusta Jane Evans Wilson," *Encyclopedia of Alabama*, http://www.encyclopediaofalabama.org/face/Article.jsp?id=h-1072

Harvey, Gordon. "Public Education in Antebellum Alabama," *Encyclopedia of Alabama*, http://www.encyclopediaofalabama.org/face/Article.jsp?id=h-2599

Hawkins Jr., Jack. "Alabama Institute for the Deaf and Blind," *Encyclopedia of Alabama*, http://www.encyclopediaofalabama.org/face/Article.jsp?id=h-1855

"History: The Town of Blakeley," http://www.blakeleypark.com/history.asp

"History of Old St. Stephens," http://www.oldststephens.com/history_of_old_st_stephens.htm

Hubbs, G. Ward. "Birmingham-Southern College," *Encyclopedia of Alabama*, http://www.encyclopediaofalabama.org/face/Article.jsp?id=h-1844

———. "Methodism in Alabama," *Encyclopedia of Alabama*, http://www.encyclopediaofalabama.org/face/Article.jsp?id=h-1857

Jolly Jr., James L. *Encyclopedia of Alabama*, "John Gorman Barr," http://www.encyclopediaofalabama.org/face/Article.jsp?id=h-2455

Lee, J. Lawrence. "Alabama Railroads," *Encyclopedia of Alabama*, http://www.encyclopediaofalabama.org/face/Article.jsp?id=h-2390

Lewis, Herbert J. (Jim). "Canoe Fight," *Encyclopedia of Alabama*, http://www.encyclopediaofalabama.org/face/Article.jsp?id=h-1815

———. "Charles Tait," *Encyclopedia of Alabama*, http://www.encyclopediaofalabama.org/face/Article.jsp?id=h-2338

———. "Daniel Pratt," *Encyclopedia of Alabama*,
http://www.encyclopediaofalabama.org/face/Article.jsp?id=h-1184

———. "Horace Ware," *Encyclopedia of Alabama*,
http://www.encyclopediaofalabama.org/face/Article.jsp?id=h-1174

———. "Lafayette's Visit," *Encyclopedia of Alabama*,
http://www.encyclopediaofalabama.org/face/Article.jsp?id=h-2152

———. "Sam Dale," *Encyclopedia of Alabama*,
http://www.encyclopediaofalabama.org/face/Article.jsp?id=h-2460

———. "Old Cahaba," *Encyclopedia of Alabama*,
http://www.encyclopediaofalabama.org/face/Article.jsp?id=h-1543

———. "Old St. Stephens," *Encyclopedia of Alabama*,
www.encyclopediaofalabama.org/face/Article.jsp?id=h-1674

———. "Tuscaloosa," *Encyclopedia of Alabama*,
http://www.encyclopediaofalabama.org/face/Article.jsp?id=h-1654

———. "William Phineas Browne," *Encyclopedia of Alabama*,
http://www.encyclopediaofalabama.org/face/Article.jsp?id=h-1119

Mellown, Robert O. "Steamboats in Alabama," *Encyclopedia of Alabama*,
http://www.encyclopediaofalabama.org/face/Article.jsp?id=h-1803

Moore, Andrew S. "Archdiocese of Mobile," *Encyclopedia of Alabama*,
http://www.encyclopediaofalabama.org/face/Article.jsp?id=h-1070

Padgett, Charles Stephen. "Spring Hill College," *Encyclopedia of Alabama*,
http://www.encyclopediaofalabama.org/face/Article.jsp?id=h-1029

Robertson, Ben P. "Lewis Sewall," *Encyclopedia of Alabama*,
http://www.encyclopediaofalabama.org/face/Article.jsp?id=h-3004

Sledge, John. *St. Stephens Historical Overview*, The American Center for Artists,
http://www.americanartists.org/art/article_st_stephens_historical_overview.htm

Tate, Adam L. "Joseph Glover Baldwin and *The Flush Times of Alabama and Mississippi*,"
Encyclopedia of Alabama,
http://www.encyclopediaofalabama.org/face/Article.jsp?id=h-1566

Thomas Jefferson to John Holmes, April 22, 1820. Manuscript Division, Library of Congress
Internet site, http://www.loc.gov/exhibits/jefferson/159.html

Toulmin, G. H. comp. "Judge Harry Toulmin—A Sketch," The Northern Toulmins,
http://www.toulmin.family.btinternet.co.uk/GeorgesWebPage/AppL.htm

Waddell, Joseph A. *Waddell's Annals of Augusta County, Virginia, from 1726 to 1871*,
Roane County, TN Family History Project, http://roanetnhistory.org/
bookread.php?loc=WaddellsAnnals&pgid=326#section68

Wallace, W. Jason. "Presbyterian Church in America (PCA)," *Encyclopedia of Alabama*,
http://www.encyclopediaofalabama.org/face/Article.jsp?id=h-1626

Wells, Elizabeth Crabtree. "Judson College," *Encyclopedia of Alabama*,
http://www.encyclopediaofalabama.org/face/Article.jsp?id=h-2492

White, Cynthia Quinn. "Johnson Jones Hooper," *Encyclopedia of* Alabama,
http://www.encyclopediaofalabama.org/face/Article.jsp?id=h-2514

Williams, Benjamin Buford. "Alexander B. Meek," *Encyclopedia of Alabama*,
http://www.encyclopediaofalabama.org/face/Article.jsp?id=h-1127

Index

Visit us at *www.quidprobooks.com.*